Moving Stones

THE VISUAL ARTS OF AFRICA
AND ITS DIASPORAS

*A Series Edited by Kellie Jones
and Steven Nelson*

MOVING STONES

About the Art of Edmonia Lewis

Jennifer DeVere Brody

Duke University Press
Durham and London

2 0 2 6

© 2026 Duke University Press

All rights reserved

Printed in the United States of America on acid-free paper ∞

Project Editor: Livia Tenzer

Designed by A. Mattson Gallagher

Typeset in Garamond Premier and Ogg

by Westchester Publishing Services

Library of Congress Cataloging-in-Publication Data

Names: Brody, Jennifer DeVere author

Title: Moving stones : about the art of Edmonia Lewis /
Jennifer DeVere Brody.

Other titles: About the art of Edmonia Lewis | Visual arts
of Africa and its diasporas

Description: Durham : Duke University Press, 2026. |
Series: The visual arts of africa and its diasporas |
Includes bibliographical references and index.

Identifiers: lccn 2025037228 (print)

LCCN 2025037229 (ebook)

ISBN 9781478038528 paperback

ISBN 9781478033639 hardcover

ISBN 9781478062127 ebook

Subjects: LCSH: Lewis, Edmonia—Criticism and interpretation |
African American women artists—Biography | African American
sculptors—Biography | Sculpture, American—19th century |
Neoclassicism (Art)—Influence | Sculpture—Social aspects

Classification: LCC NB237.L487 B76 2026 (print) | LCC NB237.
L487 (ebook) | DDC 730.92 [B]—dc23/eng/20260108

LC record available at https://lccn.loc.gov/2025037228

LC ebook record available at https://lccn.loc.gov/2025037229

Cover art: yétúndé olagbaju, *Edmonia Lewis: Shooting Star*,
2024. Courtesy of the artist.

For Sio

. . . who is Edmonia Lewis? All of us
have heard of her, and yet nothing very
definitive about her.

The Elevator (San Francisco's Black newspaper), 1879

As the War was drawing to a close, an
entirely new and unexpected star
burst forth in the firmament of American
Art in the person of Edmonia Lewis.

Freeman Henry Morris Murray, *Emancipation
and the Freed in American Sculpture: A Study in
Interpretation,* 1916

Contents

Illustrations

Foreword

Here her brown face, rendered two-dimensional, appears pasted on the corner of an unaddressed envelope—destination unknown—looking out at us from the confines of a USA Forever stamp. There she is, perched in the middle of my computer screen—a pixelated Google Doodle, chiseling a cartooned version of her magnificent statue The Death of Cleopatra. *Next, I see her in my mind's eye near Niagara Falls in the 1850s, a precocious girl, selling beaded moccasins, elaborate pin cushions, and woven baskets—art she learned to make with her Anishinaabe (Ojibwe) family on her mother's side—to sell to tourists visiting the nature-made spectacle of cascading water. Here, in 1862, she sketches, by the light of a wax candle in her boardinghouse room in Oberlin, Ohio; she is drawing the goddess Urania as a wedding gift for her classmate. There she sits in Boston, now a young woman, wide-eyed as she witnesses the Black Union soldiers of the Massachusetts 54th Regiment marching past on their way to battle, led by a youthful white colonel astride a horse, heralded and guided by white silk banners—a vision of thrilling formation in the eyes of this budding artist. Soon after this event, after the deaths of most of the men on a sandy shore in South Carolina, she stands before the passport clerk on August 21, 1865; according to the notary public for the county of Suffolk who filled out her application in Boston, she is "4' high, about age 20, with small chin, medium mouth, and hair, eyes and complexion all Black—who displayed great talent as a sculptor." Passport in hand, she speeds across the vast Atlantic on a steamship bound for Europe and, not long after her arrival on the continent,* sets up her artist's studio in central Rome at the Piazza Barberini, where she sees Bernini's fountains on her daily outings. She sips a drink at the famed Antico Caffè Greco near her studio—the very same workspace that once belonged to the famous sculptor Antonio Canova. In her artist's loft, she strums her guitar for her supper guests. While in Rome, she carves the first sculptures of formerly enslaved, now "forever free" people from the United States alongside fictional Native subjects from Longfellow's epic poem The Song of Hiawatha. Over the years, her various Roman studios host dignitaries, Pope Pius IX, President Ulysses S. Grant, and many other voyagers, many on the grand tour, who come and come again to watch her—this genius of the art world—carve Carrara marble into lifelike forms. In the 1870s, on a visit to the States, she poses before the photographer in his Chicago studio on State Street, wearing her sculpting garb and other telling costumes captured during the session. Now she smiles as King Emmanuel II of Italy presents her with a Gold Medal at the International Art Exposition in Napoli. Later, she rides the new transcontinental train to present her wares to markets in northern California. In the parlor of a San Francisco hotel, she finds herself surrounded by a throng of "white beauties"—all admiring her person. In 1876 she stands beside her monumental sculpture of Cleopatra as paying audiences view her work at the Centennial Exhibition in Philadelphia. Now it is 1887 and she travels via train to Italy, accompanied by Frederick Douglass and his second wife, to view the ruins in Pompeii. Soon she moves to Paris, then as the century turns, on to London—her final resting place. There, after her death from Bright's disease in 1907, she is laid to rest in the Catholic cemetery, in a grave sheltered by a willow tree, under a plain slab headstone. In my dreams, she is back in Rome, hovering just above the winding streets composed of ancient Roman stones, as if she were a revenant, floating up, up, up the Scalinata di Trinità dei Monti to see the vista across the seven hills of the sacred city. And now, here, she still moves about the globe, and her touch forever inhabits her sculptures, which retain the residue of their maker . . . Miss Edmonia Lewis.

Introduction

Moving Stones is a book about an extraordinary artist named Edmonia Lewis. In her lifetime, she was also known as Mary, Ish-scoodah, Wildfire, and most importantly, "an American sculptor of undoubted genius."[1] Edmonia Lewis, who was of Anishinaabe (Ojibwe) and, likely, African Haitian descent, was born free in 1844 in upstate New York, "on or near the traditional territory of the Mississauga people in present-day Ontario," and was buried in St. Mary's Catholic Cemetery in London in 1907.[2] Lewis led a peripatetic life, garnering fame (if not fortune) as the "only colored professor who ever attained eminence in [the sculpture] department of the fine arts," to quote a prominent nineteenth-century "colored" newspaper's description of her.[3] An anonymous 1870 tract explained her remarkable journey: "God's gift to Edmonia Lewis is unconquerable energy, as well as genius; and these two combined enable her to *rise* above all *prejudices* of *race* or *color*, and command the respect and honor of all true lovers of art."[4]

Lewis succeeded in her determined quest to become a neoclassical sculptor, although avoiding prejudice proved impossible.[5] In 1878, at the height of her fame, she reflected, "With color and sex against me, I've still achieved success."[6] Over the years, she experienced and resisted racist and sexist violence at the liberal Oberlin College in Ohio, the patronizing comments about her abilities in the abolitionist stronghold of Boston in the 1860s, and disparaging words from luminaries in her expatriate artist community in Rome, as well as in the international press. Although subject to opprobrium and faint praise throughout her life, in addition to genuine regard, her defiance never let others define her. She managed to carve out a life in art and, in so doing, experienced significant freedoms. Lewis forged her own refuge, and her fame as an artist resulted in her ability to frequently transcend the strictures expected of her by virtue of her era, race, nationality, class, sexual subjectivity, and gender.

Lewis told the *New York Times*, "I was practically driven to Rome, in order to obtain the opportunities for art culture, and to find a social atmosphere where I was not constantly reminded of my color. The land of liberty had no room for a colored sculptor."[7] Lewis felt both propelled and compelled to find a new life beyond the confines of her birthplace. She set sail for Europe on August 26, 1865, four months after the end of the Civil War, visiting London, Paris, and Florence and ultimately settling in Rome. Like many American sculptors in the generation before her, she moved to Italy to have proximity to Carrara marble and skilled Italian carvers. Thereafter, Lewis became a "transatlantic commuter" (to use James Baldwin's term avant la lettre), crossing the Atlantic Ocean no fewer than eight times on steamers, to say nothing of her journeys on foot, in horse-drawn cabs, and by rail.

More than just a woman who traveled, however, Lewis became a diasporic subject who had to flee her birthplace. Her improbable journey included shifts among cultures, languages, and communities during her exile.[8] We can think about Lewis's exilic life and her work as emblematic of the term *diaspora*, which is derived from the Ancient Greek verb διασπείρω (diaspeirō), "to scatter," "to spread about."[9] To tell her story, one must grapple with the many disparate geographical, ideological, linguistic, and aesthetic trajectories her life and art entailed. Her movements across continents and throughout the Atlantic world connect her to recent and past migrations not only of African-descended migrants who have traversed large, dangerous bodies of water to take refuge, if they survive, in the colonizing nations of Europe, but also of millions of Indigenous refugees, again past and present, whether Black, Native American, or from whatever nation across the globe.

I imagine Edmonia's initial leave-taking must have been difficult, even if ardently desired (and here I am thinking of Louise Erdrich [Ojibwe] who wrote: "There can be no traveling unless there is a leave-taking. And the traveling is all the more in earnest if the leave-taking is difficult.")[10] These journeys and leave-takings remain fractious, fraught with danger and, often, life-threatening travails. Such crosscurrents still move many, amid our global crises, propelled by profound inequity, climate change, ethno-racist wars, the perpetual (re)construction of borders, and the rise of many nefarious forms of neonationalism. These profound movements were present as pressures in Lewis's life (albeit in different forms) and impacted her art. Edmonia's legacy and her deferred gift to us is to allow us to understand her already-complicated web of interrelation as a feature of our own. Her story challenges our own categories of inclusion and exclusion and our powers of interpretation. It is my modest, if earnest, wish for this project that the reader learn something about Lewis as her star, once again, rises in the firmament.

The pages that follow reveal more about Lewis's remarkable leave-takings and arrivals. For now, let us turn to explaining this book's interdisciplinary and intimate approach to Lewis's art and life.

Moving Stones approaches Lewis as a thoroughly modern subject whose neoclassical sculptures and life narrative afford us the opportunity to ask new questions about sculpture and embodiment in the diasporic Black and circum-Atlantic worlds.[11] As a person of Anishinaabe and African descent, Lewis's own complex subjectivity defies racial and disciplinary divides. It is difficult to grasp her significance from a single point of view: Her chosen mode of artistic expression, figurative sculpture, personifies the natal details of her life. The homology between her art and life exemplifies the logic inherent in three-dimensional sculpture, made in the round. Such lifelike sculptures cannot be accessed in their "totality" from any fixed position. Figurative sculptures are often made with a frontal view in mind; one side is more "finished" and presents a preferred view for public consumption. I argue, however, that such sculptures can be valued from all sides, generatively.

Most of Edmonia Lewis's sculptures were made and meant to be viewed "in the round." Mimetically, both her art and her life can be understood as multifaceted and volumetric: We must move about them, both physically and imaginatively, in order to understand them. Accordingly, this study takes a poetic and imaginative approach that seeks to amplify multiple dimensions of Lewis's art and life—to help round out, circumnavigate, and circulate the marvelous, burgeoning archive of all things Edmonia Lewis.

Put differently, this book eschews a straightforward biographical or strictly historical approach to Lewis's astounding life and art. Its methodological tools hew closer to Black feminist, performance, and queer studies as it seeks to carve out unexpected aspects of her work through its close readings of Lewis's sculptures, including not only her well-known portrait busts, literary Indians, mythic and biblical subjects, but also minor aspects of her work—her feminized flowers, a sculpture of clasped hands, and her cherubic children—all made of magnificent marble. In addition, this study asks about how Lewis performed her raced, gendered, and sexualized subjectivity as she posed in the few known photographic portraits of the artist. These precious artifacts were not the product of her own hand but rather, given the fact that they were taken at the height of her stature as a mature artist, we surmise that they may have been composed with her input.

This book hopes to reveal Lewis as a force in the world, past and present. To this end, its chapters mostly center on Lewis in her time and are then supplemented by interstitial interludes that examine twentieth- and twenty-first-century artists (many queer, of color, and feminist) who are meant to be seen as following in Lewis's footsteps and whose work complements her aesthetic and political concerns even, or especially, when they do so in media other than Edmonia's specialty, sculpture.

Thus, the book's jagged method moves about the work, mimicking the viewpoint we might see through the lens of a handheld camera. It zooms in to focus momentarily on specific aspects of Lewis's life and work. By doing so, this study seeks to mobilize the "cut," a term from film and Black studies.[12] Following this visual perspective requires us to think about moving stills, such that we are aware of how things are produced and created. Here, we think about editing: about how the splice sutures views, how the gap is productive, and how the viewer's knowledge that she has arrived at another viewpoint or moment is determined rather than inevitable. We do so in an attempt to attend to the "ungraspable" totality of Lewis and her sculptural work.

This brief discussion helps us think about the cultural work that the terms *moving* and *still* do to blur the boundaries between different media such as sculpture and photography and to pay attention to various contexts, processes, and lenses through which we see and understand art and life as well as their interrelations.

The relays between the shot and the scene of movement that compose cinema exist within the purview of sculpture that, like "cinema by other means" or photographs in the mind, is connected via a complex interplay of the stable and the sequential.[13] Our binocular vision prevents us from seeing beyond a singular viewpoint in any three-dimensional image. As a result, we must see "the whole" of a three-dimensional sculpture in successive movements that may resemble a series of "cinematic stills." Several of these ideas about movement and stasis are born out in a conversation between Tina M. Campt and film director Arthur Jafa. Specifically, the two theorists discussed their understanding of the difference between movement and motion: "Movement means 'change in position of an object in relation to a fixed point in space.' Motion, on the other hand, is a change of location or position of an object with respect to time."[14] When looking at the relation between moving and being still, I posit that they are inexorably connected and contingent, not oppositional. Stasis is the genesis for movement. Similarly, movement momentarily concludes in stasis.

As viewers, to see three-dimensional sculptural works, we must move around them, and in doing so, we create a connection between movement and stasis. In this way, we can begin to see how sculptures and photography worked together in the nineteenth century to create new perceptions of moving stones. This is an understudied aspect of Lewis's sculptural works that allows us to think about them in the purview of new visual technologies such as photography. Photography stilled the motion of life in order to preserve an instant in time. When the industrialist and former governor of California Leland Stanford Sr. wanted to find out if his racehorse lifted all four hooves off the ground when it galloped, he funded the work of Eadweard Muybridge, whose photographic motion studies became the successive or sequential stop-action photographs that many consider to be a key moment in the birth of cinema. In these famous images, the horse is ridden by a Black jockey. These famous "Animal Studies" again place professionalized Black people in the main frame of technological innovation.[15]

I mention these innovations in "moving stills" not only to highlight their connections to "moving stones" as another way of understanding sculpture, but also to touch on communities of other professional Black workers in the West, and northern California in particular, where Edmonia Lewis and her work circulated in a consequential sojourn in the 1870s (discussed in chapter 4). Sculpture can be read in relation to cinema, even before the advent of such technology entered the scene. We can even think about sculpture in the round as a kind of prelude to cinematic technology and in relation to the invention of other viewing machines of the nineteenth century such as panoramas, stereopticons, magic lanterns, and even galleries of art. I take such technological innovations of art projection developed in the Victorian era seriously as a way of opening up a space for scholars of cinema and sculpture.

Methodologically, then, I ask that we move about Lewis's work as if we were taking a cue from the camera movements featured in the seven-minute experimental film *Static* (2009). Black British filmmaker Steve McQueen (b. 1969) made this short independent film to be shown exclusively in art galleries. The roving camera in the film moves around one of the most famous neoclassical sculptures, *Liberty Enlightening the World*, better known as the Statue of Liberty (versions of which were designed by Lewis's contemporary, French sculptor Frédéric Auguste Bartholdi [1834–1904]), installed on Ellis Island in New York in 1886.[16] McQueen's avant-garde film remakes this iconic nineteenth-century sculpture by showing it abstractly. The film's disjunctive cuts and shots defamiliarize the neoclassical sculpture through the skillful use of montage. One of the key effects of McQueen's camera work is to render the magisterial and massive "Lady Liberty" in a new light. The film plays with our perception of moving images on screen, in particular, their size-distance ratio and even the speed with which they were shot. Its opening sequence features an extreme close-up that shows only the oxidized corrosion of the surface of the colossus, rendering the figure abstract and disorienting and thus allowing viewers to see the sculpture anew. In the film, Bartholdi's iconic neoclassical female figure appears as sheer texture, without clear form. I contend that Lewis's figurative work can also be viewed from such an abstracted and disjointed perspective.

These technical issues point out the problem of locating oneself in space and explore the idea of the statue's liberation from its historical setting and the way the film's deep focus can undo how we see relationships between its form and content.[17] I play with the idea that Lewis's sculptures can be read in these productive, postmodern ways that distort and perhaps reveal different aesthetic experiences. This approach seeks to understand the latent capacity of her work that might engage more views, move viewers—literally and figuratively—such that we see her works as dynamic moving stones that are also traveling across space and time. In this way, Lewis's figurative, free-standing marble sculptures can be seen as fractured and fragmented depending on how, from where, what angle and at what moment in time one views them. We understand that Lewis's statues were, and are, subject to change and dislocation as they move about galleries, in different ship's holds that crossed the Atlantic, over railroad tracks that traversed the United States, and now on trucks that speed along highways in specially made crates as well as in the holds of airplanes that fly about the globe.

By tracking McQueen's camerawork, I ask less what Lewis's sculptures *mean* in strictly art historical terms (what they represent iconographically) than what they *do* in, for, and about inhabited worlds of the past, present, and future. I examine how her sculptures elicit and solicit our affect and performative desire. Such queer takes on Edmonia Lewis are meant to flesh out unlikely aspects of her work and to serve as oblique references to my subjective readings that provide unexpected ways of thinking about Lewis and her art.

Such concerns bring us to another experimental filmmaker, Sir Isaac Julien, whose own critical and artistic vision serves as another intertext for Lewis's work. Julien is an auteur who graduated from St. Martin's School of Art in London and whose work often references art historical objects. Several of his films feature the museum as a privileged mise-en-scène. Julien was instrumental in promoting other Black British independent filmmakers in the 1980s and 1990s through his participation in groups such as Sankofa, Ceddo, and the Black Audio Film Collective. While still a student at St. Martin's, Julien codirected the experimental documentary *Territories* (1984), about the police brutality taking place in the Notting Hill neighborhood of London. As would become his signature, the film wove together fragments of material that included footage from Notting Hill's annual Carnival, televised bits of the ensuing riots in 1981 that protested the ongoing police violence, and other images, all set against a nondiegetic soundtrack of voices, music, and street sounds. This film produced a visualscape that eschewed Realism and straightforward storytelling in favor of imagistic, imaginative, and emotionally truthful scenes from actual life. Julien's own critical-artistic visions and ever-sculptural cinematic installations serve as an impossible, queer inspiration for interpreting Lewis's work.

Julien's vast knowledge of art history extends to the way he captures classical paintings and sculptures in many of his films, which also include angels as leitmotifs (chapter 4). His short-format art films featuring the museum include *The Attendant* (1993) and *Baltimore* (2003). *The Attendant* is set in a museum of slavery, Wilberforce House Museum in Hull, England, and a theater where scenes from the opera *Dido and Aeneas* are performed. This eight-minute film, with its largely nondiegetic score, presents a series of montages that create a surrealistic fantasy. While a full reading of this complex narrative work is beyond the scope of this project, I mention it because it showcases one of the earliest instances of Julien's interventions in art-historical conventions. It is one of the first films he made that features sequences and close-ups of white, neoclassical sculptures made in the mode of Edmonia Lewis's works.[18] There are other filmic features such as angels (or putti) who twirl in 360-degree circles or paintings that transform before the spectators' eyes from two- to three-dimensional form, following the Victorian practice of tableaux vivants. In *The Attendant*, the large-scale history painting *The Slave Trade (Slaves on the West Coast of Africa)*, created by François-Auguste Biard in 1833, comes to life as actors replace the painted characters and enact imaginary scenarios.

In the past decades, Julien's film work has been installed *in* museums, as he sets out to explore, if not explode, tensions between two- and three-dimensional forms, bringing the screen to life in actual, architecturally open spaces. Julien's multiscreen, multichannel video installations themselves challenge generic categories as well as ontological differences between film and sculpture in what he has named "the sculptural possibilities of the moving image." These works are experienced in what one critic calls "sculptural multiscreen architecture."[19] Their installation also critiques the hierarchical and even historical categories of these supposedly distinct artistic genres: Julien has exhibited his film stills as works of art and displayed screens such that they appear to be resting on plinths, like sculptures.

In Julien's now classic film *Looking for Langston* (1989), the director deployed collaged montage techniques similar to those once described by the famed Russian film theorist Sergei Eisenstein, who also concerned himself with new forms of perception and memory, promoted by the use of the montage in cinematography. Eisenstein deconstructs different logics for viewing architecture, which in his example includes sculpture. Eisenstein's essay clearly describes the alternate means of perception from "the imaginary path followed by the eye . . . [such as] impressions in front of an immobile spectator. In the past, however, . . . the spectator moved between [a series of] carefully disposed phenomena that he absorbed sequentially with his visual sense."[20] Eisenstein showed the difference between how movement works for a stationary viewer of cinema and the peripatetic "roving" spectator required by sculpture. Julien's oeuvre also engages different embodied modes of perception. In *Looking for Langston*, a queer homage to the Black Harlem Renaissance poet Langston Hughes (1901–67), Julien makes brilliant use of tableaux vivants, and moving tracking shots of still figures show how film works to elicit dynamic responses.

The changing temporality created by Julien's works that rely on the device of the tableau creates a disjunctive rhythm that depends on the cut as the spatial referent that sutures the moving image. Julien has said that his work seeks to "make theoretical films of desire" as a means of contesting racism and homophobia in British culture and throughout the diaspora. These questions about race, gender, and sexuality matter in both Julien's and Lewis's art. Julien's recent hybrid sculpted/filmic installations are designed to move us queerly through different times, spaces, places, and emotions in ways that resemble how we can approach Lewis's sculptures that have been installed in museum settings. All such works are moving and move us: they defy a singular stance, literally and figuratively. An aspect of these works always exists beyond the curve or the boundary mobilized by the cut and therefore require a subsequent imaginary suture.

Julien's celluloid gilded putti appear in a number of his films and were included in a 2016 installation of stills at the Jessica Silverman Gallery in San Francisco.[21] Notably, young actors portraying these figures first appear in *Looking for Langston*, and they flit in 360-degree turns throughout *The Attendant*. Nina Kellgren, Julien's cinematographer for both works, studied sculpture as well as photography. This fact grounds the arguments here in terms of connections between sculpture and film.

Kobena Mercer has written about this phenomenon in his book on Alain Locke, the gay philosopher and eminence grise of the Harlem Renaissance. Mercer discusses the cleansing trope of classicism that both uncovered and recovered the homoerotic sculptures made by Harlem Renaissance artist Richmond Barthé, whose work was featured in Julien's 2022 installation *Once Again . . . Statues Never Die*, as well as in *The Harlem Renaissance and Translatlantic Modernism*, a show curated by Denise Murell at the Metropolitan Museum in New York in 2024. Julien's winged putti, filmed as cutouts that spin around and around in different moments of Julien's film, are rendered in black-and-white and color: They might be read as the queer progeny of Lewis's cupid discussed in chapter 4.

Sir Joshua Reynolds wrote in 1780: "The sculptor's art is not unlike that of Dancing, where the attention of the spectator is principally engaged by the attitude and action of the performer."[22] I trace how sculptures, when literally animated, can be seen to "come to life"—or become "live," enlivened entities, with results akin to those of kinesthetics (movement or dance), to reiterate Reynolds's analogy. Notably, Enlightenment pronouncements such as Reynolds's preceded the invention of kinetic (actually moving) sculpture, which we now think about as "mobiles," to use the neologism coined by Alexander Calder (1898–1976) in the early decades of the twentieth century. Calder's mobiles were inspired by the movements of a dancer he saw in Paris: the multitalented Black American performer Josephine Baker. The invention of the mobile marks another moment of moving sculpture whose source is concomitant with the movements of a

Black woman. Calder's mobiles were made of wire so as to be suspended from the ceiling, like the performances of Black female high-wire artist Olga Kaira, known as "Miss La La," who was painted and drawn by Edgar Degas (1834–1917). In Degas's *Miss La La at the Cirque Fernando* (1897), the off-kilter, contorted perspective from which we see the high-wire performer conveys a sense of motion since the subject, Miss La La, is frozen in the midst of a whirl on the wire. The painting captures the performer in medias res, suspended within a dizzying rotunda whose architecture, with its rhythmic triangular segments, reinforces this sense of a moment, moving. According to Griselda Pollock, the art historian Aby Warburg (1866–1929) saw a similar concatenation of stilled movement in the "petrified stasis of classical sculpture's gestural repertoire [which he described further as] a repository of once-animated performances and dancing rituals, that carried in mnemonic form the legacy of once-enacted rituals and sacrifices, themselves the register in social and collective action of materially determined—if psychically experienced—emotions about life, death, desire and want."²³ These ideas reference a long-standing tradition of connecting sculpture and movement. Think, for example, of Shakespeare's *The Winter's Tale* (first performed in 1611), where the drama culminates in the moment in which the audience witnesses an actor playing a statue transmogrify into a living being. In this famous scene (act 5, scene 3), the actor playing Hermoine gives viewers pleasure by juxtaposing the proximity between art and life that sculpture enacts. Such practices of vivifying stone go back to Ovid's *Metamorphoses*, itself a source for Shakespeare's drama.

Here, I draw on these ideas to animate the affective valences of sculpture that extend, or rather emanate, from this medium as such. The performative acts staged during the nineteenth century known as tableaux vivants are another iteration of such transformations that bring two-dimensional pictorial images to "life" in dramatic ways—either at home in parlors or in theatrical productions. In these popular theatrical events, actors composed themselves into scenes from famous paintings for the pleasure of the viewing audiences seated in the theater. They would hold themselves still to produce the moment of "realization." In so doing, these staged events transformed artworks known two-dimensionally into three-dimensional forms. They proposed and staged a relay between "striking a pose" and "freezing a frame," a relationship of connections between stasis and movement that were *realized* in the fullest sense of that verb, or in Martin Meisel's sense of "realizations" that looks at the connections among the representational arts of theater, dance, and sculpture in the Victorian era as well as in the Julien films mentioned above.[24]

Sculptures perform "types" and resonate with specific contexts and ideas. They move us, literally and figuratively, as they carve space and beckon us to move about them. Adrienne Kennedy explains that one of the impetuses for her brilliant play *Funnyhouse of a Negro* (1964) was "the statue [she] saw of [Queen] Victoria in front of Buckingham Palace.... [It] was the single most dramatic, startling, statue [she'd] seen. Here was a woman who had dominated an age." She continues: "In my play, I would soon have the heroine, Sarah, talk to a replica of this statue. Finally the dialogue with a statue would be explicit and concrete. And the *statue* would reply; the *statue* would inform my character of her *inner* thoughts. The *statue* would reveal my character's secrets to herself."[25] It should come as no surprise that Kennedy, the student of Victorian culture who teased out her era's repressed hysteria, imagines this surrealist scene of an externalized "body double" in dialogue with an actor on stage—engaging the possibilities of projection and introspection among these propped objects before us.

Beginning in the Victorian era, the practice of lighting statues in galleries as if they were actors became prevalent. Some were covered with red velvet cloth so that the white marble took on a slightly "rosy," almost flesh-like hue, or were given a yellow wash in the mode of Antonio Canova, or were lit so that they would be shadowed to elicit greater drama and affect. Like architecture, sculptures carve space, marking places in such a way that our bodies must negotiate them, relate to them in space and time, and engage the haptic and the optic. Event, sculpture, and film were always already sutured in the art of Edmonia Lewis's time—the time of tableaux vivants, panoramas, and other mixed-media displays of live and still, of sculpture performed as a cinematic event. As Liz Grosz says in *The Nick of Time: Politics, Evolution, and the Untimely*, "We can think of time [and, I would add, sculpture] only in passing moments, through ruptures, nicks, cuts, and in instances of dislocation."[26] Consequently, I want to think about the deep connection among sculpture and bodies, as objects in motion. If we believe that *all* matter is gestural, we might understand that pose in sculpture is the building block of theater, dance, and performance.

"How do we remember a sculpture?" David Getsy asks in his study *Body Doubles*.[27] If we imagine statues as immobile, unchanging, unseeing, and mute, they hardly seem appropriate objects for performance; but, in fact, they do change in part by the discourse imparted to them and in part through our bodily relation to them. Sculpted bodies are famously "life-like": We cannot invoke them without setting off a signifying chain, a Möbius strip of referential movement. Their formation retains residues of feeling, touch, audiences, the artist's hand, remnants that have been memorialized and transformed, transported, and translated, but remain.

In a sculpture class I took in North Carolina in the mid-2000s, we students were instructed to throw a mass of clay and then "read" its gesture. Mine landed on the far edge of the table. I felt its diagonal gesture was lurching and tentative. It was during this session that I realized that the sculpture studio is a theater of movement. It is a space of shifting glances, complex choreographies, states of being, and constant movement. I remember moving around the live nude model placed in the center of the studio. As we did so, we were able to form and reform flesh and clay, anatomy and geometry—adding muscle to maquette. We were meant to hone our technique in order to transform the figure before us, which became fodder for the imagination. We had to keep coming back into place as we engaged the live model. I learned to comprehend the moving materiality required to make sculpture, and to contemplate its mass, space, and temporality.

To make her sculptures, Lewis needed not only technical skill and technological knowledge but also philosophical and historical knowledge about embodiment that entailed understanding composure, composition, comportment, and anatomy as well as market forces. Lewis's selections were sui generis and distinct while still being in conversation with her coevals, who themselves were also arguing about notions of the "Antique," which is to say Roman-era copies of Greek sculptures, as well as the many popular updates of such idealized genres as the putti, the Native American, heroic leaders, dying queens, and biblical subjects. Neoclassical sculptors wrestled with how to make statues that were at once reminiscent of established ideals and yet somehow also innovative and newly distinct from previous models. They struck this balance by updating the subjects they sculpted (such as the many images of contemporary leaders in "ancient" guise) or molding new subjects that included modern props in the place of ancient lyres. Sculptures convey a sense of the past even as they portray modern subjects.

During her life as a sculptor, Lewis created clay studies, sketched in pencil, carved and chiseled hard marble with tools she sometimes made herself, put up her own bozzotti and polished her precious works. This was arduous work to which she committed herself over many years before she was able to employ assistants: Each strike, each perambulation about a work of sculpture in progress, required her to engage all of her senses in meaningful movements that coordinated eye, mind, arm, hand, legs, feet, and heart. In focusing only on finished products, we forget the fact of production, the forging of a work, willing it to life with one's own moving motive and emotions. This too was an important aspect of Lewis's life-long dedication to moving stones.

The Original Copy: Photography of Sculpture, 1839–Today, a large-scale exhibition at New York's Museum of Modern Art in 2010, interrogated various ideas of "moving stones" and helps us to read Lewis's work in terms of other concurrent and subsequent visual and affective technologies. For example, the invention of the photo-sculpture in France in the 1850s: This human-technology hybrid used a special room with twenty-four separate operators stationed in the round. A model would stand in the center of the room, and, when directed, the camera operators would each take a photo that was then sketched onto plates and then "drawn" into clay to produce a rough maquette of the model. This forerunner of the 3-D printer, designed to democratize and "automate" sculpture, is another example of how different visual media worked in concert.[28]

Each of these innovations paves the way for understanding sculpture as a kind of cinematic or perceptible form, and as performative to the extent that it is composed of takes, of temporality, and is not "static" space. Such ideas of sculpture's durational instantiation inform my theoretical understanding of how Lewis's motivation to be a neoclassical sculptor may not have been only commercial or whimsical but plausibly also about modernity and motion, to say nothing about her motivations to create her own genealogical formations.[29] As Kobena Mercer explains, "Art invites us into a concentrated act of looking, thinking and feeling that takes us out of the ordinary as we reflect on what we behold in the very moment of beholding it. Before we can say what art is about, our sensory engagement tells us that form comes first. The primacy of the aesthetic dimension, however, receives the least attention when it comes to black artists."[30] Close reading of Lewis's art along such lines is a central goal of this book.

Perception, then, provides an important window on the performative aspects of sculpture and its cinematic elements. "While a visual object is presenting one side to the eye," Jean-François Lyotard wrote, "there are always other sides still unseen. A direct focused vision is always surrounded by a curved area where visibility is held in reserve yet isn't absent. This disjunction is inclusive. Perceptival 'recognition' never satisfies the logical demand for complete description."[31] The lack of satisfaction fuels the desire to return to the scene of the still unseen. This brings to mind the process of carving a likeness that depends on the cut, concepts of re-memory, and the openness of the seemingly closed, complete image that is in fact on and even in the move. This is "cinema by other means," according to Pavle Levi.[32] Perhaps this is why Richard Powell titles his brilliant book on Black portraiture *Cutting a Figure*, and why Fred Moten champions "the break" as an iterative mode of Black performance.[33] Such markings make meanings memorable—creating connection and distance in the break.

Finally, the field of performance studies also helps to shed light on the work of what historically were mixed-media forms in which sculpture proper and embodied performances were realized and cathected.[34] As we move through this book, I hope that you will be attuned to various and varying feelings (presumed to reside inside the body) that are engendered by thinking about our encounter with sculptures in this "expanded field of vision"—even or especially those pieces signed by and assigned to the name Edmonia Lewis and often accompanied by the Latin phrase "Facit a Roma" (Made in Rome). This is to say that in offering some broad propositions about sculpture in the round, I mean for them to "apply" to Lewis's work in particular.[35]

During the nineteenth century, Lewis's sculptures were well known throughout the Atlantic world; however, knowledge about her became scant after her death shortly after the turn of the century, and many of the sculptures she produced were damaged or forgotten, and some still remain "lost." Although she was mentioned with some regularity throughout the annals of African American history and claimed by both feminist and lesbian feminist art and history, only in the past few decades has there been a robust resurgence of art and scholarship about her. Nevertheless, Lewis's contributions to the visual arts of an African American diaspora remain paramount, not only because of her ability to live as an artist or because of her achievements as a female sculptor in a so-called male-dominated field, but also, and more significantly, for her compositions and the skilled work evident in her copies of masterworks. In short, for the art she made. Her smooth copy of an ancient bust of Octavian, *Young Octavian* (ca. 1873), was thought to be among the very best carved reproductions of the bust being sold in Rome during her lifetime.[36]

This book reads both Lewis's less-discussed pieces and the marginalized aspects of her more famous works through a queer lens. In particular, the book analyzes two pendant sculptures of allegorized infants, a statue of a winged cupid, her sculpture of a couple's hands, and her use of roses throughout her work in order to produce queer readings and new interpretations. In so doing, it attends to the modes through which we can approach her sculptures: ekphrastic descriptions, photographs, imagined haptic encounters, and digital prints. Again, attending to the different media through which we might come to know Lewis and her work fulfills my desire to think about how different media, when read together or against one another, can open up aspects of visual culture. Scholarship by Kobena Mercer, Isaac Julien, Imani Perry, and José Esteban Muñoz, among many other queer artists and writers, teaches us that *how* we look at a subject is always already fraught with questions of unexplained desire. The book follows these and other queer studies by looking *for* as much as *at*, if not "looking after" (to invoke Kara Keeling's work) or *about*, in order to counter more straightforward, linear accounts.[37] Even the short biographical note in this chapter provides only the most basic contours about her and therefore is designed to be neither definitive nor fixed, even as it proves the thesis that "a black artist always becomes an actor in her own show."[38]

To think about the question of how Lewis acts in her work and life requires many methodological modes, each of which meets certain limits registered via silences, gaps, and breaks.[39] Lewis's work and life have been obscured by the very categories of (disciplinary) difference through which we can see traces of her—race, place, subjectivity, ethnicity, gender, and nation. Lewis's works and her life could be viewed through many lenses: Native American folklore, American history, and politics; African American and Indigenous histories and the intersections between them; transnational art history; European history; Atlantic studies; feminist, gender, and queer studies; aesthetics; movements of global capital; literary studies; histories of abolition; women's education; global nineteenth-century studies; theories of race and ethnicity; and other disciplines too numerous to name here.

Lewis's multiple movements confound ethnic notions about Black and Native female subjects in the era of mass enslavement of peoples of African descent and the continuing violence of genocide against Native Americans and other migrants across the globe—a time when Lewis's queer artistic life in Italy verged on an impossibility. Although she could be viewed as a singular queer subject for her time and ours, it is important to remember that she was not anomalous. As Philip J. DeLoria, for one, reminds us, to invoke the idea of the anomaly is to reconfirm stereotypes that limit horizons of expectation.[40] Indeed, we should assume that there were, and still could be, many more Miss Edmonia Lewises. Tiya Miles makes a similar argument in her magisterial book *Night Flyer* (2024) about another historical nineteenth-century heroine, Harriet Tubman.[41]

We expand our focus so that it is multidirectional and able to account for different media and modes of remembering, which is also to say, forgetting. The mixed methods of the transdisciplinary field of performance studies help us to unearth Edmonia Lewis's life and work. As a result, I draw on my knowledge of performance studies, visual studies, queer studies, Indigenous studies, and Black feminist theory, each of which requires one to "think otherwise" about the almost always contentious ways that race, gender, sexuality, difference, and class are curated, displayed, and constituted. I grapple firsthand with Lewis as a "transitory figure perceived through glimpses and furtive glances, by fictive traces and fugitive moves," as well as the ethical imperative of honoring such subjects' right to opacity.[42]

Lewis was a spinster, or what the novelist George Gissing called, "an odd woman."[43] She never married nor, as far as we know, did she bear children.[44] In my understanding, Edmonia Lewis led a "queer," nonnormative life by virtue of being (1) a professional, (as she would have said) colored woman artist; (2) a sculptor in stone at a time when such work was deemed "masculine"; (3) a spinster; and (4) the subject of lesbian and queer affections, past and present. In other words, the specificity of Edmonia's life and work can lend itself to evident queer readings (though some readers might consider this a tendentious approach).[45] Lewis does appear in *The Queer Encyclopedia of the Visual Arts*, and was claimed by the Guerrilla Girls as a queer "ancestor."[46] I hope, however, that thinking about Lewis via such queer approaches can bring about fresh ways of reading her art that work against essentializing or reifying her sexuality as such.

While it may be impossible to determine or define Lewis definitively as (a) "queer," it is nevertheless possible to identify and amplify queer aspects of her oeuvre. Examples include her sculptures of female heroines such as the biblical Hagar (whom she carved stating, "I have strong sympathy for all women who have struggled and suffered") and Cleopatra—both of whom have frequently been characterized as sexual outlaws.[47] In her later works, Lewis sculpted flowers and sensuous feminized forms that contrasted with her deployment of masculine poses in some of her photographs—and can lend themselves to readings from feminist and queer perspectives. Throughout this book I speak queerly about the *production* and performances of formal aspects of her work and less about her own possible queer gender performance or any idea about her "actual" sexual subjectivity.[48]

In *American Negro Art* (1960), Cedric Dover described Lewis as "an attractive young woman of East Indian appearance—many Negroes of part American indian [*sic*] origin (her mother was a Chippewa) have their twins in Asia and Southern Europe. She had, too, an appealing intensity and forthrightness, heightened by an uncultivated voice, and a tell-tale boyishness increasingly emphasized by clothes reminiscent of the more unfeminine feminists of the period." A few paragraphs later, Dover references her as "the dark brown boyish girl." Dover concluded his summary of Lewis: "Her end, like her beginning, is a mystery or a conspiracy of silence."[49] This statement was written before her grave in London had been located, at a time when she appears to have disappeared from the historical record. Dover's diction aligns with the discourse of illicit sexuality; the language to describe her might not yet have existed either in common parlance or in art historical vocabularies. While most chroniclers of Lewis's story maintain that no hint of "scandalous" sexuality exists, multiple ways of interpreting her work suggest she may have led a queer life.[50]

According to the *Oxford English Dictionary*, the etymological root of *to queer* means "to turn," "to twist," or "to curve." In following its subject, this book is speculative and performative, circuitous, recursive, queer: It asks us to train our eyes on movements and motion as a means of dissolving differences between media, the past and the future present, the now and the then, the living and the still. This is to pose (as) problems of perception not merely what there might be to see but how to see around, about, or perhaps beyond the boundaries of the archive itself. Such journeys through the archives should seek to open the fixed boundaries between the lost and the found by looking askance at, or queerly about, the purportedly ephemeral evidence.

Moving Stones offers new ways of reading Lewis's queer' life at home and abroad that reverberate in the present. I mention Lewis's interactions with other free Black women of her time, in contrast to most accounts, which tend to mention her only as an isolated anomaly in the all-white context of other American artists in Rome. I am curious about how portrait photographs of Lewis circulated among Black queer women from the nineteenth century to the present. This speculative aspect of my book thinks about her as one of many "colored" girls who led "wayward lives, [as] beautiful experiments"—to paraphrase Saidiya Hartman, who glosses the word wayward as that which is "errant, fugitive, recalcitrant, anarchic, willful, reckless, troublesome, riotous, tumultuous, rebellious and wild." While the women in Hartman's study are all twentieth-century subjects, they had their corollaries in the nineteenth century. As Hartman writes, they created "possibility at a time when all roads, except ones created by *smashing out*, are foreclosed."[51] I take up Hartman's topic of the radical lives of Black girls to illuminate Lewis's nineteenth-century work with chisel and awl—which she used literally to smash out a meaningful living. Aptly, smashing was a nineteenth- and early-twentieth-century term for queer sex as well as an adjective that signified something marvelous; it is again popular in the twenty-first century as a way to denote any sexual activity. All three of these meanings help us to see Lewis's ability "to make a way out of no way" and to forge a life for which she had few, if any, models. As was the case with her original sculptural subjects, she had to create sui generis forms that did not always conform to expectations about her.

This book's subtitle features the word *about* as an analytic and theoretical proposition. This is a book *about* Lewis's life narrative as a work of art, *about* sculptures as moving objects, and *about* the engagement of contemporary artists with both of these subjects.[52] Deploying the word *about* as both a preposition and an adverb suggests how the term denotes and connotes movement, intensity, and topicality. To be "about" something is to maintain a certain distance from the subject of an inquiry: to approach, to lurk, to approximate it.[53] The spatial valances of the word, particularly in British English, connect it to ideas of temporality and affect. Each chapter of the study resonates with the terms set out here and demonstrates how setting stones in motion produces new approaches to understanding the nineteenth century's most acclaimed international professional female "colored artist" and her works.[54]

These myriad meanings of *about* allow us to promote the idea that movement is integral to sculpture. We must look askance or awry, which is to say, behind, before, beyond, around the edges and at the bottom of her life and work—incorporating a theoretical approach that also focuses on haptic-optic relations. Although we associate the optic with relatively distant vision—that which lies beyond one's sighted stance—and, relatively speaking, we understand the haptic in relation to the proximate—that within one's sited or sighted stance, these terms are connected.[55] As the sculptor Aria Dean (b. 1993) conveys in distinguishing painting from sculpture, "Sculptors are interested in how something works, how it moves, how it enters discourse."[56] As I write these words, my computer claims it is "moving items into place." The haptic, optic, and even sonic surround us.

Moving Stones offers an approach to the artist's work and life that is rife with desire—my own and others'. A more colloquial understanding of *about* suggests being engrossed in an intense passion for one's topic. To be "all about Edmonia Lewis" is to commit oneself with the most ardent devotion.[57] Such desire for Lewis and her obscured body of work might move us to seek out the erotics of touch (hers and ours), the evidence of ephemera (in the forms of photographs, letters, clippings), and the imagined queer futurity of the archive composed of such eroticized ephemera.

Chapter 1, "A Head of Her Time," discusses my initial encounter with Lewis in an archive in the London Library and gives an abbreviated biographical sketch of the artist. Chapter 2, "Animating Stones," continues theorizing about sculptures as moving, even animate, objects and concludes with an analysis of the materiality of marble that "colors" Lewis's work. Chapter 3, "With Holding Hands," analyzes Lewis's hands as tools and provides a close reading of a sculpture she made of the clasped hands of an abolitionist couple. Chapter 4, "About the Nude," discusses naked putti that Lewis carved in the 1870s, making her among the first and likely the only female sculptor of color to produce nude statues. Chapter 5, "A Rose Somebody Knows," focuses on Lewis's penchant for sculpting roses in the latter part of her career. Chapter 6, "About Photography," looks at the significance of photography in Lewis's art and life. Chapter 7, "Engraving Edmonia," analyzes Lewis's carving of headstones and changes made to her gravesite in London before turning to a discussion of commemorative sculptures.

Since her death in 1907, many different artists and media makers (and an increasing number of curators and art historians) have paid tribute to Lewis, including poets, musicians, multimedia performance artists, novelists, children's authors, comic book writers and illustrators, photographers, filmmakers, and digital artists. A 1969 portrait by one of her early admirers and most deft interpreters, the brilliant artist Romare Bearden, presents a three-quarter-length view of a seated Lewis in a gorgeous collage—the background is a vermillion that highlights the figure's cerulean blue clothing. In this work, Lewis's brown hands are folded in her lap as if mimicking the pose of one her photographic portraits discussed in chapter 6. One of the scraps used in the composition to depict the right side of her face is a photograph of the bronze sculpted head of what looks to be Queen Nefertiti. The other side is composed of grey rough stone. A triangular white earring dangles delicately from her one visible ear. The work is titled, appropriately, *Homage to Edmonia Lewis*. It serves as an apt visual accompaniment to Bearden's superb short study of Lewis and her art in the book he coauthored with Harry Henderson, the 1993 study *A History of African-American Artists from 1792 to the Present*.

In a nod to this approach of creating a collaged compendium of artists, each of the chapters outlined above is followed by an "interlude," that focuses on an artistic work by a contemporary artist. These riffs on Lewis's work and life connect her and her art to subsequent artists well beyond her specific métier and time period. The terms and conditions of these interruptions suggest the ways that art is subject to change, in multiple senses. Specifically, I connect the following twentieth- and twenty-first-century artists (in order of appearance) to aspects of Lewis's life and art: Faith Ringgold (1930–2024), Beverly Buchanan (1940–2015), Kent Monkman / Miss Chief Eagle Testickle (Cree) (b. 1965), Mickalene Thomas (b. 1971), Simone Leigh (b. 1967), Zanele Muholi (b. 1972), and Maud Sulter (1960–2008). Each of these seven interlocutors has something to say about Lewis or an aspect of her artistic legacy: They participate in what Christina Sharpe would call "wake work" that has kept and keeps Lewis current.[58]

It is perhaps no accident that the majority of these artists identify as colored or queer, or both, and as a result, can be read in proximity to queer aspects that some readers might see in studying Lewis's art and life.[59] The ludic interludes serve as a way to look back with new eyes at her work: to perform a kind of about-face. The term *about-face* originated with the English army and was deployed in the United States during the Civil War. It is defined as a complete, sudden change in position or 180-degree turn. The interchapter sketches perform an about-face and seemingly turn against the previous views of Edmonia and her work. The idea of the about-face works with the larger theoretical framework of *about* used throughout this study of Edmonia Lewis. It too has a queer valence, for at least since the 1990s (and perhaps earlier in drag culture) the phrase "about face" has been used in queer communities, as in the About Face Theatre in Chicago or the recent art history volume edited by Jonathan Katz.[60] Without doubt, all of this collective work confirms curator Kinshasa Holman Conwill's contention that "reading both the facts and the between-the-lines emotions of the lives of [extraordinary artists such as Edmonia Lewis] is a vivid and moving experience."[61]

A Head of Her Time

She came to me cut by a white man's hand. Sometime about 1875, the Victorian author Charles Reade (1814–84) used his scissors to crop the head and torso of Edmonia Lewis from an etched newsprint portrait of the artist. Reade then pasted the rough-cut printed image onto the left edge of page 92 in his bound private notebook. Next, he used a pencil to label the top of the page "Heads." There this picture of Lewis remained for more than a century, affixed on the page of that notebook, which was kept on a low, locked shelf in the London Library, located on the southwest corner of St. James's Square. This two-dimensional version of Lewis, drawn, printed, quartered, pasted, then classified and (mis)labeled, transformed her living body into a flattened remnant and floating signifier in Reade's representational realm. Like a pinned butterfly, she remains there, a specimen flayed. *A head of her time.*

This chapter begins with a description of a single page in a notebook in the London Library because I have come to see my encounter with this random page as the genesis of this book about Edmonia Lewis. Let me explain.

1

Upon learning about Charles Reade's wide-ranging interests in so-called marginalized subjects, I wanted to look at his private journals, which he used as source material for his novels and plays. I suspect that only a few researchers have shown interest in Reade's fading notebooks, let alone looked at this specific page in the archive. Nevertheless, the works are available to view, preserved as a result of Reade's status as a well-known Victorian man of letters.

Reade's notebook resides in the London Library, a place where generations of notable writers such as Charles Darwin, Bram Stoker, and Virginia Woolf all worked, after they each had become members of this innovative research space.[1] When I first went to view Reade's bound volumes there in 1996, I too had to pay a subscription to the library in pounds sterling. The day I first visited the building, I remember leaving the bulk of my things in the coatroom on the first floor before ascending the staircase to the second floor. At the upstairs librarian's counter, I was issued the requisite white cotton gloves. Ill-fitting, they reminded me of gloves from the era of blackface minstrelsy.

Nevertheless, I managed to grasp the sharpened no. 2 pencil I was permitted to use. I had concealed a small Kodak instamatic camera in my blue leather pencil case. Perched on a hard wooden chair at one of the long oak tables in the high-ceilinged Reading Room, I recall seeing the pale amber light shining through the large neoclassical windows at the end of the room. I spotted dust particles dappling the rays.

I think it was a June morning. Having settled myself at the table, I was flipping through umpteen pages that featured Reade's bizarre collages when my eye landed on the dark visage of the female figure pasted on a page. Suddenly I found myself facing that fateful page with the word "Heads" written at the top.

At that instant I did not recognize Lewis: She was just an anonymous cutout amid a jumble of other "heads." In fact, it would be another decade before I came to know her as the once famous professional female sculptor of African and Indigenous descent Miss Edmonia Lewis. Yet, as my gloved hands grazed the yellowing page, I touched the past and felt some frisson, some visceral connection with the paper. Did an elusive presence accelerate my pulse?

There is no doubt that Lewis was there, posing as a kind of secret in the archive, as if manifesting José Esteban Muñoz's theory of "ephemera" as evidence of and for queer lives.[2] I did not go in search of her (how could I have done so when the very name Mary Edmonia Lewis was not

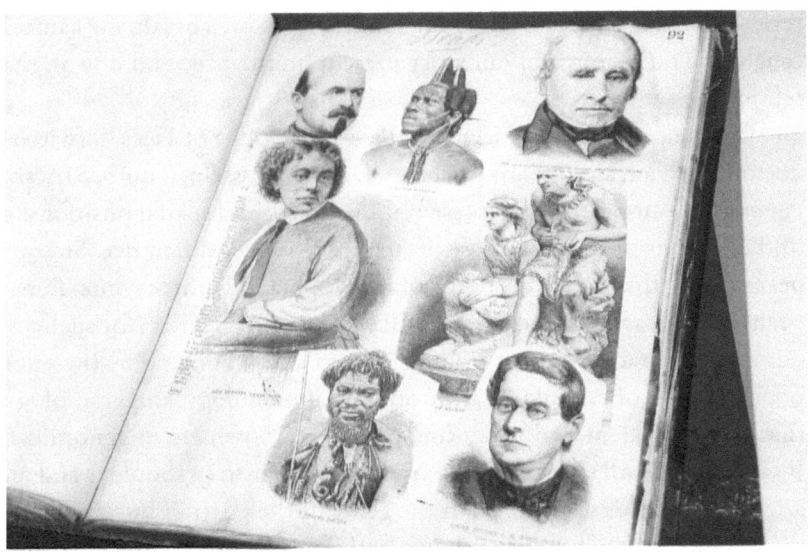

1.1 Charles Reade's notebook, page with "Heads,"
ca. 1870. Newsprint pasted on scrapbook paper. London
Library, London. Photo by J. D. Brody, 1996.

yet known to me?); rather, it is as if she appeared to have found me. By
some miracle, in that hushed space of the archive, we found our way to
each other. Then and there, I let Edmonia Lewis have me—mind, body,
and soul. Our impossible meeting across an ocean of time, a haphazard,
misbegotten, almost forgotten moment, moves me to wonder about how
such an archival fragment could foment such desire. Serendipitously, she
has refused to let me go. . . .

Here is a reproduction of the photograph of the page in Reade's
scrapbook (figure 1.1). As you can see, several cutouts of different people's
heads are displayed. Among the heads sits the sketchy image of Edmonia
Lewis.

On first viewing this strangely arranged tableau of characters, I may
have in fact overlooked Lewis as I rushed to capture and preserve the page
before me. Although Lewis clearly appears centered on the page (she is the
largest image in the group of heads), I was snapping the picture in haste
and perhaps did not stop to think about the snapshot's composition. After
all, I was using a Kodak camera without the benefit of a digital preview. I
left the outcome of the image to the mechanics of the aperture, perhaps
only subconsciously aware that there were black-and-white images on the
page. The illicit photograph you see reproduced here is the less-than-ideal

result. Breaking the rules while the librarian was on a break, my camera caught the protagonist of our story present on the page and now in the reprint you see here.[3]

On the page, Lewis is seen amid a hodge-podge of faces: a (witch) doctor, a warrior, an (Indian) chief . . . a Dakota, Prussian, Basuto, African, American, European. The representational logic and spatial positioning of these heads seem to be those of juxtaposition, of difference. She appears among the rag-tag grouping of men: apparently three white/European?/American?/Caucasian? two Black/African/Negro? (for such are our inherited racial ways of reading, forged and reinforced by the once popular, fields of ethnology, anthropology, phrenology, and craniology that were prevalent and prevailing prior to our own era of genomics). If we look carefully, we see that part of Lewis's torso (a shoulder and an arm) is present, as was typical in the genre of the portrait bust. Lewis is the only member of the group shown with a product that she devised and divined—her sculpture *Old Arrow Maker*, to her right (see figure 1.2). In order to understand this relation, we have to already know that she is the Artist habitually represented with (if not wedded to) her work, as Reade's haphazard pasting does not make this connection explicit.

These "heads" function synecdochally as distillations of racial types.[4] The head, like the "crown," condensed whole narratives of fictive (if no less efficacious) ideas that established a hierarchy of race, gender, and sexuality thought to reside in the bodily differences. These imagined hierarchies hardened throughout the nineteenth century as they were reinforced by legal, medical, sexological, scientific, ethnological, and other discursive formations. I understand the ideology of such racial schemas proffered by Reade as he created this improbable mix of "types" according to a hierarchical logic of invented difference—racial, spatiotemporal, geopolitical, sexual. The copresence and nonuniformity of these specimens may have indicated unequal references. It is possible that Reade laid out his schema of what he thought of as the primitive and the cosmopolitan, as a means of rendering them both sutured and separated.

Certainly, when I first saw this page, as an assistant professor of English at the University of California, Riverside, I was primed to think about its representation of difference. At the time, I had traveled to London on a fellowship from the Royal Society of Theatre Research that allowed me time to study Reade's archives. I was finishing a chapter of my first book, on representations (literary, visual, theatrical) of Black American women in nineteenth-century Britain. Like many other humanistic scholars who came of age in the 1990s, my intellectual formation included exposure to cultural studies, poststructuralism, and Black feminist theory. I learned always to look askance, to remember Walter Benjamin's concept of history in which "every document of civilization is, at the same time, a document of barbarism," to eschew triumphalist, often nationalistic interpretations of historical materials, and to research many models and modes of knowing. I learned to pay attention to what was obscured and jettisoned by dominant narratives of the past.[5] These ideas informed my reading of Reade's work.

Like his coeval Charles Dickens, Reade was one of the most prolific authors of "social problem" novels, or what we might now call documentary fiction. Notably, Reade was among the original founders of the London Library, which opened in 1841. The library was a first-of-its-kind lending library. He also contributed to progressive literary culture by helping to shape Victorian ideas about prison reform, migration, and the changing roles of men and women. Reade scoured newspapers, broadsides, and other texts that could be useful fodder for his writing about railways, trade unions, Catholicism, ancient and recent political history, and a thousand other topics—from the colossal to the merely curious, or what he termed "curalalia."

Throughout his long career, Reade diligently preserved these clippings in scrapbooks, creating his own personal archive. "The scrapbook," Jessica Helfand observes, "was the original open-source technology, a unique form of self-expression that celebrated visual sampling, culture mixing, and the appropriation and redistribution of existing media."[6] Another historian describes scrapbooks as "bulky, somewhat haphazard in arrangement, extremely miscellaneous, a medley in which significance is often snowed under drifts of inconsequential clippings."[7] Such volumes are understood to have limited intellectual value and, as they are notoriously difficult to catalog, are overlooked. Yet the ephemeral matter they contain can provide speculative insights about process and creative production. When I went back to look again at Reade's archive, in 2023, specifically to revisit that fateful page (and try to rekindle my archival affair?), I learned that Reade's notebooks were being digitized for online access and were not available to be perused in person. They were at that moment no longer accessible to my immediate touch: were digitally withheld from my hands, in both senses of the term.

The scraps Reade collected, while once housed in a semipublic reading room, reveal that such spaces contain erotica and countercultural artifacts. After Reade's death, some libraries deemed his writings about unwed mothers, lady doctors, and clever actresses too salacious to be kept on library shelves.[8] This judgment seems ironic in that Reade had helped to usher in the library as a place of knowledge more public and open than the libraries of monks, kings, or wealthy elite private citizens. The London Library as an institution incorporated Victorian interests in the more public circulation of ideas and the transformation of writing, journalistic and otherwise, into a paid profession.[9] It was the era of the democratization of print culture. Throughout his career as a writer—dramatist, novelist, and journalist—Reade carefully archived his fascination with actors and (especially) actresses' lives "on and off the boards." He also archived his fascination with ambiguous figures, many of whom were also actors (such as the eighteenth-century star Peg Woffington), whose protean performances he developed into scripts that complicated conventions of the day. Reade wrote dramatic tales drawn from the quotidian lives of those whom he saw as suffering systemic oppression—whether in asylums or prisons or via sumptuary laws. He was obsessed with mistaken identity, a theme that figures in many of his works, from the cowritten play *Masks and Faces* (1854) to his essay on an androgynous figure, "Woman Playing at Man" (1884), which chronicles the case of a married woman who "cross-dressed" as a journeyman painter, only to court and then fall in love with another woman.[10] His writing betrayed an obsession with paradoxes, oddities, and marginalized subjects.

Reade's curiosity contributed to the years he spent supporting and researching in the London Library. The library opened in the same historical moment as the organization of the London Ethnological Society (1847) and other institutions of learning. As noted above, the logic at work in the "Heads" images appears primarily to be about racial differences. Indeed, in nineteenth-century racial science (as well as in Western symbolic anthropology), the head served a metonymic function as the locus of "knowledge" and "power" (moral and otherwise) and came to be correlated with intelligence. In this era of craniometry—a science devised to measure intellectual capabilities that helped to establish racialized, gendered, and other hierarchies—the head purportedly bore the imprint of personality and individuality. Later proved to be deeply flawed, craniometry nevertheless supported what was then deemed objective bodily signs of criminality and deviant sexuality—overwhelmingly in nonwhite and female heads.[11] Where might Lewis land in such a ranking? How does she compare to the Black Indigenous "heads" that touch her cutout torso? Are these "colored" etchings her companions—darker figures who labor under racist and reductive labels: "A Basuto [Witch] Doctor" and "A Kaffir Warrior"? Or, given that Edmonia Lewis sports a cravat and sits in a fringed chair, is she closer to the "white" heads of state? Two are identified by their "proper" names and professions: "Chief Justice J. M. Read" and the "The Late Count Von Brunnow, Russian Ambassador to the Court of St. James."

The print of Lewis in the scrapbook is based on a carte de visite made by Augustus Marshall in 1864 (discussed in chapter 6), when such photographs were posed in the same way as sculpted or painted portrait busts. We are meant to view Lewis's visage as about her character, as the site of individuation. The page includes a third, goateed white man, unnamed, whose head is directly above Lewis's. We assume that, unlike the "Basuto [Witch] Doctor," he *has* a name and is also an individual; he does not represent a general type. Such are the conventions of portraiture that endow whites with singularity and others with general features common to their stereotype. We have been trained to read visages, physiognomies, as tell-tale signs of race, gender, and sexuality. The honored sculptor has, in common with the white heads, an honorific: "Miss Edmonia Lewis"—a name that bespeaks her gender and unusual status in the colonial world powered by what we could now call white heteropatriarchy. It is little wonder that in her book *Writing with Scissors* (2013), Ellen Gruber Garvey sees the scrapbook as a "museum" with fixed exhibits in which visitor-readers "comprehend exhibits through the . . . space [in] a structured performance . . . [that] embodies a script for moving through."[12]

Reade's scrapbook page also illuminates the way Edmonia Lewis's image has been sutured to her work. She is almost always represented in conversation with her sculptures. As Kirstin Pai Buick argues, Lewis's "subjectivity is fused with and confused by her subject matter," particularly when read in racial and gendered terms.[13] Even now, it is a rare occurrence to "see" her without reference to her work, and vice versa. In her own time, she posed and stood by her work, literally and figuratively. When her sculpture *The Death of Cleopatra* (see figure 2.2) was shown at the Philadelphia Centennial International Exposition in 1876, she stood by the work to gauge viewers' reactions. She even thought of herself as wedded to her work. While no extant photo of this side-by-side posing exists, we know about it from newspaper accounts. We should, however, be cautious about reading relations between the artist and her work tautologically. It is important to avoid essentializing and reductively reading what were and remain complicated constructions of her subjectivity.

As this book unfolds, I speak more about theories of heads in art historical and racialized-gendered terms, remembering that the head in sculpture served frequently as a locus of individuation: as the place, particularly in realistic portraits produced from life, understood to be saturated with a "self." As discussed above, the head was concomitant, if not synonymous, with the portrait bust. The head was the locus of the crucial elements of "style, subject matter, heritage, and phenotype."[14] The questions surrounding Lewis's subjectivity demonstrate one of the many paradoxes that this book discusses: How and why did it become axiomatic to think of Lewis and or as her work? This is another way of asking about our curiosity about the makers of particular works of art, which is at once a question about style, the market, and the political production of identity.

Even though Lewis frequently referred to herself as a "colored artist," such utterances, according to the literature about her, may have been deployed strategically. Naming herself and signing her work as a colored artist was at once a capitulation to and a claiming of her "difference." She could not avoid "standing out" among other, white neoclassical artists of her generation, who, while they sculpted similar subjects, did so with under adjacent ascriptions to their bodies (of work). For example, Lewis was singled out in a disparaging remark made by Henry James who called the American female sculptors who had made their way to Rome in the 1800s "that strange sisterhood of American 'lady sculptors' who at one time settled upon the seven hills in a white, marmorean flock." James noted that among the group was "a negress, whose color, picturesquely contrasting with that of her plastic material [white marble] was the pleading agent of her fame."[15] Willingly or not, Lewis's multifaceted racialized affiliations mattered. At different moments throughout her career, she spoke of her pride in her origins, and in a few instances reported in the press, she voiced racist stereotypes about both Black and Indigenous people. These remarks by Lewis were reported secondhand, however, and should be read with some skepticism as well as with an understanding of her need to perform "otherwise" to preserve her sense of self. Some contemporary critics of Lewis displayed a derogatory fixation on her "black hands on white marble." Her subjectivity seems always already to be inseparable from these objects; as in her appearance next to her statue of Cleopatra in Philadelphia or her performances in her studio in Rome (where President Grant and Frederick Douglass both visited to witness her carve her statues with a heavy lead chisel, to refine them with a sharp awl, and finally to file them with a rasp). Her life and work form the core (and corps) of what Buick discusses as her "career" rather than her "biography."[16]

Let us now return to the page with which we began to address the image of Lewis's sculpture. Clearly from the same printed source, a cutout etching of Lewis's *Old Arrow Maker* (1866) sits directly opposite Lewis's picture on the scrapbook page. This is the only image of a sculptural representation and, as such, differs from the "heads" on the page. In the drawing of the sculpture, we see two people in putatively Indigenous dress. Below the figures, the letters "Of Hiawat[—]" are visible. Lewis's sculpture was known in other copies as *The Wooing of Hiawatha* and was derived from Henry Wadsworth Longfellow's popular nineteenth-century epic poem *The Song of Hiawatha* (1855). "As a national poet in the Emersonian sense, Longfellow would sing the unsung poem that was America by focusing on historical, indigenous themes but in a distinctly sentimental vein."[17] He did so, in an era of expanded settler colonialism perpetrated by the government that involved placing Indigenous subjects in newly built prisons, executing and slaughtering them, and violently removing them from sovereign lands.

In 1866, a short time after she had settled in Rome, Lewis elected to interpret a scene from Book 10 of the epic, in which Hiawatha gives a slain deer as a wedding gift to Minnehaha. In this way, she could build on and make her own claim to the fabled tale by translating Longfellow's text into a new medium. The intertribal union depicted in Longfellow's poem involves Minnehaha from the Dakota tribe marrying Hiawatha, who is Ojibwe (even if the hero's name is borrowed from an Onondaga chief who was a founding member of the Iroquois Confederacy). Lewis's dual-portrait sculpture represents the Dakota "maiden" Minnehaha and her father, the "old arrow maker," crouching over the limp body of a recently killed fawn, gifted by Hiawatha (figure 1.2). Minnehaha's father wears a loincloth and jewelry consisting of a beaded necklace perhaps meant to represent bear claws. His long hair is styled on top at the center of his head, held by a tie. The statue, however, depicts a tenderly rendered father-daughter duo practicing their arts of arrow making and weaving. Ojibwe artists, past and present, made beautifully embroidery for blouses, belts, and shoes: Lewis mentioned several times that her mother was lauded for her novel embroidered designs and credited her with her own artistic interest in "making the form of things."

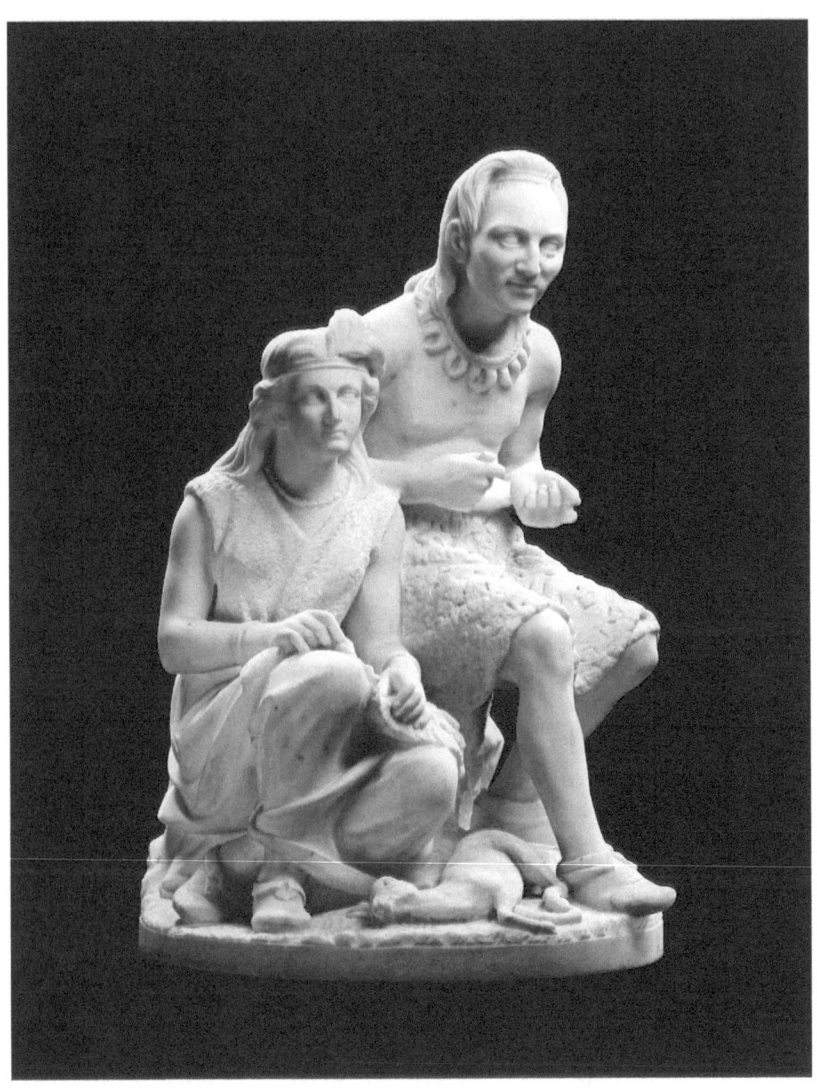

1.2 Edmonia Lewis, *Old Arrow Maker*, modeled 1866, carved 1872. Marble, 21½ × 13⅝ × 13⅜ in. Smithsonian Museum of American Art, Washington, DC, Gift of Mr. and Mrs. Norman Robbins.

Much has been written about how Indigenous people were seen as subjects fit for neoclassical transformation, rendering them at once noble, "neoclassically white," and located in the past. Unlike the dozens of idealized neoclassical statues that portrayed either "dead" or singularly "nubile" and/or inert Indian subjects carved by American sculptors in this era, Lewis's work, filtered through Longfellow's fiction so as to eschew a reductive rendering of Lewis's biomythography, stands apart. Art historian Elizabeth Hutchinson argues that, Lewis's "subtle visual language . . . used a form of ideal sculpture to counter stereotypes of Native Women."[18] Lewis elects to show two Indigenous characters who are very much *alive*, together and diligently making art (Minnehaha weaves dried bulrush while her father shapes arrowheads).[19] Here, Lewis may have tried to interrupt racist, reductively "realistic" renditions by illustrating these characters in scenes of quotidian activity, in moments of health and vigor, and as makers of art.

Lewis's sculptural production of the furrowed fur on Minnehaha's vest and her father's garment renders this work more naturalistic than traditionally idealized "Indian" subjects sculpted by other artists of her time. The naturalistic style adds dimension to the work. The kneeling figures are *grounded* in multiple senses of the term. The figures sit on a round base, which the artist has signed on the bottom, and their intricate poses beg to be seen from multiple angles. This is a small work and one that Lewis copied several times.[20] It is a beautifully detailed double portrait: Minute strokes form the wide, full feather that adorns Minnehaha's horizontal headband and decorates both figures' flowing hair. The textured elements (hair, cloth, and the aforementioned fur) were not typical of the neoclassical idealist style, which tended to valorize smooth, untextured surfaces in white marble. The decorated moccasins worn by each figure compel close looking, as do the delicate fingers of Minnehaha as they interact with the matting. Her perfectly rounded necklace is another work of art featured in the statue. The entire scene recounts a quiet if meaningful moment when the daughter is on the cusp of taking on a new identity. It instantiates in marble the ideas of change, life, death, sexuality, and transition in a work that conveys dynamic density.

Over all these years, Lewis has remained a vibrant presence alive in a corner of my mind—moving with me, moving me, indeed, consuming me. My photo of the scrapbook page remained as a material trace in my own personal archive, carted across many moves, reminding me that, as Jacques Derrida has argued, "the question of the archive is not, we repeat, a question of the past. . . . It is a question of the future."[21] The photograph has been digitized—not only on a computer but also by my fingers—as if the brush of my fingertips over the image could recover or revive her, as if she were a rosebud that could blossom under the warmth of my touch.[22] It was she, however, who possessed the power to make a bloom materialize in three dimensions, as chapter 4 shows.

Nevertheless, I have carried a copy of the four-by-six-inch glossy photographic print with me ever since that first auspicious, queer turn in the archive in 1996, not entirely knowing why. Touching the slick surface of the photograph is a revelation of affective desire and desired effect. Each time I pick it up, I engage in a proleptic fantasy that one day this no longer mysterious woman and I might meet in a space outside the archive that confines us.

In my efforts to understand this image, I seemed continually to have been confronted with lack. The persistent invisibility of categories such as "Indigenous woman" or "Black woman" in the vast majority of library and museum filing systems prevents researchers from locating Black and Indigenous histories in conventional materials. When my students looked for references about Black women in the 1990s, when the internet began, they found mostly pornographic sites: Our battle to shift the sites and sight of power continues.[23] In an attempt to expose the gross generalizations and lack of specificity found in the archives of museums, the poet Robin Coste Lewis wrote "The Voyage of the Sable Venus" (2015).

This long-form narrative poem artfully collates actual titles found in museums archives, "catalogue entries, and exhibition descriptions of Western art objects in which a black female is present, dating from 38,000 B.C.E. to the present." The multipart poem uses the language of these institutions against themselves by showing how they have (mis)characterized so many works by or about female Black figures in their holdings. Here again, Miss Edmonia Lewis makes her presence felt. Coste Lewis mentions "*The Old Arrow Maker and His Daughter,*" in section XVIII, next to the line "Untitled Negro Woman" as if to suggest a disjunction between the work and a possible maker.[24]

Robin Coste Lewis and many other Black feminist writers fixated on "invisibilized" lives argue for the value of even the most fragmentary archival traces of our enslaved, buried, or disappeared ancestors. Although these figures have been obscured and even made absent from the National Archives, at the very least, a desire for their existence remains. Although now some of Lewis's sculptures have finally made the arduous journey to a place of honor in the Smithsonian American Art Museum, "remarkably," as Elizabeth Broun, former director of the National Museum of American Art, notes, "for 135 years after the founding of the federal art collections in 1829, no work by a black American was represented in the nation's holdings."[25] The executive order "Restoring Truth and Sanity to American History," issued by the president on March 27, 2025, explicitly denounces the multigallery Smithsonian Exhibition *The Shape of Power: Stories of Race and American Sculpture*, which showcased two of Edmonia Lewis's sculptures, *Hagar* and *Old Arrow Maker*. With this pronouncement, we may again have to face the expulsion of works from the National Archives. For me, seeing Lewis's *Hagar* outshine Hiram Powers's *The Greek Slave* (the first nude sculpture of a woman to tour the United States) with which it was juxtaposed and again having the opportunity to see *Old Arrow Maker* placed "in the open" just behind a small velvet rope, was breathtaking. The ongoing controversies over how and why sculpture, in particular, shapes our understanding of power, the very theme of this show, is discussed in greater detail in chapter 7. Suffice it to say here that we should not be at all surprised that Edmonia Lewis's work was ahead of its time in speaking to these enduring questions of race, gender, class, sexuality, and subjectivity.

Lewis's savvy statues connect her to many Indigenous, African, and so-called non-Western people who continue to resist the long-standing impacts of being and having been "the collected" by Western archival and museums. Our bones, bodies, belongings, historical artifacts, religious and other precious objects, while claimed as our changing cultural legacies, also have become part of the detritus of modernity and colonialism. Numerous museums in Europe and the United States have closed exhibits, returned artifacts, and are attempting to reconcile the difficult origins, means, and meanings of their collections. In historiographic accounts—what we might call archives about archives—we learn that the repositories of libraries and archives were typically designed to be coextensive with, if not constitutive of, colonizing Western citadels. Such places were conceived as spaces to guard written records, official documents, and other empirical imperial evidence tied to the majesty and ministrations of the state. "There cannot . . . be a definition of 'archives' that does not encompass both the building itself and the documents stored there," Achille Mbembe has argued. "The institution has an 'architectural' power that produces an inescapable materiality and an instantiating imaginary."[26] In this way, archives possess the potential to represent the collective: a composite, composed gathering—a community bound and binding that creates a limit of inclusion and exclusion.

The city of London, where this chapter begins, is part of what Joseph Roach has called the "circum-Atlantic vortex." The library sits at the metaphorical center of the empire where and by which "a great deal of the unspeakable violence instrumental to this creation may have been forgotten, [and yet where] circum-Atlantic memory retains its consequences, one of which is that the unspeakable cannot be rendered forever inexpressible."[27] Archives are thus places of negotiated, negotiating, and negated power, of ordering things and therefore of engaging the dialectic between presence and absence, history and memory, the lost and the found. In such places, we may find ourselves looking at loss, making an absence present and remembering history.

The London Library belongs to the vast British Library (formerly part of the British Museum). The building and its contents index Great Britain's powerful imperial reach and rule, perhaps epitomized by its long-standing connections to the global slave trade. Sir Hans Sloane (1650–1753), who is credited with starting the British Museum when he donated his collection of objects, built up his vast holdings with wealth derived from sugar plantations worked by enslaved West Africans and owned by his wife's family.[28] His home is now itself a museum in London.

Here we might ask, following Rebecca Schneider, "What does it serve to remind ourselves that this privileging of the site-able remains in the archive is linked, as it is the root of the word *archive*, to the prerogatives of the archon, the head of state?"[29] The link between the archive and the head of state suggests the often belated entry into museums and libraries of such categories as Women in the Arts, African Americans, Native Americans, Enslaved Peoples, Victims of the Holocaust, and Lesbian Herstory Archives, all of which are meant to contravene the many collections of the merely "othered," peoples who have been "museumified" and "collected." As ethnographic specimens or spoils of war from the many years of "discovery," these peoples have provided the basis of major museum collections from the British Museum in London to the American Museum of Natural History in New York City. National archives are fortresses that have also served as residences for residual memories and moments that run counter to the stacked, stocked, and locked documents in those purportedly stable locations. This is a crucial concept for understanding how Edmonia Lewis's life in art can be narrativized, collected, and recalled.

The cultural wealth preserved in England's capital buildings is a result of the slaughter and brutal toil of enslaved people across the globe in its far-flung colonies in the Americas, Africa, and across the East and

West Indies. The continuing consequences of this traffic in human beings and violent resource extraction are profound. "There is no document of civilization which is not, at the same time, a document of barbarism," as Walter Benjamin put it.[30] Indeed, every invocation of the library and the museum, these venerated archives of knowledge, contains a connection to the constitutive violence of these original "holdings." We must grapple with the ethical quandary that Christina Sharpe presents: "If museums and memorials materialize a kind of reparation (repair) and enact their own pedagogies as they position visitors to have a particular experience or set of experiences about an event that is seen to be past, how does one memorialize chattel slavery and its afterlives, which are unfolding still?"[31] Although our Afro-Native subject was never enslaved, she was among the first artists to memorialize chattel slavery, in two sculptures that valorized freedom while (as if, impossibly, mindful of Sharpe's critique) representing these figures as "unfolding still."

Neither you nor I can escape being enmeshed in the lethal exchanges of human beings that occurred in the Atlantic, given the fact that slavery was and is the stock-in-trade of racial capitalism that formed and informs our modern world. In many ways, the constitutive collision of racism, colonialism, dispossession, imperialism, and capitalism spurs us to question the space of the archive and how we understand what might be lost and found there. Although Edmonia Lewis was not enslaved or forced off of tribal lands, her story cannot be read without invoking this world-historical dispossession.[32] For more than four hundred years (and into the present) such global journeys transformed millions of lives, producing the modern world of capital, goods, services, insurance, governmental and official religious records, stocks, bonds, and deeds, which is to say, death itself.[33] Lewis was propelled from the United States, however, because she was aware of its enormous capacity for violence against the Others living within its national borders, egregiously vilified, among whom she could have been and indeed was counted.

My analysis moves among and between the encounters of histories and memories, archives and repertoires, things and bodies in which "the archive and the repertoire are not mutually exclusive; but rather mutually constitutive."[34] I remain attuned to the many absences and losses that the abundance of archives only serves to magnify.[35] Each instantiation of official history is haunted by passing shadows that mark its building: Containment is never complete. History changes; the impulse to preserve is one that encodes a vision of, for, or about the future. The time of the archive, therefore, moves as much as motivates its formation.[36] These larger questions have contributed to the obscuring of Edmonia Lewis's story. We turn now to an abbreviated narrative of her life that seeks to unearth some of the facts of her being that have been buried . . . in the archives.

Edmonia Lewis always wanted to be an artist. In an interview printed in the *Lorain County News*, she claimed that she "always wanted to make the form of things." She furnished a maternal genealogy for this desire: "My Mother was famous for inventing new patterns for embroidery on moccasins and perhaps the same is coming out in me."[37] Lewis's heritage, as she identified it, was Ojibwe (formerly "Chippewa" and now Anishinaabe) on her mother's side and probably Afro-Haitian on her father's side. Her mother, Margaret Groat Mike, may have been the daughter of a formerly enslaved man, John Mike, and an Ojibwe woman known as Catherine. As is so often the case, the exact circumstances of her family genealogy continue to unfold.[38] What is clear is that Lewis was orphaned: Both her parents died before she turned ten years old.[39] After their deaths, she lived with her mother's sisters. She said, "My Indian aunts took care of me; the tribe moved away to Canada but they sometimes came down as far as New York City to buy beads and such things."[40] She learned how to produce Indigenous souvenir art (beaded moccasins, weavings, and the like) for the tourist trade that flourished around Niagara Falls. To paraphrase Buick, the selling of souvenirs is like playing Indian, by which she means that this act was a calculated move that traded on the nostalgic idea of an aboriginal identity unadulterated by the modern world.[41]

Such a move (of which there were many throughout her life) suggests that Lewis cannily deployed racialized discourse to further her own survival. She sought to maintain references to her origins even as she attended private schools (New York Central College in McGrawville, New York, and Oberlin College outside Cleveland, Ohio) and moved to Europe. Moreover, she often referred to her own origins as "wild" in a subversive move to counter the racist presumptions of interviewers who may have sought to denigrate her identities. Instead, Lewis often boasted that her difference was in fact the basis of her artistic and intellectual triumphs. During her life, her half-brother, Samuel Lewis, helped support her endeavors by paying her tuition, assisting with rent, and assuring her that she would not be without sustenance. Samuel, who was known as well by the name Sunrise, had moved West where he prospered as a barber in San Francisco and worked as a miner during the height of the California frenzy that took place just after the discovery of gold in the city of Coloma in 1848. As a miner in the state at mid-century (the "rush" was said to last until 1855), his work, while lucrative, also contributed to the destruction of local Indigenous peoples and the land, with its abundant natural resources, over which they had previously had dominion. This historical fact complicates how we understand the sources of wealth that help to sustain Lewis in that Samuel maintained banking interests in the state until his death in 1896. In Bozeman, Samuel became the proprietor of several real estate holdings; he rented properties, built a substantial home for himself, and helped the community.[42]

Lewis attended Oberlin for three years before she was forced to leave the progressive, avowedly abolitionist college (the first in the nation to admit non-white students) after a scandal. She falsely was accused of poisoning two white female students—for which she was acquitted in a trial. The lawyer who defended her was John Mercer Langston, who later became the dean of Howard University Law School. In the wake of the initial accusations, Lewis suffered a violent attack. After the entire ordeal, a callous and calculating administrator, Marianne Parker Dascomb, who was the principal of the Female Department at Oberlin, prevented Lewis from enrolling for her final credits when she was again falsely charged with stealing art supplies and forced to move on from the school.

Lewis used her connections to prominent abolitionists to assist her with letters of introduction to colleagues in Boston and moved to that more hospitable city in the Northeast. In 1865 she received her passport to sail to Europe, whereupon she settled among an established expatriate community of American-born artists, first in Florence and ultimately in Rome, Italy.

She arrived in Rome in the middle of December 1865. Shortly thereafter, she dined on "turkey and plum pudding" with three female acquaintances, one of whom had helped her to secure her studio and rented rooms (a sitting room and adjoining bedroom) in the city. She was welcomed by the American-born Williams sisters, Mary Elizabeth (1825–1902)and Abigail Osgood (1823–1913), along with their close friend Florence Freeman (1836–83), another American sculptor. Lewis proved to be a welcoming host, not only serving food in her modest studio but also entertaining her guests by playing her guitar after meals. Lewis loved music and attended the opera frequently—this was the case even at Oberlin, which is still known as an excellent school for the musically inclined.

The start of Lewis's professional career as an artist coincided with the final years of enslavement in the United States and the increasing violence of Native American removal. Her work was supported by and contributed to abolitionist activism. Much of her work was difficult to sell; nevertheless, she held true to her artistic vision. Much of her correspondence pertains to queries about payments. She would take commissions but also might create work that she would either gift or even sculpt with the belief that the work would find a buyer. Her statues sold for hundreds of dollars, a fine sum in the era. Still, it is remarkable that Lewis lived on the sales proceeds of her art, with only intermittent assistance from her beloved brother.

The relatively more welcoming world Lewis found in Continental Europe allowed her to make her own way and to avoid the overt racist violence she more readily experienced in the United States. She managed to circumvent the customary assumptions that would have curtailed her freedom as a "colored woman" and an artist. As Buick argues in her brilliant study of Lewis, "Between 1866 and 1876, her heroism lay not in subversion . . . but rather in the musical sense of inversion or counterpoint in which upper and lower voices are transposed or in which a single melody is applied in the opposite direction."[43] Lewis's career shows her not as a revolutionary tout court, but rather as a woman who whittled a smooth new shape against a racist and sexist grain that would otherwise render her warped and disfigured. Above all, she maintained her commitment to carving sculptures.

Lewis sculpted more than thirty portrait busts during her prolific career. Several were of Black patrons and heroes, including Frederick Douglass, Rev. Daniel Payne, and perhaps Phyllis Wheatley (a bronze bust of whom is purportedly lost), and others were of Jesus, President Lincoln, Longfellow, and the lesbian actress and doyenne Charlotte Cushman, who hosted Lewis in Rome. Among Lewis's most important busts was that of Col. Robert Gould Shaw. She sold more than one hundred plaster copies of this work for $15 apiece, amassing a sum that famously financed her move to Rome in 1865. These relatively affordable souvenirs of the revered white leader of the all-Black 54th Massachusetts Regiment (to which one of Frederick Douglass's sons belonged) were crucial to the launching of her career abroad. It is notable that at least one Black artist of the period, Nelson A. Primus (1842–1916) of Hartford, Connecticut, who knew of and admired Lewis and her work, remarked that he "wished [he] had money so I could go to Europe to study coupple [sic] of years."[44] Lewis's achievement in setting up a studio abroad takes on more significance in light of such statements.

In 1868, Lydia Maria Child wrote to her friend and fellow abolition-ist Harriet Winslow Sewall that Edmonia Lewis was "very poor." Child blamed Lewis's financial condition on her inability to understand the concept of budgeting money—a fact she attributed to the artist's race and ethnicity: "I have observed that she has no calculation about money: what is *received* with facility is *expended* with facility. She is not to blame for this deficiency. How could it be otherwise, when her childhood was spent with poor negroes, and her youth with wild Indians?"[45] Although one of her early champions, Child, like so many white philanthropists and art patrons, past and present, maintained a stance of superiority over the "objects" of her charity. Child wanted Lewis to work in wood, a less expensive material, or to become a "technical" carver of stone who made architectural pieces that, in her opinion, required less skill. Such pieces were also "unsigned" and did not have the value of works created by a named artist.

Patronizingly, Child "suggested to [Lewis] to work in stucco-molding for architects, which I have been told employed a good many hands in Europe. . . . She might have, meanwhile, kept trying her hand at statuary during [after] hours, and if, in the course of years produced something really good, people would be ready enough to *propose* to put it in marble for her. I have also thought of *wood* carving as a means of subsistence for her" (emphasis in original). Child believed that "neither her mind nor her hands [were] yet educated enough to work in marble."[46] She even considered one of Lewis's early sculptures, *Forever Free* (also known as *Morning of Liberty*) (1867; see figure 4.1), not "worth putting in marble."[47] Lewis was obdurate, holding fast to her determination to work in marble despite pressure from the likes of Child who would want her to choose an "easier" medium. Child's admonitions were but one of enumerable ra-cial slights Lewis endured in her quest to become a professional sculptor. "Many people praise me because I am a colored girl: but I do not want that kind of praise," Lewis declared. "I would rather critics point out my faults for that will teach me something."[48] Lewis was adamant that she could achieve success at the level of the great masters of her medium. She would not be daunted and worked to attain what was understood by art critics of the time as "ideal excellence that must be assigned in art to any creation in marble. Sculpture cannot depend on any accessories of the surrounding, but solely on its own character. The limitation of its mate-rial peculiarly isolates it from all other arts. Its true place is in immortal-izing for us types of humanity or epochs of thought."[49] I credit Lewis for choosing to create sculptures made of the most valuable medium of her day. I see her selection of marble as her medium (in both senses of the term?) as a striving for sculptural significance and an appeal to permanence. Surely she succeeded in this quest since her marble works remain as testament to her . . . art.

In Rome, Lewis produced the majority of her known sculptures in a highly productive decade between 1866 and 1876. Lewis worked in several different studios in Rome, all of which over the years were listed in guidebooks and known to be a stop on the Grand Tour (the customary travel to Europe whereby wealthy young men "completed" their cultural education). Lewis's studio, then, was a desired destination among the travelers from the upper echelons of the era—from the British Marquess of Bute, who bought some of her Catholic-themed pieces, to US President Ulysses S. Grant, whose bust she sculpted, to writers and activists such as Longfellow and Douglass, and even Pope Pius IX. Overwhelmingly, this impressive cadre of international visitors celebrated her for her achievements as well as her welcoming manner. A majority of visitors over the years commented on her brilliance, persistence, and wit, as well. In Rome, Lewis circulated among a mostly white expatriate artistic community where she was able to sculpt and live in relative freedom. A number of the other women sculptors were supported by and joined the lesbian coterie generated by the actress Charlotte Cushman, which also helped Lewis (even if, on occasion, its members also denigrated her).

Lewis followed in the path of many other American sculptors who had moved to Rome before her, such as William Wetmore Story (1819–95), Anne Whitney (1821–1915), and Harriet Hosmer (1830–1908), to name only three. She was the only "dark" member of the excoriated and exalted group of artistic expatriates living in Rome at mid-century. These artists were immortalized in Nathaniel Hawthorne's novel *The Marble Faun*, published in 1860. Based on Hawthorne's visit to Rome in 1858, the novel helped publicize the group American women who worked as painters in the Eternal City before Edmonia Lewis's arrival.

Lewis apprehended that living in Rome, a veritable city of stone, afforded her access to the magnificent marble quarried from the lustrous white cliffs of the Apuan Alps in northern Italy. In carving out her own territory as an artist, Lewis chose to work with the challenging material of marble stone in the tradition of the master sculptors Michelangelo, Bernini, and Canova (whom chapter 3 discusses further). She always had faith in herself as an artist. She converted to Catholicism shortly after her arrival in Rome and carved many religious statues during her career.

Unlike some of her older colleagues, Lewis overwhelmingly did her own carving, not only to curtail the exorbitant cost of paying technicians to do this laborious work but also to prove that she was capable of doing it herself. She, like her American colleagues, worked in the neoclassical style, making marble statues of freed people, abolitionists, Civil War heroes, literary Indians, notable citizens, copies of classical works, portrait busts of US presidents, and putti, as well as historical, mythical, and biblical figures.

Frederick Douglass visited Lewis's studio in Rome in January 1887 while on honeymoon with his second wife, Helen Pitts Douglass. During this visit, Douglass remarked on Lewis's collection of books about classical Roman art and history: She lent him several of these texts before journeying with him and Helen via train down to view the ruins at Pompeii and Herculaneum.[50] In a describing this encounter in 1961, scholar Arna Bontemps noted that Frederick and Helen

> had a chance meeting with Edmonia Lewis in Rome. . . . The oddly dressed woman, whose clothes had a masculine look, materialized suddenly before Douglass as the couple strolled on the Pincian Hill. If not herself a relic or a period piece, Edmonia at least belonged to another world, and that is where she was. Douglass had met her before. She had attended Oberlin and may have been present when he and William Lloyd Garrison engaged in a public debate with [the school's] President Asa Mahan. . . . By the time she took up sculpting in Boston as a young woman, she was known for her personal peculiarities. Stories about her . . . made an impression on readers of Negro newspapers throughout the United States.[51]

Douglass said of Lewis in his diary, "Here she lives and here she plies her fingers in her art as a sculptress. She seems very cheerful and happy and successful."[52] In a time when the vast majority of Indigenous and Black people were subject to white colonial rule, enslavement, and displacement, Edmonia Lewis was able to find a way to live a determined and apparently joyful life free of such direct domination.

Lewis's older half-brother, Samuel "Sunrise" Lewis, as noted earlier, contributed to her livelihood, until his death, whereupon he left her some of his estate. This fact counters the fate of many Indigenous siblings during this era who were forced apart by the United States' draconian Indian Removal Act, passed in 1830 under President Andrew Jackson. According to her selected executor, Rev. Charles Cox, a Catholic curate in London, when Lewis herself died in 1907, she was able to give £489 pounds and 1 penny to Catholic charities (about $80,000 in current dollars).[53] Again, her access to funding, even when not altogether sufficient, placed Lewis in a more secure position than most other artists of color enjoyed at the time.

During Lewis's long life, she stood both within and outside multiple categories.[54] Historian Nell Irvin Painter mentions Edmonia Lewis as one of many famous Americans whose "Indian ancestry disappeared beneath the more culturally conspicuous black identity. . . . But Lewis, at least, depicted her dual ancestry in her work by sculpting Indian as well as African figures."[55] Racially, she could be seen as one of many Afro-Native individuals who, as Jack Forbes (Powhatan-Renape) contends, were read as Black—in a sociopolitical environment ruled by an "epidermal schema," to quote Frantz Fanon.[56] Here we must contend with the insane contradictions that "racial classification" contains. Forbes argues, "There is hardly a racial term which has a clear and consistent meaning over time (and space) . . . in attempting to grapple with Black African–Native American mixture and especially with the question of to what extent African-Americans throughout the Americas are part American Indian, we [must clarify how] such racial and ethnic terms were used in the colonial and early national periods."[57] In another work, he parses, in numerous languages, "key words" such as "mulatto, *pardo*, colored, free colored, negro, zambo, . . . mustee and mestizo."[58] These attempts at nominative denominations are themselves part of the problematic of racial difference.

These matters of historical racial relation are not merely academic but deeply ethical. They require us, as Kyle Mays explains, "to understand what it is that draws African Americans to Native America in the past and in the present, that divides Afro-Native people from other Native Americans, that propels blacks to claim Indian ancestry while at times dishonoring living Indigenous peoples and cultures, and that leads some Native Americans to refuse a response to the call of their African-descended kin."[59] At issue is the question of belonging—of affective and effective racial and familial assignment. "Race," despite its fictitiousness, nevertheless functions materially to create and sustain ideas about family, emotional bonds, identity, inheritance, citizenship, community and access.

Frank Naurice Woods Jr. suggests that Edmonia's mother may also have been Afro-Native, having had a Black father. He notes that had this been the case, she would have been excluded from receiving annual government payments from the Canadian government to the Mississauga tribe. Many people consider Lewis's Afro-Native heritage to be the most captivating of her attributes. This is also misguided. She herself said she hated to be "pointed [to] as a colored artist." In naming these details about her heritage, I do not wish to reinforce fantasies about blood quantum that work in concert with dangerous ideologies of racial purity. Such ideologies profoundly affect people's right to "life, liberty and the pursuit of happiness," since, in our liberal democracy, property rights have been privileged above human rights. We should be exceedingly careful to disaggregate any connections between property rights (whiteness being a "property" of its own), human rights, and civil rights. These questions become even more fraught if we look to citizenship in the sovereign Indigenous nations, which did not become enfranchised in the United States until the 1924 Indian Citizenship Act.

Lewis was born an American citizen, and her passport was issued by the US government, even though by necessity, most of her life was spent living in Europe. Her passport (in the National Archives) contains the following information: "Boston, on the twenty-first day of August, Eighteen Hundred and Sixty-Five, in the Commonwealth of Massachusetts, there appeared before Jonathan Amory the notary public of Suffolk County a 20-year-old female citizen of the United States with black hair and black complexion, a high forehead, and standing 4 foot high, who swore to defend the constitution and Government of the United States against all enemies. She signed her name, Miss Edmonia Lewis." A statement written by hand on the lower left edge of the printed document reads: "M. Edmonia Lewis is a Black girl sent by subscription to Italy having displayed great talents as a sculptor."

From that auspicious launch to the present moment, Edmonia Lewis continues to fascinate us in part because of the supposed fission between her subjectivity and the subjects—and perhaps especially the style—of her art. Lewis's exiled existence as a colored woman artist working in white neoclassical marble upends our understanding of nineteenth-century narratives about the limits and possibilities for such subjects.

She may in some ways have been conscripted to perform as a racialized spectacle. Her visage and body were frequently displayed next to her work and, indeed, continue to be sutured to them when displayed. Depending on the scenario, such suturing served to point out the supposed shock of the fact that she, a "colored woman," originated these rarified and idealized white sculptures and vice versa. Darby English captures Black art's dilemma as "a tendency to limit the significance of works assignable to black artists to what can be illuminated by reference to a work's purportedly racial character."[60] Such presumptions constituted and confirmed the racialized and gendered logics of reading that undergirded and continue to inform the idea that Black, Red, and white subjects impossibly should remain in separate domains. Whatever may have been the "intent," the gesture to see her with her work was always performative. Lewis may have been complicit both fostering and fighting against such gendered and racialized performances—those that seemed to understand her as cross-cast in her own time.

In removing herself to Rome, Edmonia Lewis became a figure able to position herself outside the confines of a post-Confederate United States and beyond the reach of Indian Removal. Lewis spoke some Ojibwemowin or Anishinaabemowin and was fluent in English and ultimately Italian. After going with her to Pompeii, Frederick Douglass wrote that her accent was unplaceable. In light of these multiple coordinates, she serves as a quintessential diasporic subject—an exemplar of the "wide nineteenth century" that allows us to "undiscipline" Victorian studies by unsettling, challenging, and contesting conventional parameters.[61]

Her work as a "maker: of white men and women" was questioned by at least one of her patrons, as noted above, the liberal abolitionist and champion of the rights of "others," Lydia Maria Child (1802–80). Child believed Lewis was not talented enough to sculpt a credible likeness of the white male subject whom the young mixed-race sculptor set out to figure: in particular, Lewis desired to create a commemorative bust of the white Col. Robert Gould Shaw (1837–63), whom she saw leading the all-Black 54th Massachusetts Regiment to war—and to their tragic deaths at Fort Wagner in Charleston. The bust was, in fact, a resounding success.

Gloria Jane Bell's excellent reading of Lewis and her work and life in Rome in her book *Eternal Sovereigns: Indigenous Artists, Activists, and Travelers Reframing Rome* (2024) distinguishes neoclassical works that made race perceptible in the physiognomy and "character" of the form.[62] Frederick Douglass believed that "Negroes can never have impartial portraits at the hands of white artists . . . it seems impossible for white men to take likenesses of black men without most grossly exaggerating their distinctive features. And the reason is obvious. Artists, like all other white persons, have adopted a theory respecting the distinctive features of Negro physiognomy. We have heard many white persons say, 'Negroes all look alike.'[63] In an essential study, *The Color of Stone: Sculpting the Black Female Subject in Nineteenth-Century America* (2007), Charmaine Nelson has queried Lewis's work for its representations of "black and Indian" subjects exclusively in white marble, as was the convention of the day. In the time of the Greek and Roman empires, marble sculptures were painted, but by the nineteenth century they were left "bare," denuded of the very skin and mistakenly assumed to always already have been "white." Lewis's choice to produce neoclassical sculpture can be read as a refusal to conform to stereotypes of visibility by providing a modicum of abstraction, as when she chose allegorical figures such as Hagar and Cleopatra, characters from literature and one a symbolic freed slave.[64]

The racial dynamics of Edmonia's work challenged stereotypical expectations derived from standard racial scripts and interactions with "scriptive things."[65] In an era when many believed that colored people were incapable of creating great and beautiful works of art, she proved these presumptions erroneous. Many of the illustrious visitors to Lewis's ex-pat studio came to marvel at her "handiwork"—the proverbial Black hands on white marble—yet many left having witnessed the work of a consummate artist. In short, although she was conscripted to perform as a racialized spectacle and had to grapple with the effects of how her race perpetually impacted ideas about her capability, her dedication to her craft remained resolute. In this dedication, Lewis resembled her admired predecessor in the literary arts, Phillis Wheatley, whose abilities were denigrated famously by President Thomas Jefferson in *Notes on the State of Virginia* (1785) as "below the dignity of criticism."[66] The focus on Lewis's heritage constantly colored her art and life. Her choice to enter into the tradition of the white "Old Masters" was read at the time as even more daring than same choice when made by the white women artists in her circle, who counted race and class among their privileges. By contrast, Lewis's interactions with other free Black women and other Native women remove her from being seen only as an anomaly in the all-white context of other American sculptors in Rome. Melissa Benbow Flowers, in her doctoral dissertation "Before Black Bohemia: Edmonia Lewis in the Post-Bellum, Pre-Harlem Period," makes an important corrective that contextualizes Lewis in African American print culture, as do the many scattered references to Lewis in the writings of her Black contemporaries such as the Remond sisters. This is all to say that we need to think about how we contextualize artists of color in particular narratives.

This book gives only a rough, "gestural" study of Lewis—something that itself anthropomorphizes and approximates an idea, by challenging the idealization of the whole and complete. Whatever facts about Edmonia Lewis I offer may remain stunted and stilted. We may yearn for more modeling and affect, more moving detail and dimension. But, as Erin Manning writes, "any pose, any stilling of the image is simply another durational stratum in the complex experience of a lived perception."[67] This insight troubles our sense of perception to the extent that it questions bounded temporality. The pose is not stopped but is rather, functions as a caesura, a momentary resting place that portends future action with its stilling. We pause here as we have gleaned a sense of Lewis's comings and goings—her habits and haunts from recorded traces—her passport, bills of sale for her works, ships' logs, friends' diaries, secondhand correspondence, church bulletins, court cases, newspaper articles, scrapbooks, photographs, and the pictures of the sculptures. These documents show how her sculptures could be read, following Robin Bernstein, as "scriptive things [where] archive and repertoire are one."[68] I offer a critical method that seeks to recall the dimensional, perspectival, and proprioceptive properties of the "moving" sculptural medium itself. For things that are round we can never see in full or "in totality," given the "scripted" blind spots of binocular vision that constrict our vision.

Still, we have glimpsed the entwined performances of Lewis's race, gender, class, ethnicity, and sexuality that dwell at the core of so much of her work. Lewis was far from being a rebel in her time, nor was she a heroic figure; rather, she was a savvy survivor who "made a way out of no way" (to quote the African American proverb). I agree with Buick that Lewis was more of a complicated "counterpoint" who effectively deployed her shifting subjectivity for her own gain. As an outsider in the American expatriate community, her subject position and insistence that all women be included in the Cult of True Womanhood caused a shift in expectation and perspective for her white comrades.[69] In other words, Lewis used tactics and appeals to humanity similar to those the formerly enslaved woman author Harriet Jacobs (writing under the nom de plume Linda Brent) used in appealing to all mothers (an appeal that sought to unlink what at the time was an oxymoron—an "enslaved mother"). Lewis sought to include Black and Native women as *women* who suffered. Her art, however, originally conceived, still conformed to certain expectations of her time, given that it was legible to her contemporary audiences and potential customers. She made inroads in the field by producing some of the first works of freed peoples ever conceived in neoclassical American sculpture.

More than a third of Lewis's sculptures consisted of portrait busts. The selection of Abraham Lincoln as a subject speaks to Lewis's interest in championing antislavery figures, such as John Brown, the daring dissident who died fighting the evils of slavery; Col. Robert Gould Shaw of the 54th Massachusetts Regiment; and Black Sergeant William Harvey Carney (1840–1908), also of the Massachusetts 54th (the last-named sculpture remains lost). These individual portrait busts were stable sources of income that Lewis relied on to support carving her more ideal sculptures. She lacked access to investors and, to generate income, had to work harder than her coevals, several of whom came from wealth.

In the winter of 1863 she arrived in Boston, where she encountered a statue of Benjamin Franklin that purportedly prompted her to want to learn sculpting. To form stone was for her perhaps a way to realize animate beings (as discussed in chapter 2). After having been rejected by several white sculptors who did not want to educate a "colored" pupil, Lewis worked for several weeks with the neoclassical sculptor Edward Augustus Brackett (1818–1908). Her first assignment was to copy a baby's foot with her lump of clay; she then got on very well when asked to sculpt "a woman's hand" which she did with ease. Next, "as her own master, Edmonia Lewis began to model creatively."[70] She made the aforementioned medallion of abolitionist John Brown and then, from a photograph, the celebrated plaster busts of Colonel Shaw, which financed her one-way journey to Italy.

Lewis survived the 1867 cholera epidemic, which killed some six thousand people in Rome, by being prepared, as she said, with "Bible and brandy by her bedside. If one gave out, I can take up the other."[71] Over the following two decades, she was able to return periodically to the United States to exhibit her work in major venues such as the Centennial Exposition in Philadelphia in 1876 and the Columbian Exhibition in Chicago in 1893—both featured her magisterial *Death of Cleopatra* (see figure 2.1). Lewis sent this 3,015 pound sculpture, carved in 1876, to the all-white jury committee for the Philadelphia exhibition anonymously so they would judge her work on its own merits, without a prejudicial racialized lens. Throughout her career she artfully alternated between wishing not to be judged by the color of her skin and foregrounding her race, depending on which she surmised might serve her audience better in the particular context. Nevertheless, to this day,

A Head of Her Time   **47**

and indeed, even in this book, Edmonia Lewis the artist appears always already to have been sutured to her artistic works. The very intimate connection between maker and made was read in term of racialized gender, as a statement confirming a difference. One could see the conjunction of Lewis and her work as evidence for an argument either for or against this artist of color.

How, then, to tell her story? I have opted to think about Lewis's work disjunctively via contemporary artists' engagement with aspects of her artwork. What follows is a patchwork account that stitches together dense and colorful segments into what I hope will register with readers as collated text—something beautifully colored, kaleidoscopic, an aesthetic homage to this consequential figure of nineteenth-century art.

Thus we begin our storytelling again. This time with a story quilt in which a portrait of Edmonia Lewis appears among an imagined group of artistic peers.

Interlude

Faith Ringgold

You asked me once why I wanted to become an artist and I said I didn't know. Well, I know now. It is because it's the only way I know of feeling free. My art is my freedom to say what I please.

> **Willia Marie Simone,** "Letter to Aunt Melissa," caption 4, in Faith Ringgold, *Picasso's Studio, The French Collection, Part I, #7, 1991.*

This statement from the fictional alter ego of Black feminist artist Faith Ringgold (1930–2024) serves as a credo for her oeuvre. It comes from a series of "story quilts"—Ringgold's neologism—and is echoed later by Willia Marie Simone in her "Colored Woman's Manifesto of Art and Politics": "Today I became a woman with ideas of my own. Ideas are my freedom. And freedom is why I became an artist."[72] Here, you see a reproduced image of a quilted canvas with black handwritten script painted around its outer border that depicts a motley group of Black artists gathered outside a café in Paris (figure 11.1). The painted quilt has been sewn as well and, as such, is a work of mixed media. It is one panel from the twelve distinct story quilts that compose the linked series made between

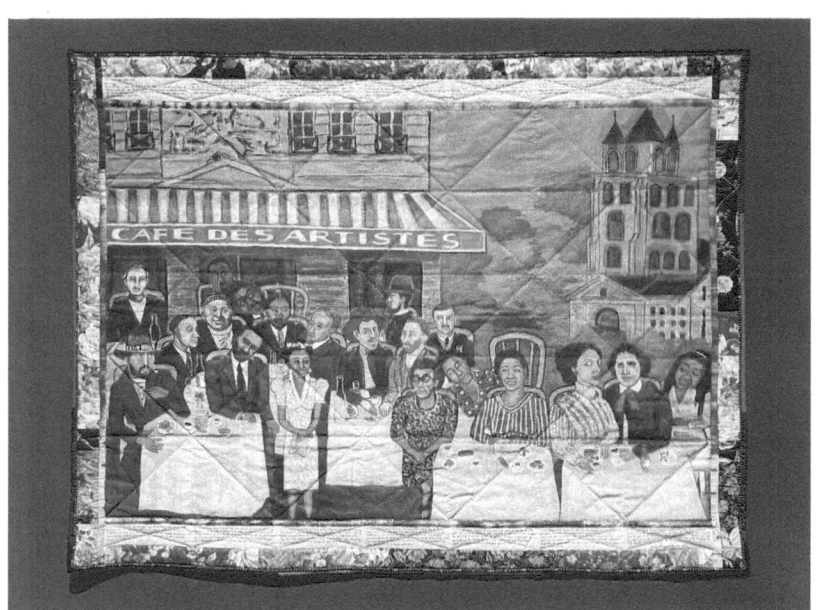

ii.i   Faith Ringgold, *Le Café des Artistes, The French Collection Part II, #11*, 1994. Acrylic on canvas; printed, tie-dyed, and pieced fabric, 79½ × 90 in. Collection of Juanita and Michael Jordan.

1991 and 1997 by Ringgold titled *The French Collection*.[73] This panel, titled *Le Café des Artistes* (1994), uses acrylic paint and sewn fabric that has been both printed and tie-dyed.

Ringgold had "a lifelong interest in sewing," Lisa Farrington tells us, "which she had inherited from her mother, a local dress designer, who assisted the artist" in sewing the story quilts.[74] This is similar to Edmonia Lewis's oft-repeated decision to credit her mother, Catherine Groat Mike, for instilling in her daughter a love of art. Lewis's mother's skill in making moccasins and weaving inspired Lewis's interest in "making the form of things," albeit in a different medium. Ringgold received her BA and MA in visual art from City College of New York in the late 1950s. Regarding the story quilts, Ringgold said that she was "motivated by textile-bordered Tibetan *thangka* paintings" that she had seen and reproduced earlier in her career.[75] Ringgold first used the term "story quilt" in the late 1970s about the same time that Black feminist writer Ntozake Shange (1948–2018) invented the "choreopoem" to describe her mixed-media theatrical work, which combined poetry, dance, music, and narrative. Both Black feminist artists gave the world new genres of art.

To make these large-scale story quilts—which were meant to be viewed on museum walls—Ringgold "'unstretched' her own canvases . . . [and,] by removing the frames and wooden stretchers from her paintings and edging them instead with quilted and brocaded soft borders, was able to minimize the expense and logistical difficulties of transporting and storing her works (which were now literally foldable like clothing)."[76] They were monumental and yet portable, exemplary of the handiwork of making crafts for and within the home and yet signed, durable works of art to be viewed in museum contexts. As such, these works elevated what was considered the tactile textile work predominantly associated with women's work, by creating art for the paying viewing public on a grand scale.

In each iteration in the series of quilted panels, Ringgold patches together a harmonious collective in a "traditional" Africanist-derived abstract form—the patchwork quilt—at the same time that she parodies many of the most famous "masterpieces" in the Western canon of art. The panel called *Le Café des Artistes* features the fictional heroine whom Ringgold names Willia Marie Simone presenting her manifesto before a crowd of famous Black and a few white artists representing multiple eras and media. The series of twelve panels, as an aggregate, places Black people as central to iconic moments from the story of (white) Western art history. As a whole, Ringgold's series riffs and "samples" iconic paintings such as Édouard Manet's *Le Déjeuner sur l'herbe* (1862–63) and Picasso's *Les Demoiselles d'Avignon* (1907). Ringgold chronicles Simone's experiences as an artist and model who navigates modernist circles in 1920s Paris. The series is one of many critical commentaries on the history of Western art that, as Ringgold understands it, has denigrated both "colored folk" and "folk art." This is to say that both quilts and the sometimes-anonymous people of color who made such "functional" or "ethnographic" works were excluded from the annals of art history and the hallowed halls of major museums and exhibition spaces. When their art was displayed, it was often under the sign of "anthropological artifacts" rather than the hierarchically ranked "high art" of the academy. Ringgold's canny work claps back at such exclusionary categorizations by making oversize quilts that feature Black artists in the (dis)guise of "great" "white" artists. In so doing, she revises the history of "Western art" as such, proving that "no important change of a modernist nature can go on without the colored woman."[77]

Ringgold's decision to highlight images of various Black artists who have been excluded from the Western art historical canon, and to feature snippets from her own life through her fictional avatar Black feminist artist Willia Marie Simone, is an act of not only of Afro-fabrication, but also of "afro-fabulation."[78] Eschewing historical fidelity, Ringgold elects to gather all the "ancestor" artists together in one colorfully vibrant frame. She said that this story quilt is "a surreal meditation on things we've never done but would have liked to have done."[79] In the scene, Willia delivers an artistic sermon to the eclectic group of artists who are scattered in the foreground, listening to her proclamation. The lecture, entitled the "Colored Women's Manifesto of Art and Politics," is a fictional account purportedly from Willia to her Aunt Melissa. Encasing each of the larger pictorial scenes, these handwritten epistles compose the "story" of the story quilt series.

When one faces the singular quilt *Café des Artistes*, depicting the Boulevard Saint-Germain in Paris, one's eyes take in a crowd of intricately rendered individuals stitched together into a jocular collective. Some figures are standing, others are sitting, all are mingling. The figures spill out of the café and populate the entire central horizontal plane of the canvas-quilt. On second glance, one realizes that many of the posed figures are engaged in a relay of gazes that animates the quilt and provides its inherent, internal drama. The entire hanging is framed by a handwritten black script that explicates the visual narrative in the frame while also, of course, being part of the entire work of art. On the quilt's far lower-right edge, one spies a square table covered with crisply folded white linen. The table seemingly floats almost as if it were about to topple from the two-dimensional frame. If we look carefully, we may be able to recognize at that table the image of one Miss Edmonia Lewis (figure 11.2).[80] Indeed, here is Lewis seated at the café table with two other Black women artists: on the left, the sculptor Meta Vaux Warrick Fuller (1877–1968), and on the right, a (self-)portrait of the quilt's creator, Faith Ringgold. In this lower quadrant of the quilt, one sees Ringgold's warm brown left hand, with its manicured fingers painted with white fingernail polish, gently grasping the dark sleeve of Edmonia's jacket from the right. Edmonia sports red lipstick, along with what we now think of as her signature cravat—here also painted in a bright scarlet red. She wears a dark jacket, and her white blouse is visible at the collar and in the open front of the jacket. The other Black woman sculptor, the aforementioned Fuller, is seated to Lewis's right. Fuller wears a high-collared white-lace, striped "Gibson Girl" blouse, as she did in many of her iconic photographs from the 1890s, when her fame

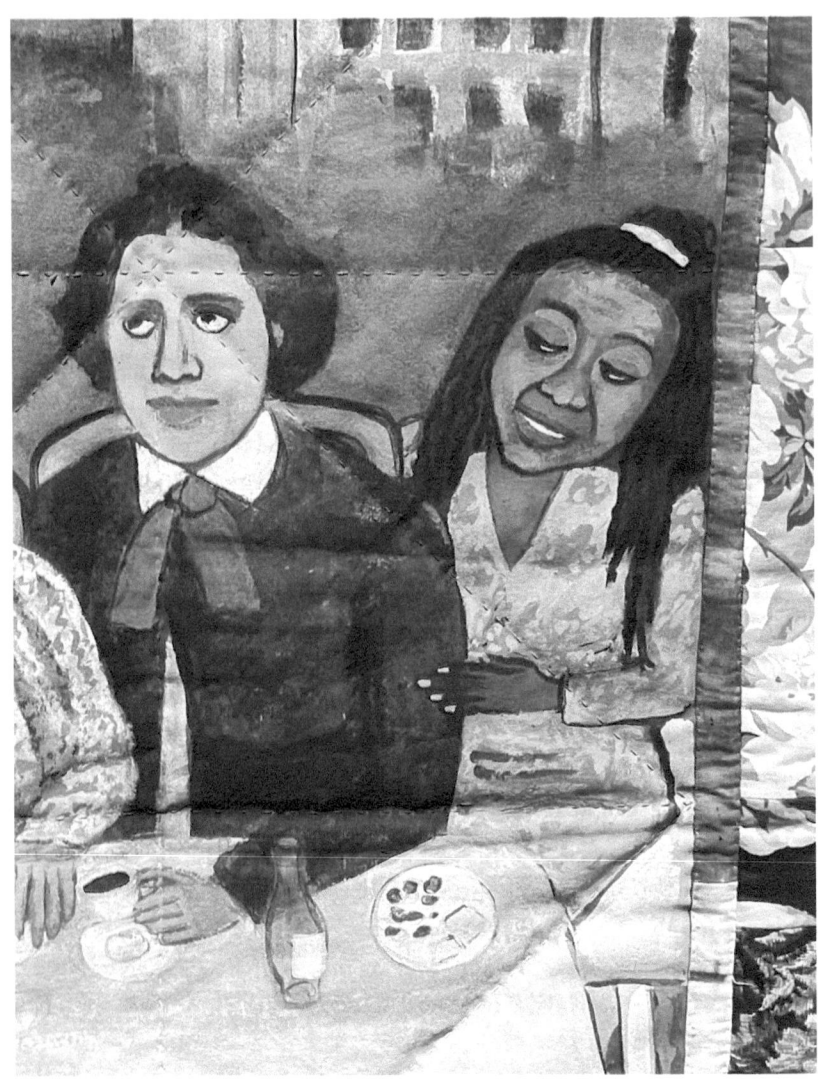

11.2 Detail of Faith Ringgold, *Le Café des Artistes, The French Collection Part II, #11*, 1994. Acrylic on canvas; printed, tie-dyed, and pieced fabric, 79½ × 90 in. Collection of Juanita and Michael Jordan.

was on the rise. There is a bottle of rosé wine set on the table before this august group of three Black women artists, each from a different time period but here sharing a welcome table in the same tableau. This cross-hatched, mixed-media strategy juxtaposes time and space.

Ringgold portrays her predecessor-cum-compatriot Edmonia Lewis drinking an espresso from a dainty white demitasse cup (perhaps like those from which Lewis would actually have sipped at the Caffe Greco, near her studio in Rome). Ringgold's head is tilted over her left shoulder as she smiles dreamily at her Lewis, who looks out at us, beyond the frame. These stylized gestures show the two to be companions, intimates, sharing a convivial moment. In contrast, the third artist, Meta Vaux Warrick Fuller, sitting at what really is a table for two, is giving us the side-eye. This image contravenes the truth of history in which Fuller knew of Lewis's legacy and corresponded with Freeman Henry Morris Murray about her. Ringgold's hair is styled like that of the father figure in Lewis's dual-portrait sculpture *Old Arrow Maker*: a top knot on her head with the rest of her hair flowing. Fuller's hair is parted in the center and coiffed in an elaborate updo. As was her custom, Lewis's short hair frames her face in soft, pillowy dark waves. These three represent one half of the Black women depicted in the quilt (excluding Willia, who stands in the front, at the center of the canvas).

In this quilted panel, Lewis can be identified by her costume and accoutrements, which in turn were known from the circulation of her photographic portraits (discussed in chapter 6). Ringgold's portrait of Lewis shows her with red cravat (and, here, lips painted red); velvet brown skin; white collared blouse, black jacket, rippled black hair surrounding an oval face, and large rounded, knowing eyes. These accoutrements have become part of her iconic style. In Ringgold's quilt, Lewis's eyes are open and direct, gazing slightly upward. The viewer can see a small ring on Lewis's finger that resembles the one visible on her hand in an actual photograph (discussed in chapter 6). The quilt's stitches converge on her right temple, creating a star effect as if her visage were emanating light. Stripes of floral fabric are visible on the border. Ringgold wields a knowing smile as her manicured hand touches the folded arm of her coconspirator in what we now understand to be a tradition of Black feminist art. I find it fascinating that Ringgold chose to place herself right next to Lewis at the table with Fuller. Although Ringgold made soft, three-dimensional doll-like figures, as well as quilts, she was not known as a sculptor per se. Still, she sees herself paying homage to this earlier generation of professional Black women artists, "beginning," we might say, with Lewis. In contrast to other artworks that remember Lewis explicitly, Ringgold's includes Lewis in a genealogical community of Black artists, standing or, more precisely, sitting in a place of honor with other Black women artists at the proverbial table. Such a welcoming table is something Edmonia Lewis coveted in her life, if we are to believe one of the few extant letters she wrote, one that was published in a Black newspaper. Here is Edmonia's missive, responding to the commission by a Black women's association to have her make a bust, initially of a Black pillar of the church, a commission that ultimately became a request from the group for Lewis to do a portrait bust of the famed Black poet Phyllis Wheatley (ca. 1753–84):

> *Dear Miss McCandless,*
>
> *My price for a life-sized bust in bronze or marble is always $500 to $600. But I will not stand on price now after so many years of my life are passed and never before have the colored people given me such recognition. So you must know that I did feel proud when I read in the paper you sent me, the* Commercial Gazette *"Action Taken." I will therefore execute in bronze the life-size portrait bust of Rev. Avery for the agreed price of $300. Send me good photographs or engravings, front view and also profile, as there is no time to be lost. I will guarantee good work or not any. May I trouble you to send me the names of the women who are doing this? I want them for myself. This is indeed a little history and always to be remembered. Thank them all for their appreciation of me.*
>
> *Sincerely yours,*
> *Edmonia Lewis*[81]

The letter is itself a little history, always to be remembered. It gives a sense of the courtesy Lewis generated even in what is essentially business correspondence. Lewis's stated regard for being recognized and appreciated by others in the colored community is notable. It suggests that she valued being part of such a community and, indeed, there are numerous examples of her expressing appreciation as part of larger circles of relation that cut across traditional exclusions of ethnicity, religion, class, gender, and race.

Ringgold completed her portrait-tribute to Edmonia Lewis the same year that she made a quilt titled *Marlon's Quilt*, which honors filmmaker Marlon Riggs, who had succumbed to an AIDS-related illness that year, 1994. Since that time, numerous other Black feminist artists and critics (myself included) have been so drawn to Lewis's story that we too wished to embrace her as Ringgold does in her story quilt, to bask in Lewis's visage, and to behold her as part of our element where we imagine her as a formative American (Black and Native), diasporic, queer subject. Lewis is the lodestone for ever-emerging webs of interrelation. I do not believe that we can ever know her wholly—her evolving story will never be finished; even so, Edmonia's partial presence, full of holes, can be stitched and pieced together, as it has been in the fashioning by Ringgold's hands. Ringgold says, "Art historians must . . . [find] the fragments that have been ignored and reconnect them." We can pattern her quilt in endless variations and designs, write along their edges, rearrange the details that make up an artist's life. Indeed, this is the artistic process Faith Ringgold created to commemorate Edmonia Lewis; inaugurating many patchwork memorials made to revere Lewis and reveal her as a key figure in the "Ur-story" (and herstory) of American art.[82]

Animating Stones

There is no adequate way to stage the problem of either vision or desire without recourse to a tactile relationship with the object world . . . our psychic lives become intricately bound up in things (commodities or art), and sculpture and its repetitions offer the most charged course to untie the knot of eroticism, repetition, and commodities that governs our daily lives.

Helen Molesworth, "Eros and the Readymade"

2

Stones are hard matter. They are elemental. Since time immemorial, stones have shaped and mediated our existence; we live in a world composed *of,* if not *by* or *about,* stones. Stones are our *habitus*—environmental, inescapable, symbolic, cosmic, and phenomenological: They help to form, inform, and shape our perceptions of space, place, time, and history.[1] Stones perform: They are a substance, underfoot, through which we make meaning of our world. They appear in the sky as meteorites, falling stars whose visible flames spark wonder.[2] They are megaliths that greet those who walk in open fields or about ancient environs. Stones can mark separations between *here* and *there*, between city and country, between *ours* and *theirs*. For example, in 2021 archeologists uncovered a slab of travertine stone dating from 49 CE that delimited the boundary of the city of Rome during the Roman Empire. Known as a pomerial stone, it was used as a sacred, religious, political, and military marker delineating where the city of Rome began or ended.[3]

Stones are moving *about* us continuously, in formation. Igneous lava stones erupt from volcanoes, sedimentary stones move through currents in brooks and streams (the idea motivating the proverbial smooth pebble indexing eons), and metamorphic stones, such as marble, form as a result of the tremendous movement of forces of time and temperature. Stones seem always to be on the move via the rotation of the Earth, the shifting of tectonic plates, the interplay of atmosphere, gravity, water, and other forces. Some stones even appear capable of moving themselves: In California's Death Valley National Park, for example, geologists and artists have witnessed the astounding movement of rocks as far as 1,500 feet across the desert floor, leaving grooves and trails in the ground behind them. This natural phenomenon, known as "sailing stones," is not yet understood, but some posit that it happens as a result of the expansion and contraction of ice, water, and earth, revealing that stones possess the power to remove themselves as well as mark location.[4] In these ways, stones engage in movement across space and time. Stones are "vibrant matter" that are meaningful in their own right.[5] Stones even develop in fruits and in our bodily organs. In some cases, stones are understood to be the bearers of rights. For example, the Ojibwe language, the word *asiniins* means both ancestor and rock, and *asiniinsag* themselves have rights as sentient beings.[6]

When she moved to Italy, Lewis became part of an Indigenous presence in Rome that could be dated to the first rapacious European collections of Indigenous artifacts in the vast holdings of the Vatican.[7] In 1867, a year after Lewis arrived in Italy, a visiting reporter remarked on the

> busts of three ancestors in terra cotta, the line of which well suits their copper colored skins. They are natural in expression and, though not of high rank as works of art, yet are perfect types of the Indian character and lineaments. She [Lewis] speaks of them with a frankness and a naiveté that is quite amusing, and as she was pointing out the face of "my uncle, Sunrise," she, a colored sculptor from America here in the city of the Caesars, I must say I experienced a new sensation.[8]

This statement, despite its condescending tone and mistakes (e.g., Sunrise was, as we know, Lewis's brother), supports a reading of Lewis's possible perception of stones as ancestral figures.[9] The point here is to build out worldviews that could reshape how we imagine the past as well as the inexorable shifts of ideas over time.

This chapter muses about the importance of a specific stone, marble, with which Edmona Lewis developed a close relationship. Lewis interacted with this medium nearly every day of her artistic career. Carrara marble was part of what drew her to Italy. In the tradition of ancient stonecutters, Lewis created work that was as much about marble as it was in or of marble. Like so many Greco-Roman classical and Renaissance sculptors, such as Michelangelo (1475–1564), Lewis thought that blocks of marble stone contained figures that, once found there, could be set free.[10] Lewis may also have seen her marble works as animated stones.[11] She worked almost exclusively with this readily available marble during the years she lived within the palimpsestic white pasts of the imperial city. Her black boots tread the cobblestones and climbed the stairs to her gabled upper studio, where she transformed the history of art.

The matter of marble cannot be separated from its material production, beginning with its geologic formation, then its mining from the earth's core, and its transport, purchase, cutting, and shaping by people. Marble is composed of carbonate mineral material in addition to recrystallized calcite or dolomite, as well as the DNA of thousands of (almost exclusively) male quarry workers, many of whom died while mining this valuable material.[12] In this vein, we can understand, as Kara Thompson observes, that "marble is alive with death. Like other materials that derive from fossilized creatures and plants, marble is a non-renewable resource. To excavate it from deep inside the earth where it has lain for millions of years is to touch nonhuman worlds and temporalities."[13]

Ideas about the transformation of such "natural" resources into art are at the heart of the performance and practice of resource extraction in the larger geological and ecological world. Starting in the sixteenth century, Carrara marble was increasingly exported, due in part to the influence of Italian sculptors but also to improved transportation options, more efficient industrial mining practices, and more effective marketing by merchants. Nicholas Penny, the former director of the National Gallery in London, estimates that by the mid-nineteenth century some forty thousand tons of marble were extracted from Italian quarries every year, and that by 1914 more than one million tons were mined annually.[14]

The exponential increases in the rapidity and rapaciousness of this major industry continue.

As an artist working in Rome from 1865 to the 1880s, Lewis would have witnessed and participated in the monumental changes in the extraction methods required to access Carrara marble. She likely visited the quarries in northern Italy and would have known how the process of harvesting stone relied on technological advances. In her lifetime, she saw industry move such mountains of material faster, easier, cheaper. Many of these advances were (and indeed remain) by-products of warmaking: part of a military-industrial-aesthetic complex. The increased demand for marble stone for making art and architecture encouraged the "introduction of explosives, the successive use of waterpower, steam power and then electricity for saws and polishers, and the invention of cranes, cableways, railways and of wire saws."[15] Marble sculptures, as commercial objects, cannot readily be severed from questions of locality, science, modernity, coloniality, or materiality.

The architectural use of limestone, such as marble and travertine, has been historicized as quintessentially Roman: Local marble "was the preferred material of Roman emperors, including Augustus, who 'vowed to make it . . . the very fabric of Rome.'"[16] Carrara marble represents the most prized material with which to make neoclassical sculptural works, and the famed quarries around Carrara have produced high-quality alabaster and marble stone. Lewis almost bankrupted herself when she purchased the large block of Carrara marble that she used to carve the affecting upright, life-size figure of *Hagar* (1875; see figure 4.8). Many of her works are smaller, since sculptures on that scale were less expensive to carve; Lewis modified their design with the cost of materials in mind. She was only too aware that, for some working artists, as she put it, "pay-day [was] an unpleasant time. . . . [We] must sell our work if we want to live."[17] A few of her works were made of less pure, less costly marble that contained gray veins. The art market went hand in hand with colonial and commercial concerns; her artistic decisions were not based solely on aesthetic ideals.

I follow those art historians who discuss the materiality of works of art—who think about them as durable things and not solely as iconographic representations. As Michael W. Cole writes, "The marble from which a statue is made was always a 'found object' in a sense that bronze was not, because the block always remained present to the sculptor to whom it could suggest ideas as well as limitations for his work, present to patrons and viewers who were apt to think in terms of how a sculptor had dealt with the thing he had been given to carve."[18] The facticity of such marble sculptural objects confronts viewers by complicating their orientation to these three-dimensional occupiers of space. We cannot conceive of such stones without thinking about them as matter that matters. The substance of a stone and the form and content of a statue cannot readily be separated; form and content are hardened by their instantiation.[19] The nature of the material as stone remains, regardless of form, content, or reference; a "rock solid" connection in which surface and substance are sutured. To destroy the statue is to damage the stone; to destroy the stone is, potentially, to create the statue.

Classical scholar Mary Beard stresses the significance of the artist's work in production, highlighting the *making* of sculpture and rethinking the *how* of sculpture by returning the work to its formation.[20] Reading statues as works in progress and in situ allows us to think about sculptures as things that are produced and developed. An article written about Lewis in 1866 a few months after her arrival in Rome described the sculptures in her studio in their various states of development. It reads:

> As she has been here only two months she has not much to show. A bust of Colonel Shaw, who commanded the first colored regiment ever formed, is a meritorious work, and has been ordered by the family of the brave colonel who died fighting for his country.
>
> Another bust, of Mr. Dionysius Lewis, of New York, is nearly completed as a commission. The first ideal work of our young artist is a freed woman falling on her knees, and with clasped hands and uplifted eyes thanking God for the blessings of liberty. She has not forgotten her people, and this early dedication of her genius to their cause is honorable to her feelings.[21]

Beard, too, reminds us that Lewis was carving her popular bust *Young Octavian* in the same place and time that she was working on her celebrated statue *The Death of Cleopatra* (figures 2.1 and 2.2) and several others.[22] Indeed, any image of a sculptor's studio of the era shows work in various stages of production, along with raw materials, live models, tools, and maquettes. Beard calls on us to look at Lewis's work in its formative stages, to remember that sculptures take shape as part of a moving, performative, iterative process—and as labor. This strategy contrasts with reading sculpture exclusively for its "finalized" representational qualities

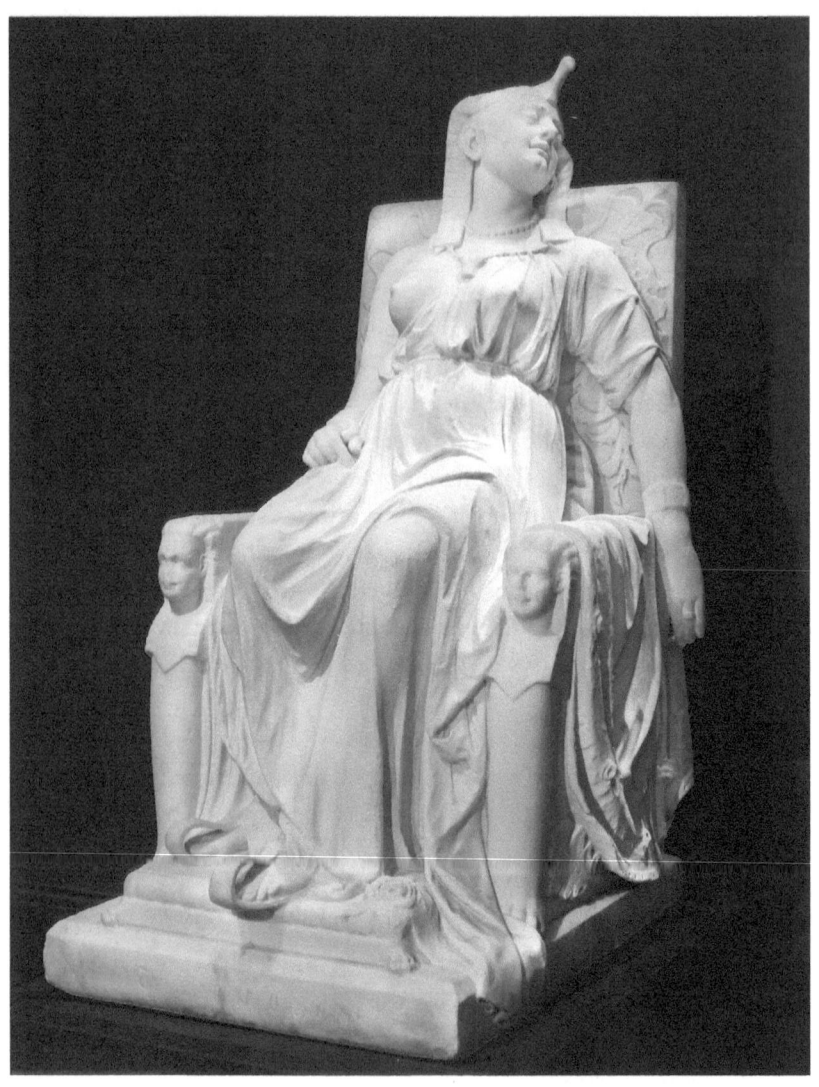

2.1 Edmonia Lewis, *The Death of Cleopatra*, 1876. Marble, 63 × 31¼ × 46 in. Smithsonian American Art Museum, Washington, DC, Gift of the Historical Society of Forest Park, Illinois, 1994.

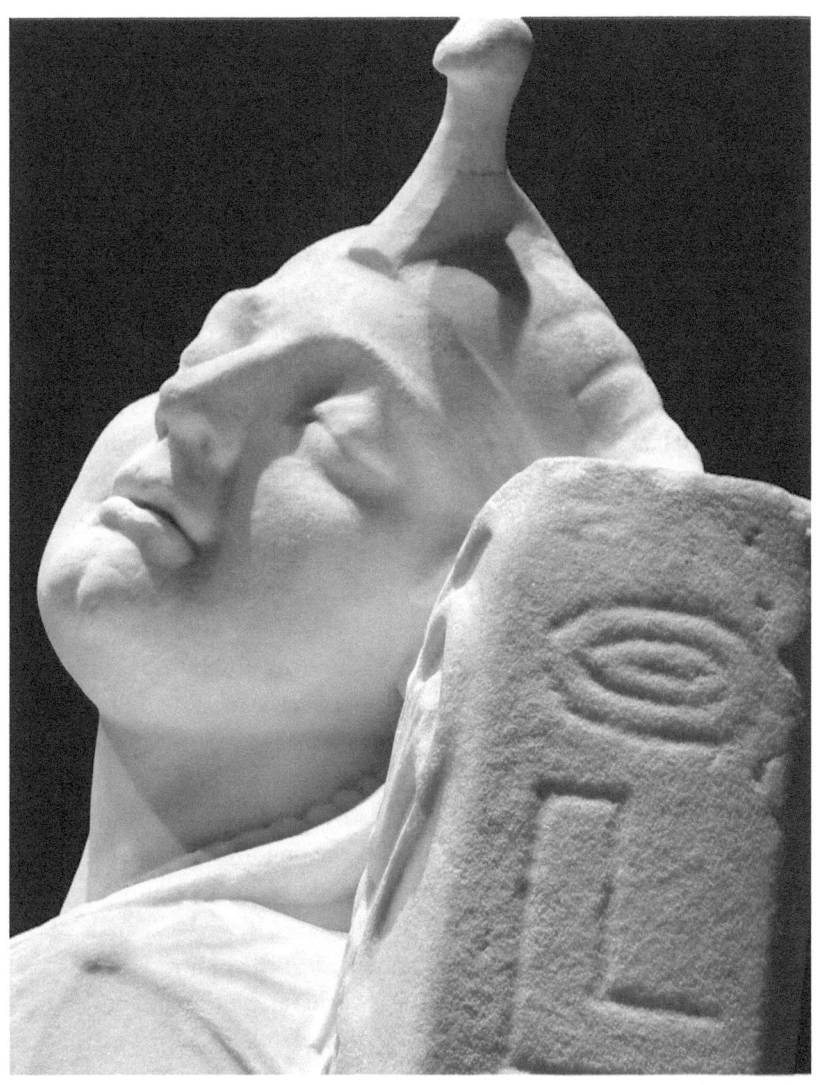

2.2 Detail, Edmonia Lewis, *The Death of Cleopatra*, 1876. Marble, 63 × 31¼ × 46 in. Smithsonian American Art Museum, Washington, DC, Gift of the Historical Society of Forest Park, Illinois, 1994.

(e.g., here is a woman, there is the angel, before us the freedman and his wife). Lewis manipulated the make and model of her marbles in a dialectic sculptural action.

Although we tend to think of sculptures as fixed in place, singular and inanimate, they are in fact alive with meaning and motion. They move and make us move. We cannot know them unless we engage with them, move around them, aware of our own physical movements and the way sculptures demarcate space. In a discussion of globalism, postcolonial critic Arjun Appadurai suggests that to be modern is to live in an era characterized by objects in motion: "It has now become something of a truism that we are functioning in a world fundamentally characterized by objects in motion. These objects include ideas and ideologies, people and goods, images and messages, technologies, and techniques."[23] Lewis and her marbles can be read as indexing the continued circulation and performance of such artistic objects on the global stage.

This is to say that Lewis's oeuvre exemplifies the global movements of Black art, always already diasporic, moving about the Atlantic and at least three vast continents—Africa, the Americas, and Europe. Although Lewis's art in particular traveled mostly between America and Europe, it was part of the movements of vital matter and world-historical events, the traffic among race, place, bodies, space, and aesthetics, all of which were (and indeed are) undergoing processes of profound transformation. (The previous run-on sentence references the ongoing movement.) These works cannot escape the global flows of modernity; as Leigh Raiford asserts, "'Black Art' is composed of 'elsewheres.'"[24] Lewis's art, made of the marble she carved, is inextricably connected to the movements of racial capital that produced the Black Atlantic world (and its attendant technologies of gender, enslavement, life, and death).[25] "Indian" subjects, too, were world-historical travelers whose journeys—both forced and chosen—were formed through such global traffic.[26]

When thinking of stones as carriers of living history, I remain haunted by a photograph of a mortarless stone auction block featured in Katherine McKittrick's book *Demonic Grounds: Black Women and the Cartographies of Struggle* (2006) (figure 2.3). McKittrick shares the following description of the markers' construction, written in the 1960s by a surveyor assessing the now defunct plantation: "Stone table, approximately 3′ square and 3′ high. It is supported by four rectangular stones set upright into the ground. A bottom stone is shaped as a cross to fit between the posts, while the top stone slab rests directly upon the

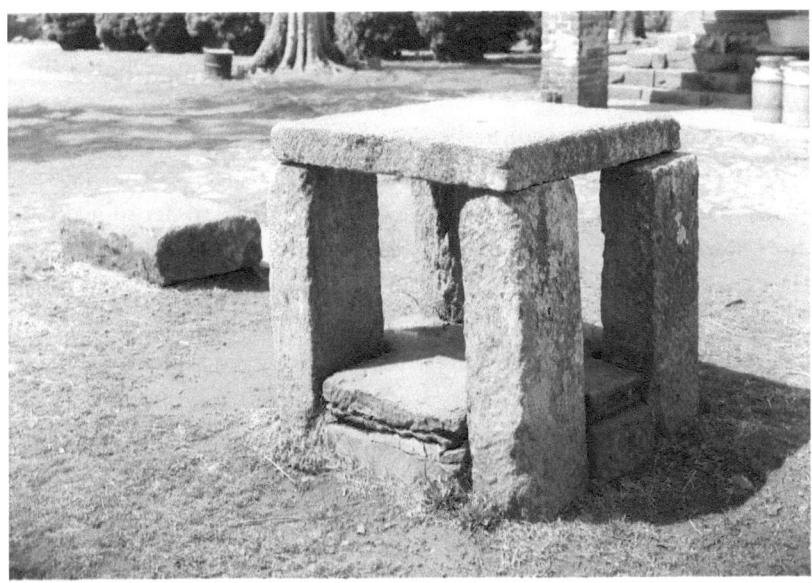

2.3 Jack E. Boucher, *Green Hill, Slave Auction Block, 378 Pannills Road (State Route 728), Long Island, Campbell County, VA*, n.d., documentation compiled after 1933. Prints and Photographs Division, Library of Congress, Washington, DC.

four posts at each corner. Top stone about 3″ thick; bottom stone about 2-½″ thick. No mortar used.″[27] When I read this clinical description, included as part of a larger report on the buildings and grounds of the plantation, its final sentence struck me: "No mortar used." I imagine the slippage in the near rhyme between mortar and mortal, its double meaning of a person and an invocation of death.[28] The stone and the person are never far apart.

I build my language with rocks.

> **Édouard Glissant,** *A Poetics of Relation*

Lewis, as an Indigenous Black diasporic artist, forged a complex relationship to art, language, and self. The invocation of living properties latent in stones cuts both ways: In trying to understand her own self-exoticization and the primitivism imposed on her by others, she also connected to other ways of knowing the world. The sharp distinctions drawn between her youth in the "wild" outdoors with her Native mother and her subsequent formal education in Western traditions of art amount to a kind of false dichotomy deployed for opposing political purposes throughout Lewis's life. Over the years, press interviews quoted her as expressing awareness of her identity and her contradictory viewpoints about it that served to deflect as well as define her difference from a European norm. Speaking generally, I think it fair to surmise that when it came to her subjectivity, she knew more than she told.

The multilingual Edmonia may have known some of the Ojibwe language. Poet and novelist Louise Erdrich (Ojibwe) writes that, in this language, "when it comes to nouns, there are . . . no designations of gender, no feminine or masculine possessives or articles. Nouns are mainly designated as animate or inanimate, though what is alive and dead doesn't correspond at all to what an English speaker might imagine. For instance, the word for stone, *asin*, is animate. After all, the preexistence of the world according to Ojibwe religion consisted of a conversation between stones."[29] Intimate familial relations exist between people and stones; stones were immediate ancestors, offering one way to commune and communicate across generations. Stones are moving—thinking, doing, acting, and connecting: "People speak to and thank the stones in the sweat lodge, where the *asiniig* are superheated and used for healing. They are addressed as grandmothers and grandfathers. Once I began to think of the stones as animate, I started to wonder whether I was picking up a stone or it was putting itself into my hand. Stones are no longer the same as they were to me in English."[30] One wonders if the stones that Lewis carved could, in fact, have chosen her.[31]

For speakers of Anishinaabemowin, as noted earlier, stones are ancestors. Lewis likely would have known—even if just in her body's memory—about "asin"—animate, living stone.[32] I imagine that she may have understood stones themselves as "alert, responsive, communicative," to quote the geologist Marcia Bjornerud (who grew up near Ojibwe homelands in Minnesota and Wisconsin). "Once one becomes attuned to the language of rocks," Bjornerud suggests, "it is obvious that Earth is vibrantly alive and speaking to us all the time."[33] We can posit that such Indigenous philosophical concepts about animate objects offer another way to think about Lewis's life and artwork. Might Lewis's divining of a stone's sculpturability include such ways of knowing (in addition to her "classical" training in art and her practical need to weigh the cost of marble)?[34] One can use only the interrogative to address these questions given that "as an African and Native American sculptor, [Lewis] became both the subject and object of her own oeuvre, allowing for the simplistic readings of her work as 'self-portraiture.' She manipulated the dichotomy of otherness but did so in a semiotic slippage so elegant that art historians across the board still are not quite sure how the known object became her own knowing subject."[35] My turn to readings of animate stones in this chapter is not a naïve attempt to unquestionably suture her identity and her art; rather, I seek to pose new ways to think about her artwork at the juncture where ontology meets epistemology.

Contemporary African Native studies scholar Tiya Miles links such Native American Indigenous ideas to Africanist epistemologies:

> Having been treated as possessions and deprived of ownership of themselves, their families, crops they nurtured, and objects they made and maintained, African American survivors of slavery recognized the world of things. . . . Despite the prominence of a Cartesian duality in Western philosophy that proposed a clear split between spirit and matter, enslaved Blacks knew that people could be treated like things. . . . Awash in this awful knowledge, African Americans may have been theorists of the mercurial nature of things. In this understanding, they would have joined Native Americans, the first thing-thinkers on this continent who affirmed in their stories and lived through their actions a belief that many things have a kind of spirit and are capable of relationship. In their everyday lives, Indigenous North Americans recognized the animated nature of things as well as the innate relationality of people, non-human animals, and plants all of which, scientists now confirm, share common fundamental elements (such as cell structure, chemical makeup and DNA).[36]

This work expands the ways we can think about Lewis's devotion to working in and with stone, adding the insights of Afro-Indigenous epistemologies and perspectives. Edmonia Lewis was and is also known by her Indigenous name, Ishkoodah, translated as "Wildfire." She claimed that she spent a childhood in nature learning from the woods and that, though she would have preferred to have remained "in nature," "her love of sculpture prevented it." At other times, Lewis claimed that the so-called wild life of her youth provided her inspiration to become a sculptor and that her mother's artistic skills were part of her own practice: "The same thing is coming out in me."

Again, this chapter's account of Anishinaabe ideas of stone is not meant to suggest that Lewis, who may have known some Anishinaabemowin (as the language is called), was beholden to this faith, these worldviews, or even this knowledge, per se. She converted to Catholicism in early adulthood, but also spoke disparagingly of her early education, saying, "The 'Black Robes' taught us a few prayers—that was all." Her usage seems a transliteration of the Anishinaabemowin word *mekadewikonayewini-iniwag*, "the black-robe men" or Jesuit priests.[37] We may imagine that her spiritual and epistemological orientations were as layered, complex, and contradictory as other parts of her life.

Still, she may have had passing knowledge of such African or Indigenous religious confluences and generational memories—those "traces in blood, bone and stone" (to quote Gerald Vizenor's poem that lends its title to Kimberly Blaeser's volume of Ojibwe poems)—that suggest a complex transference between persons, things, and conceptions of subjectivity.[38] Indigenous and African American scholars have studied the meanings of survival and sovereignty in the face of both colonization and enslavement, and as Tiya Miles reminds us, "Although it may seem counterintuitive at first, attention to material things, especially ones elaborated by words or pictures, opens a route to accessing intangible feelings and desires that can evade the documentary record."[39]

We think of stones as moving in terms of the emotional, affective, and even life-giving ideas that create us as humans and as living matter. I want to expand the habits of classification that calcify and limit connections between "us" and "them," between "we" and "it." As we learn from Miles, there is a chiasmic relationship between the human and nonhuman as well as the inhuman. Frederick Douglass's famous chiasmic statement "You have seen how a man was made a slave; you shall see how a slave was made a man" redoubles the equation of the "human" and the "thing," the "man" and the "slave."[40] Lewis's decision to sculpt only free or freed persons (and recall that she was one of the very first to do so), references the long, entangled history against which so many enslaved and colonized "colored" subjects fought against their objectification. People of African descent who escaped slavery were called contraband even when they were captured while fighting as soldiers in the Civil War. Lewis's decision to dedicate her sculptural practice solely to the portrayal of the free and freed helped to humanize people of color and became part of the larger discourse about so-called men and things that are the sine qua non of ongoing debates about racialized humanity. In the words of Huey Copeland, "The slave emerges as a thing-that-is-not-one, a form of readymade that not only challenges the status of the artwork, but that also intersects with and reframes theorizations of the "thingly"—the commodity, the sculptural, or the material itself—within Western cultural discourse."[41] As we think anew about connections among bodies and objects in the "life-like sculpturing" of Edmonia Lewis and others, we come to a "yes, and": We recognize the profound task of remembering those who were (and continue to be) dehumanized by being viewed as objects. Simultaneously, we elevate objects or matter, stones in particular, as things sentient and alive, imbued with the power to reconnect broken lineages and histories and to affirm one's place in the firmament. Lewis's marvelous marbles were made as a means of marking her existence. The works were born of a meeting of her mind and hand and inscribed in marble stone, for eternity, "Edmonia Lewis, facit a Roma."

Interlude

Beverly Buchanan

Edmonia Lewis's legacy and enduring stone work provide a precedent for the twentieth-century works of Beverley Buchanan (1940–2015), an African American sculptor and mixed-media artist whose work takes up and extends Lewis's preoccupation with the matter of stone. The artist's statement "Notes on Wall Column," written for a 1980 group exhibition that featured her work titled *Wall Column*, includes a poem Buchanan wrote expressly to accompany this sculpture. The poem, "Cast Cement" reads like a calligram (a concrete poem that mimics the shape of its subject).

> Each piece of the sculpture is cast
> separately and placed individually, one at a
> time. Placing each piece involves a long
> time of looking and moving—shifting—
> replacing and looking some more. The
> slight weight and emphasis on my right
> to left orientation continues in this piece.
> The small front half slab was placed first.[42]

The artist's statement and poem are about moving "stones" made of cast concrete. The key gerunds are *placing, looking, moving, shifting, replacing, looking some more*; they define the labor of making this statue that replicates the look of weathered stone. The stones are singular, as if they could be "individuals." Read vertically, the tail end of the lines on the right explain: "cast / one at a / long / shifting / the / right / piece / first." Her detailed description is at once concise and expansive—like the blocks themselves that bind and radiate in her sculptures, combining past, present, and future in one placement (and notice here that we have moved about the poem in an effort to both understand and defamiliarize its features).

There exists a doubled black-and-white photograph, labeled "Untitled (Double Portrait of Artist with Frustula Sculpture)," of Buchanan taken in the 1980s that presents two images of the artist standing next to her work *Wall Fragments* (1978). The vertically layered sculpture to the right of Buchanan is nearly as tall as is she. The distinctive parallel pose seen in the photographic diptych suggests an equivalence between the sculpture and the sculptor, between the person and the rocks. It is only when one looks carefully at both images that one sees minute differences in the artist's stance (legs open, legs close together, arm up, arm down), and that one understands the spatial and temporal disjuncture between the two juxtaposed photographs. The diptych shows movement across space and time in her minute changes in posture. "As a sculptor, Buchanan was interested in what she described as the 'inexhaustible number of ways in which and from which the composition is seen.'"[43] As discussed here and throughout *Moving Stones*, these rock figures are anything but static. Their composition conveys change. Even the specific frustulas changed as Buchanan moved the individual blocks of mud-infused cement in varying arrangements.

In a single photograph of just the sculpture *Wall Fragments* (figure 2i.1), we see squared-off blocks of cement that are piled to resemble ancient markers. Some have been carved with vertical lines that look a bit like Greek columns while others have a smooth texture. All have been painted. Buchanan documented these sculptural arrangements with her own camera. In this photograph of *Wall Fragments*, six rock-like forms are visible. Two rough forms balance precariously atop the group of lower stones that are clustered at the bottom. An open gap reminds viewers of this take on the sculpture of the importance of negative space amid the positively present forms.

Much of Buchanan's artwork could be classified as land art: Her sculptures mark and remark on sedimented landscapes bloodied by the deeds

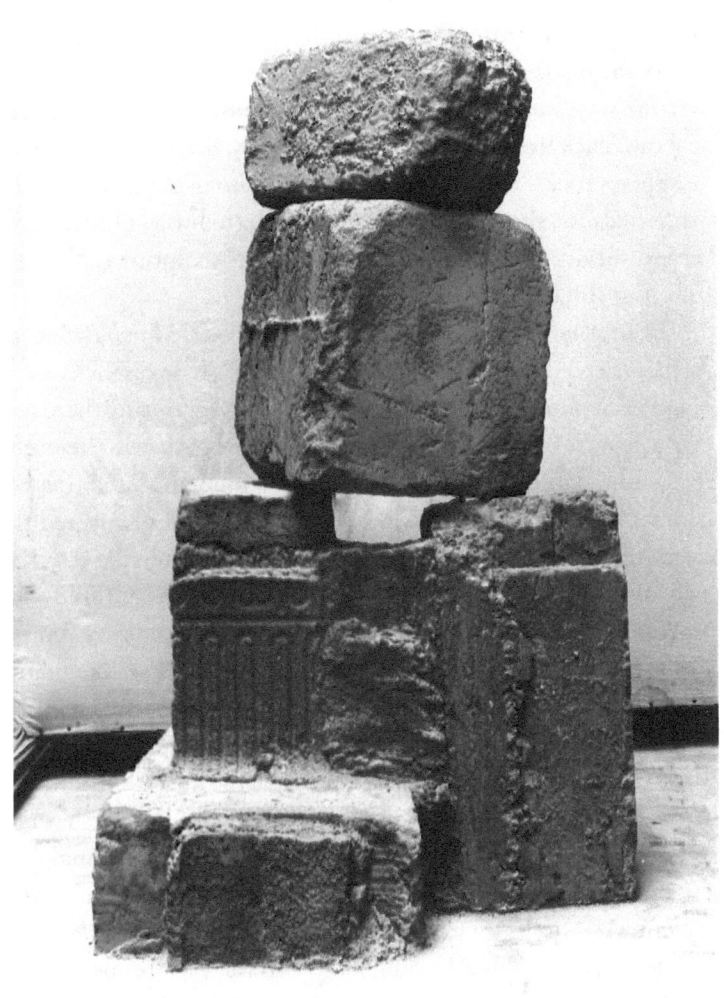

2i.1 Beverly Buchanan, *Wall Fragments*, 1978. Cast concrete with acrylic paint. Courtesy of the Estate of Beverly Buchanan and the Andrew Edlin Gallery, New York.

of the past. They transform our understanding specifically of the stratified places where racial histories—especially the forgotten histories of the enslaved—live and reside. Her first tribute to her ancestors, *Ruins and Rituals* (1979), was built at a site in Macon, Georgia, near the cabin of a racist author and apologist for slavery. Buchanan's work commented on this space by placing cast-concrete blocks of various sizes directly on the earth in groupings that look like sarcophagi—meant, symbolically, to mourn the enslaved. She repeated this performative gesture throughout the art she made during her life. She often placed stone or clay markers in overrun graveyards, in sandy marshes and near fields. Such was her effort to show Black lives (as) matter. Accordingly, Buchanan's work anthropomorphizes rocks. She included the word *ruins* in the titles of several of her works because, she thought, "that tells you this object has been through a lot and survived—that's the idea behind the sculptures . . . it's like, 'Here I am; I'm still here!'"[44]

In another major work of temporal land art, *Marsh Ruins* (1981), Buchanan selected an area called the Marshes of Glynn on the Georgia coastal island of St. Simons. She made a monumental sculpture there to memorialize a group of Igbo people who in 1803 chose to drown themselves rather than submit to enslavement. Buchanan commemorated these ancestors with stones: She "planted three concrete forms and covered them with layers of tabby, a mixture used in slave living quarters. *Marsh Ruins* gradually disintegrated back into the marsh. Buchanan captured that erosion process on video."[45] Tabby is made of lime expressed from burned oyster shells, mixed with ash and water to make a concrete-like material. This raw material was often used for construction since the process required to make it is not complex. Cultural geographers and theorists understand work such as Buchanan's as activating spaces rife with meaning, evoking memories of the conquered, the suppressed and buried that require the redrawing of maps as a means of redress.[46] Buchanan makes manifest the ancestral lineages that are still threatened by violence and erasures in the present. As Michel de Certeau put it, "What the map cuts up, the story cuts across,"[47] to which I would add, "and the rock re-members."

Edmonia Lewis's stone work anticipates Buchanan's significant placements of her cairn-like structures. All such works with stone can be understood as contradictory, at once commenting on the ceremonial and the commercial, the eternal and the eroding. Stones are endowed with the capacity to reinscribe and revive histories: They bear a ritual energy and can remind us of the politics of the auction block, the pedestal, the pomerial (boundary) stone, the artist's uncut block of marble, the potentially endless signifying iterations of these living objects in our midst.[48]

With Holding Hands

And truly women have excelled indeed
In every art to which they set their hand.

    Ludovico Ariosto, quoted in Giorgio Vasari,
    The Lives of the Artists

From childhood, she [Lewis] has had wonderful power
with her hands. In shaping, fashioning, executing. It began
with beads and wampum, and ended, as we see, with clay.

    The Elevator (San Francisco) (1879)

Lewis's intelligent, intelligible hands both shaped stone
and forged her professional identity. In her life and in
her work, Lewis's "freedom to do, to achieve [was] won
by her own hand."[1] Exploring the meaning-making capacity of her hands is, therefore, central to understanding her sculptural prowess. This chapter seeks to revive
tactile traces of Lewis's work as a means of exploring
the sensational affective power produced by the touch
of her hands. Hands convey more than the potential
for active gestural repertoires or the capacity for transformation: Ideal hands with their opposable thumbs

and moving digits are metonyms for the making of human form more generally (just as the paleolithic handprints on the cave walls at Lascaux evoke the whole human body, alongside the deer and horses). Her human hands worked as "organs of performance," leaving tangible digital imprints of her life and times.

Our imaginative faculties can revive the intimacy of the artist's touch, retrace the movement of her palms and fingers about her sculptural forms, replace caresses forgotten long ago. One wonders if some of Lewis's sculptures bear the mark of her hands. Is it possible that a trace of her fingerprint appeared in the clay bozzetti she modeled? Does an imprint remain as the center of a rose she carved in one of her later works?

Edmonia Lewis came from a family of individuals who worked brilliantly with their hands: Her mother and aunts were moccasin makers; her father was a "gentleman's" servant, a job that required nimble fingers for opening and closing fine jacket buttons, tending to the employer's physical form, and carrying out innumerable manual tasks. Her half-brother, Samuel, or Sunrise, was a barber, miner, and a sleight-of-hand artist, a practitioner of legerdemain, who could manipulate objects as only a performative magician can. Hands are among the many things Lewis's statues depict; one of her little-known (formerly misattributed) sculptures, *Hands of Gerrit and Ann Smith* (1872) shows *only* a pair of clasped hands (see figure 3.2).

Lewis carved many hands during her career. One of her early assignments during the short period she apprenticed with Boston-based sculptor Edward Augustus Brackett was to sculpt a lady's hand. Notably, this hand became one of the first sculptures that she ever sold; it generated the handsome sum of $8.[2] The hand, likely sculpted in clay, no longer exists, nor is there any photographic record; all mentions appear only in writing. Throughout her oeuvre, we find hands clasped in prayer, wringing with worry, joined to represent the bond of matrimony; hands wielding weapons, making arrowheads of jasper, weaving fabric, holding scrolls, pulling hair; a cupid's hand caught in an iron trap; hands cradling the curls on a baby's head; hands resting over hearts, grasping morning glory stems; a hand raised in a fist signifying freedom from bondage, with a broken chain dangling from the wrist. We see even the delicate carved hand of a dead Cleopatra limply draped over the arm of her throne.

At least two separate sculptural representations known as *mani in fede*, Italian for hands clasped in fidelity or marriage, deserve closer examination. The first, a full-scale, full-body sculpture titled *Hiawatha's Marriage*

(1870), includes the clasped hands of the fictional characters Hiawatha and Minnehaha as they stand next to each other. The second is the sculpture of only the hands and wrists from the actual abolitionist couple, Ann Carroll Fitzhugh Smith (1805–75) and her husband, Gerrit Smith (1797–1874).[3] These sculptures of two individuals holding hands, cements their matrimonial bond, here held together in Lewis's sculptural homage.[4]

Let us look first at the hands in *Hiawatha's Marriage* (figure 3.1), based on Henry Wadsworth Longfellow's exceptionally popular epic poem *The Song of Hiawatha*. *Hiawatha's Marriage* differs greatly from the stereotypical representations of idealized "Indian" subjects in the neoclassical tradition; these are usually depicted as single-figure male warriors or maidens, as other scholars have noted. Lewis's depiction of the Native couple Hiawatha (Ojibwe) and Minnehaha (Dakota) is an original conception, though based on fiction. She conceived this sculpture in Rome and first carved it in marble in 1866, then in a different version in 1870. Her decision to sculpt this moment of celebratory, cross-tribal marital bliss, out of the hundreds of images in the stanzas that compose Longfellow's poem, is significant.

Most scholars reference the artist's own Indigeneity when viewing this piece; for example, in discussing the 1866 version (once owned by Camille and Bill Cosby), David Driskell argues that, "As romantic as she was neoclassical, Lewis . . . romanticized . . . holy matrimony using [her] Mother's people, the Mississauga." The sculpture's use of "Roman togas rendered in the classical style," Driskell continues, universalizes the figures, even as "Hiawatha's hairstyle, the necklace he wears, and the moccasins the newlyweds wear show this composition to be in the genre of 'Indian' lore."[5] Kirsten Pai Buick cautions us against assuming, as Lewis's contemporaries did with ease, that, "by virtue of her birth, Lewis was the embodiment of Indigenous themes . . . her art and her self were collapsed into a neat tautology."[6] To counter this stereotypical conflation, perhaps Lewis chose only to represent Indian subjects imagined by Longfellow (even if she included selected sartorial aspects from life). The majority of her known so-called Indian sculptures reference figures from Longfellow's poem; an exception is her sculpture *Indian Combat* (1868), housed at the Cleveland Museum of Art. This complex and beautiful work depicts three wrestling, entwined figures, whose hands and gazes defy the title's expectation.

We must wonder about Lewis's sculptural motivations. Might she have been resisting expectations that she would or could only make autobiographical representations, sculpting Black people and Indians? How

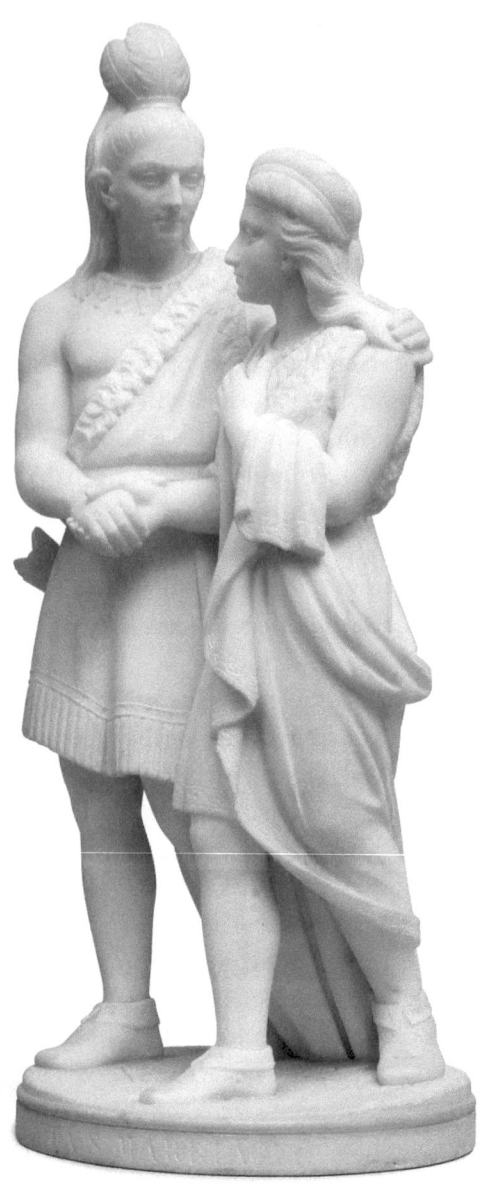

3.1 Edmonia Lewis, *Hiawatha's Marriage*, 1870. Marble, 32¼ × 15 × 10½ in. Stark Museum of Art, Orange, Texas, Purchase of the Nelda C. and H. J. Lutcher Stark Foundation.

did she negotiate the pressures to value white forms or forms derived from European poetry? Was she symbolically linking her sculpture to a massively popular poem as a savvy marketing move, knowing it would give people an anchor to understand and discuss her sculpture? Was she strategically choosing an image of Indigenous love in the poem as a way to critique the poem's overall theme and plot? Certainly, no other neoclassical sculptor in Europe at the time would have known any details about Ojibwe culture, dress, and adornment better than Lewis did. This specificity may have allowed her to bring to life the representations of the characters in this poem in a way that might have steered the popular imagination toward an actuality and away from brute stereotypes. Or, she may simply have been moved by the lyrical poem and its black-and-white illustrations. We should always consider her choices through multiple valences and possibilities.

The 1866 and 1870 versions of the sculpture contain significant and subtle differences. The earlier take has the two figures gazing at each other at almost eye level. Minnehaha's left hand rests at her midsection, holding classical drapery about her waist. The base on which the figures stand has flowers carved in relief. A Greek key pattern appears at the bottom of Minnehaha's toga. In the later take, no Grecian symbols appear. In the 1870 version, Minnehaha's eyes align with Hiawatha's chin. They exhibit the same contrapposto stance but from these varying heights, they appear less equal. Minnehaha's left hand is held up by her breast as she gazes up into her new husband's face. They stand on a base with leaves protruding from the sculpture. The trim on Minnehaha's robes has been changed from the Greek key to fringe, echoing the drapery surrounding Hiawatha. His feathered hairstyle is higher and has two feathers, rather than one, and is larger and more dramatic.

In *Hiawatha's Marriage*, Lewis placed the clasped hands of the couple at the literal center of the full-scale sculpture. Their hands mark the space where the figures touch. Their hands are the fulcrum point between them, drawing our eye to their firm, warm, intimate embrace of relaxed figures during a momentous event. As such, their joined hands perform the consolidation of romantic love and, simultaneously, merging of assets: the hands themselves manifest this new union. When the work was displayed as one of five pieces Lewis brought west to San Francisco in 1873 to sell (it sold for $550), local papers debated its quality. The *San Francisco Chronicle* covered the event—the first display of sculptures made in Europe in the area—but damned the work with faint praise:

There is so much labored finish to [the sculptures] that very little expression is left. The chisel has been used with too much mechanical nicety, and even if the conceptions were originally beautiful, the over careful manner in which they have been carved out would prevent them from ever taking a high rank in art. Miss Lewis is a skillful manipulator of marble and the polish she gives is very fine, but compared to the works of Powers and other eminent sculptors her efforts make a poor show. It cannot be denied, however, that she has acquired a certain excellence in art.[7]

A rejoinder quickly followed this critique. In the Black-owned paper *The Elevator*, Lewis sculptures were lauded and praised for their

originality of conception and their beautiful finish. There are no rough or neglected points as much care has been spent on the reverse as on the obverse sides. The pose of "Hiawatha and Minnehaha" is perfectly natural: there is an ease and gracefulness which is really charming. The adjuncts are also in keeping: the wampum belt, the fringe on the robe, the quiver and arrows, the wildflowers on the ground: the whole tout ensemble carry out the idea and illustrate Indian life.[8]

Despite these differing opinions, it is important to note that both reviews comment on Lewis's work with her hands.

Lewis's second sculpture of wedded hands featured disembodied hands as a sculpture in their own right. The work was a commission from a living couple who had been married for decades by the time she was called to commemorate their bond: Ann and Gerrit Smith, who used their stately home in the town of Peterboro, New York, as a site for abolitionist work. According to Gerrit Smith's diary, Lewis visited the home in August 1872: "Edmonia Lewis of Rome, Italy comes to take the first steps in putting up my statue in marble."[9] After Smith communicated that he did not want a full-size sculpture of himself, Lewis chose not to create a smaller-scale portrait bust or a medallion of him. Rather, she decided to represent Gerrit Smith conjoined, coterminous, and coequal with his wife, Ann, committing a *pair* of hands to marble. This pair of hands, cleaved together, becomes the subject of what we can read as one of Lewis's abolitionist sculptures.[10]

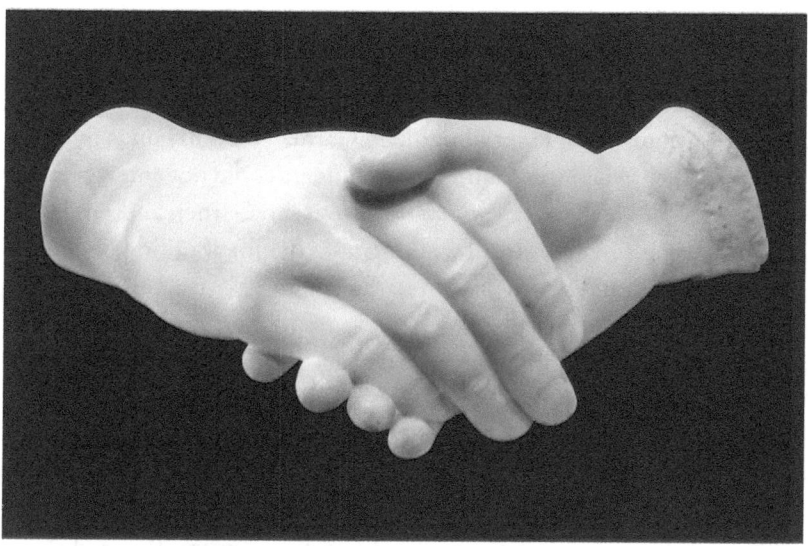

3.2 Edmonia Lewis, *Hands of Gerrit and Ann Smith*, 1872.
Marble. Madison County Historical Society, Oneida,
New York.

The sculpture of Gerrit's and Ann's hands was done just a few years before their deaths, though the representation does not portray (or betray) the advanced age of the sitters. The hands feature smooth, unblemished skin and evince a sense of youthfulness. They end at the wrist, they float in space, separate(d) from "the whole."[11] The hands themselves are bare; they wear neither rings nor gloves. A one-inch ribbon of marble lace adorns Ann Smith's hand and a simple cuff frames Gerrit Smith's wrist. Decisive details abound: veins mark flesh; weight and warmth are rendered via the interstitial lines; negative space and points of contact that keep the hands both bound to each other and apart. Gerrit's hand has pronounced knuckles and smooth, even fingernails.[12] Ann's small right thumb is positioned prominently at the top of the sculpture and her hand casts a shadow over the middle and index fingers of Gerrit's right hand. Her index finger can be seen below his pinky finger which runs the length of her other, curved digits. Gerrit's pinky bends with the pressure from her hand toward his ring and middle finger. The fact that the hands are semidetached from a body does not prevent them from seeming, in our mind's eye, connected to fully formed figures, with hearts, brains, and other invisible extremities registered only through context. This representation indexes tactility at every turn.

The Smiths devoted their lives to the abolition of slavery and other progressive causes. Smith assisted hundreds of escaped slaves on their journeys to freedom, including the young Frederick Douglass. The well-known Black abolitionist Rev. Henry Highland Garnet (1815–82) once quipped that there were two places southern slaveholders could not enter: Heaven and Peterboro, New York. The Smiths, Reverend Garnet, and Frederick Douglass were close friends, all working together for abolition and racial justice. Douglass and Smith organized the Fugitive Slave Convention, the only such meeting to take place on American soil. Gerrit was also passionately involved in promoting interracial coeducation—he helped give the land and funding for Oberlin College in Ohio, the first school to offer integrated classes for men and women, Blacks and whites, together–and the very college Edmonia Lewis attended.

A close reading reveals subtle clues about the race, gender, and class statuses of the subjects of the wedded-hands sculpture. We read these markers in the details: the hands' different sizes, their placement (depending on how the sculpture is displayed), the color of the stone, and the remnants of vestments visibly framing each hand's wrist. Where most sculptures of differently gendered held hands "present" the female-coded hand on top of the male hand, the latter playing the supporting role (as is the case in Harriet Hosmer's version of the Brownings' hands, discussed below), here, Gerrit's fingers rest gently in Ann's palm. We can venture to read this as a feminist intervention (the two did indeed champion women's rights) or even a suggestion that the Smiths had an unusually progressive relationship. One wonders if Ann herself had a hand in the striking placement that communicates feminine support and strength leading from the bottom.

Edmonia cast the hands in plaster before carving them in marble. To complete this casting process, their hands would have been slathered with a slick, viscous substance to prevent the plaster from sticking to their skin. The rapid hardening of plaster casts required the artist to work quickly and to entreat her models to remain still. I wonder if Lewis held each of these subjects' hands as a means of researching this work. Might the artist have measured the weight, pressure, the feel of the skin and palms of the subjects? Might she have joined their intimacy? Was she able to register the temperature, the texture of their skin? What might she have felt? In the nineteenth century, clasped "ungloved" hands symbolized more than just a romantic gesture. They conveyed a sense of erotic, if not sexual, contact: The viewer surmises that Gerrit and Ann's

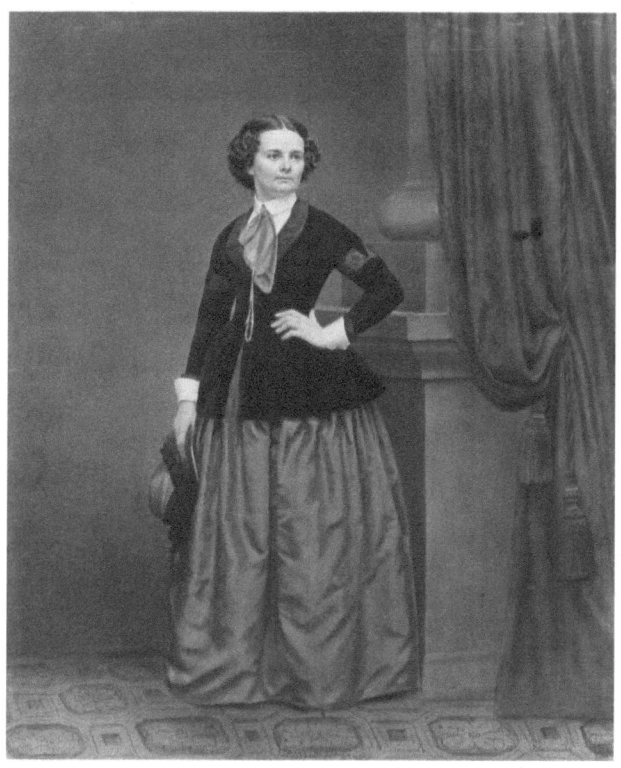

3.3 Mathew B. Brady and Studio, portrait of sculptor Harriet Goodhue Hosmer, 1857. Salted paper print, hand-colored with black ink, 17¹⁵⁄₁₆ × 14⅜ in. Harvard Art Museums.

touching hands have, indeed, held other body parts.[13] This sculpture fused the two hands as one complete object connected, in the round.[14] In this sense, they are moving stones. This three-dimensional sculpture retains the impression, the residue of the artist's touch and, by extension, the possibility of our own.

For insight into the contemporaneous questions of color, race, and gender and their representation in art, we may look to another iconic set of sculpted hands—hands made by the sculptor Harriet Hosmer (1830–1908; figure 3.3), who lived with her lover, the actress Charlotte Cushman (1816–76) in the center of Rome. Hosmer cast the hands of her friends the poets Elizabeth Barrett and Robert Browning in plaster in 1853 and made several versions, including at least one in bronze (figure 3.4). This is surprising since Robert Browning wrote to "Hattie" (Harriet) that "bronze

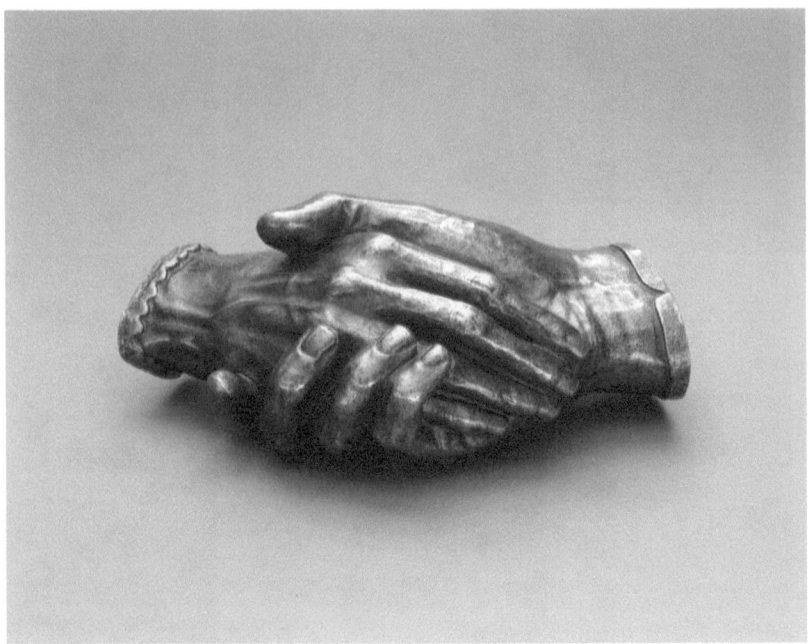

3.4 Harriet Hosmer, *Clasped Hands of Robert and Elizabeth Barrett Browning*, 1853, cast after 1853. Bronze, 3¼ ×
8¼ × 4¼ in. Metropolitan Museum of Art, New York, Purchase, Mrs. Frederick A. Stoughton Gift, 1986.

is such inadequate stuff for the expression of flesh, compared with marble."[15] Although it was made a decade prior to her arrival, Lewis would have
been familiar with this famous sculpture, this pair of hands. It was so well
known that Nathaniel Hawthorne mentioned it in his novel *The Marble
Faun* (1860), a fictionalized account of Hosmer and her circle. The novel's
narrator states that the sculpture was made to "symbolize the individuality and heroic union of two highly poetic lives." To this day, the hands are
described as "tiny but iconic hands [that are] immortal."[16]

The plaster versions of the Brownings' hands are currently in the
Schlesinger Library at the Radcliffe Institute for Advanced Study at Harvard. The library's notes on the sculpture state that the plaster from which
it was made "bears traces of a light wash of paint to mimic flesh." Other
studies of the work suggest that Elizabeth Barrett Browning consented
to having the "life-cast" done only if her dear "Hatty" did the mold with
Hatty's own hand, thereby rejecting sitting for a "formatore," an artisan
workman."[17] Perhaps the intimacy of the casting process may have made

Browning skeptical of a male stranger's rough touch. Robert Browning may have referenced the process in his poem "Andrea del Sarto" written in 1855. This dramatic monologue written from the perspective of the painter del Sarto for his wife, Lucrezia, states in lines 21–22, "Your soft hand is a woman of itself / And mine the man's bared breast she curls inside."[18] Such lines bespeak the erotics of touch that can be present in the production of sculpture.

Thinking about the production of a "finished" work allows us to remember the arduous process of making it. This attention transforms our reading of the temporality of a work: It shows again how sculptures are objects not merely of emotion but also of motion. Among the arts, sculpture is uniquely imagined to be cathected to the body of the artist. Antonio Canova (1757–1822), the most revered neoclassical sculptor, whose work was known through Europe, epitomized this concept. Lewis rented the late Canova's former studio in Rome when she first arrived in the city. As a neoclassical sculptor herself, Lewis would have followed his techniques, working first by molding clay maquettes and finally shaping forms into gleaming marble bodies with the finishing technique known as the *ultima mano* (literally, the "last hand" of the sculptor, or last touch). As scholars of Canova's works suggest, "Even . . . finished marbles retain something of the memory of clay's manipulability. In [Canova's] pursuit of the pliability of marble—in his desire for stone to become living flesh—Canova seemingly translated the defining quality of one medium into another. [He famously] 'kissed' and 'caressed' his marbles into existence rather than chipping or carving—imprinting his own body onto the stone, pressing against it to create form."[19] This is an eloquent way of consolidating the connection between the sculptor and "his" creations. The pressure exerted between the maker and the made, the coming together of flesh and stone, sparked desire.

Canova sometimes applied a stain of yellow wax to his sculptures in an attempt to render his white marble stones as if they were "warm flesh."[20] Color conveyed concupiscence: It was salacious rather than sensuous. Some critics sought to censure Canova (and other sculptors) for creating sculptures that hewed too closely to living flesh. This is another aspect of the interlacing issues surrounding how physicality and materiality meet (in) sculptural representation, thereby returning us to the knotty question of color.[21]

In my view, racial conceptions color every aspect of neoclassical sculpture; the neoclassical style, invented in the eighteenth century, dovetails with histories of racial hierarchy and white supremacy. Nineteenth-century viewers associated whiteness with purity: For many Victorians "Greek sculpture was white—a further badge of virtue. Time and again Victorian writers let their thoughts play around the whiteness of statuary, often using it as an emblem of purity."[22] Statues such as *The Greek Slave* (1846), by Hiram Powers (1805–73), were lauded as the apotheosis of perfection since the white marble of the work was highly polished and gleamed. (Lewis's work was compared to Powers's on more than one occasion in her era, and recently her *Hagar* was juxtaposed with it in the 2025 Smithsonian exhibition *The Shape of Power*). In contrast to Powers's purportedly perfect work, the color-washed sculpture known as *The Tinted Venus* (1850–62), made by British sculptor John Gibson (1790–1866), invoked invective and was read as vulgar and vile. The work's flesh tones represented indecent sexuality, and its color detracted from its dignity. All of this color symbolism was, ironically, based on a misinterpretation of the classical aesthetics of Greco-Roman works. Modern artists of the nineteenth century, in their reverence for ancient sculptures, ended up reifying an erroneous representation of the "original" and the "antique," overlooking the fact these sculptures were originally painted to resemble colored flesh. The question of how such statutes should be presented for a viewing public and for artists themselves permeated international art culture in the era.

These questions of color also present themselves in two distinct versions of the white Brownings' hands made by the white artist Harriet Hosmer. Initially, Hosmer made the hands in white plaster in the winter of 1853. She then rendered them in white marble, and ultimately decided to cast them in bronze. In a deft reading of the sculpture, Katherine Fein observes: "The pale tone of plaster more closely matches the white skin of the Brownings, whereas the eight bronze versions featuring varying patinas, ranging from deep brown with hints of blue and green to nearly gold, do not."[23] To ask if these dark hands appropriately approximate the pale skin of the Brownings is to repeat the question asked of Edmonia Lewis's sculptures of "colored" subjects that she rendered in white marble. Focusing on the form of flesh does not ever render the question of color immaterial. Again, this is to remember that "lifelike" sculptures construct bodies as forms of embodiment. The color of sculptures and the "color of stone" that was debated as a racial issue throughout the nineteenth century has remained an enduring aspect of all discussions about Lewis's neoclassical work.[24]

Nineteenth-century debates about racial differences intersected with parallel discussions about the use of polychrome in sculpture. As opposed to monogenesis, the belief that there is one race of "Man," polygenesis subscribed to the belief that multiple types of beings existed under the categories of white "Men." Working from the hierarchical schema developed in medieval and Renaissance thought and known as the Great Chain of Being, later adherents of this schema, which ranked entities by placing God at the pinnacle and mere minerals at the nadir translated these ideas into a modern racial hierarchy. In this ranking, the lowest type was the so-called black (African), on the bottom, followed by red (Native American), then yellow (Asian), and capped off by white (European), at the top. As Charles Mills explains:

> A color-coded morality of the Racial Contract restricts the possession of this natural freedom and equality to *white* men. By virtue of their complete nonrecognition, or at best inadequate, myopic recognition, of the duties of natural law, nonwhites are appropriately relegated to the lower rung on the moral ladder (the Great Chain of Being). They are designated as born *un*free and *un*equal. A partitioned social ontology is therefore created, a universe divided between persons and racial subpersons, *Untermenschen*, who may variously be black, red, brown, yellow—slaves, aborigines, colonial populations—but who are collectively appropriately known as "subject" races.[25]

Building on such beliefs, intellectuals and the general public debated whether iterations of skin color were simply variations of a single human race (a more liberal view), or if the variation signified the existence of many separate races with different immutable variations. The polygenecist view asserted the fixed valuation of being that drew on racism to conceive of differences as absolute. Such differences correlated with moral values that asserted the purported purity and superiority of white over Black, to quote the famous title of Winthrop D. Jordan's book about attitudes toward the Negro.[26] In contrast, the monogenecist viewpoint proffered that color was superficial and that one's inner "soul" could be white in the moral register (and here I am thinking about William Blake's illustrated poem "The Little Black Boy," written in 1789, whose speaker proclaims, "I am black, but O! my soul is white").[27] It was still a problematic view; monogenecists valued "whiteness" as the apotheosis of ideal virtue, arguing that whatever one's outer skin color, all souls could be white in the eternal light of God.

Like every sculptor working in the neoclassical style, Lewis had to choose between at least three options: whether or not to use colored stones or to cast her work in bronze, to paint or tint stone to create the illusionary realism, and whether to work with white marble, which emphasized form and formalist abstraction over functionalist colorism. The fact that she represented Black as well as Indigenous people in white marble in accordance with Idealist aesthetics has been a feature of her work ever since it was first made. The neoclassical devotion to creating sculptures exclusively in white marble held sway at the time because most Victorian sculptors of the era erroneously believed that the great works of the ancients were intended to be bare white stone. In fact, as noted, these revered works were originally painted—but the paint had worn away in the years since antiquity. Thus, nineteenth-century sculptors worshipped a false notion of the antique.

While other sculptors of Lewis's era and genre (such as Jean-Antoine Houdon and Jean-Baptiste Carpeaux) chose to craft figurative sculptures of African and Native characters in black marble, onyx, or ebony, or used various techniques to color their work, regardless of the race depicted in the subject, Lewis overwhelmingly adhered to the neoclassical use of white marble, regardless of subject matter. She did make a few portraits of white men in red-toned terra cotta, rendered some Indigenous figures in copper, and proposed a bust of Phillis Wheatley in bronze (if it was produced, its whereabouts are unknown). An example of her minimal use of polychromy appears in a thin line of gold paint that adorns the top of the garment worn by her portrait *Bust of Christ* (1870). This exquisite bust depicts Jesus with lanky locks that curl over the figure's shoulders. Here, he wears a serene pupil-less expression, a highly creased garment, and a full bushy beard and thick mustache. This work was found in 2015 languishing in a random cabinet in Scotland's Gothic Revival Mount Stuart castle, once owned by Lewis's Catholic patron, the Third Marquess of Bute, John Patrick Chrichton-Stuart. The bust remains as one of only two known works by her in the United Kingdom.[28]

The author Henrik Ibsen wrote to his British friend Edmond Gosse on January 15, 1874, "We are no longer living in the age of Shakespeare. Among sculptors there is already talk of painting statues in the natural colors. Much can be said both for and against this. I have no desire to see the Venus of Milo painted, but I would rather see the head of a Negro executed in black than in white marble. Speaking generally, the style must conform to the degree of ideality which pervades the representation."[29] This statement concurs with the conservative sentiment pervasive in so much Victorian (and current) discourse about difference: the compulsion to police, the anxious, phobic responses to ambiguity, the ardent desire to see "blacks" as black, and "whites" as white, segregated into separate realms. As Caitlin Beach, argues, "figures of jasper, marble, bronze, Parian, and plaster were bodies produced—literally and figuratively—in relation to broader economic and legal negotiations of ontology and animacy of the period."[30]

The historical and ongoing investment in racial realism deeply influenced Lewis's work and its reception. Neoclassical sculptures encode and exude, if not reify, racial difference, often in the form of realism. Since figurative sculptures were likenesses that sought to be "like life" and were made "from life," they were also the result of projection—a psychological transfer wherein perceptions, attitudes, and actions are ascribed to an Other. As Kirsten Buick argues, "We are reminded that 'realism' is an ideology, couched in the seemingly objective charge of 'life-like.' As an ideology, realism could be weaponized; and this was certainly the case in the critical reception of Lewis's ideal works."[31] As a "colored" sculptor, Lewis could not escape this phenomenon, which affected her aesthetic choices, personally and politically. Her choices were critiqued by multiple constituents. For example, when her monumental sculpture, the 3,015 pound *The Death of Cleopatra* was selected from hundreds of entries to appear in the 1876 Centennial Exhibition in Philadelphia (the only sculpture by a colored artist), many found her depiction of the dead queen appalling, ostensibly due to the graphic realism of portraying the subject as a corpse (see figures 2.1 and 2.2). Naurice Frank Woods Jr. surmises that "such a bold move from a woman and person of color exposed . . . deep seated prejudices and thus allowed for less-than-favorable observations." He quotes another critic who, in Woods's estimation, "came close to deconstructing the inevitable racist and sexist biases that surrounded her." Woods quotes an account of the reception Lewis had in 1878 "[She] received any amount of rudeness and insult from boors who will not believe that such a beautiful creation could come from colored fingers. They should learn to think more of the article and less of the epidermis."[32] When, as she often did, Lewis put her body on the line by standing next to her work in order to claim it as her own, not only was she the subject of racial defamation, but on at least one occasion, she was even physically attacked by white men who "deemed her an intrusive imposter."[33]

While she may have made a daring choice in deciding to depict the Egyptian queen as already deceased, she was less decisive when it came to representing her as fully "African." Lewis depicted Cleopatra with distinctly Greco-Roman features similar to those she had seen on ancient, gilded coins that she had studied in Rome. The debate about how to depict Cleopatra's so-called racial features has yet to be resolved; the mere subject always already raises the question of race given that Cleopatra ruled Egypt, on the African continent.

Contemporary poet Jeanne Atkins writes:

Artists reveal. Artists hide.
Edmonia remembers a dream of Europe.
Can she swap clay the color of her hands for pale marble?
Carve entire bodies instead of life broken at the shoulders
and live where the ground is never hard and white?[34]

Here, the poet references the proverbial problem of how to understand Lewis as a "colored" artist whose dark hands worked on white marble in what some of her coevals considered to be an act of miscegenation. Lewis, however, was at times able to eschew the Black-white binary that others used to fix her. Her all–white marble, "white-appearing" subjects, whether meant to represent so-called Red, Black, white, or Brown people, create a certain undecidability of racial designation. They break the purported fidelity to type to which she herself was so often subject.

On at least one occasion, Lewis's colleagues presumed that her prowess as a sculptor meant that she must have had "white blood." "White blood" was believed to be the ultimate source of "intelligence" and artistic talent at the time. Such a phenomenon verges on the impossible, since race is a discursive and not a biological category. Yet this fact does not mute the power of its metaphoricity to organize and divide populations or manage questions of life and death.[35] For her part, Lewis absolutely denied what she considered to be the aspersion of having "white blood" and frequently spoke of her cultural difference—her coloredness—as a key source of her success. "No, I have not a drop of what they call white blood in my veins," she once said. "My father was a full blooded Negro, and my mother was a full blooded Chippewa" (recall that *Chippewa* was the name frequently used in Lewis's time to designate people of Ojibwe heritage). While this statement may make use of the idea of different kinds of blood quantum, it did so in a reversal of the idea of the differential value of different races' blood. This approach was not without its complications. Throughout her life, Lewis was reported to have voiced racially inflected views about her own subjectivity and occasionally was cited as having made disparaging comments about others who shared her racial designations. Lewis was quoted in 1866 in the *Boston Commonwealth* as saying, "My features I take from my father, but my spirit, my industry and perseverance I get from my Indian mother," a statement that remains equivocal, perhaps as much about gender as it is about race and ethnicity. Despite such lifelong equivocations about her own racial, ethnic, and tribal designations, Lewis acknowledged her genealogy and its significance and sometimes did so in unexpected ways. Most reportage of her words is secondhand: What surfaces through her entire corpus and life story is that race mattered.

Despite her at times complicated statements about her own racial makeup and sentiments about race, Lewis used her art to champion those who fought for abolition and liberal political causes. Returning to the sculpted pair of hands of Ann and Gerrit Smith, we may posit that sculpting these hands marked a deeper entrée into abolitionist circles and communities for Lewis. The association with the Smiths may have afforded Lewis the opportunity to meet Frederick Douglass—or they may have met when Lewis was a student at Oberlin between 1859 and 1863, before her gruesome attack. Gerrit Smith funded Douglass's abolitionist paper, *The North Star* (published from 1847 to 1851). The two worked together over many years to generate ideas for ending the reign of terror and greed that was the slavocracy in America.[36] Smith sold a farm from his vast landholdings to John Brown; Brown lived there during the time he was planning his armed revolt against slavery, an action that followed the tradition of other armed rebellions across the Atlantic world, including those led by Black revolutionaries such as Denmark Vesey (1767–1822). As he became more radicalized in the fight for manumission, Gerrit Smith gave money to aid Brown's 1859 armed rebellion, one of the first insurrections against enslavement to have been fronted by a white person. This entered the annals of history as the raid on Harper's Ferry, Virginia, where the US government manufactured and stored firearms. John Brown's interracial coalition included armed freedmen and galvanized further abolitionist sentiment, though it was not successful in its immediate aims and Brown was arrested, tried, and hanged for this collective action against the state. He became one of the most popular folk heroes in the country and is the subject of numerous tributes by African American critics and artists, from W. E. B. Du Bois's 1909 biography *John Brown* to the four spare narrative gouaches that Jacob Lawrence (1917–2000) made to honor Brown that constitute his powerful series *The Legend of John Brown* (1941).

Edmonia Lewis sculpted a medallion of John Brown in 1864, before she left America for Rome. Her portrait of Brown in profile was made to hang on walls in homes whose residents, we may imagine, revered Brown's messianic commitment to freedom. Lewis advertised her medallion in the antislavery magazine *The Liberator* (to which she subscribed) and gifted a copy of her John Brown marble bust to Rev. Henry Garnet. By 1878, Lewis had made no fewer than nine versions of the likeness of Brown, who, she said, "had done so much to help my father's people." Her art contributed to the generative circle of abolitionists who championed Brown as a revolutionary hero.[37]

After John Brown's organized insurrection against the state, while he was still imprisoned in Charlestown, Virginia, Lewis's one-time mentor Edward Brackett (a white northerner with abolitionist sympathies) became one of the first artists to sculpt Brown before his eventual death at the hands of the state. At first Brackett was denied access to the incarcerated revolutionary, which prompted him to devise a surreptitious scheme with the assistant jailor that would allow him to get close enough to the imprisoned Brown to create his portrait bust. Brackett recalled the story decades later:

In anticipation of this movement, I had prepared a conventional drawing of a head. Taking the drawing and my measuring instruments and accompanied by Mr. Griswold, I went to Brown's cell. Mr. Griswold entered and explained to Brown my purpose. . . .

Now came our consideration of the under jailer's fears. For his sake I must be able to swear, if questioned, that I had never entered his prisoner's cell. So I stood on the threshold, sketch in hand, almost near enough to Brown to touch him, while Griswold, with my instruments and by my minute directions, made each measurement. These I noted down in their several places on my sketch, photographing the subject on my brain the while.

The bust as you see it, is a little poetized. A man who paints a picture of a great man and puts no greatness into it, saying that he sees none, errs both in perception and in art. In this case the idealization is elusive—not to be located in any one feature. But it exists, and purposely, the more truthfully to express the character of the subject. Yet John Brown was not himself a great man, but rather a forerunner of great things. He was a blind instrument, blindly cutting the way to the death of thousands and the birth of a new age.[38]

By characterizing Brown as "a blind instrument" who served as a harbinger of justice, Brackett's recollection demonstrates that neoclassical portrait busts function not only as representations of specific individuals but also as idealized figures symbolizing distinct ideologies. Thus, the details of production that Brackett recounted were in the service of *extradiegetic* properties—aspects that exceed the frame of the individual portrait as such. Every distinct portrait of an "individual" concretizes cultural valances, carrying ideas about history, politics, race, and so much more.

Sculptural technique served the most ardent human desire for creating change. Lewis was motivated by a desire to sculpt heroic figures, and she would have adhered to the same general methods as Brackett followed, deploying measuring instruments, pencil sketches, and her imagination to produce sculptures. In making some of her most famous portrait busts, she relied on her memory of having seen her subjects, sometimes from afar. In this way, she, too, "photograph[ed] the subject on [her] brain." Brackett and Lewis parted ways in 1862. Lewis made several sculptures of the same subjects that Brackett did; and, on at least one occasion, she seemed to have outdone him. Henry Wadsworth Longfellow, whose image Lewis sculpted in Rome, said that he preferred the bust she had made of him to the one Brackett made.

When Edmonia Lewis left the United States, she hoped to find a more welcoming community abroad: "a social atmosphere where I was not constantly reminded of my color." While she may have found that environment, her community of American expatriate artists retained many racist ideas. When she was not being accused of having white blood, she could be rendered crudely as a kind of chimera. Lady Cholmondeley, one of the female sculptors she knew in Rome, made a portrait bust of Lewis (now lost). She sculpted Lewis with her hair "divided" in a ridiculous bifurcation that had short "negro" curls atop one side of her head, and long, lank "Indian" hair on the other side. One can only wonder what combination of anger and hurt this offensive portrait may have caused Lewis. Lewis's interactions later in life with other Black women were more welcoming. She met two colored ladies during a stop in 1878 in Indianapolis, where, during an hour's visit, the three spoke candidly about Lewis's life in Rome, including her interactions with Sallie Mercer (a colored woman who worked for Charlotte Cushman for thirty-five years), her devotion to sculpting, her reading and speaking knowledge of four different languages, and her understanding of herself as a racial subject. The report of this encounter in the *St. Louis Dispatch* made a point of explaining that upon greeting Lewis, who "wore a short traveling suit of brown woolen goods [and] . . . shook hands with" them, the two women "could but notice their shape and expression. They were small, plump, with tapering fingers and of a polished smoothness, and her grasp was a firm and characteristic one."[39]

What shifts when we think about race as *felt* (haptic) rather than only *seen* (optic)? In proprioception, color cannot be "felt." Our perceptions of the world rely on haptic sensing, combining touch and kinesthesia: "Unlike the visual system, where information such as color and shape of an object [are] available with minimal effort, to acquire haptic information we must move our fingers across an object's surface to perceive its texture . . . to determine if it is hard or soft."[40] In this larger discussion about haptic-optic relations, we must caution against reading these senses as diametrically opposed, as if "the boundless haptic [could replace] the evil optic." The haptic is "the link between touching and feeling."[41] There is always already a gap, a space between any touch that we fill in with desire.

Hands interpret a surface in terms of its shape (round, square, curved, linear—) its texture (rough, viscous, smooth), and its temperature (hot or cool). Such "surface reading" does not privilege the visual, per se. The emphasis on "feeling" sculpture complicates and highlights questions of color and racial dynamics thought to cohere in the color of one's skin. What would we make of the curled waves on the head of Edmonia's freedman, were we to feel them with our hands instead of seeing them with our eyes? What would we know from touching the roughly rendered deerskin, the textured flint, and the beaded moccasins made of marble in her *Old Arrow Maker* (see figure 1.2)?[42] Lewis's highly textured sculptures such as the *Old Arrow Maker* shift our racial readings toward the tactile: textured waves of hair, fullness of lips, cheekbones. Of course, to recite these physiognomic details—which are stereotypical "racialized" features—also risks essentializing difference. We find ourselves again confronting the coiled construction of race; one that Edmonia Lewis's sculptures perform at the intersection of the haptic and optic ways of knowing. We "feel" and "see" the texture of her work, read details via titles, "adjuncts," and accoutrements, all to produce a felt racial reading of her work.

How did Lewis conceive of "colored" art in the face of her benefactors and audiences? How do we understand the work that Black and colored artists make *as* "Black art"? Kirstin Pai Buick argues that, paradoxically, Edmonia Lewis was "present as an artist but absent as the subject or object of her art."[43] Lydia Maria Child said that Lewis's determination to be an artist was so strong that she "could cut through the Alps with a penknife."[44] We could take "the Alps" to be the mountains considered the sine qua non of whiteness in the era, made so by a generation of Romantic poets such as the Shelleys and Lord Byron, and later by the art critic John Ruskin, famous for writing the treatise *The Stones of Venice*. This damning praise then provides us with potent new metaphors to consider: the cut, cutting, and the whiteness of stone.[45] By refusing to depict the Black body as a screen or mirror for the white other, Lewis may have frustrated or foiled some of her white viewers. She allowed them to *see* her subjects—via the use of the "white" marble they may have imagined to reflect their own "universal" idealized white identity through which they understood "humanity" to shine through.

Works of the era often demonstrated the phenomenon of portraying "whitened" or "white-appearing" subjects whose proximity to whiteness served as their purported badge of honored humanity. Such "toning" was being read as a liberal gesture toward humanizing colored subjects and "lessening" the broad and demeaning stereotypes attached to them. But as art historian Freeman Henry Morris Murray understood, writing in 1916 about Edmonia Lewis's portrayal of the freedwoman in her work *Forever Free* (1867; see figure 4.1), "What Black Folk really need and should strive for, is not 'the Caucasian's physical features, but the Caucasian's opportunity.'"[46]

In the early twentieth century, Freeman Murray, himself a "colored" man, provided important, new art historical analyses of Lewis's work. With valuable input from the sculptor Meta Warrick Fuller, Murray wrote about Lewis's work with true sympathy and empathy. Although he had yet to see her sculptures in person, he imagined himself in the position of this "cultured young artist [who] though descended from the two races mentioned, was yet by American custom identified wholly with the Negro." This was Murray's way of referencing the rule of hypodescent that legally classified anyone with "one drop" of the imaginary "Black" blood as a Black person. He argued that,

When Miss Lewis was modeling her "Freedwoman" in 1867, reaction—reenslavement, I had almost said—had set in. If, perchance [white sculptors of freed Black subjects] had observed it, Miss Lewis and "her people" had felt it. The Sun of Emancipation which had risen in

1863, had seemingly reached its zenith in 1865 with the passage of the 13th Amendment prohibiting slavery. But already the sheriff's handcuffs were taking the place of the former master's chains; already the chain-gang stockade was supplanting the old slave pen. Another constitutional amendment, the 14th, was being pushed to bolster up the 13th. The freedwoman was being told that it would be better for her children, even in the North, to go to "separate schools."[47]

Murray guides us toward the reception of Lewis's works—asking us to imagine how and to whom her sculptures spoke and the different voices they may have represented for her audiences, which were diverse in terms of their nationality, color, gender, sexual orientation, class, and cultural formation. Murray attributes the emotional conflicts that many twentieth-century people felt when viewing Lewis's work as, in part, a response to what became known as Jim Crow—the post-Reconstruction system of brutal racial inequity and white supremacy both de facto and de jure (codified into law with the US Supreme Court's infamous *Plessy v. Ferguson* decision in 1896, declaring segregation of the races constitutional). Lewis may well have presaged the Jim Crow era in her sculpture. Murray concludes his entry on her, "Miss Lewis, being an intelligent and educated woman, could not help seeing, feeling, and interpreting. So, while she was purporting to portray the freedwoman as of the time when she received tidings of her liberation [in 1863], it was impossible that the conditions prevailing and threatening at the time—1867—as well as her own feeling and emotions, should not find some expression in Miss Lewis's work."[48] Murray's words give us a sense of the political stakes of the moment and offer deeply felt insight into the artist's possible ideas and feelings about the subjects she sculpted.

Another example of how Lewis's works were read and received come from John P. Samson, a Black minister and leader of the American Methodist Episcopal Church who attended the 1876 exhibition in Philadelphia, where Lewis's *Cleopatra* was on view. Samson's narrative offers further insight into views about Lewis's racial sentiments:

I had not thought about the American colored lady who had made it when . . . a very ordinary looking colored girl (as I thought) offered very kindly to show me other statues carved by the same lady. She took me to another department where I saw several beautiful carved statues . . . all of which seemed to be the center of attraction,—in the class of statuary in which they were found. I am no critic in aesthetics, and yet I could see that her works took the popular eye. I was more surprised when I found that my guide, a plain and unassuming young woman was the veritable sculptress herself. After some conversation, I soon found Miss Lewis to be a downright sensible woman; a young lady of no foolishness, a devoted lover of her race, a woman courageous in the faith of her final triumph and the fullest recognition of the equal brotherhood of the race she so successfully represents. She spoke of her trials and said she rested under the burden of two despised races, the Indian and the Negro. Some of her own people who had been more favored in point of opportunity, gave her no encouragement but came to criticize her work, of the merits of which they knew nothing; it was presumptuous; she said she had no time for them; and instead of fooling her with our people aping the prejudices of the whites, that she "was going back, to Italy, to do something for the race—something that will excite the admiration of the other races on earth."[49]

Rather than asking what her sculptures mean or even what they depict or represent, we might ask how they perform and for whom. How do they elicit and solicit viewers' affect and performative desire? By whom are they appreciated and why? In what ways has their presence been discussed and understood, even or especially when such presences are partially obscured? Did the images she sculpted of "whitened" femininity play into problematic racial hierarchies? Were they representations of "how she wished to be seen," as Buick argues? Are they meant to raise questions about physiognomy and stereotypes of crises of "being and having," as Diana Fuss has theorized?[50] Though the issue is undecidable, I do think that such figures were produced not "in her image" but certainly in her aspect and in accordance with her identifications.

I believe that we can never know anything fully, that comprehension is compromised by the conditions of possibility of apprehending a subject spatiotemporally, discursively, and materially. Richard Schechner claims, "Performativity is a pervasive mood or feeling—belonging not so much to the visual-aural realm (as performances do) but to the senses of smell, taste, and touch. . . . 'I was touched by what happened' [is a way] of apprehending the performative."[51] Edmonia Lewis was not merely "touched by what happened" but also happened by what she touched. This touchstone helps us focus on her as an actor and producer, not just a projection screen for competing identity claims. With her, I am content to grasp at the ineffable, to work with only a partial view—the always-already mediated aspects of archival materials and storied narratives that continue to accumulate meaning and therefore change over time. Three-dimensional sculpture, with its multisided and -sited aspects, complicates our view of any work in its totality. All is necessarily skewed, partially viewed, like the sculptures of Edmonia Lewis.

Edmonia Lewis's hands were not only her tools. They were also her weapons in a racist, sexist, and homophobic world that at best doubted her ability to succeed in her profession and at worst negated her genius and cast her as an impossibility.[52] Biographers Harry and Albert Henderson ask readers to "think of Edmonia Lewis as an artist at war. As her heroes took to the gun, the pen, or the pulpit to attack the cruel social order of the 1800s, she weighed in with artistic gifts and tools meant for clay, plaster, and marble. In the grand struggle for respect, she was a regiment of one."[53] In considering her hands as weapons, we can also turn to Pulitzer Prize–winning postmodern poet Tyehimba Jess and his homage to Lewis's life story in his formally innovative text *Olio* (2016). Jess's work sings of Lewis's solitary resistance. The speaker in one of the series of poems "Edmonia Lewis: Provenance" says: "I am the sound of one / mallet against history's / pale fist."[54]

In an interview I conducted, Jess said that the idea of Lewis's hands haunted him so much that he commissioned a visual artist to render them pictorially in his book of poems. Jess said that initially he wanted to "see" Lewis's hands in a realistic mode; however, the Black artist he hired, Jessica Lynne Brown, produced a highly abstract black-and-white drawing of a menacing, moving group of hands (figure 3.5). The image highlights the hands of those men who made Lewis an object of their hate; the hands of the group of men who violated Lewis in a brutal attack when she was a college student at Oberlin in the winter of 1862.

In Brown's illustration that accompanies the section of the book about Edmonia Lewis, ten rough-drawn monstrous petrified hands move about a central figure. Knotted and gnarly, each of these abstract, free-form, five-fingered "disembodied" hands (attached only to jointed limbs) reach in a different direction. The drawing connotes movement through its multiplicity. All but two of these hands seek to grab the floating supine feminine figure with flowing hair at the center of the whirling vortex. They appear arched, spread-eagled, and vicious.

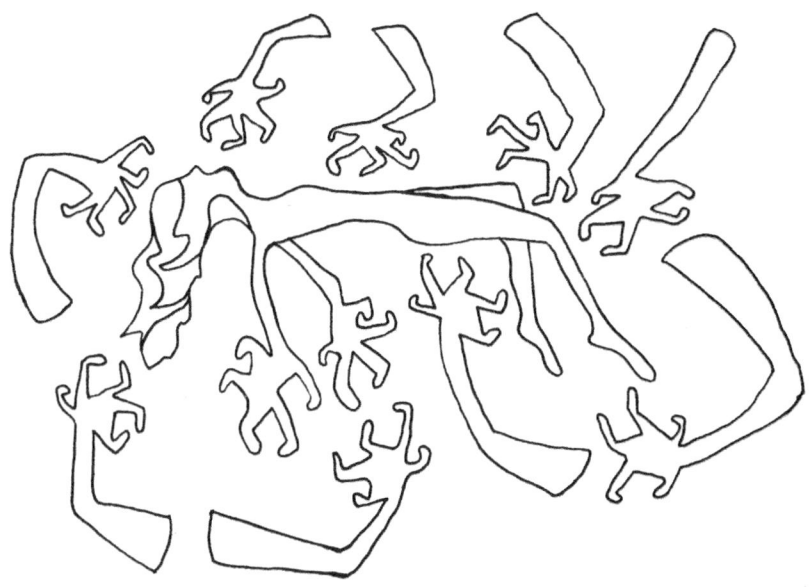

3.5 Jessica Lynne Brown, line drawing accompanying a section of poems about Edmonia Lewis in Tyehimba Jess's *Olio*, 2016.

Jess renders the terrifying Oberlin attack in the poem "Alabaster Hands, Edmonia Lewis, 1862":

Let me tell you how
white hands kilned me
in the moonless middle
of night. How they stripped
and spittled and smeared me
in an open field hardened
with ice. How they worked so
diligently upon me with palm
and fist and angry sweat,
with knuckle and dirty nail,
until I was struck still as stone,
until I was one with the dust
of the Earth that called my name,
whispered to me from its labyrinth
of lava and buried bone. My truth

was honed there, deep in the fated
crease between life and loss.
It willed me to rise from the dirt
and staggered me home.
I claimed for my own
what they'd strived to strike
from me. I scraped myself
up from what they'd tried
to beat down. And now
I let them witness how
artfully their curses fold;
how ruthlessly I mastered
their death-less hands
beneath the weight
of my mercy-fraught mold.

Jess references the cold Ohio winter night during which Lewis was torn from her room in Rev. John Keep's home, stripped, violated, and discarded in the snow at the edge of the wilderness in Oberlin. She had been falsely accused by two of her white classmates of giving them Spanish fly (cantharides) in their spiced wine before they went out on a sleigh ride. At her trial for the alleged poisoning, she was defended by the renowned Black lawyer John Mercer Langston, who argued that the contents of the "victims'" stomachs could not be examined and, therefore, could not be determined. This defense was successful.

Several details that affected Lewis's career are worth noting. A local paper reported that Lewis "came to court badly battered with her arm in a sling from a broken collar bone."[55] This painful injury would have been slow to heal and, for a sculptor who relied on torso strength, potentially devastating. One news account mentions that "her clothes were torn off"—she was denuded, a state Jess characterizes as "a nakedness she had never known." She was acquitted, but this "incident" in the life of a free colored college girl hastened her departure for more habitable and hospitable hosts. After being accused of stealing art supplies the following year, Lewis moved to the abolitionist stronghold in Boston and ultimately to Rome.

Jess's prose poem renders the event as "one slap, then another, a torn cloak, a knee to spine, a fist into cheekbone, a / clamored clawing for safety, a blood spray across snow."[56] I want to re-member Lewis's fragile flesh. Although she was born free, she was, nevertheless, at times, stripped of the limited protective coverings of her class, context, gender, and education. Her career as a sculptor bears the weight of this event and testifies to Lewis's endurance. The double and triple entendres in this persona poem, the use of the near rhyme between "killed" and "kilned," express Edmonia's identity: forged from the earth, battered into a new form, triumphant through the practices of her art. As Jess tells us *how* this incident formed her, the raw material of clay shifts meanings over the course of the lyric. Jess's work continually reveals the ways "violence is constitutive of identity," to quote Gayatri Spivak.[57]

Lewis's sculptures bear the imprint of her working hands and mark every aspect and avenue of her historic life. She used them to pray, to ply her trade, to shape her destiny, to write her letters, to fashion her world, and to touch other bodies. Lewis's hands manifested her life in art.

Lewis dedicated her life to the durational practice of carving blocks of marble stone. She spent years of arduous labor shaping stones into idealized statues. Lewis touched many stone surfaces with a depth of feeling particular perhaps to carvers of marble, which is to say that since she had to polish her works with tools and interact with them constantly, her hands were trained to touch stones with a specific "professional" feeling. She said that she made her own tools of ebony, shaped by her rasper. When she left Boston for Europe, she was gifted "a handsome ivory mallet" by the well-wishers at her bon voyage party.[58] The few extant letters that she wrote stress both the years that she spent working on a single block of stone and the amount of money she spent procuring marble in the marketplace. To put it succinctly, "sculpture's political efficacy was not limited to iconography, its ability to create an enduring image of a monarch or other personage: its potency was also a consequence of its materiality."[59] Lewis's act of forming these works involved "touching and retouching," which in turn created an erotics of touch that was bound to produce moving sensations.

Frederick Douglass mentions Lewis "plying her fingers" as she worked happily in her Roman studio. We long to touch the surface of these works, whether smooth or rough. It is the texture of sculpture, which is visible to the eye of the beholder, that may simultaneously activate and awaken our desire to touch them. Because so many of Lewis's sculptures were abandoned and left untouched, unattended, "alone," virtually all of them have been retouched over time. Students at Howard University worked to restore *Old Arrow Maker*; with gloved hands and restorer's tools, they brushed away the dirt of neglect that had settled in the many crevices of

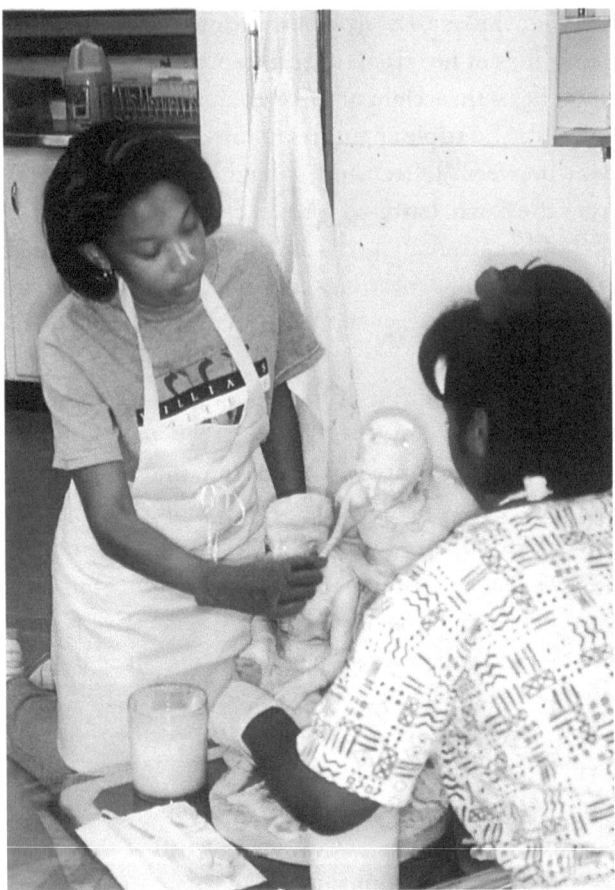

3.6 Student interns Tamara Holmes and Kelli Hall retouching Edmonia Lewis's *Old Arrow Maker* at the Howard University Art Gallery, summer 1997. From Richard J. Powell and Jock Reynolds, *To Conserve a Legacy: Art from Historically Black Colleges* (Andover, MA: Addison Gallery of American Art; New York: Studio Museum in Harlem, 1999).

the highly textured sculpture (figure 3.6). The restorers rely on haptic-optic knowledge.

We live in the era of the museum industrial complex, shaped by nationalism, economics, and the politics of display, among many other factors. At their heart, museums as places for the display of power pose acute ethical questions. Museums function as sites of preservation, display, and ownership. As such, they are now being critiqued as compromised institutions built on colonization and on the theft of Indigenous works from around the globe. The historical practices of many colonial museums founded in the nineteenth century are being questioned about the ways they constitute Art with a capital *A*. We must critique how and whose cultural memory is adjudicated in the space of collections. It is not insignificant that from *The Death of Cleopatra* (whose circuitous journey of restoration is discussed in chapter 7) to the award-winning *Asleep* (discussed in chapter 4), many of Lewis's sculptures moldered in industrial hangars, drafty palaces, and dusty basements for decades. Some are still in such spaces: gone but no longer forgotten. All of these works, like the life narrative of Edmonia Lewis herself, have been and will continue to be subject to retouching. This book is no different. What matters is that we acknowledge the significance of touch in the formation of art, life, and knowledge. As the oft-quoted unsigned pamphlet entitled "How Edmonia Lewis Became an Artist" states, Lewis's "beautiful *Hagar* is the result of patience, hope, of a thousand delicate touchings and retouchings."[60]

Once sculptures are installed as museum objects, beyond our physical touch, they—and we—lose an aspect of their knowability. We can no longer apprehend them haptically. I want to take down the walls of glass in which many sculptures are encased so that we can stroke them, feel their volume, take their temperature, as if we could know them as lifelike in proximity to our bodies. I want to take them off their pedestals, move them closer to our hands, and bring them more fully within our grasp.

Interlude

Kent Monkman

Postmodern visual artist Kent Monkman (Cree) (b. 1965) works in several media to dismantle canonical works of Western art. Like Faith Ringgold (chapter 1) and Mickalene Thomas (chapter 4), Monkman is known for radically revising "classic" artworks by celebrated white male artists through sly inversions, translations, and additions. Many of Monkman's large-scale paintings, for example, are decolonial works that pervert the revered genre of history painting with campy sensibility and biting wit.[61] He paints bacchanalian scenes that he sees as celebrating the more liberated views on gender and sexuality that are "native" to traditional Indigenous cultures. His works deploy nudity, bawdy jokes, overt sexual situations, and a cacophony of characters in unexpected positions as a means of poking holes in the venerated values of the Great White Master who colonized his people. Monkman invented a "gender-fluid alter-ego," Miss Chief Eagle Testickle, to perform throughout his oeuvre as the embodiment of the bravura he saw other "great" artists enacting. Miss Chief Eagle Testickle, with their punning honorific, appears to create mischief and is a manifestation of Monkman's serious play with the political plight of Indigenous peoples throughout the globe.[62]

Of the many Native modern artists working today, I included Monkman in this book about Lewis to serve as one of her artistic descendants because of the way both of these artists deploy humor: At times, their wit suggests a fierceness that is not afraid to speak back to cultural naysayers. Lewis's Indigenous heritage is also being recognized anew, and there is a logic to thinking about her as being part of a history of modern, global, and urbane Indigenous artists.

Moving from our discussion of Lewis's nineteenth-century sculptures of hands in the previous chapter, then, we turn to Monkman's work *Miss Chief's Praying Hands (Red)*, made in 2016 (figure 3i.1). Monkman made sculptures of his own hands that resonate with this chapter's discussion of how sculpture in particular hails, if not invites, engaged haptic responses. *Miss Chief's Praying Hands* provides a critical revision of the way "disembodied" sculpted hands in prayer can be read as profane vehicles of queer performativity.[63] Monkman, in his guise as the artistic alter ego Miss Chief, molded small-scale sculptures composed of silicone rubber dyed red or black. Silicone is a material frequently used to produce modern sex toys. (It is flexible and is used as well to make other hand-held household items such as cooking utensils.) The molds are not only made by the Indigenous artist's own hands—they quite literally are Monkman / Miss Chief's hands. These pliant replicas of the artist's hands can be purchased in two difference colors of silicone: either neon red or slick black. Each set of hands in silicone rubber sits on a flared round base, cut off at the wrist, and has been made to resemble a butt plug. As inspiration for this work, the artist cites the famed "self-portrait" drawing of *Praying Hands* made by German artist Albrecht Dürer in 1508.

Monkman / Miss Chief includes a "Certificate of Authenticity" with their praying hands sculptures as a means of critiquing the very idea of

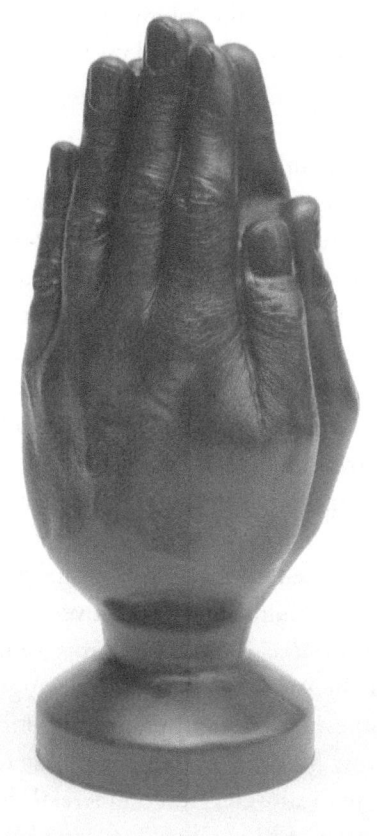

31.1 Kent Monkman, *Miss Chief's Praying Hands (Red)*,
2016. Molded silicone rubber, 4½ × 10½ in., edition of 10
plus 1 artist's proof. Courtesy of the artist.

"authenticating" Indigenous artwork. The artist is ever mindful of Western systems of domination and settler colonialism:

> My First Nation, Fisher River, was part of Treaty Five, which was signed
> in the late 1870s. And the treaties, from my perspective, were about going
> into kinship, and for many, from the original perspective, which I share,

is that we were going into kinship with the settlers. As Indigenous people we are already in kinship with all living beings. It was a way of speaking to our responsibility, but also of the settlers to be in kinship with each other. And, of course, the colonial project has been a project of white supremacy and of genocide, and my community, all Indigenous communities are still experiencing the effects of present-day colonialism.[64]

All of Monkman's multimedia art—paintings, prints, drawings, beaded stilettos, carved rocks, books, and films—reference the historical and ongoing repressive colonial Christianity taught throughout the North American system of Indian boarding schools to which he, like thousands of others, was subjected, and where many perished.[65] Monkman uses his work to reveal Canada's complicity with genocidal policies. For example, his new media and film work frequently exposes destructive policies such as the residential schools sponsored by the Canadian government. "Monkman often employs montage and juxtaposition to challenge the notion that sociopolitical indigenous issues are resolved in a post-colonial Canada. His recent series of video paintings speaks back to static historical paintings and European representations of indigenous peoples."[66]

As the artist explains in the voiceover for his 2019 short film *Miss Chief's Praying Hands*: "The colonial project on Turtle Island [an Indigenous term for the Americas] has forced the 'gift' of European religion, education, sickness, shame, and prejudice upon Indigenous peoples for generations. Now Miss Chief Eagle Testickle is giving it back! Evoking the style of dramatically elegant commercials for decadent status items, the glistening form of Miss Chief's Praying Hands inserts a piercing yet playful perspective into the conversation on reconciliation and Indigenous resilience."[67]

The film features different shots of Monkman's *Praying Hands* as a leitmotif. They are sometimes the gloved hands of the artist shot in vivid color and languorous motion. The gloves are shown alternatively in either black or red satin—often bejeweled with rings made of turquoise or brilliant faux diamonds that glisten in the light of the studio where they were being filmed—they appear as moving hands, without a connected or corresponding body. This creative (dare we say colorful) use of the red and black masked hands performatively evokes the racially tinged and sexualized aspects of Miss Chief Eagle Testickle's identities. Lewis's hands played a part in shaping the world, perhaps joining those of Monkman in ongoing performative acts of Indigenous resilience.

About the Nude

Denude: verb. 1. *transitive.* from the Latin verb *nudare*—
to lay bare, or leave unprotected. To make naked or bare;
to strip of clothing or covering; *spec.* in *Geology* of natural
agencies: To lay bare (a rock or formation) by the removal
of that which lies above it.

   Oxford English Dictionary, online edition

I have shown you the outside of that life, and just as sculptors who study the Florentine statue by looking in to the
mirrors which surround it, see only a reflection of marble superficicies [*sic*] . . . it may be, that you see nothing,
know nothing of my interior self. . . . I stand in conscious
hiddenness.

   Harriot Kesia Hunt, *Glances and Glimpses, or Fifty Years
   Social, Including Twenty Years Professional Life*

Edmonia learns to chip away what's softer than what
remains. / She breaks marble and memory, practicing
the art of taking away, so people will see / only what she
chooses to save.

   Jeanne Atkins, *Stone Mirrors: The Sculpture and Silence
   of Edmonia Lewis*

4

During her career as a sculptor, Edmonia Lewis had to grapple with the art historical category of the nude. Lewis's partially nude sculptures and her few fully nude ones contribute to debates about how Black artists represented this contested genre. Naked flesh and body parts appear throughout Lewis's oeuvre; however, little has been written about the impact of her work on histories of the nude in Western classical art as they intersect with Black feminist visual studies and queer studies.[1] The body parts Lewis formed from clay and cut in marble created noteworthy interventions into narratives about the naked and the nude. Although Lewis's nude sculptures conformed to the aesthetic codes of the time, the fact that *Lewis* carved them at all suggests one of the ways she was able to defy limits placed on her own creativity.[2] This chapter explores how Edmonia Lewis's work effects genealogies of the nude.[3]

Before we turn to her statues, however, let us discuss the art historical genre of the nude. As an aesthetic genre invented and upheld by Western European academies of art, the nude has functioned as the sine qua non of idealized human form. Since classical times, sculptors, in particular, have contended with the mythology of the nude as a specific type of representation. It is considered settled knowledge that the "ideal" sculptural subject in this tradition has been the *kouros*, a Greek term denoting a perfectly proportioned, standing, European male figure, usually unclothed: the model of Beauty.[4]

Few Black or Native women (or persons of any gender in the global majority)—were deemed to be *ideal* subjects in this genre. When such subjects did appear under the sign of the "classically beautiful," they seemed to do so almost exclusively under the sign of an adjectival descriptor in their title (e.g., the *Sable* Venus or the *Indian* Maiden).[5] The making of such "beauties" beyond the imaginary boundaries of the young, white, male ideal was discouraged by the standard bearers of artistic value. Perhaps as important for the composition of such nude figures was *who* was permitted to mold and make this form. In Lewis's era, for example, women sculptors could not readily create nude figures of any gender, because, in formal academies, they could not sculpt from live models. To sculpt a nude was deemed an erotic act—so much so that the production of this ideal subject was believed to engender love for the figure one had created in stone. This was the logic of the prohibition that constrained many women and colored artists at the time.

The complex choreographies conscripting and creating the production of the nude hinged on the bodies or, more precisely, ideas about bodies and their interrelation and potential interaction. Thus, in order to grapple with the nude, we must simultaneously confront the politics of the body and bodies. The body understood here exists not as an essential ontological phenomenon but rather as form of performative embodiment—an ideological concept mobilizing cultural, linguistic, medical, juridical, religious, ethical, aesthetic, and historical discourses. Categories of difference such as sex, sexuality, race, ethnicity, gender, nationality, ability, class, and the like affect our understanding of the body as a "historical situation."[6]

Let's think about nude sculptures made in the neoclassical mode during the decades prior to Lewis's arrival in Rome in 1866. Hundreds of neoclassical nude sculptures were made by European artists in the last decades of the eighteenth century. Most of these works referenced ancient models in some shape or form while sometimes also representing modern contemporary subjects related to the changing historical moment. Many of these modern nudes, as was the case with ancients as well, depicted female forms, some of whom were enslaved. The long era of the abolition of slavery in the Atlantic world intensified during the eighteenth and nineteenth centuries—and this intensification impacted Lewis's early career as a sculptor (recall that she began sculpting in the 1860s, in the midst of the Civil War and that she created one of the first statues of a freed woman).

With greater frequency, scholars are attending to the inescapable issues of racial projection and formation in nude sculptures from this era. Most of this work critiques and fleshes out the understanding of the nude as the purified pinnacle of perfection throughout Western art discourse (especially the eighteenth and nineteenth centuries). The perception of these nude statues as racially "white" and sexually "pure" stood in contradistinction to the merely "naked" representations that axiomatically were understood to be Black and "impure." In such a diabolical Manichean schema, "nakedness ([became] a racist discourse [that]) signals raw, animality, dumb flesh, the inhuman other."[7] To see the world through such fixed dichotomies as white-Black and nude-naked was to accept a foundational if fictional fallacy in which the hyphen violently breaks what could otherwise be read as a founding connection, as a binary opposition. Lewis, working both with and against these limiting conditions of possibility—the many competing expectations about her artistic abilities as they inevitably intersected with her identities—chose for the most part to make her figures in white marble (even those not commissioned as portraits of individuals such as the ones she made of Henry Wadsworth Longfellow, President Ulysses S. Grant, Anna Waterson, and Charlotte Cushman). Again, the material, the conventions of the day, her artistic abilities, questions of cost, time, and labor, all affected how, whom, what, and why Lewis carved.

There can be no doubt that Edmonia Lewis thought deeply about the problem of "the body" in Western art and life. It was her life's work. Lewis knew that her own castings were being made in an era in which "nude flesh, the essence of the classical sculptural tradition, could not be shown in the representation of the contemporary hero."[8] These strictures curtailed how one might show nudity in concert with contemporary heroic figures, and affected debates about the representation of enslavement and the enslaved. We cannot look at nineteenth-century *sculptures* of bodies, which were displayed as objects for sale, without also grappling with the fact that some living human bodies were (and of course are) also actually for sale. This correspondence between body and flesh colored Lewis's artistic choices: She was attendant to the politics of representation. The impossible social death and subject position of chattel—the state of being a thing and a person simultaneously—and the imagined "dead and gone" Indigenous subjects of art so prevalent during her lifetime likely troubled Lewis. To understand Lewis's oeuvre as a whole, and her contributions to and interventions in the larger concepts of the nude, we need to survey both her efforts and her origins.

To investigate how she came to shape the few nudes she sculpted, let us look first at her artistic training, both formal and informal. Lewis learned how to sew and bead moccasins, how to weave baskets, and stitch and stuff pin cushions. She may have had art classes during her early education at the private New York Central College.[9] She excelled at sketching and drawing at Oberlin. As we recall, as part of her education in sculpting, Lewis began by shaping smaller naked body parts "piecemeal." In Boston, she started with a baby's foot, which she worked on for weeks until it satisfied her teacher at the time, Edward Augustus Brackett; then she moved on to "a lady's hand." She told a St. Louis reporter that "she worked on the Lady's hand and got on nicely."[10] Next, she moved on to medallions and portrait busts. One of the goals of any sculptor's education was to make these disarticulated, smaller sculptures of individual body parts in the service of learning how to, one day, carve a full, three-dimensional ideal figure.

Like many "colored" students at the time, Lewis was denied entry to any of the traditional art academies in the United States. Poet Elizabeth Alexander tells the story in her book of essays, *The Black Interior* (2004):

> Lewis sent an application for admission to the Corcoran School of Art in Washington, D.C. The application was evaluated, "pronounced excellent," and Lewis was admitted. When Lewis showed up in that selfsame black and female body, "in propria persona" as [her friend the formerly enslaved black feminist] Anna Julia Cooper put it, all promises were revoked. The school superintendent then told her in plain unartistic English that of course he had not dreamed a colored person could do such work, and had he suspected the truth he would never have issued the ticket of admission.[11]

As a student at Oberlin College, Lewis took several classes with a female drawing instructor in 1859: Oberlin at that time did not have a full-scale art program. The college art gallery, where Lewis no doubt studied individual works and learned more about various artistic traditions, supplemented her informal education.

Some of her contemporaries in the circle of women sculptors in Rome had somewhat greater access to academic training than Lewis did, based on their various race and class privileges. For example, sculptor Harriet Hosmer's father, Hiram Hosmer, a medical doctor, desired to give his daughter the same advantages as he gave his two sons.[12] Harriet, who showed artistic talent and interest even in childhood, sought to formally study medicine in order to learn anatomy. Medical schools, however, were open only to men. She was instead given access to her father's library of medical books for her study of the human form. These books contained detailed and explicit drawings of human bodies—certainly a significant advantage for her craft. Hosmer consulted privately with her father's colleague Dr. Joseph Nash McDowell about anatomy.[13]

Crucially, Lewis credited *her* upbringing *outside* educational institutions for her prowess in learning how to sculpt the nude. She claimed that she had something more than any medical school or tutor could have provided her: her "wild education," which gave her the chance to study the human form. Her lived experience as a youth was in striking contrast to those of most of her white colleagues. As she put it in an interview with the *Milwaukee Daily Sentinel*, "I felt the strangest sensation putting on dresses.

I had never worn anything but blankets. (Laughing) You see, I had good opportunities for studying the nude."[14] This remark speaks simultaneously to gender, ethnicity, and sexuality—as well as her savvy deployment of types. Lewis's use of the word *blankets* may be an example of her frequent references to her own ethnic exoticism—unique details or embellishments that made her stand out. Speaking of blankets, nineteenth-century Ojibwe people wore both their traditional dress and all manner of Western clothes procured in the tourist trade, consistent with contemporary American dress. Although we do not know what Lewis wore as a child, this statement about styling her body reveals her interest in deploying her difference, playing up or about, rather than *into*, stereotypes about her racial, gender, class, and "other" identities. She held a complex understanding of the politics of her own body as a metaphor and as what Daphne Brooks would call a "body in dissent" that performed acts of deferral and defiance.[15]

Once in Europe, Lewis learned to train her eyes outside the classroom by observing idealized nude sculptures in museums and ateliers in Florence, Rome, Paris, Naples, and Pompeii. She visited the Native American artifacts compiled at the Vatican by Cardinal Borgia, and she would have been aware of Il Gabinetto Segreto (secret cabinet), a locked collection containing the erotic and pornographic frescoes and statuary of Pompeii. It was opened to the public by the Italian general and revolutionary leader Guiseppe Garibaldi when the country was unified in 1861 and became the nation of Italy. Il Gabinetto Segreto remained famously off-limits to women, youngsters, priests, and many others; only European gentlemen could enter the locked room.

In Rome, Lewis could study classical nudes at almost every turn; she knew of the ancient nudes at the Vatican as well as the more modern ideal nudes created by the late Antonio Canova, in whose studio at 27 Via della Frezza she worked years after his death. Canova's sensuous sculptures, famous throughout Europe, were not beholden to the Roman copies of Greek forms that preoccupied the more Germanic versions of neoclassicism. Rather, they were dancing, lithe, stylized, fanciful sculptures full of light, characterized by serpentine forms and famous for the complicated choreography of their entwined figures. Canova's sculptures were valued for their tactility and grace. "When nudity is pure and adorned with exquisite beauty," Canova argued, "it deflects us from mortal preoccupations and transports us to those early times of blessed innocence—all the more so if nudity approaches us as spiritual and wise, elevating us to the contemplation of things divine. These latter, since they cannot be manifested to the senses because of their spirituality, can only be indicated to us by their excellence of form so that they inflame us with their eternal beauty."[16] Whether or not Lewis was thinking of Canova's words, she made her own forays into sculpting the nude.

Black feminist art historian Judith Wilson contended that Lewis was the only "colored" artist to carve nudes in the nineteenth century.[17] Wilson encountered Lewis when she was on a quest to find female nudes made by Black artists that may have served as precedents for the collaged nudes made by Black American artist Romare Bearden (1911–88) in the 1960s. Wilson, to her surprise, found only three fully nude figures thought to have been made by an artist of color in the nineteenth century, and all of them were carved by Edmonia Lewis.

Wilson was on this poignant search for Black female bodies in art *made* by Black artists—and, specifically, she was looking for bodies that had not been "raped, maimed, murdered," or colonized, according to the late Black feminist artist Lorraine O'Grady (1934–2024), who thoughtfully characterized Wilson's work. About Wilson's contributions to Black and feminist visual critiques that continue to be generative, O'Grady observed, "It is no wonder that when Judith Wilson went in search of nineteenth-century nudes by black artists, she found only three statues of nonblack children—Edmonia Lewis's *Poor Cupid* (1876); her *Asleep* (1871); and one of the two young children in her *Awake* (1872)."[18] This single sentence in O'Grady's germinal article enshrines not only Wilson but also Lewis in the annals of Black feminist visual culture. To give but one example of this ongoing tradition: Lisa Gail Collins quotes O'Grady's statement in a prelude to her chapter on Black female nudes. Collins's reading begins with Lewis's sculpture *Forever Free* (1867; discussed below). About that statue's representation of a just-freed kneeling Black female figure, she writes: "Portrayals of the Black female nude are rare. . . . Missing from most formalist and feminist scholarship on the nude is the discussion of the unclothed black body in art. White artists and white models, as well as white viewers, are typically assumed. [Moreover,] the black female body could not unequivocally signify the promise of freedom, for she was already too entangled in her charged flesh."[19] Collins also credits Judith Wilson with documenting the profound absence of Black nudes *produced by Black artists* until the mid-twentieth century, when Black nudes became "a permissible subject" in art—after the Black Power movement and the sexual revolution of the 1960s. Again, in thinking about the nude, we must attend to suppressed yet pressing issues of race, gender, class, and sexuality as we seek to uncover connections among nude sculptures, the erotics of sculpting, and the politics of race and gender that give creative substance to Lewis's sculpture.

The only entirely naked figures that Lewis carved were two statues of young children and one of a putto. We know that Lewis refrained from depicting her Black and colored women subjects in the nude (even as we might imagine that she may have wished to sculpt a female nude). Her naturalistic sculpture *The Death of Cleopatra* (1875; see figure 2.1) was one of at least two known sculptures she made that depicted a bare-breasted female figure. In this case, Queen Cleopatra is shown with a refined visage and notably "Greco-Roman" rather than "negroid" nose. Her right breast with its erect nipple points firmly at the viewer, while the rest of her body slumps down on her throne, just moments after her death. When this magnificent work was displayed at the 1876 Philadelphia Centennial Exhibition, one anonymous viewer complained of its partial nudity. According to a local paper, this observer of Lewis's statue said directly to the sculptor, "Miss Lewis, that is a very beautiful statue, but don't you think it would have been more proper to drape it. Clothing is necessary to Christian art." Lewis replied: "Said I, Madame, that is not modesty in you. That is worse than mock modesty. You see and think of evil not intended. Your mind, Madame, is not as pure, I fear, as my statue."[20]

Lewis's reply was bold: it shows her authority and her ability to clap back at her white critics, turning the mirror back on them, "reading" *them* for misreading her intentions. The dialogue distills much about how nudity played in the minds of Victorian audiences and, what is more important, demonstrates Lewis's understanding of the risks involved in making her work—and her sense of her own power. Lewis's cheeky response could also be an attempt at throwing the viewer off the scent, if you will, of what in fact may have been unseemly aspects of the statue in question. I think we can also read this scene in Philadelphia as Lewis's participation in "a culture of dissemblance," to use Darlene Clark Hines's phrase suggesting that Black women in the period actively sought to invisibilize and shroud themselves in a world in which they were overexposed and therefore vulnerable.[21] It was perhaps an act of "stand[ing] in conscious hiddenness," as Harriot Kezia Hunt put it (see p. 105, epigraph).

We can see a similar tactic in Lewis's representation of the kneeling "white-appearing" female figure in her abolitionist sculpture *Forever Free* (also called *Morning of Liberty*; figure 4.1). This now well-known dual sculpture portrays a standing Black male figure with curls and a defiant

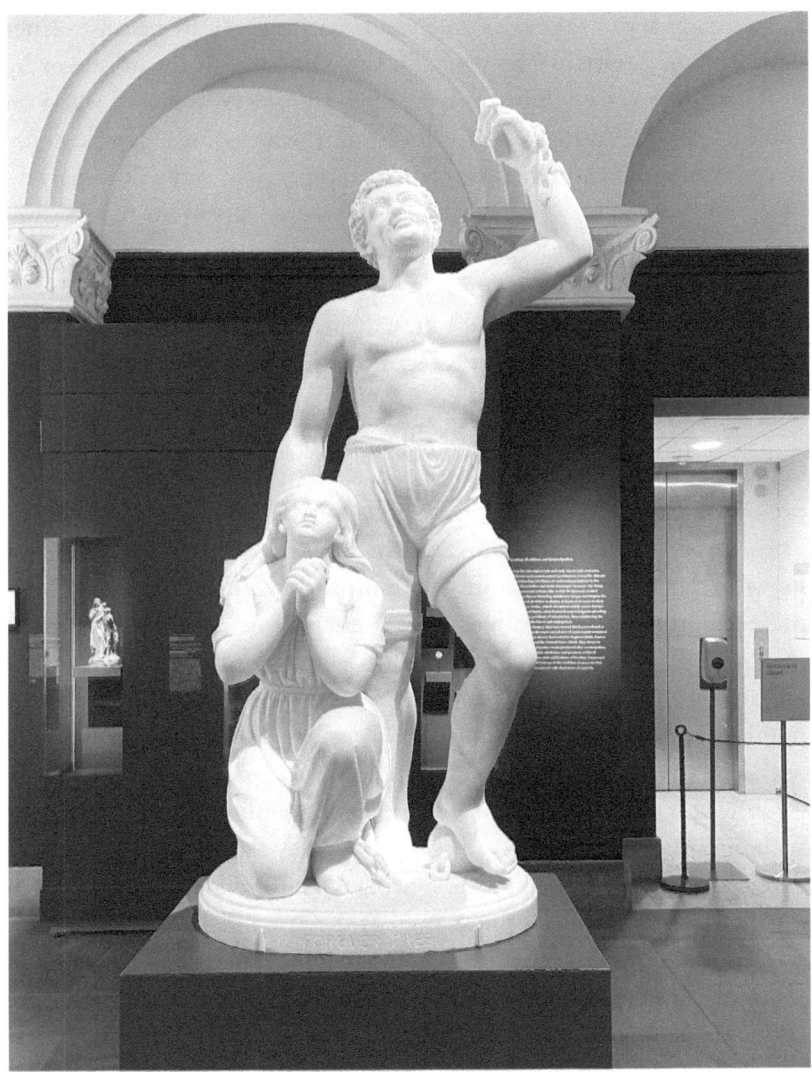

4.1 Edmonia Lewis, *Forever Free*, 1867. Marble, 41¾ × 21½ × 12⅜ in. Howard University Art Gallery, Washington, DC (67.9.S). Photographed at the Metropolitan Museum of Art, New York, 2022.

raised fist that bears the remnant of a broken wrist manacle. His female companion is shown on her knees with shoulder-length flowing hair and fine facial features. Her race and age seem ambiguous. We know from the title of the sculpture that she too has been manumitted from slavery. Her appearance conforms to the "octoroon" figures that served in the white racial imaginary of the era as the most beautiful, delicate because of her perceived proximity to whiteness. She was deployed as the most worthy of rescue in the minds of many a white abolitionist or sympathizer with "liberal" views.[22] As Lisa Gail Collins reads the newly freed female figure in *Forever Free*, "Her blackness is removed from view, and visible markers of her adult sexuality are largely hidden. Perhaps wary of the relationship between visibility and assault, Edmonia Lewis attempted to 'veil' her freed woman and, in this manner, protect her from harm."[23] In a similar vein, we may say of Lewis's nude sculptures, that they too "veil" visible markers of adult sexuality in order to protect them from easily being read as degraded images of sexuality.[24]

Surely, Lewis understood the difficulties involved in creating a Black Venus that could withstand the perpetual attempts at reduction and appropriation by viewers and critics deploying fast-changing racist tropes. These tropes were always at the ready to disfigure Black women, no matter how reverent their presentation or prominent their position. Many of the nude sculptures of Black subjects in the era became subject to anti-Black readings even when they conformed to "white" forms of idealism. (The controversy surrounding Hiram Powers's *The Greek Slave*, discussed later in this chapter, serves as a prime example of the desire to empathize only with "white-appearing" subjects.) Conventions for depicting individualized Black female models changed through the nineteenth century, but such figures were always already stereotypically raced, classed, and gendered. Lewis took care to sculpt her Black and Indigenous figures with the dignity of wearing clothing, even as she also mocked such aesthetic standards. As we discuss bodies, dressed and undressed, we are in fact also stitching together ideas about race, freedom, gender, and propriety. The art historical genre of the nude required whiteness as the cloak of respectability; perhaps to counter this requirement, Lewis elected to show her women of color attired.

Some statues of the era were called "anti-slavery sermons in stone."[25] Lewis herself made two such sermons—first with a figure of a recently freed woman and child (a statue currently lost that exists only in descriptions) and a second with *Forever Free*, one of her earliest full-bodied works, whose Black male subject is bare-chested and wears only a draped cloth tied at the waist and rolled about the groin, falling to his mid-thighs.[26] The figure of the formerly enslaved man, even in his moment of standing up for freedom, was not yet thought to be an "Ideal" subject for representation in neoclassical art, as Elizabeth Barrett Browning theorized when she wrote in her sonnet "Hiram Powers' 'The Greek Slave'" in 1850, "They say Ideal beauty cannot enter / The house of anguish."[27]

Antislavery sculptures had great sentimental value and were purchased for their edifying effect. They were often designed to elicit moral reflection, yet their existence as commodities, in some ways, seems reminiscent of the purchasing of slave bodies. As we see in the engraving *Sale of Estates, Pictures and Slaves in the Rotunda, New Orleans* (1842) by William Henry Brooke,[28] nude statues were installed as decorative art in the niches of the great neoclassical rotunda in the St. Louis Hotel and Exchange in New Orleans, where one of the most lucrative slave markets was held. In the same halls where human bodies were sold, sculptures and paintings of the human form were, at times, auctioned. While the two types of sales are in no way comparable, they are linked. Mirroring the performative conventions coextensive with the slave markets, these artworks were (and continue to be) on view prior to sale and made available for examination to potential bidders. Their display was similar: As Joseph Roach explains, human goods "were placed on a raised stone or table so that everyone might see and handle them even if they did not wish to purchase them."[29] Auction houses dating back to classical Greek and Roman times sold goods, women, and slaves (hence the term "marriage market"). Auctioning transforms subjects, making them (also) into commodities; this same cash-nexus system "creates value" in the world of the art and flesh markets.

My perception is that any auction bears the gestural memory of the estate sales that included auctioning off enslaved people, sending members of enslaved families in different directions, to different masters. This fact re-members a brutality echoing from the center of the rituals performed in auction houses such as London's Sotheby's, founded in 1744, and Christie's, opened in 1766. If enslaved people were not already naked, purchasers took care to have them stripped to be examined from all sides."[30] Such an act closes the distance between the naked and the denuded.[31] Perhaps the reason that Lewis never sculpted an enslaved person (she sculpted only freed slaves) and sculpted her works only in white marble was related to the fact that she did not wish to reiterate, symbolically or conceptually, negative associations with the still-fresh trade in Black bodies.[32]

Let us turn to the five of Lewis's known sculptures that feature nude or partially nude figures. Fully nude figures appear in the pair *Asleep* (1871) and *Awake* (1872) (figures 4.2 and 4.3), and *Poor Cupid* (or *Love Ensnared*) (1876) (see figure 4.6). The partially nude figures appear in the two famous works that depict a female figure with one breast revealed: *Hagar* (or *Hagar*

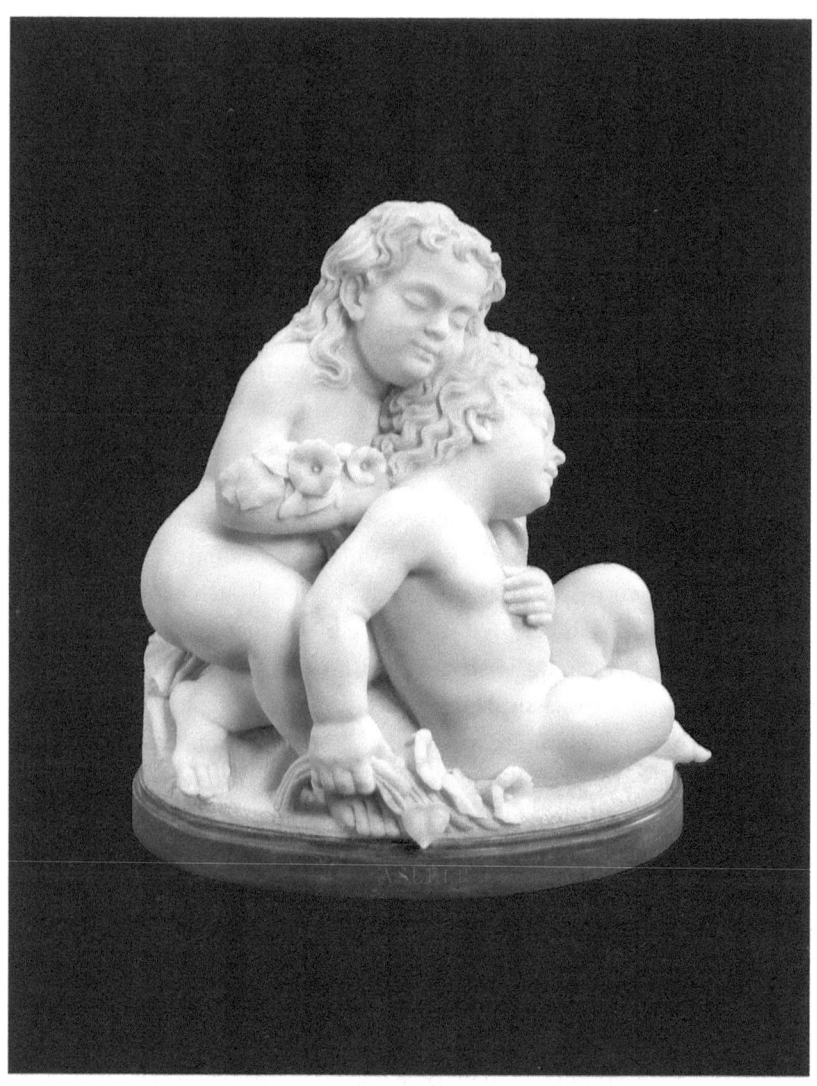

4.2 Edmonia Lewis, *Asleep*, 1871. Marble, 24 × 193 × 15 in. San Jose Public Library, San Jose, California; Gift, Sarah Knox-Goodrich, before 1914. Photograph by John Janca, commissioned by the author.

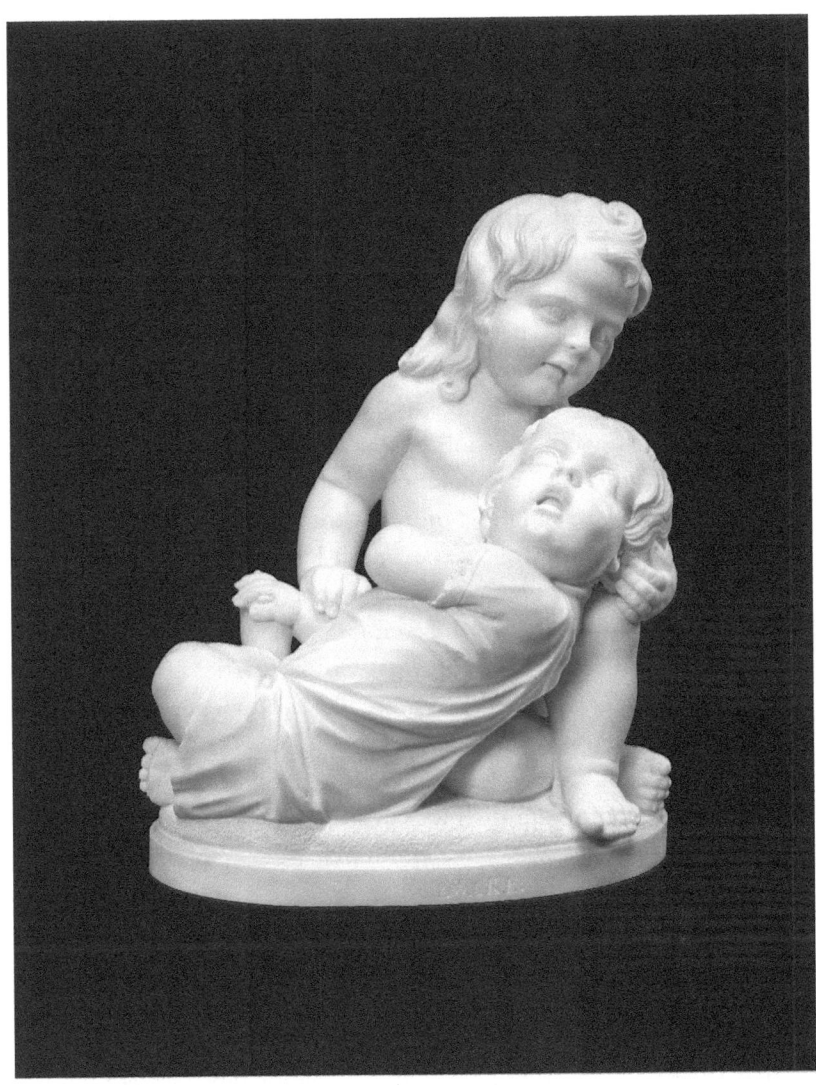

4.3 Edmonia Lewis, *Awake*, 1872. Marble, 24 × 19⅜ × 15 in.
San Jose Public Library, San Jose, California; Gift, Sarah
Knox-Goodrich, before 1914. Photograph by John Janca,
commissioned by the author.

in the Wilderness) (1875) (see figure 4.8) and *The Death of Cleopatra* (1876) (see figure 2.1). Although they are most often dismissed as Lewis's "minor" sculptures in contemporary art historical scholarship, her strange *Poor Cupid* and the nude, entwined toddlers of *Asleep* and *Awake* display her "mastry" of neoclassical nudity.[33] The works were produced during her most productive decade, the 1870s. Each could have been viewed in various stages of development by visitors to her atelier in Rome. *Asleep* won first prize when it was displayed at a national exposition in Naples in 1872; King Victor Emmanuel II personally presented Edmonia with a gold medal to mark her triumph. According to Harry and Albert Henderson, "The Italian art world adored the pudgy tots, usually male and naked, that they called *putti*. Edmonia's prize-winning touch made alchemy with marble. It turned the cold, inert stone into adorable baby fat, silkily expressing every sensuous ripple, finger, and toe. Indeed, confirmed by Italian judges and the sophisticated committee of the Union League Club, her skills were entirely on par with the better-known sculptors of the day."[34]

Asleep and *Awake* are prime examples of dual-portrait sculptures, a distinct feature of Lewis's body of work. Unlike Harriet Hosmer's sculpture *The Sleeping Faun* (1865) and more like the dual portrait of a "parent" and "child" in her *Waking Faun* (1866), Lewis's work is nominally in the same vein; however, her conceptions are wholly original. These two sculptures depict four distinct putti figures; two entwined pairs of toddlers. *Asleep* shows two young children in a close, intense embrace.[35] These supine cherubs are unclothed and yet are perceived as innocent due to their very young age.[36] They appear to be between one and three years old. One figure cradles the other from behind, left hand caressing the lower figure's hair. The one caressed tilts his head tenderly toward the shoulder of the other with lips upturned.[37] They are distinctly *not* asleep: Their eyes appear to be closed in romantic rapture, yet their positions and gestures are distinctly awake and vibrating with awareness of the other's body. Their languorous figures mimic the bodies of mature entwined lovers seen in many other neoclassical works. The marble seems alive with echoing forms, with a rhythmic geometric symmetry between the fingers and toes; the stamen of the morning glory and the phallus (figures 4.4 and 4.5). The left side of the figures is draped with fabric polished smooth. The back of the sculpture shows detailed musculature around the spine, hips, pelvis, and buttocks of the upper figure—almost as if it is the miniature back of an adult, curving into an arc of rough-hewn stone.

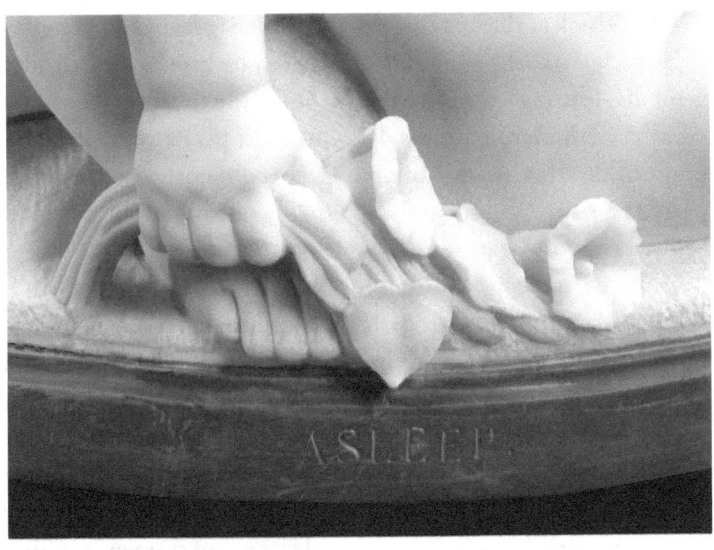

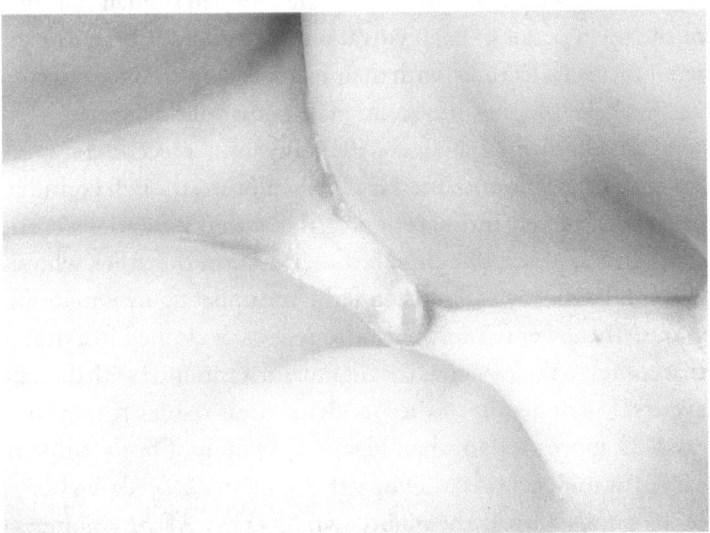

4.4 Detail of toes and flowers, Edmonia Lewis, *Asleep*, 1871. Marble. San Jose Public Library, San Jose, California; Gift, Sarah Knox-Goodrich, before 1914. Photograph by John Janca, commissioned by the author.

4.5 Detail of child's genitalia, Edmonia Lewis, *Asleep*, 1871. Marble. San Jose Public Library, San Jose, California; Gift, Sarah Knox-Goodrich, before 1914. Photograph by John Janca, commissioned by the author.

Let's look at the extreme close-up of the foregrounded figure in *Asleep* (figure 4.5). Among the folds of his flesh lie his naturalistically rendered genitalia, leaning left of the child's thigh. The tiny member sits at the center of rotund marble thighs. Viewers must peer closely into the meeting point of the thighs and abdomen to become privy to the small "private part," the penis peeking out. The small scale of this bit of sculpted flesh belies its historic stature and significance.

There is a certain androgyny to the figures in *Asleep*. Both have wavy shoulder-length hair with curls that seem to lick their necks. There is an odd disjuncture between their bodies, faces, and gestures. Some viewers have read their sensuality as sapphic, despite the microphallus. The flowers in *Asleep* bear particular significance for our reading of the genders and sexuality of the figures (figure 4.4). The lower nude figure gently holds a garland of cut morning glories; the marble flowers have pronounced stamens that resemble clitorises. A single rounded stamen rests in the center of the open petals of each vulval blossom. Could the statue's somewhat feminine facial features, with their mature expressions of ecstasy, and those flowers belie the tiny, innocent, male bodies of the figures?

Let us look now at *Awake*, the companion piece to *Asleep*, also carved from one solid block of marble. This sculpture, though considered "innocent," is extremely intimate and carries with it potentially erotic connections. In the statue, one child rests in the lap of the other, who sits upright and cradles the lower figure tenderly. The upper figure is nude and androgynous. The lower figure, also androgynous, is clothed in a thin nightdress that comes to their thighs. The nightdress is trimmed with delicately carved eyelets. (Such details of the "modern" dress render this more neo- than classical, more modern than Ideal.) The pupils of both children's eyes are carved at their centers to signify that they are, indeed, "awake"; the shape of the pupils mirrors the nightgown's eyelets and the children's delicately carved, life-like fingernails. The lower child lies in the upper child's lap with their torso partially twisted, turned toward the upper one. This position inspires inquiry; the lower child's left hand is mysteriously hidden as the child reaches, stretching its arm, toward the lower torso of the upper figure. Presumably, the hand is not visible because it is reaching lower than the point where their bodies meet. With their other hand, the lower child grasps its own big toe, mouth open in what seems a gasp, revealing their tiny tongue.

It is imperative to think about *how* Lewis posed the figures she carved, and to contemplate the style of their poses and gestures, as these aspects are connected to larger questions about representations of the body.[38] In both *Asleep* and *Awake*, texture, volume, and arrested movement are palpable. While most sculpture of the time was carved with a frontal view, this pair of cherub sculptures do not emphasize frontality. They rather resemble Antonio Canova's famously undulating, entwined figures, best viewed from multiple directions.[39] They invite our movements, ask us to walk around them, taking our time to admire them as moving stones. As in *Asleep*, several toes of the children in *Awake* extend beyond the base, as if the figures could, soon, leave their perch and move about the room. The child that cradles their companion gazes downward, with a look of love. The child sits cross-legged, their left hand stroking a curling lock of hair of the other child, lying across their upright left knee. Their right hand cups the wrist of the lounging child. The upper figure's hair boasts a pronounced curl carved on the very top of their tilted head; a curl that resembles a rose with its perfectly rounded swirl. The hair of this toddler is long and rests in tendrils on the child's shoulders. They appear to be slightly older than the young child in their lap; their muscular chest is visible from the side view. Again, these figures convey a subtle eroticism.

We can surmise that Lewis had multiple reasons for making *Asleep* and *Awake*, including claiming her place as a master neoclassical sculptor. The statues' titles are written on the front of the base in gilt letters (see figure 4.4); Lewis's signature appears on the backs of the works: "Edmonia Lewis, Roma, 1871" and "Edmonia Lewis, Roma, 1872." Carving the putti resolved the artistic problem of making an example of the nude, the consummate artist's achievement, in a socially acceptable style despite its potential implied eroticism. Given the fraught power relations of looking at the nude in art in an era when the fear of the female form was ubiquitous, Lewis handily avoided the problem by carving childlike figures. The generic children she carved in *Asleep* and *Awake* may have provided her predominantly white audiences and buyers with images that could appeal to a narcissistic(?) desire for idealized white subjects.

References to sexuality were thought to be inoculated by the constant redeployment of powerful "classical" discourses that painted these erotic little figures as exemplars of piety and purity. In the same way, the whiteness of the marble and the childlike figures worked to counteract any sense that they are untoward or overly erotic, given that these features—whiteness and infancy—connoted sexual innocence. The invention and proliferation of representations of the pure, white innocent child (like depictions of the immaculately conceived, white baby Jesus) helped to ease the erotic display of the many corpulent cupids. Similarly, the invention of the Victorian child as a tabula rasa (a concept introduced in 1690 by philosopher John Locke in his *An Essay Concerning Human Understanding* and still prevalent in the Victorian era) became a touchstone for pure innocent whiteness. Such whiteness is epitomized by the apotheosis of Harriet Beecher Stowe's Little Eva in the transatlantic best seller *Uncle Tom's Cabin* (1852).[40]

Lewis's decision to make these nude babies was both practical and prudent. Always savvy to marketing, she knew this subject matter was popular and had a fine chance of selling; the market value of these desirable Victorian types was proven. For example, when Harriet Hosmer had carved her small, winged, cherubic marble Puck in 1855, the work proved to be her most lucrative sculpture: Hosmer sold at least fifty copies of the work at $1,000 apiece (about $20,000 today)—including one to Prince Albert.[41] For Lewis, carving two figures from the same stone for her dual portraits was both a more efficient and a less costly way of carving an extremely expensive block of marble. Posing each of the putti in close proximity to each other, one resting on the other, also "diminishes the empty spaces that would have had to be cut between them, saving labor."[42] These doubled figures contrast with the single figure of her *Poor Cupid* (figure 4.6).

Lewis sculpted only one true cherub, or cupid with wings. Her marble *Poor Cupid*, was modeled in Rome in 1872 and carved in 1876: The statue shows a standing, corpulent toddler-angel whose facial features bear a distinct resemblance to Harriet Hosmer's (see figure 3.3). Hosmer was described by some of her contemporaries who visited her Roman studio as a "small, brisk, wide-awake figure of queer and funny aspect, yet not ungraceful . . . [having] a curly head . . . her face was bright and funny, and with small features, as a child's."[43] To provide more evidence for this interpretation: We know that in neoclassical portraits "pupils were drilled into the eyes. Any line marring the brow . . . signified extreme emotion."[44] This generic cupid has a furrowed brow and drilled pupils. This was Lewis's fifth infant statue with a near-adult-sized head and a mature, individualized expression. Lewis's *Poor Cupid* provides some original twists on the ancient theme of the cupid caught in a trap with flowers at its feet. Lewis's winged cherub has a quiver of arrows slung across its back, and another quiver on the rear base and was said to have been "baited by a rose."

A tall, horseshoe-shaped iron trap that comes up to the level of the child's waist is open at the top and has closed on the figure's right wrist, so that the poor thing's entire hand is caught in the trap's arched labial

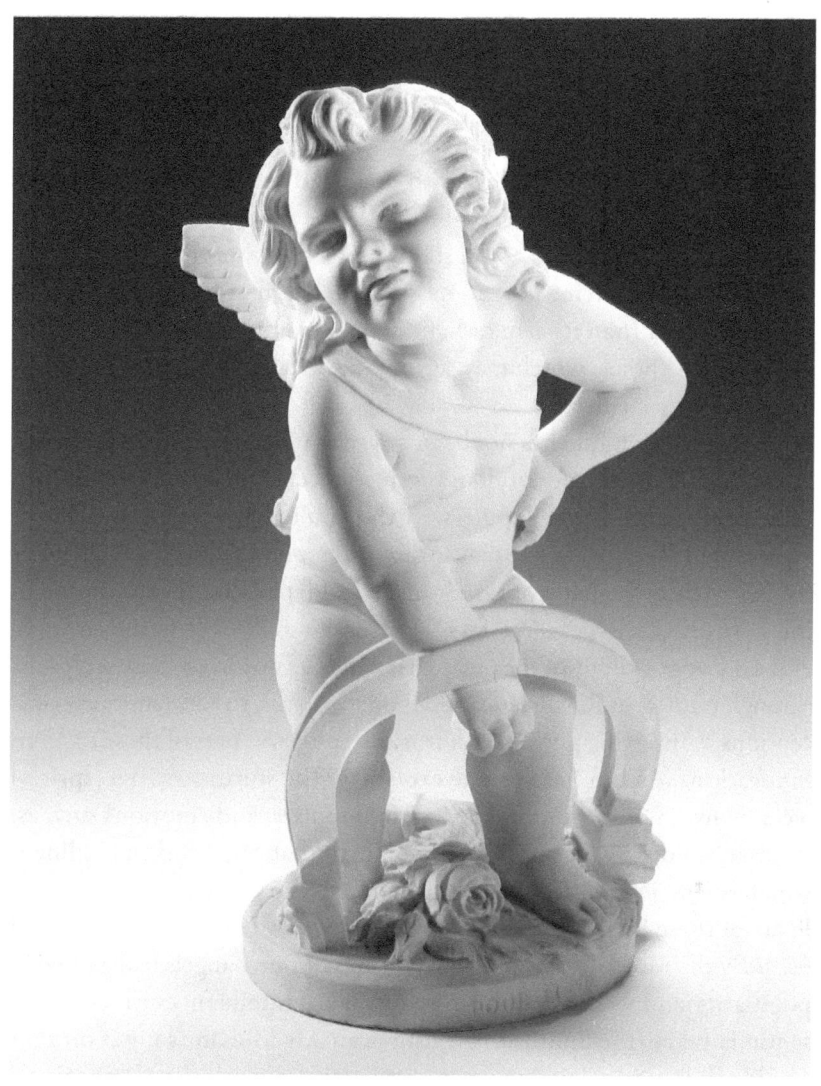

4.6 Edmonia Lewis, *Poor Cupid,* modeled ca. 1872, carved 1876. Marble, 27 × 13¾ × 12¼ in. Smithsonian American Art Museum, Washington, DC, Gift of Alfred T. Morris Sr., 1984.

mouth. The right hand reaches down to the blooming rose that lies below the figure's pelvis, on the exact same vertical line. The left hand rests sassily on its hip, and its torso leans forward with desire. It is arrested, however, caught and unable to grasp the rose or any of the limp flowers that resemble faded tulips or lilies (with one petal peeled back, revealing a stamen) strewn about the feet—feet with one sandal on and one sandal off. This queer, contorted cupid stands out somewhat from other representations of this theme in that, most often, the figure's foot is caught in the trap, rather than its arm or hand. We may inquire about the significance of this choice, which may, again, be a coded reference to off-limits or risk-laden sexualities.

Clearly, this figure has not been sent from Heaven above but, rather, resembles the sensuous quotidian angels connected to the realm of romantic love on earth.[45] Initially, putti were thought to have been impossible to represent in "bodily" form because they were spirits. Early conceptions of the *putto* (from the Latin *putus* for "male child") in sculpture are found in the work of Renaissance "masters" Donatello and Michelangelo, and provide a queer genealogy of the putto that winds its way from these sculptors, through numerous Renaissance and modern works, to contemporary conceptions.[46] Investing putto with form *and* spirit was part of these modern innovations. As Lin Vertefeuille explains, "The spiriti sensitivi [sprites] were many, varied, and caused random impulses, and emotions such as: surprise, sudden erotic arousal, panicky disturbances, drunken giddiness, wonderment, joy. . . . The putto-spiritello was the physical representation in art of these invisible spirits that evoke emotion and thought in all of us."[47] By the nineteenth century, sculptures of putti-angels had gained in popularity and were often taken to be maudlin references to Victorian sentimentality (the Smithsonian American Art Museum's notes on *Poor Cupid* call it a "frivolous" sculpture).[48] Putti also marked sarcophagi and were seen as guardian spirits between realms—which is why they still adorn many gravesites.[49]

Putti, as hybrid figures, occupy ambiguous spaces between the secular and the sacred, the form and the spirit. They simultaneously embody a slip between the sentimental and the sexual. Imaginary characters (in the nineteenth century, sometimes called "fancy works," with a root connected to "fantasy" and "fantastical") have existed for millennia and were present in, and before, Greco-Roman times. Hybrid and fancy figures referenced a fascination with transmogrification: of men becoming gods, animals becoming men and vice versa; of history becoming myth; between biblical

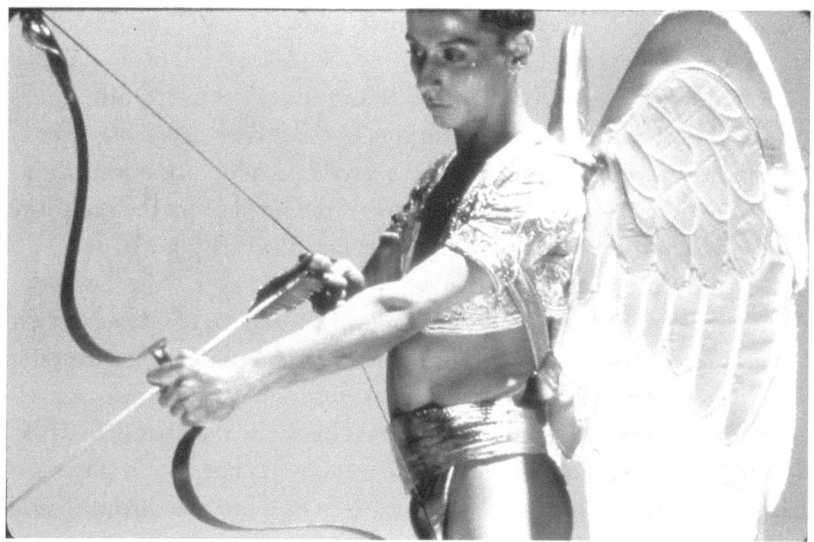

4.7 Angel in Isaac Julien, *The Attendant*, 1993 (still).
35 mm film, color, 5.1 surround sound; 8 minutes, 10 seconds. Edition 1/4. © Isaac Julien. Courtesy of Isaac Julien Studio, London.

versions of Heaven, Hell, and Earth, and many more liminal or shifting locations. Since their invention, hybrid figures that combine body parts of one or more beings, such as human and animal, have appeared with regularity in the annals of art history. Ovid's *Metamorphoses* is a key source for the concept of Cupid, descended from the Greek god Eros and a consort of Venus/Aphrodite, who carried a quiver of arrows to strike unsuspecting mortals with love (figure 4.7). By Roman times, Eros was portrayed as a child, the figure we now call Cupid. In book 1 of the *Metamorphoses*, we see "a blind, winged child armed with a bow and arrows."[50] These figures, combining human and nonhuman aspects such as arms and wings, tap into the long history of tropes that the great classical sculptors chose to represent. No wonder Lewis, with her ambition to succeed as a great sculptor, sought to make a "babe with weapon piercing heart," to quote the poet S. D. Allen (see chapter 5, interlude).

Let us turn from consideration of Edmonia Lewis's sculptures to those of her contemporary Hiram Powers. Powers was among the most famous sculptors of the nineteenth century; Lewis would have known his work well. Powers's statue *The Greek Slave* (1846) was the most celebrated and revered nude of the century (rivaled only by the Apollo Belvedere, a Roman marble copy of a Greek bronze, discovered and put on display at the Vatican in 1511).[51] Powers's *The Greek Slave* certainly would have informed Lewis's ideas about the nude and about her own work, as was true of almost all the sculptors working in the wake of Powers's success. His statue was one of the first nudes carved by a white American sculptor in the decades before the outbreak of the Civil War. The sculpture depicts a beautiful, ideal, fully nude woman whose wrists are bound with chains, and represents a Christian woman captured by the Muslim Turks. Although Powers's statue presents an allegorical defense of Christianity, it was also read as an allegory for the contemporary political debates about slavery in America. Even the earliest reviews took the sculpture as a reference not only to the trade in enslaved Greeks by the Ottoman Turks during the Greek War of Independence (1821–32) but also to the transatlantic slave trade. *The Greek Slave* was seen by many as a direct, critical comment on chattel slavery, a symbol of resistance. It became a lightning rod for criticism of the inhumane practice of human enslavement. The great interpreter of African American art Freeman Henry Morris Murray called it "American Art's first anti-slavery document in marble" in his ground-breaking book, *Emancipation and the Freed in American Sculpture: A Study in Interpretation*, published in 1916.[52] Even Frederick Douglass owned a copy of *The Greek Slave*, which he displayed in his Washington, DC, home.[53]

Strikingly, Lewis never chose to depict an enslaved person in chains. All of her statues of formerly enslaved people depict them in a state of freedom—one even still wearing a broken manacle. Lewis sculpted at least four formerly enslaved people (aside from historical figures such as Frederick Douglass—another of Lewis's sculptures that is missing from the archive). Of these four, three show women; one of them, *The Freedwoman* (1866), has been lost. In *Forever Free* (see figure 4.1), a female kneels next to a standing male figure who holds broken chains. This leaves us with the third, *Hagar* (1875), which remains among Lewis's most revered and idealized sculptures (figure 4.8). This exquisite statue shows Hagar with furrowed brows, eyes that are watching God, and beautiful hands joined in prayer. One of the most striking aspects of this work is the sheath Hagar wears, which gathers in dramatic folds about her lithe body. When viewed in profile, the work has a pronounced forward motion: It looks as if Hagar is walking, about to step off her perch. Lewis has made a wonderous work: a woman at once strong and supple, a supplicant who stands firm in the face of struggle.

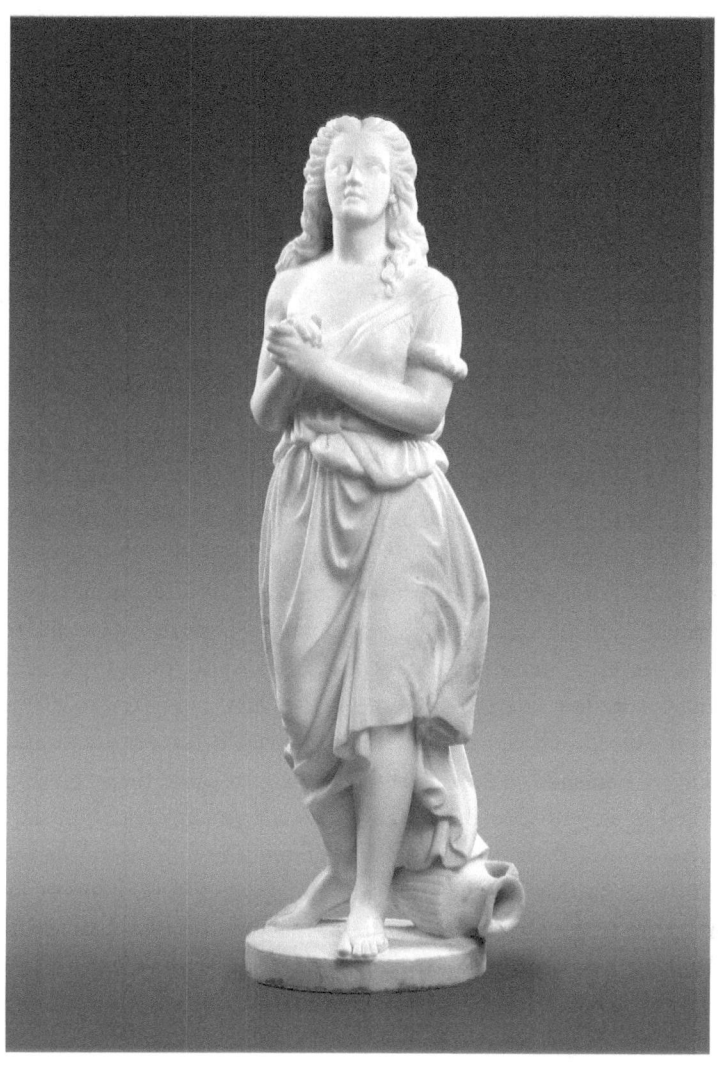

4.8 Edmonia Lewis, *Hagar*, 1875. Marble, 52⅝ × 15¼ ×
17⅛ in. Smithsonian American Art Museum, Washington,
DC, Gift of Delta Sigma Theta Sorority, Inc., 1983.

And what of this face that is thought to bear the trace of race?

According to Kirsten Pai Buick, Lewis "purged . . . [her racialized
women rather] than risk [the appearance of an] obviously black or Indian
woman."[54] Others have read this work as racially ambiguous. Again, we
find ourselves cast about in search of stereotypical features. What does a
Black woman look like? How do we recognize her?

Lewis dedicated this statue to "all women who had struggled and suffered."[55] Hagar, the Egyptian woman enslaved by Sarah, the wife of the biblical Abraham, was, as depicted by Lewis, a woman who struggled and suffered. Lewis portrays her partially nude. Her dress of draped muslin exposes her right breast and shoulder; her hands, with their lifelike tensile fingers in an open curl, are clasped in prayer and obscure her otherwise bare nipple. The partial nudity allows the figure to retain its modesty. She gazes upward away from the eyes of her onlookers. An elaborately carved water jug is tipped over next to her right foot, symbolizing Hagar's search for water when she was in the desert. Her legs and hips, in contrapposto, appear ready to move.

The sculpture marks a shift in Lewis's work toward sculpting biblical characters with greater frequency; the biblical context provided Lewis with a potent allegory for transatlantic slavery. When Sarah learns that she is unable to conceive, she "gives" Hagar to her husband as his slave and sexual concubine. Hagar indeed becomes pregnant and is treated with exceptional cruelty by the couple during her pregnancy. Hagar runs away and temporarily takes refuge in the wilderness. She is the first person in the Old Testament to be visited by an angel of God, who instructs her to return to her captors, where she gives birth to a son, called Ishmael. After some years, mother and son are banished to the desert where they are cared for by God.[56] Women like Hagar, who gave birth to the master's progeny, had no legal standing to determine their own or the child's fate—the child was bound to "follow in the condition" of the enslaved woman who bore them, or so said the doctrine of *partus sequitur ventrem*, enacted into law in colonial Virginia in 1662. This heartbreaking tale spoke to many nineteenth-century Black women, enslaved and free, who viewed the narrative allegorically as a story about the plight of the "slave mother" and the practice of male slave owners having unrestricted access to rape and defile women they "owned" and to thereafter own or sell their children.

Here, let's reposition ourselves so as to be able to see yet another perspective that, in a sense, returns us to the imaginary scene of Lewis's initial making of her statue of Hagar. What might Edmonia Lewis have felt about or toward the figurative, full-bodied sculptures she made? We can only surmise who her models for such works may have been, if she used models, and this leads us to ponder her sense of the Nude. In creating these works, Lewis had to mold the body in full. Her hands shaped clay to model the hidden breast of Hagar and the exposed breast of Cleopatra, then carved every inch of their forms in stone. Lewis, as far as we know, did not sculpt female figures in overtly sexual situations: None of her works show a female figure in a state of open repose, as an odalisque, posed for consumption. Rather, her female figures for the most part convey dignity, determination, or deference.

Deeply entrenched heterosexist presumptions reign in most sculptural discourse: the maker having more power than the made; the desirability of a feminized passive object; hierarchical relationships (Adam and Eve, for example) in which the female subject is an extension of the male creator. Many accounts of Renaissance sculpture valorize male, homoerotically inclined subjects—sculptors and sculptures alike, such as Michelangelo and his David or Donatello and his chaps-clad Amor-Attis. Many fewer works have considered how questions of desire may have affected female sculptors. The same-sex erotics that can exist between female artists and their subjects deserve more research and inquiry (the following interlude, about contemporary Black lesbian artist Mickalene Thomas, touches on this topic).

The ur-case of the Western artist's desire to *make*—particularly the female form and its erotic revelation—is the myth of Pygmalion falling in love with his sculpture of Galatea. Every sculptor had to grapple with this mythic story and the indelible idea of the artist enamored with his own creation, and to figure out how it touched their own process. In most depictions of the artist Pygmalion, his sculpture Galatea is presented without clothes. Ovid recounts this story in book 10 of the *Metamorphoses*. There are, of course, numerous translations of the passage, including the largely bowdlerized nineteenth-century version with a chastened Christian overlay. Most translations include Pygmalion's "empty bed," referring to his lack of a wife or female companion, and mention his hands touching the at-first hard and then miraculously fleshly, naked gleaming-white body of Galatea in repose, with its ability to return the enlivening kiss. In Charles Martin's translation, which I quote in this chapter, Pygmalion "runs his hands over the work, tempted as to whether it is flesh or ivory. . . . He kisses it and thinks his kisses are returned, and speaks to it, and holds it, and imagines his fingers press into its limbs, and is afraid lest bruises appear from pressure."[57]

As the myth relates, "Pygmalion dresses the body . . . but it appears no less lovely naked." Ultimately, the sculptor imagines, wishes, that *she* could "move," that she could be a moving stone. In Ovid's version of the myth, Pygmalion "again and yet again, gives trust to his hopes by touching her with his hands." His anthropomorphizing of the body double extends to the question of the doubled relation of the denuded or (un)dressed.[58] In much neoclassical sculpture, even clothing suggested nudity. The thin "classical" swaths of sheer material, valued for their technical difficulty to render in stone, allowed the sculpted body simultaneously to reveal itself and to be covered. Even in the process of producing clothed sculptures, artists could make figures first as nude bozzetti (the sculpture in its rough clay form), suggesting that the nude and the dressed were temporally related, rather than opposite categories.[59] Again, we must look to artistic production to see the nude in its formation.

In her work surveying white female painters and Black female models from the 1850s to today, Denise Murrell discusses the crisis that critics experienced over the idea of female painters having to touch their female models, which was also expressed as a prohibition on any possible racial dynamics present in such interactions (and therefore bearing on the case of Edmonia Lewis). "Critics [of women artists]," Murrell explains, "also described their revulsion at the juxtaposition of black skin and luxurious white fabrics, especially given the presumed contact between the white female painter and the sitter necessary to drape the fabrics, which carried strong connotations of illicit eroticism."[60] This concept of racialized female-to-female eroticism through touch is intensified regarding the practice of sculpture.

The entire era, awash as it was with chastened ivory nudes and enthralled by iterations of the Pygmalion-Galatea myth, seemed fixated on the "ivory" bodies of an imaginary female nude. The term *nude* frequently denoted a "white" subject, as we have seen. Black and Indigenous female forms required a distinguishing adjective—*Black* Venuses, or *Indian* maidens. Acceptable nakedness demanded the cleansing trope of a mythologizing classicism that purified ancient figures such as Cleopatra or the biblical Hagar. By contrast, to sculpt a living or contemporary white-appearing woman's breast was indelicate. Denise Murell writes, "By 1800 the nude breast was considered by critics to be too erotically charged to be acceptable in portraits of known living subjects; from the model's subject position, this nudity could well have been more reminiscent of the practice of stripping black women to the waist at slave markets."[61] Sojourner Truth famously bared her own breasts during an antislavery speech as proof of her womanhood. This self-revelatory performative gesture, made in public, was meant to show the "truth" of her body as a means of making the case for Black women who were enslaved *as* female. Her accompanying statement for this gesture, "Aren't I a woman?" has functioned as a kind of rallying cry in some (Black) feminist circles.[62]

Contemporary viewers of Lewis's *Hagar* no doubt read it differently than did viewers in its initial era of reception; the sculpture continues to inspire homages in various media that seek to represent liberation of all kinds. For example, poet Tyehimba Jess, in his poem "Hagar in the Wilderness, Edmonia Lewis, Marble, 1875," reimagines Lewis's statue as participating in a sensuous encounter with Lewis. In its last section, the narrator of this personal poem shifts perspective, and *Hagar*, the statue, speaks in a dramatic monologue. This literary Hagar, anthropomorphized, claims to have kissed Lewis's brown fingertips, to have known her maker's caress—as if the two women had been forged in the same crucible and reborn in each other's image. The voice of the statue valorizes Lewis as her maker, deeming her a "dark and mortal God":

> I have been touched by my God
> in my creation, I've known her caress
> of anointing callus across my face.
> I know the lyric of her pulse
> across these lips . . . and yes
> I've kissed the fingertips
> of my dark and mortal God.
> She has shown me the truth
> behind each chiseled blow
> that's carved me into this life,
> the weight any woman might bear
> to stretch her mouth toward her
> one true God, her own
> beaten, marble song.

The two female figures of African descent "stretch out their mouths" to create a generative song together; the homoerotic valences of the poem—"the lyric of her pulse / upon these lips"—are evident. While we cannot speculate about Lewis's understanding of her gender identity or sexual orientation using contemporary language, many scholars read her as both queer and as leaning toward a "female masculinity" in her self-presentation.[63] Thinking about Lewis's "queerness" or queer desire and her sensuous engagement with her subjects opens up new ways of understanding her art; from this view, Lewis's sculpting process can be understood as passionate performances involving dedication, devotion, and perhaps even erotic desire and love. The statues exist as "wild visions of continuance."[64] They carry and convey memories of touch.

We have traces of her to study through this lens. Lewis, in a letter to her benefactor Lydia Maria Child recalled her first meeting with Harriet

Hosmer, an avowed lesbian, on April 5, 1866, at Hosmer's studio in Rome: "[Hosmer] took my hand cordially . . . and then, while she still held my hand, there flowed such a neat little speech from her true lips." The flowering of friendship is fomented in the flow from hand to lips. Like Hosmer, Lewis demonstrated a lifelong assumption of masculine attitudes, willfulness, and an unfeminine occupation, often wearing masculine attire above the beltline and skirts below, like other women sculptors of the era. Chapter 6 examines this costume in the series of six daguerreotypes made by Henry Rocher in his studio on Rush Street in Chicago circa 1870. Lewis attended the private New York Central College in McGrawville, where she may have encountered Amelia Bloomer, who popularized the divided garments for women's lower body known at the time as Reform Costume and considered by some to be risqué and masculine. This pre-pants-for-women garment represented greater freedom in both the private and public spheres.

Harry B. Henderson and Albert Henderson, writing in 2012, rejected any notion that Lewis may have had same-sex inclinations, insisting on her "propriety." "She might have fared better with male critics and buyers," they wrote, "if she [had] offered female nudes. Adult nudity, essential for so many artists and buyers, was not in her repertoire."[65] I question this assertion. It is not that adult, specifically female, nudes were not "in her repertoire"; surely she could have excelled at any form she chose. It may have been the case, rather, that to sculpt the female nude would draw unwelcome speculations about her own inclinations. We will treat the subject of Lewis's gender presentation and possible sexual presumptions more fully in chapter 5, "A Rose Somebody Knows."

The American West proved to be a place where Lewis's celebrity and her professional acumen generated fervor among new admirers, many of whom happened to be women. As it turned out, women became her *main* buyers. The *San Francisco Chronicle*'s write-up of her visit noted the "throngs of beauties who stood in line to meet her at the Fair." In the fall of 1873, Lewis carted her smaller sculptures of putti across the Atlantic to New York and then across the United States to California in order to raise funds to finish her version of Cleopatra. When her commissions and sales in the eastern United States lagged after the abolitionist communities in Boston and New York had already purchased her work, she shrewdly went west.

During this consequential sojourn in California, Lewis became the first international artist from Rome to visit the Bay Area. The five marble statues she carried across the Atlantic via steamship and then across the country by rail, included the pendant pieces *Asleep* (1871) and *Awake* (1872), as well as her *Poor Cupid*, the *Bust of Lincoln* (1871), and *Hiawatha's Marriage* (1870). These works were exhibited at the newly opened Art Association gallery on Pine Street in San Francisco and subsequently at a Catholic fair in San Jose. The established African American press in the Bay Area praised her work. "Over sixteen hundred persons visited Miss Lewis's beautiful exhibition of sculpture at the hall [in San Jose] last week," a local paper claimed.[66]

That September, two of the five sculptures, *The Death of Cleopatra* and *Hiawatha's Marriage*, sold at the San Francisco Art Association on Pine Street. She had the remaining three works—a bust of Lincoln, *Asleep*, and *Awake*—brought down by horse-drawn cart to San Jose for its agricultural exhibition. A wealthy white widow and suffragette, Sarah Knox-Goodrich, one of the largest landholders in the area, whose family quarry supplied the stone to build Stanford University, was encouraged to purchase Lewis's statues by the groundskeeper of her estate. He was a Black man who was a regular reader of the Black press and knew of Edmonia Lewis from *The Elevator*. A full-page announcement in the paper read:

> The Beautiful creations of this Young Artist are of Real Merit, and have received the encomiums of Professors and Connoisseurs of Art in Europe and America, and cannot but fill our hearts with pride as a contradiction of the assertion that we have never produced an artist of true genius. Those who fail to see these works will miss an opportunity which may never occur again. The bare announcement of the artist's name should be sufficient inducement to fill the house with our people alone every night.[67]

The sculptures attracted women, men, and children of all races. Lewis's trip to California arguably helped to galvanize the growing population of wealthy patrons in the Gilded Age Bay Area to collect European statuary. Lewis's exhibition at the Pine Street gallery, attended by the mayor, marked a high point for the San Francisco Art Association (that later transformed into the San Francisco Museum of Modern Art). The *Pacific Appeal* noted that, "Her statuary, which was on exhibition, are [*sic*] magnificent works of art, and every piece in the group was fully in keeping with and in beautiful contrast with the fine oil paintings that adorn the walls of the Art Gallery. The 'Marriage of Hiawatha,' 'Asleep and Awake,' infant statuary, present life-life expressions of grace and beauty and innocence that none but a master of the statuary art can portray with the chisel."[68]

Nearly a century after Sarah Knox-Goodrich purchased *Asleep*, *Awake*, and *Bust of Lincoln* and donated the sculptures to the San Jose Library (now the Martin Luther King Jr. Library), a local chapter of the Black women's philanthropic organization The Links, Inc., donated three wooden bases on which to display them. They remain in use today. These works have been exhibited only three times outside the library: at *Two Centuries of Black American Art*, organized by David Driskell for the Los Angeles County Museum of Art in 1976; at a show curated by Marla Novo at San Jose State University Art Museum, in 1995; and at *Edmonia Lewis: Indelible Impressions*, a show organized for the Cantor Museum at Stanford University in fall 2025.[69] The works were requested for an exhibition at Vassar College in April 1972, titled *The White Marmorean Flock: Nineteenth-Century American Women Neoclassical Sculptors*, but were not permitted to leave their West Coast home, in part because they were estimated to weigh over five hundred pounds apiece.

The two nudes and the bust languished in the library basement for nearly a hundred years until they were rediscovered in the 1960s, coated with dirt and in a neglected state. The library director at that time, Philip Montesano, described his first encounter with the statues: "My fingers tore at the dust and grime until the pure marble glowed softly." He could then read the inscriptions: "Edmonia Lewis, AWAKE, 1872, Roma, [it] said. . . . I turned to a third statue and rubbed until the words appeared magically under my hand, Edmonia Lewis, ASLEEP, 1871, Roma. Asleep indeed [I] thought, crouching on [my] heels. For too many years . . . As [I] photographed all three statues, questions raced through my mind. How did they get here? And what of Edmonia Lewis?"[70]

"And what of Edmonia Lewis?" is the question we also ask throughout this monograph. To tear "at the dust and grime until the pure marble glowed softly" is also our work (though some may say that critics, in fact, add more dust and grime). The physical and the critical are not separate realms when it comes to sculpture. Edmonia Lewis's foray into the genre of the nude reveals how questions of sensuality, the erotic, and concealment feature in the act of sculptural creation. Without her work, the agency of a woman's sensuous touch would have been missing from the archive. Lewis was never a mother, and her nudes—unlike many of the era—seem not to feature a maternal touch. Rather, they appear to be calculated to dissemble, deliberately measured to suggest certain desires but not reveal them; they are passionate, yet premeditated and designed to secure commercial success but also, strangely, something else. We may inquire about how her contemporaries and critics of the day perceived "female-on-female" sculpting and how she may have both embraced and contravened Victorian perceptions. We can question what she was thinking and feeling in creating the breast of another woman and a toddler who resembles an adult; and we must imagine a way to think about open possibilities in the process of performing sculpture.

Mickalene Thomas

If we agree that Lewis deserves a place in histories of the nude; then so does Mickalene Thomas (b. 1971). Thomas is among the most important contemporary artists; indeed, her fame is comparable to Lewis's celebrity in the nineteenth century. In many ways, Thomas can be thought of as part of a new genealogy of Black women artists who wrestle with the nude. Thomas is among the first Black women artists who, according to her gallerist Susanne Vielmetter, was "radical," because in 2007 Thomas was one of the few artists "making portraiture of female Black figures from a perspective of female desire."[71] The two artists' body-centric aesthetics and interest in sexual imagery and unconventional subjects could link them.

Figure 4i.1 is a photograph of Thomas taken by the Haitian artist Widlene Cadet (b. 1992, in Pétion-Ville, Haiti) in Thomas's New York studio. The photo accompanied a 2021 *New York Times Magazine* feature titled "Mickalene Thomas Is Reinventing Nudes."[72] Part of the purported "reinvention" has to do with the connection between artist and artwork. Thomas unwittingly re-creates the situation of Lewis in her studio a hundred years before, molding a model breast, open lips, and idealized beauties. The photo shows Thomas in the left center of the frame, wearing a short-sleeved pink canvas shirt splattered with different colors of paint, as she works on one of her signature large-scale mixed-media collages. The artist's muscular upper body dominates the image; hair in thick upswept locks, her handsome face obscured by a pair of glasses and a black KN95 mask that leaves only her brown eyes visible—the photo was taken in the midst of the COVID-19 pandemic. At the center third of the horizontal plane of the photograph, Thomas's braceleted right hand touches a pair of cut-out hot-pink lips, pasted on

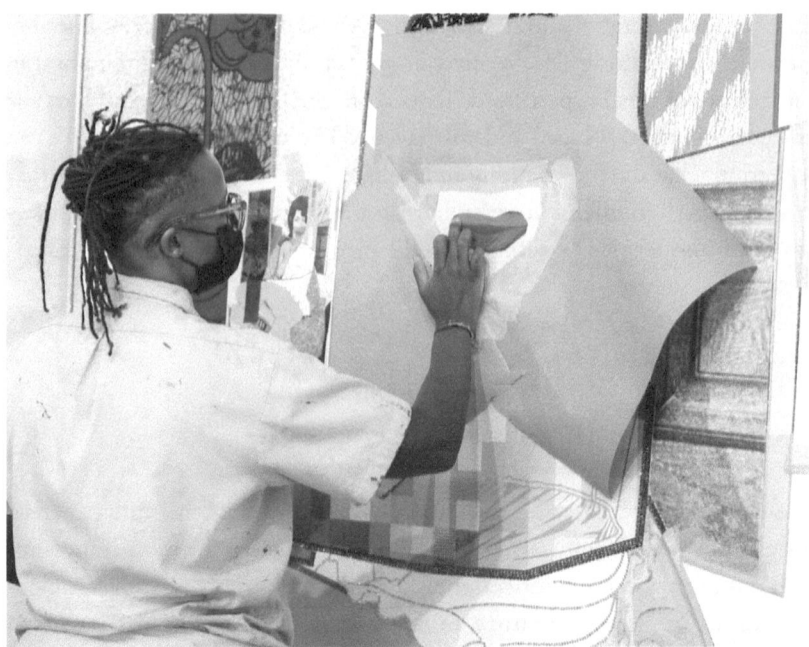

4i.1 Mickalene Thomas in her Brooklyn studio, 2021.
Photograph by Widlene Cadet for the *New York Times*.
NYTimes.com. Courtesy of the artist.

white paper framed by a triangle of yellow painter's tape. The lips sit at
the perfect center of the canvas: They hold together pieces of light-brown
butcher paper. Two sheets are placed diagonally and a third one is placed
vertically above the lips to produce the image of a vulva. The curve of
the paper that would be in the position of the "thigh" in this landscape
creates a shadow and adds sculptural dimension to the figure. Thomas
fingers the image suggestively. In the background, Thomas's trademark
sequins and glitter make up the edges around pixelated X-ray boxes.
Thomas suggests via this covering technique that the blurred-out images
include nudity, porn, or are X-rated photographs.

On the wall behind her in the photograph are other pasted bits of
paper: architectural sketches, hand drawings, and collaged fragments.
The colors in this vibrant image include collages made out of other tactile
pieces of material: flame-stitched warm corals, bits of blue, gray, and
tan broken by intermittent vertical lines of Thomas's sparkling ruby red
sequins—lines that divide the canvas of the wall and, by extension, the
photograph.

Thomas's work can be read in the context of the writer S. Diane Bogus's short story "Dyke Hands," about queer women's hands as sex tools. The story toys with the idea that hands appear and disappear in their varying performances of quotidian work (like making art?) as well as in creating sexual pleasure.[73] We find ourselves again contemplating hands that, in touching stone, find flesh. Mel Y. Chen's *Animacies* includes a lyrical discussion of "a stone—as it has been encoded and applied to . . . a particular erotic and sexual economy of affect in which [in some butch or femme lesbian cultures] the butch's sexual pleasure can emerge from the touch instigated by her . . . the stoneness of the butch can also refer to masculinities of expressive life for butches: feelings held in, the appearance of unfeeling. 'Being stone' is thus not merely a queer affect; it also tugs at and traverses the animacy hierarchy's affective economy with regard to both feeling and touch."[74] These sculpted hands are primed to play an important role in various erotic scenarios: They are endowed with the capacity to become moving stones.

At the opening of Thomas's first major solo exhibition, *Mickalene Thomas: All About Love* at the Broad Museum in Los Angeles in 2024, audiences were in awe of her shimmering, larger-than-life collages. Her work refuses to abide by patriarchal rules around sexuality and art making. Denise Murrell writes, "While the centuries-old presumption of an objectifying male viewer is now dematerialized as an empty chair, it is the figure herself, rather than the relationship with the viewer, that is the source of pictorial interest. This radically new black muse transcends an antecedent history of subordination and obliteration and assumes the power of her central subject position. Thomas resurrects the self-assured demeanor of her previous portraits of black female subjects, but now in the iconic trope of the reclining nude."[75]

To my eye, Cadet's photograph is composed to reveal Thomas's interests in Black women's nudity, queer sexuality, and beauty. It is an image "all about love" that centers the queer hand of the lesbian artist in the frame.[76] We've noted that there are few commentaries about women artists creating images of other women: as if such female desiring looks are an impossibility. Roxane Gay, in the first monograph focused on Thomas's work, admires the fact that the artist "does not shy away from nudity or sexuality or explicit desire."[77] Thomas's artist's hands retain the memory of her desire: One of her models is her wife, and several others were her lovers. Her layered and textured portraits of Black women from among her friends and family (including her mother) beguile with their bold use of glitter, vibrant, in-your-face colors, and scattered patterns—to say nothing of the averted gazes of her model subjects, who epitomize Beauty. One can imagine that Edmonia Lewis may also have brought members of her intimate community and her local area into the studio as subjects and inspiration.

The charged subject of nudity in art has often been overtaken by narratives of men's desire for the nude, and we forget that consumers of the nude include women and nonbinary people. In disidentifying with the tradition of the nude, we should always ask other questions, such as, *How do we look at the work—and how do we look* in *the work?* Looking at the work of both Thomas and Lewis, we may ask further, *Whose nudity is this, and for whom does it appear?*

A Rose Somebody Knows

CLEOPATRA: What, no more ceremony? See, my women!
Against the blown rose may they stop their nose
that kneel'd unto the buds.

   Shakespeare, *Antony and Cleopatra,* 3.13.45–47

5

I wonder, I wonder if anyone knows,
Who lives at the heart of this velvety rose?
Now is it a goblin, or is it an elf,
Or is it the queen of the fairies herself?

   Nursery rhyme

This chapter begins with quotations about roses because Lewis sculpted these flowers with frequency in the latter part of her career. For centuries, roses have been conflated with love and sexuality in an imperialist and colonial context that colors how they have impacted the (racial-sexual) economies of the global world. Roses have occupied a prized place not only in sheets of parchment or in reams of paper but also in visual art and iconography. Sometimes, as noted in the previous chapter, the rose functions as a queer emblem in addition to an objective correlative of female genitalia.

The first epigraph quotes lines from act 3 of Shakespeare's *Antony and Cleopatra* (1606–7) that likely would have been familiar to Lewis since she was known to have done extensive research before carving her monumental statue *The Death of Cleopatra* (see figure 2.1). Given her education and inquisitive nature, Lewis doubtless read many other works by Shakespeare and would thereby have encountered the author's more than one hundred references to the rose, his most frequent and perhaps favorite floral citation. Indeed, we could say that Shakespeare cultivated the manifold nature of the rose in Western culture.[1] For example, sonnet 130, one of the series of so called "dark lady" sonnets that the bard penned in the persona of a lover, reads: "I have seen roses damasked, red and white, / But no such roses see I in her cheeks."[2] This statement, which goes against the laudatory tradition of comparing one's lover to nature's beauty, comes after the speaker in the poem has spent the previous quatrains inverting the love sonnet's metaphorical logic. In this anticonventional poem, the speaker still considers their "love as rare / As any she belied with false compare," even if the object of affection differs from the norm.

So, why carve a rose? Or, more pointedly, why might Edmonia Lewis have sculpted stone roses? What might the floral forms repeatedly plied by her fingers have foretold? This chapter offers readings of the leitmotif of the rose that appears in several of Lewis's sculptures made in the 1870s, namely *Cupid Caught in a Trap* (1872), *The Death of Cleopatra* (1876), *Portrait of a Woman* (1873), and *The Veiled Bride of Spring* (1879). In tracing Lewis's recurrent romance with the figure of the rose, I understand the issue of the rose to be a thorny topic; I approach it with care.

Roses are painted in still lifes often to suggest the life cycle—as is the case with virtually any flower featured in the genre of memento mori. It is beyond the scope of this chapter to provide a critical genealogy of the symbolism of the rose in art. Lewis sculpted these flowers with ever-greater frequency during her career. As such, they are worthy of notice and in what follows, I give close readings of a number of these sculpted roses.

In the 1970s French feminist Hélène Cixous pointed out that "men say that there are two unrepresentable things: death and the feminine sex."[3] In the many readings of Lewis's dead (rather than dying) *Cleopatra*, I think about *nature morte* (still life), as Lewis seems to have sought to represent both death and sex in her *Cleopatra*. There is something deeply moving about the roses, cherubs, and other queer subjects in some of

Lewis's sculptures. Kirsten Pai Buick identifies the use of the rose in Lewis's statue of Cleopatra as a significant departure from other sculptural representations of the great queen: "In Lewis's statue alone the cut rose appears at the foot of the figure. . . . Only after she has died does a cut flower accompany Cleopatra: it is a sign that she is, in her death, a lady." Buick then notes the connection to an 1870 painting of the dead queen by Valentine Prinsep that includes the cut rose. "Something is borrowed from Prinsep's celebrated oil painting 'The Death of Cleopatra,' but upon this the touch of Miss Lewis's chisel is certainly very obvious. There is no Iris dead at the queen's feet [as] in Prinsep's painting for such things would be too elaborate for sculpture."[4] Here we see a technical impediment as an influence on her decision to carve a rose, since carving an iris "would be too elaborate." This may very well have been the case; however, I think we could also read Lewis's choice as building on the "floral symbolism [that] was widespread in nineteenth-century art and literature," as feminist art historian Griselda Pollock notes, symbolism that artists such as painter and poet Dante Gabriel Rossetti "made . . . use of in particular meanings associated with specific flowers."[5]

Nineteenth-century artistic images of Cleopatra rarely include a rose, even though, in an era of robust sentimentality, the rose, dubbed "the queen of flowers," symbolized love. The rose was known throughout the ancient world for its healing power, as evident in many sources from the Greek myth of Aphrodite, goddess of love, to the myth of the far older Egyptian goddess Isis, whose symbol was the rose. According to Charmaine Nelson, "Lewis's deployment of Cleopatra's costume demonstrated an awareness of ancient descriptions of the queen's adaptation of the symbolic costume of Isis for her office, particularly in the detailed floral and organic decoration of the robe's fringe which is draped over the left side of the throne."[6] Stories abound of Cleopatra strewing her rooms with rose petals during her trysts with Mark Antony. Cleopatra was said to have loved the aroma of roses. The Victorian painter Sir Lawrence Alma-Tadema (1836–1912), in his work *The Meeting of Antony and Cleopatra* (1885), depicts Cleopatra's boat sailing down the Nile adorned with huge sprays and garlands of bright pink roses, some of which are shedding their delicately painted petals. Again, this is a rare depiction of Cleopatra and roses that stands out for its profusion of the queen's flower, which also appears in Alma-Tadema's painting *The Roses of Heliogabalus*.[7]

Only once in the 1606 folio of *Antony and Cleopatra* does Shakespeare's character Cleopatra utter the word *rose*. Addressing the women in act 3, scene 13, the queen deploys the rhyme of "nose" and "rose," speaking of the scent that may "stop their nose." Here, the rose is redolent. Also significant is the fact that these lines are not in iambic pentameter. Lewis's famed sculpture *Death of Cleopatra* and the stories of Cleopatra that Lewis most likely studied emphasize the powerful queen's own deployment of the rose to foment her performance of desirability. A case in point is Cleopatra's documented use of rose water in her bath and her toiletry. The thought and gesture of smelling a rose, of moving one's body close enough to catch the fragrance of the flower, index the proximities and approximations of the live and the dead, of bodies and sculptures and all manner of moving interactions. In Egypt, roses were believed to be endowed with magic and their fragrance was thought to waft from one's grave. Rose fragments have been found inside burial tombs as a sign of the connections between the realms of the dead and the living.[8]

Finally, it is worth noting that the color of roses is another aspect of their symbolic meaning. Kim Hall has written about the long history of English associations with red and white roses in the context of female beauty in the Renaissance. In an article on the sculptures of Simone Leigh, Erica Moiah James explains, "Roses have extensive significance in global cultures. As with the 'English Rose' they often signified something to be cherished and adored. Roses are so much a part of contemporary life that their significations are commonly known. Red roses signify romantic, passionate love; yellow roses mean friendship and warmth. White roses can be signs of mourning, innocence, hope, or rebirth. Lavender are for adoration and love. The term 'sub-rosa' (under the rose) originally meant that anything said in a space sanctioned by the presence of a bunch of the delicate flowers was confidential."[9]

In almost every description of Lewis's award-winning *Cleopatra*, first shown in at the Centennial International Exhibition in Philadelphia in 1876, the focus has been on the just-dead figure's visage as an indication of her racial heritage. Descriptions comment on the sculpture's lyrically limp "body," her bared breast, and, to a lesser extent, the iconographic hieroglyphs that decorate the sides of the throne on which she slumps.[10] In the many truly excellent close readings of this major work by Lewis (I hesitate to write "her masterpiece," given that term's loaded patriarchal genealogy), which is now taught in many art history surveys and acknowledged by many art historians as Lewis's greatest achievement, there is little mention of the rose that appears at the base of the statue. This single, literally debased part of the grand multi-ton work is a seemingly insignificant detail—a mere adornment.

Nevertheless, when I first encountered the sculpture at the Smithsonian American Art Museum in Washington, DC, on a day when the official portraits of President Barak Obama and First Lady Michelle Obama were on display (and where I had come from attending an anti-gun-violence rally organized by students from Marjory Stoneman Douglas High), it was the rose that captured my gaze. I wonder if the rose functioned like the many other floral insignia that symbolized queer sexuality. Here, the rose seems to function in her work as one of the many queer codes that were to become pervasive in modern culture—from Wilde's carnally coded green carnation to Georgia O'Keeffe's labial lilies. As Griselda Pollock observes, "Flowers have often been used as a metaphor for women's sexuality, or rather their genitals."[11] We see this especially in Janelle Monáe's witty invocations of "pynk flowers," including the fabulous silk and tulle pink labial "vulva" pants she wore in the 2018 video version of the song "Pynk," which were designed by Duran Lantink.

The rose arose in my line of sight so close, its scent seemed to rise to my nose. Like Roland Barthes's punctum, the moment in the narrative that stops my roving eye and provides the close-up is the rose.[12] The rose, protruding from the area near the statue's toes, arose for me almost as if my nose could nestle there and smell its faded perfume. A dimpled depression forming a hole distinguished its center, surrounded by four fleshy rounds, the folds fluttering here and deepening there to create a whole inviting flower fixed at the base. Its hollow beckons us to enter its labyrinth, explore its furrows, make contact with its folds. There is little mystery. Can you imagine hands caressing this round mound of marble? Are you thinking of Edmonia's hands touching these rippled folds, hardened for eternity? Can we sense her tongue taste its surface?

The Death of Cleopatra, like the artist herself, led a spectacular peripatetic life. Any scholar writing about Lewis is obliged to study this gorgeously grand work depicting the partially disrobed dead queen with her right breast exposed. Superb readings of the sculptural and other representations of Cleopatra have focused on race and sexuality, as well as changing art historical styles—usually from neoclassicism to naturalism and Realism. There is no question that Lewis's *Cleopatra* is her most meritorious work. Indeed, in her own time, reviewers of Lewis's *Cleopatra* claimed that her rendition of the queen's nose was appropriately Greco-Roman rather than African, reflecting Cleopatra's Alexandrian origins. Greek? Roman? Egyptian?[13] Historically, attention has centered on the queen's racial composition—especially on the question of whether or not Cleopatra's nose somehow might indicate her racial makeup. Even more than discussions about the color of her epidermis, the nose became the locus of generations of debate.

Rather than talk about this absolutely significant aspect of Lewis's statue, I focus on a seemingly minor detail: the rose that lies at the base of the sculpture, near Cleopatra's foot. The romance of the rose, like Cleopatra herself, does not endure without death as its fulcrum. In *Egypt Land: Race and Nineteenth-Century Egyptomania* (2004), Scott Trafton argues that, "when African American lesbian sculptor Edmonia Lewis sent her larger marble statue The Death of Cleopatra from Rome to Philadelphia to be shown at the Centennial International Exhibition in 1876, she was staging a radical intervention." Trafton's insight provides the first extended close reading of Lewis's work as lesbian or queer. "Like almost all of the other makers of Cleopatran imagery," Trafton writes, "[Lewis] understood that to portray the body of the infamous Egyptian queen was always already an act concerned with far more than aesthetics or history . . . her [sculpture] was an intervention into the general dynamics of inner and outer, concealment and display, and veiling and unveiling that so widely structured nineteenth-century American signs of Ancient Egypt."[14] I supplement Trafton's queer reading of Lewis's work through a closer reading of roses as another emblem of sexual significance.

Here, at the base of the statue, exposed between folds, is another of Lewis's sculpted roses, like the one we see on the base of her *Poor Cupid* (see figure 4.6). Like stopping the rose with one's nose, one may find oneself about the fleshly bodies lying underneath flowing, undulating gowns. It is in such moments of proximity, actual and imagined, that the power of moving stones may be revealed.

Lewis's friend the formerly enslaved Anna Julia Cooper introduced Lewis to readers in her now classic Black feminist text, *A Voice from the South* (1892). Cooper prefaces her remarks about Lewis with an anecdote about the "songs" or poems of famous eighteenth-century enslaved writer Phillis Wheatley whose works Cooper admired: "That girl paid her debts *in song*," Cooper concludes.[15] The connection between Wheatley and Lewis was solidified in the work of Black women's clubs and organizations. Later in the century, Lewis even proposed sculpting Wheatley. Both women are hailed in Cooper's text as exemplary, admired for their artistry as well as their industry. Before Lewis appears in the text (again via the repetition of the exaggerated, apocryphal story of her viewing of a statue of Ben Franklin in Boston), Cooper digresses to tell the story of the colored Loiseaux brothers from South Carolina. These brothers

> own and conduct one of the most extensive and successful farms in this country for floriculture. Their system of irrigating and fertilizing is the most scientific in the state, and by their original and improved methods of grafting and cultivating they have produced a new and rich variety of the rose called *Loiseaux,* from their name. Their roses are famous throughout Europe and are especially prized by the French for striking and marvelous beauty. The Loiseaux brothers send out the incense of their grateful returns to the work in the *sweet fragrance of roses.*[16]

We have added another sense to our affective response to sculpture: In addition to thinking about haptic-optic relations, we may imagine the sensation of scent. Indexing the aroma amplifies the sensuous response to sculptural forms. In this instance, it brings to mind the fragrance of perfumed flesh, a key aspect of Cleopatra's corpus.

When Lewis's *Death of Cleopatra* was selected to be shown at the 1876 Centennial International Exhibition in Philadelphia, the statue appeared in the Men's Pavilion rather than the controversial Women's Pavilion (where, not surprisingly, most of the work was rated inferior by contemporary critics). Lewis had shipped her work to Philadelphia hoping that it would be judged without prejudice. Once it was chosen, she accompanied the work by standing next to the statue to guide and observe viewers' thoughts about it. Edmonia Lewis grappled with the proper subjects to sculpt, in what style, and with what substance. She had long wished to make a major statue of Cleopatra, who had become a popular subject among her American colleagues in Rome.

Lewis's *Cleopatra* sits upright on her throne, in contrast to other, mostly supine depictions of the dying queen. Mrs. N. F. (Gertrude Bustill) Mossell wrote in 1908, "Along the line of Art we have one noble representative: the work of Edmonia Lewis, the sculptress, is so well known that it scarce needs repetition; her 'Cleopatra Dying,'' [*sic*] exhibited at the Centennial Exhibition, received a medal of honor. Most of her works have been sold to titled persons of Europe."[17] Mossell, like

Anna Julia Cooper and other black female reformers, labored to point out Lewis's work as pure:

> Some years ago a poor and lowly orphan girl stood with strange emotions before a statue of Benjamin Franklin in Boston. Her bosom heaved and her eyes filled as she whispered between clenched teeth, "Oh, how I would like to make a stone man!" Wm. Lloyd Garrison became her providence and enlarged her opportunity; *she paid for it* in giving to the world the *Madonna with Christ and adoring Angels*, now in the collection of the Marquis of Bute. From her studio in Rome Edmonia Lewis, the colored sculptress, continues to increase the debt of the world to her by her graceful thoughts in chaste marble.[18]

This statement gestures toward the existence, noted previously, of a Black female world of love and ritual in which, as Farah Jasmine Griffin writes, so-called genteel Black women experienced "seeing themselves through each other's eyes."[19]

Further evidence for this phenomenon comes from Jasmine Nichole Cobb, who expands our knowledge about the existence of such communities when she writes about Black women such as Sarah Mapps Douglass (1806–82). Douglass was an educator, philanthropist, and artist whose delicate paintings appeared in intimate albums about her students. These scrapbooks were meant to be shared in female spaces, among and with other Black women. Lisa Farrington discusses Mapps Douglass as part of the first generation of professional Black women artists, which includes Lewis. She writes, "Douglass has the distinction of being known as the earliest documented African-American woman painter. . . . Her command of the medium can be seen in an 1836–37 watercolor of a rose, which she painted in the 'album' of a student, Elizabeth Smith. . . . In Smith's album, Douglass inscribed between her painted rose, 'Lady, while you are young and beautiful, "Forget not" the slave, so shall "Heart's Ease" ever attend you'" (figure 5.1). Cobb concludes that this work "animated the life of the flower to avoid reproducing an image of the Black female body on the page. She denied the prevailing visual animus toward Black Women through the personification of the flower."[20]

The sharing of this imagery between Black women as a token of affection appears frequently in the archive. Evidence for its feminine valence comes from Frederick Douglass, who spoke of "inducing greater pleasure in the experience of rocks than at gazing upon the most luscious flowers in a

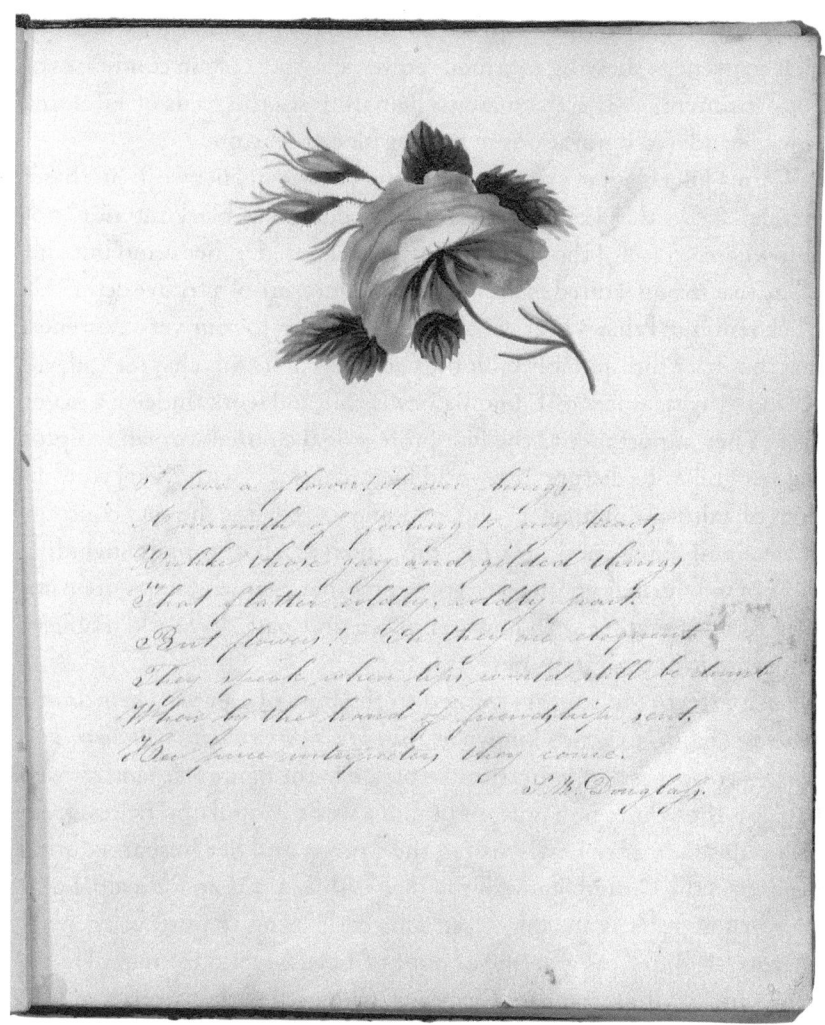

5.1 Sarah Mapps Douglass, *I Love a Flower*, 1833. Water-color and gouache. The Library Company of Philadelphia.

black woman friend's album."[21] Douglass's aversion to viewing the "luscious flowers" echoes, no doubt unwittingly, John Ruskin's assessment of a painting by Dante Gabriel Rossetti made in England circa 1863. Rossetti's pre-Raphaelite painting *Venus verticordia* is a seminude image depicting "the figure of Venus ris[ing] out of a bower of rampant roses and blood-striped honeysuckles all painted with a remarkable insistence on their finger-like tendrils." Ruskin mislabeled the painting, calling it "Flora" and was said to have disliked it precisely for its imagery, claiming that the flowers "were wonderful to me, in their realism; awful—I can use no other word—in their coarseness: showing enormous power, showing certain conditions of non-sentiment."[22] These comments help us to see the seeds of Edmonia Lewis's gendered innovations in making blooms in stone.

Anna Julia Cooper's characterization of Lewis and her work "in chaste marble" shows that Lewis's art was the product of a "black interior" not only where "graceful thoughts" were manufactured in her mind but also where that manufactured matter produced a measure of affective debt. This Black feminist value—that we owe Black women for our very existence, that they have indisputably built the nation—colors this chapter and will be lauded as an aspect of Edmonia Lewis's life and work. Indeed, a major part of her importance as the first professional colored woman sculptor was her ability to disrupt "art world hierarchies ... [with their] conventions of cultural dominance" and, in doing so, redefine the very contours of what and how American art is constituted.[23] All historians, including those of us who may go "in search of our mother's gardens," to quote Alice Walker, must grapple with how to find a usable past.[24] We ask: usable to whom, and for what purposes?

A perfect rose appears pinned to the bust of Lewis's *Portrait of a Woman* (figure 5.2), also known as *Bust of a Woman with a Rose in Her Hair*—a title that highlights the rose placed in the figure's elegantly waved hair. It is thought to be a portrait bust of a wealthy "mulatta" heiress from St. Louis made after Lewis visited the woman and her husband during her trip to the United States in the 1870s. This bust is an individual portrait that appears as an allegorized subject. It seems to portray a generic "Beauty." It differs, as was true of most of Lewis's work, from her French contemporary Jean-Baptiste Carpeaux, who used dark materials such as ebony marble to render his "Black" beauties. As mentioned previously, discerning the racial specificity from other(ed) features—hair, lips, nose—was one way of marking racial difference when looking at figures rendered in white marble. The St. Louis Art Museum, which owns the sculpture now, describes the bust on its website as having "Soft facial features, a delicately carved lace bodice, and wavy hair adorned with a flower communicate not only the taste and beauty of the unknown sitter, but also Edmonia Lewis's skill as a sculptor."[25] The question remains: Was this an image of a specific woman?

Lewis said that she was "wedded to her art." Lewis wore a ring on her finger when she became a more dedicated Catholic in Rome (it is visible in one of the Rocher images discussed in chapter 6). There was a rumor, as well, that she may have been engaged to a man; however, she never became a bride. She did, however, produce at least two sculptures of brides: the full-scale figure of the bride Minnehaha appears in the dual-portrait sculpture with husband, Hiawatha, in Lewis's significantly titled *Hiawatha's Marriage* (1870; see figure 3.2); and a second image, entitled *The Veiled Bride of Spring* (figure 5.3).

Lewis's *Veiled Bride of Spring* was noted in reviews at the time for its secular, pagan qualities. It was displayed as part of a fund-raising bazaar in Cincinnati, Ohio, in 1879. The elaborate veiled allegorical figure that Lewis produced appears to wear roses as much as she does sheer cloth. Other flowers adorn the sculpture. The figure of the veiled woman was an Orientalist trope in art, valued in sculpture as much to showcase one's technical virtuosity as to convey sensuous symbolism. Again, Lewis sought to prove herself as a highly skilled, original sculptor who met (and often exceeded) the bar to claim her place as a consummate artist.

Where the work was shown in Cincinnati, one walked past floral arrangements, pottery, and hand-carved furniture crafted by local women, past china sets, glassware, clothing, quilts, and foodstuffs, before coming upon Lewis's "almost life-size" four-foot-tall (the same height as the sculptor) *Bride*. Apparently, Lewis worked on the sinuous statue for two years while living in Paris. The organizers prominently featured it under a skylight in the southwest corner. The *Daily Star* described the *Bride* as "a female figure, removing the vail [*sic*] of winter from her face, while slightly stooping among the flowers. The expression of the face, which is seen through the vail, is the admirable point about the statue."[26] The sculpture can also be read in a biblical context as a woman wearing a rosary or a crown of roses, an adornment attributed to the Virgin Mary, whom Lewis credited as an inspiration after having been confirmed as a Catholic in 1868. It is worth noting that in Rome, rose festivals are annual events and that during the height of the city's imperial reach, its local warriors wore rose perfume (roses were not at the time equated with femininity). While the iconography of the rose in Western art suggests many contradictory significations, Lewis's lavish, lovingly carved roses read as queerly feminine to my eye. This seems especially true in the very excess of roses that creep up the figure from its base to the crown. The figure virtually undulates with serpentine swags and swerves. The statue's left hand reaches for one of the roped roses below—its thumb and forefinger skimming the top of the ripe rose. The "bride" is barefoot, standing in a contrapposto stance, enwrapped in the full-length "veil" that reveals her full figure and soft-featured face.

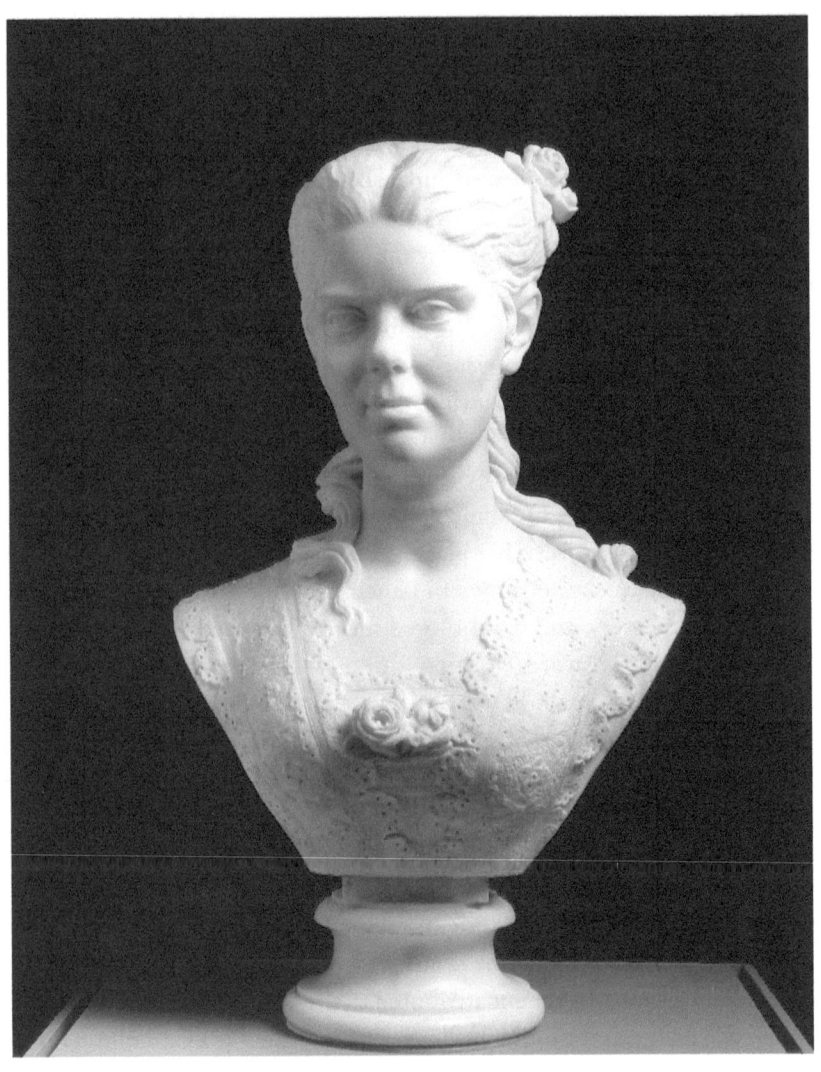

5.2 Edmonia Lewis, *Portrait of a Woman*, 1873. Marble,
23 × 16½ × 11¼ in. Saint Louis Art Museum, St. Louis, Missouri; Museum Minority Artists Purchase Fund and partial
gift of Thurlow E. Tibbs Jr., 1997.

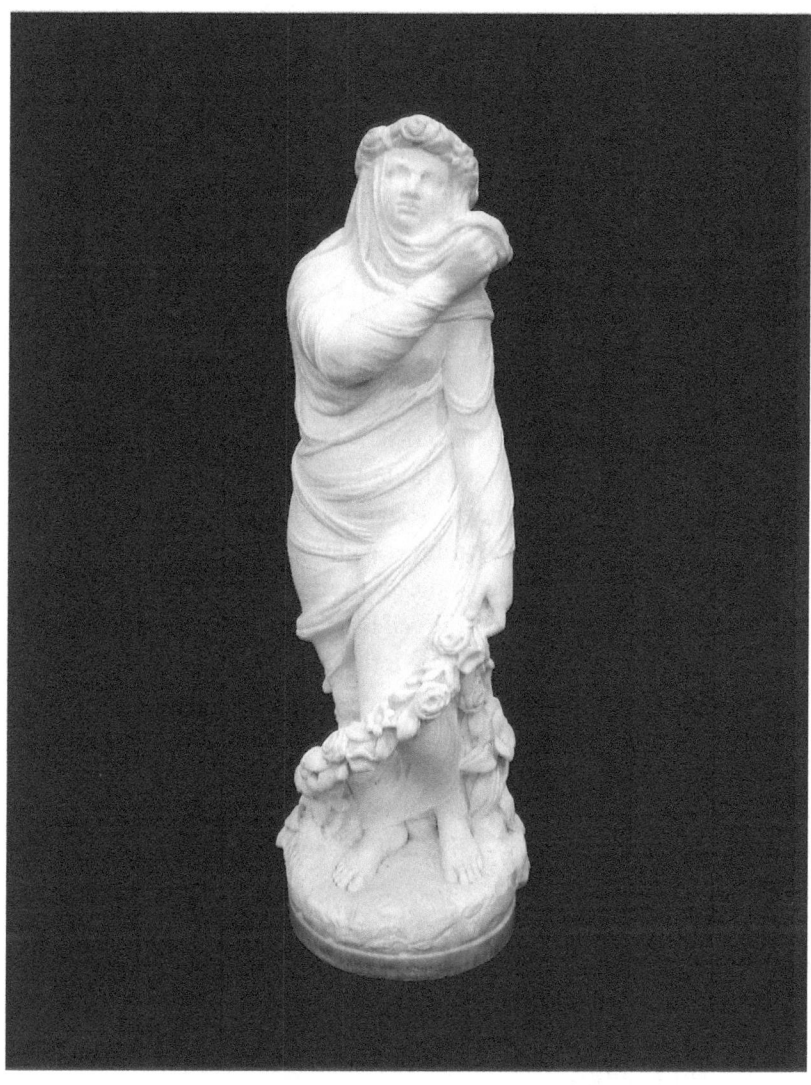

5.3 Edmonia Lewis, *The Veiled Bride of Spring*, 1879. Marble, 48 in. high. Private collection. Purchased at Cowan's Auctions in Cincinnati, Ohio, October 2007.

This work is at once sensual and spiritual; perhaps it functions as a visual equivalent of rhythm and blues, with its roots in religious practice.

Like Lewis's *Cleopatra*, the sculpture moved when its previous resting place in a hospital was moved. One of the physicians there took, was given, or bought Lewis's statue and placed it in his flower garden in Paris, Kentucky, where it became weathered and worn: Much of the statue's delicately sheered, veiled, flower-crowned head withered. Eventually, the statue made its way to the Paris-Bourbon County Library as the "pretty lady" in the corner that greeted visitors. Not until 2006 did Buck Pennington suspect that the statue was Lewis's *Bride of Spring*. He then confirmed his suspicion with the Smithsonian American Art Museum, and in October 2007, it was soon auctioned off by Cowan's Auction House to a private bidder.

The *Cincinnati Enquirer* wrote about Lewis's technically difficult work in creating *The Bride of Spring*:

> The only robe of the figure is a veil, which shows the form to fine advantage, and yet one of the characteristics of the work is its chasteness. The feet are bare, and prettier feet a bride never had. The veil entirely covers the face, and the expression is seen through it. Artists appreciate the difficulty of this work. It combines painting and sculpture. Examined closely the effect is lost, but at the proper distance it is very fine. On the head of the figure and over the veil is a wreath of flowers. Also, in the hand is held a rope of roses, which is thrown carelessly over the limbs."[27]

For a time, the work ended up as a gift to a nun in the Catholic parish. Lewis, like so many of her Victorian colleagues, would have been steeped in floriography—the language of flowers. Her roses signified multiply as they multiplied in her art. With each fold, and unfolding, a fresh interpretation blooms.

Interlude

Simone Leigh

In order to tell the truth, you need to invent what might be missing from the archive, to collapse time, to concern yourself with issues of scale, to formally move things around in a way that reveals something more true than fact.

Simone Leigh

Simone Leigh (b. 1967), who identifies as a (queer) Black American feminist artist and whose work is addressed particularly to other Black women, won the Golden Lion in 2022, the highest honor awarded at the Venice Bi-

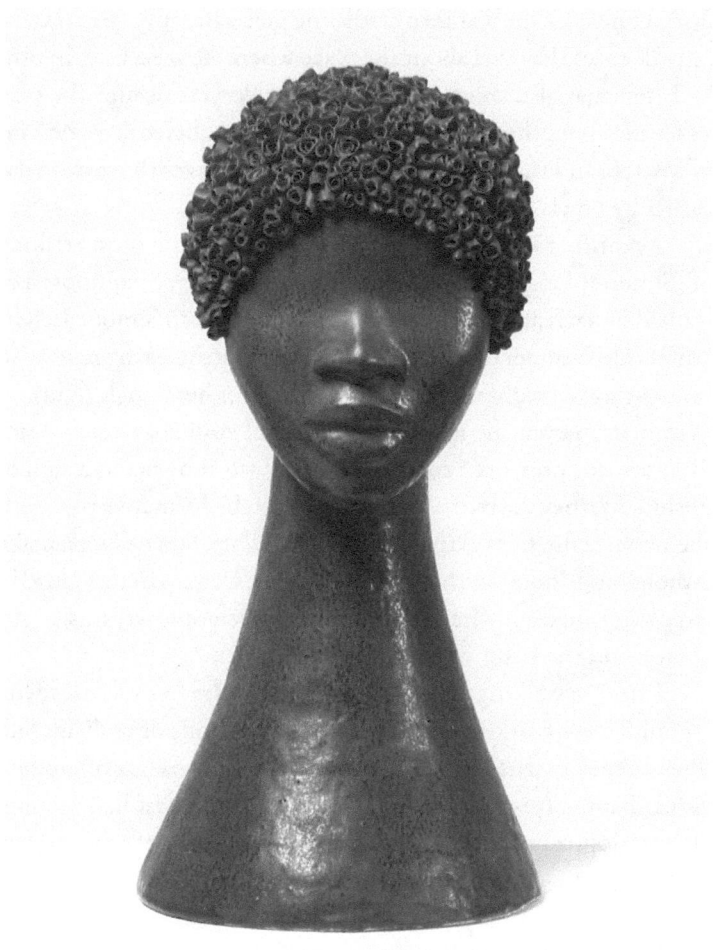

5i.1 Simone Leigh, *107 (Face Jug* series), 2019. Salt-fired stoneware, 19 × 8 × 7 in. Private collection.

ennale, for *Simone Leigh: Sovereignty*. Primarily a sculptor, Leigh includes roses and faces, and roses as faces, as a leitmotif in some of her works; we might view the explicit use of roses in Leigh's sculptures as an iteration of Black women artists who do so dating back to Lewis.

In Leigh's work *107 (Face Jug* series), made in 2019, roses appear as the face-jug's curled crown of hair (figure 5i.1). Each rosette has been made by hand with great care. Viewers are invited to drink in the shimmering blue of the subjectified object with its distinct facial features (full mouth, distinct nose). One wants to cradle the piece, literally, to caress the coiffed "afro'd" roses that curl about the place where we see a face. In other works by Leigh that also showcase rosettes, the flowers occupy the place where a face may be; others sprout from oval forms labeled "cowrie." Leigh's use of rosettes and roses recalls, calls forth, and revives those carved a century earlier by Lewis.

According to Erica Moiah James, "One of the most striking aspects of [Simone] Leigh's *Las Meninas* (2019) is its 'face,' [composed of] a void framed by a wreath of rosettes." James notes that in Simone Leigh's oeuvre, "an untold number of roses, in a range of white hues, from gray-white to a yellow-tinged bright white, frame the faces of her female figures. On close examination even the interior of the facial void is covered in small roses. They are not presented to her as a gift or worn by her as a sign of accomplishment; they are part of her."[28] I see Leigh's formative roses as figures in their own right, figures that also obscure Black female faces, making them "whole" and "hole" in the same framing gesture.[29] In this closed yet open circularity, made of whole holes, her roses resemble wreaths, or doughnuts (Lewis said the latter were her favorite food).

I find it striking that Leigh deploys a surfeit of roses where faces "should" be—working here against conventions of realism. Such canny dis- or replacements are related to the work of roses proffered in the previous chapter. It is no accident, I think, that the first major compendium and catalogue raisonné of Leigh's gorgeous body of work features many stunning close-ups of her handmade roses.[30]

Leigh also uses cowrie shells in much of her artwork. The African-derived cowrie shell, with its pinkish brown center and intricately slit cavity formed around its curving, vertical glossy labia, is vaginal. Leigh herself has noted that she "would describe the cowrie shell as a stand-in for the female body, or a body in general, or a representation of an absence as well as a presence."[31]

The fact that both Lewis and Leigh depict *wreaths* of roses is suggestive. In practice and performance, wreaths bestow many meanings. Among them, in ancient Greece, men participating in symposia often wore crowns of roses, and such decorative emblems "crowned" a person in rituals of becoming. Wreaths were worn on the head, the highest point of the body, as honorific symbols or to mark one's passage to the grave. The wreath of roses, of course, also calls to mind the circular repeated lines from Gertrude Stein's emblem: a rose is a rose is a rose.

Sonia Boyce, who, along with Leigh, took home a top prize at the 2022 at the Venice Biennale for painting, created the picture entitled *She Ain't Holding Them Up, She's Holding On (Some English Rose)*, made in 1986. Erica Moriah James suggests that this work "reminds us of the fraught relationship Black women have had with the racialized feminine interpretations of the rose."[32] As foretold in the controversy surrounding Judy Chicago's *The Dinner Party* (1974–79), including plates that featured faces in the place of vaginal imagery for the two Black women included "at the table," there remains a question about Black women and how to represent our genitalia.[33]

This phenomenon influences the lyrically powerful study of eroticism between women in the Caribbean by Omise'eke Natasha Tinsley, who argues that "flora and female sexuality cease to lie still like *so many things* and begin to turn insistently like *so many actions*—like ongoing choreography that can always be interrupted and redirected"—to which I would add, like so many moving stones. More specifically, this line deepens her earlier discussion about the significance of creative landscapes or "interactive ecologies" in the Caribbean and other colonized spaces that were subject to manipulation—by field hands, as well as painters, planters, and other patriarchs. Tinsley explains:

> Like the women themselves, roses . . . transplanted to the region by European colonists—perform another move to enter this ecology. They travel from the position of commodity to that of living being and interlocutor, talking to the women as the once thingified women talk to the river. This move is not simply a "cultural difference" in viewing landscape but a challenge to the empiricism of empire. As these imaginary mappings refuse the passivity and statis *nature morte* (still life) and *nature à l'état brut* ("unimproved nature"), they . . . reshape land that conquistadors hoped would stand still under their feet.[34]

Further evidence for the symbolic, figurative relations among roses, nonbinary gender relations, and queer fem sexualities comes from Tinsley's second book, *The Color Pynk: Black Femme Art for Survival* (2022), in which she lauds transgender activist Marsha "Pay It No Mind" Johnson's distinct, frequent, and even iconic use of "a haloed . . . crown of roses, carnations, daisies, peonies, and baby's breath." In one of Tinsley's "favorite images [Johnson] poses at Gay Pride in a shimmering, rose-gold gown, crowned with a wide-open wreath of pink and red flowers and adorned with a lavender sash embossed STONEWALL."[35] Why share these sensuous imaginings

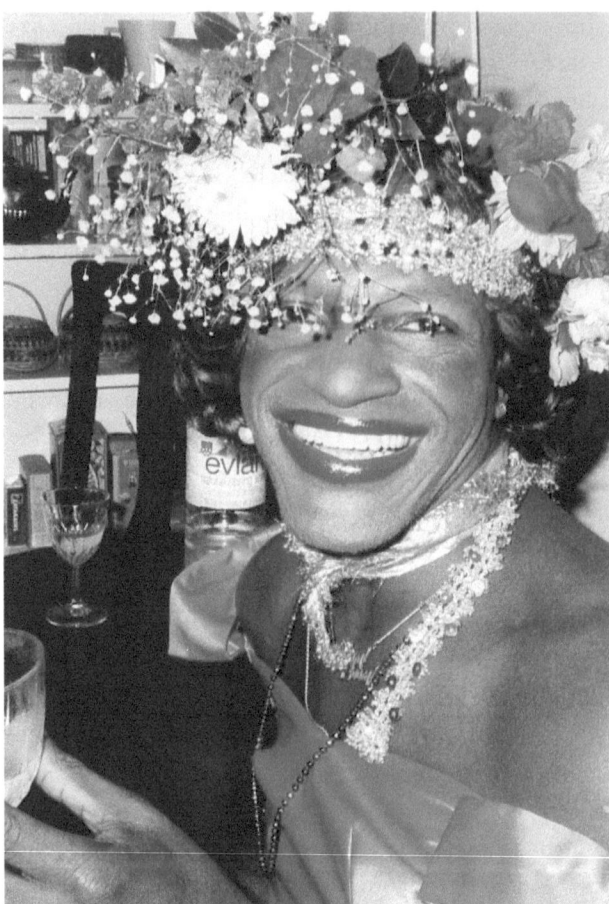

5i.2 *Marsha P. Johnson Wearing a Hot Pink Top While Lifting a Glass and Smiling*, n.d. Photograph by Randy Wicker. Marsha P. Johnson and Sylvia Rivera Collection, The Lesbian, Gay, Bisexual and Transgender Community Center in New York, New York.

about Cleopatra's rose? This distinct detail, hiding in plain sight? Because the rose may be a locus of queer desire. This previously marginalized rose plays in our reading of Lewis and the long legacy of queer looking.[36]

In my queer view (which aligns with the theoretical work Tinsley has done on black fem reading), there is an echo, a rosy resonance between the floral crowns adorning Lewis's *Bride* and those worn by STAR (Street Transvestite Action Revolutionaries) cofounder Marsha P. Johnson (1945–92) (figure 5i.2). The flowers denoted Johnson's spirituality: her belief that friends who had died of AIDS became flowers "living inside her." The Transgender Law Center, in Oakland, California, in conjunction with Gender Justice Leadership Programs, made such a connection when it titled a recent initiative "Roses." The Roses Program grew out of the center's TRUTH Program and its commitment to support trans girls of color. Its philosophy reads:

- We know Black and brown trans girls often experience higher levels of violence at home, school, and work.

- We also know that trans girls and women have BEEN organizing in the community and within their chosen family to keep each other alive and their resources sustainable.

- The Roses program is creating space built by and for trans girls of color, sculpted to not only welcome girls in but to uplift their voices and power.

- We are building a world where trans girls of color are taking the roses for themselves. A world that not only affirms but is safe for trans girls of color and where they can be and find love. . . . Black, brown, and Indigenous trans girls and nonbinary fems between 14–18 throughout the US are welcome to apply!

The creation of a National Transgender Day of Remembrance deploys the anthem "Give Us Our Roses While We're Still Here."[37] For more than two decades this commemoration has afforded participants the opportunity to hold candles and single roses as they march to honor lost members of trans communities. While noting the "myriad meanings of love" (to quote James Baldwin) that cohere in the symbol of the rose, organizers for the Transgender Day of Remembrance add that roses are ritualized in mourning the dead, calling on a tradition dating back at least to the time of Edmonia Lewis.

We shift our senses as we are drawn to the rose as a sign of racialized sexuality. It is as if Lewis, ahead of her time, beckons the coming again of Gertrude Stein's famous reiterating emblem "Rose is a rose is a rose is a rose"—three licks around completes the circular movement.[38] Stein's eternally returning ring, carved on a tree, was poetry in the making, "a completely caressed and addressed noun." And, in that way, she theorized that "civilization begins with a rose" as she wrote in the short narrative "Melanctha"—the

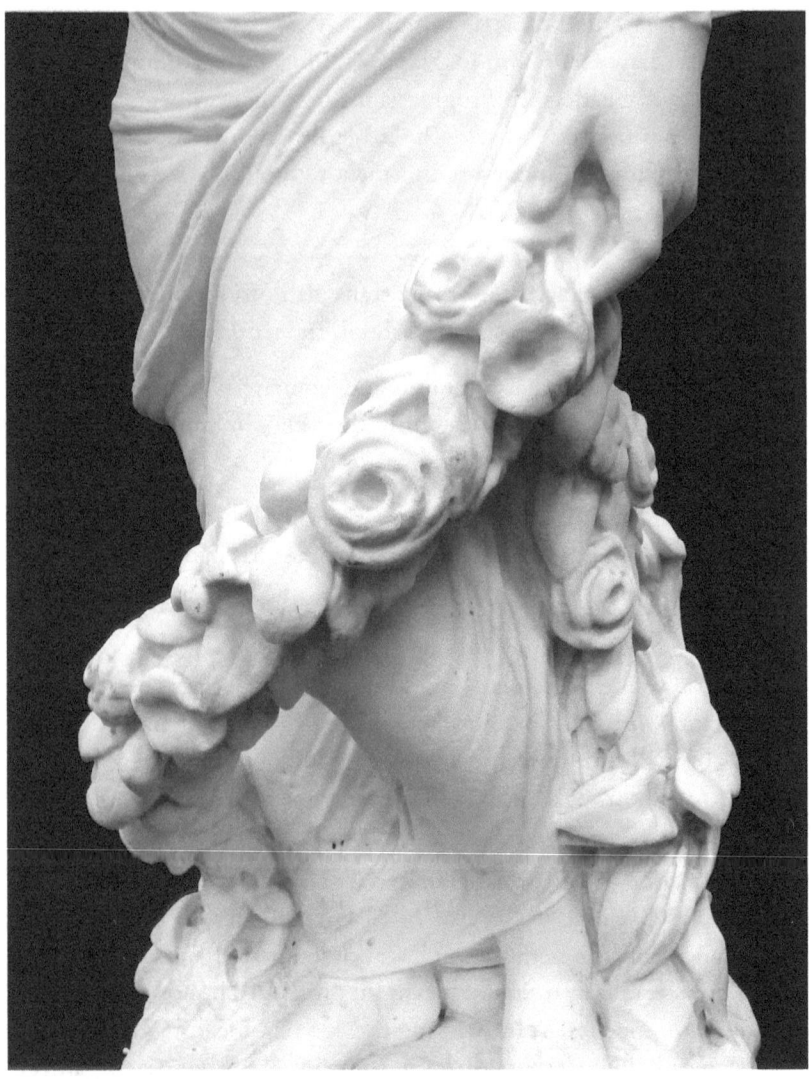

51.3 Detail of garland, Edmonia Lewis, *The Veiled Bride of Spring*, 1879. Marble. Private collection. Purchased at Cowan's Auctions in Cincinnati, Ohio, October 2007.

only "colored woman" featured in Stein's brilliant classic, *Three Lives* (1909), which was published a mere two years after Edmonia's death.[39]

Lewis's marginalized roses reverberate (figures 51.3, 51.4, 51.5): They beckon a queer future that we can read in S. D. Allen's poem (quoted in full below) included in the groundbreaking anthology *Erotique Noire / Black Erotica* (1992). Like the asynchronous attachments, or "time binds," theo-

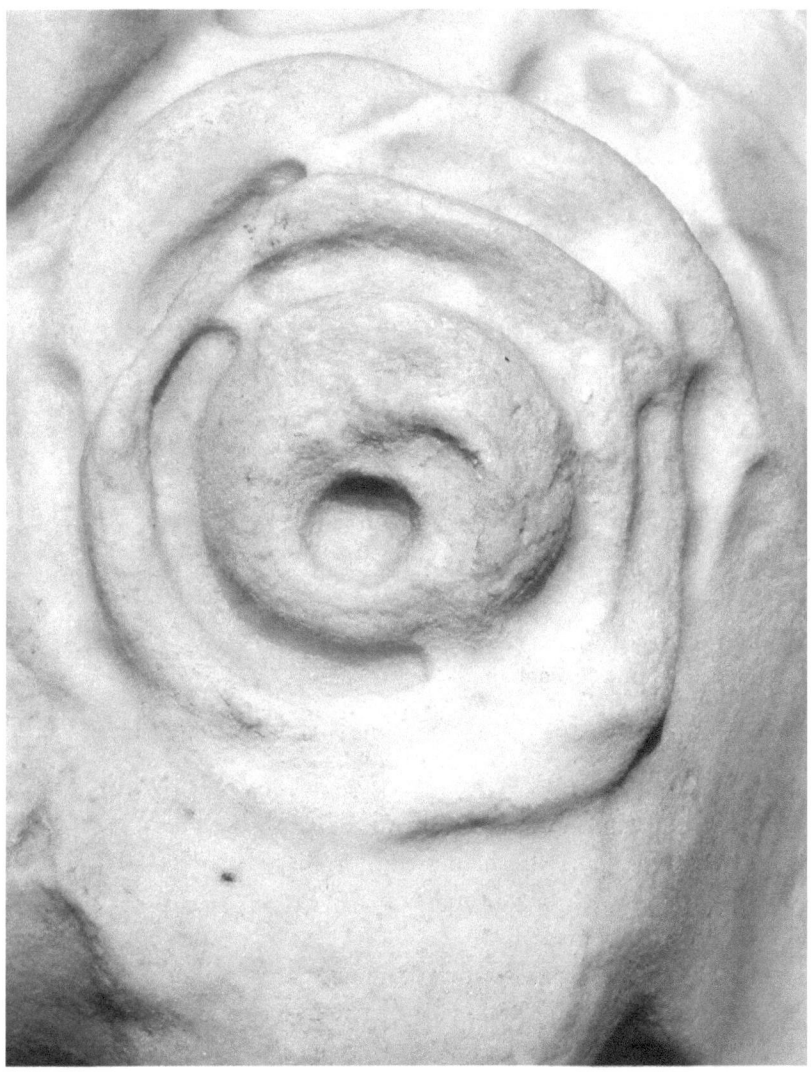

51.4 Close-up of a rose, from Edmonia Lewis, *The Death of Cleopatra* (detail). Photograph by the author.

rized in Elizabeth Freeman's work on queer time, I argue here that we can risk discussing colored women's sexuality in these terms. Such sensuous language confronts what Farah Jasmine Griffin called "the burden of a historical legacy that deems Black women 'over-sexed' [thereby] making the reclamation of the black female body difficult."[40] And yet there is a reclamation, a declaration, to be carried out: even for our single rose, Miss Edmonia Lewis.

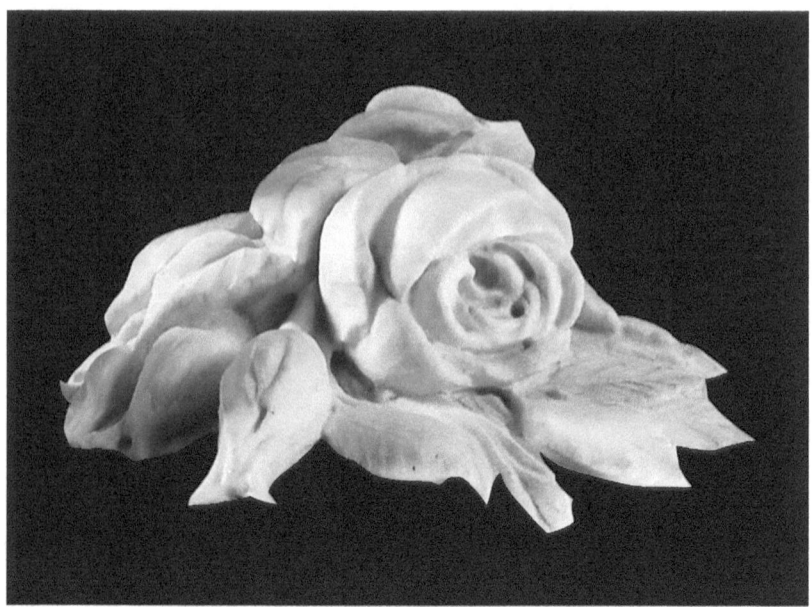

5i.5 Rose, from Edmonia Lewis, *Poor Cupid* (detail). Digital image by yétúndé ọlágbajú.

A Single Rose

In my solitude on this eve, resisting capture by fatigue
I watch this vulnerable blood red thorn head
And contemplate how brutal, how naive it is
For love to conquer all.
I know the babe with weapon piercing heart,
The seduction in the dark with a gentle scent rising.
Dared by desire to feel, I forget and stare,
And stroke, hold too close, and love.
Stoking this long stem softly, pains
Toiling to keep it, tires
For the perfect beauty of the guarded bloom briefly stays
Held inside my vase—then fairly fades.
Not to fret, it is truly a loss without regret
The warmth tonight will bring a flame
To light a new day once again
I turn in.[41]

About Photography

The commercial value of the human face was never tested to such an extent as it is at the present moment in these handy photographs. . . . No man, or woman either, knows but some accident may elevate them to the position of hero of the hour and send up the value of their countenances to a degree they never dreamed of.

Andrew Wynter, "Cartes de Visite," 1869

6

Edmonia Lewis's human face accrued value when it was transformed into a handy photograph. Her countenance on cartes de visite crossed the Atlantic and traveled across the United States and throughout Europe, increasing her fame—a head of her time, to echo chapter 1. She again has become the heroine of the hour whose countenance possesses a value of which she may never have dreamed. Much of the fanfare she received was the result not only of her sculpted handiwork but also of her canny use of a new technology: photography. Although portraits of artists have existed for millennia in the form of paintings and sketches (whether by the artists themselves or by others), in the nineteenth century visual and theatrical artists began to have themselves photographed for professional portraits. As print culture expanded and photography became more affordable, the use of the medium to advertise and publicize one's self and one's art became increasingly common. As with so many inventions, photography introduced new vocabularies and ways of seeing and therefore knowing.[1]

It should come as no surprise, then, that during the second half of the nineteenth century, Lewis relied on photography to make her art, to mark herself as a professional artist, and to cultivate an international following. Photography contributed another tool through which we know of her existence—of her exploits and her art—and by which we can access some vestige of her verity. The eleven extant photographs of her are objects in their own right: They help tell a story about her. Nearly every text that discusses Lewis and her work incorporates a photographic portrait; indeed, sometimes these narratives include a photograph of her as prima facie evidence of her existence. These portraits of Lewis are "image-objects," to use Siobhan Angus's term—made things as well as interpretative works.[2]

Photographic technology affected virtually every aspect of nineteenth-century global culture. Its advent shaped a panoply of discourses and events from civil society to law and medicine, from journalism to individual memories. The invention of this technological medium helped to transform scientific inquiry, generating new areas of study such as anthropology, psychology, and criminality. Photography also changed artistic practice. Lewis took part in this epistemic shift. In fact, Edmonia Lewis and the photographic era came of age together. A mere five years separates the "birth" of photography in 1839 and Lewis's birth on July 4, 1844. Lewis's work and life were concomitant with the spread of photography among increasing numbers of people, and she capitalized on the use of this new medium to sustain her artistic career and passions. The concentric overlap between Lewis's life and the age of photography was significant: It facilitated her identity as a modern diasporic subject.

Although many people feared that the picture-taking possibilities of the new photographic machines would decimate the desire for other modes of representation—such as art made by awls, brushes, pencils, and human hands—it turned out that the eventually cost-effective technology helped to prop up and promote, rather than completely replace, "traditional" or "classical" modes of portraiture produced through painting, drawing, and sculpture. During Edmonia's lifetime, sculptors began to use photographs rather than, or in addition to, death masks, plaster casts, and live models. Indeed, Lewis relied heavily on photographic images in producing her "life-like sculpturing," to quote a term from an 1870s review of her work.

Among those who hailed photography's potential was none other than Lewis's friend Frederick Douglass, who became the most photographed formerly enslaved person of the century. In his brilliant treatise on photography published in 1849, he asserted, "It seems to us next to impossible for white men to take likenesses of black men, without most grossly exaggerating their distinctive features. And the reason is obvious. Artists, like all other white persons, have adopted a theory respecting the distinctive features of negro physiognomy. We have heard many white persons say that 'negroes look all alike.'"[3] He saw the mimetic possibilities of photography as a means to counter racist representations.

In one of the few surviving letters we have in Lewis's hand, written to Maria Weston Chapman from Rome on February 5, 1867, the artist comments on her use of a photograph in the process of creating a sculpture. Lewis writes, "You were quite right in your criticism and as soon as I have the group all modeled I will send you another photograph."[4] A few other letters reprinted in newspapers of the time document Lewis asking potential Black women commissioners for frontal and profile images of a living person they wished her to sculpt; and she relied on a photograph of President Lincoln before his murder to create her posthumously made *Bust of Lincoln* (1871). Marla Novo claims that "as early as 1867, [Lewis] had sent photographic reproductions of her *Wooing and Wedding of Hiawatha* to the newspaper office of the *San Francisco Chronicle*."[5] Each of these instances shows that Lewis used photography to make her sculptures.

We also know that Lewis relied on a few photographs to create her well-received bust of Col. Robert Gould Shaw.[6] Lewis was able to construct a marble portrait bust of him that the Shaw family deemed superb—even superior to many other busts made of their famous son after his death. In fact, the family commissioned the studio photographer Augustus Marshall (who later took pictures of Lewis) to photograph the beautiful bust of their son that Lewis had sculpted. She sold copies of the photograph to those who could not afford to buy one of the hundred plaster casts of this work which she sold for $15 a piece. Recall that it was the sale of these casts that propelled Lewis to the top of her artistic circle in Boston and, shortly thereafter, helped to finance her move to Rome.[7] Thus, Lewis's skill as a sculptor allowed her to profit from this white man's image, in a reversal of the longer history of so many white men and women who relied on the labor of Black folks to build their wealth and careers.

Lewis joined a very small cadre of artists who relied on the professional photograph to produce modern portraits of "colored artists." Looking at these formal studio photographs allows us to learn about Lewis as sculptor. The photograph had the ability to animate affect, to produce impressions, to develop professional standards, to challenge property rights, to create scientific facts, to change journalism, and occasionally to propagate portraits as forms of "vision and justice."[8] Although the photographers with whom Lewis worked were white men, she no doubt knew about the photographic studios operated by Black men that existed throughout the United States, including that of the well-known daguerreotypist who owned a studio in downtown Hartford, Connecticut, Augustus Washington (1820–75). Lewis's knowledge about the images made by "colored folk" who worked behind the camera as well as in front of it may have impacted her own view of herself as a portrait maker. Certainly, she saw value in having her own photographic portrait taken and reproduced. We are fortunate to have so many images of her, even if we may wish for more. More important, the photographic prints that have survived portray Lewis in the best light (no pun intended).

In each photograph, she poses herself in a dignified stance. Her countenance seems calculated to counter the many photographs taken in her time that were made to create negative evidence (pun intended) of visual differences thought to indicate a propensity for depravity inherent in a subject's perceived bodily attributes. Over the course of the century, scientific researchers—those with vested interests in medicine and ethnology (to say nothing of white supremacy)—began to use photography (literally, light writing) as "scientific proof" of these differences.[9] It is in this context that we can begin to appreciate how significant photographic portraits of those freed and free subjects such as Frederick Douglass and Edmonia Lewis were in what became a debate about inscribing truths in images. Both Douglass and Lewis understood that their photographic images played a key role in this embattled representational drama. Both deployed themselves as sitters for photographic portraits such that the negatives presumed by dominant ideologies became "a form of resistance on behalf of the normally unpictured."[10]

Before proceeding with a close reading of selected photographic portraits of Lewis, I want to say a bit more about how the medium of sculpture came to be cathected with the new medium of photography. We may be surprised to learn that sculpture was among the first subjects of the daguerreotype.[11] Named for its French inventor, Louis J. M. Daguerre (1787–1851), this early photographic process required objects in its view to remain absolutely still for at least fifteen minutes in order to capture the image on iodized copper. While daguerreotype technology necessitated slow, long takes and almost absolute stillness, information about the process spread with a rapidity that is difficult to fathom. "By the spring of 1839," Deborah Willis notes, "newspapers in the United States began to publish accounts of Americans experimenting with the daguerreotype process . . . by late August, newspapers in Paris and London were describing Daguerre's process in detail. So extraordinary was this development that the *Great Western*, one of the fastest transatlantic steamers of the early Industrial Age, docked in New York on September 10,1839, carrying aboard French and English newspapers filled with descriptions of the daguerreotype process."[12] Thus, the daguerreotype quickly became a sensation throughout the circum-Atlantic world.

In one infamous set of daguerreotypes taken by photographer J. T. Zealy and produced in 1850 in South Carolina, an enslaved person named Renty Taylor and several others from the same plantation—Jem, Alfred, Deilia, George, Fassena Drana, and Jack—were photographed as specimens of a negative racial type for the work of the Harvard ethnologist Dr. Louis Agassiz, a former student of the naturalist Georges Cuvier.[13] Before the lens, wielded almost as weapon by Zealy, Renty Taylor and his relatives and colleagues, all enslaved, were doubly objectified by becoming photographs. Each of these individuals had to endure interminable sessions in which they did not move so that the camera could capture them. They had to repeat the process as they were shot from the front, the side, and the back. They became specimens as "the daguerreotype process proved a useful tool for dissection as it insisted upon a static, fixed subject."[14] The excruciating effort required to keep their bodies absolutely immobile served as part of their continuing extractive labor, which they, as enslaved chattel, as objectified "things," had little power to resist. In the photographic studio–turned–scientific lab, they were required to gaze directly into the white man's apparatus. They were forced to transform before the eyes of these lenses. Ultimately, the actual daguerreotypes were hidden from view in the museum as each one was kept in an expensive bifold case lined with embossed velvet. Suzanne Schneider describes these photographs as pornographic, noting that the full-frontal, full-body nude shots of the men in the frame differed from phrenology's fetishization of the head to focus on sex as the primary distinguishing feature.[15]

Still, the entire enterprise resulted in what we can only describe as a profoundly dehumanizing performance: It included being stripped naked to reveal their musculature as a means of instantiating their status as different from that of their presumed white overlords. Agassiz's scientific inquiry sought to secure his perpetually insecure position as a white supremacist (but it also betrayed his lurid interest in these bared bodies). Cruelly, as others have argued, the photographed were conscripted to perform this work as "evidence" of the inferiority that then justified their enslavement. This technology developed during an age of slavery: It was deployed to uphold white supremacy. As Lisa Gail Collins reminds us, "Early photography and the institution of slavery are linked . . . photography was being used in efforts to document the essential difference of people of African descent. . . . Photography is burdened by [its] legacy of visual violence."[16]

Harvey Young analyzes the production of Zealy's daguerreotypes in his book *Embodying Black Experience* (2010) by focusing on the length of time the enslaved "objects" were forced to sit or stand still.[17] He explains that "in conflating sculptural objects and enslaved subjects, [such] practices accent the inability of figurative modalities of representation alone to address the structural logic of slavery and its ongoing effects."[18] As many scholars have noted, these images were uncovered in the 1970s as part of the holdings at Harvard University's Peabody Museum (which Agassiz helped to found) and became the basis for a lengthy court case that ultimately concluded in the restitution of the photographs to family members descended from the enslaved. In being removed from the holdings of the museum, they became ancestors, family: no longer mere "scientific profiles, Negroid types, [examples for] anthropological debate, and photographic subjects," to quote selected titles from Carrie Mae Weems's *From Here I Saw What Happened, and I Cried* (1995–96), a brilliant series Weems created that appropriates Zealy's images, enlarges them into chromogenic prints, tints them in red, and etches text on the glass frames as a means of reclaiming via literally reframing them. "Through these reinterpretations, [Weems] aims to restore a level of humanity and dignity to these men and women who historically have had no voice."[19]

Nineteenth-century photographic images of Black people—those enslaved and even those who were free—transform our understanding of race and vision in profound ways.[20] As Leigh Raiford explains, "Since its inception in the United States in 1839, photography has been both a cultural site of subjugation and a technology of liberation. Throughout the nineteenth century, African Americans understood the capacity of the medium to publicly convey notions of black criminality and inferiority as well as to project images of dignity and gentility. Scientists used photographs as visible evidence to support theories of anthropomorphic difference and racial hierarchy. Abolitionists circulated photographs of 'whip-scarred' slaves to solicit sympathy, anti-Confederate sentiment, and financial contributions."[21] Among the most famous formerly enslaved subjects to sit for the picture-taking process (and of their own volition) were Frederick Douglass and Sojourner Truth. They sat for portraits from which carefully cultivated images of integrity and respectability emerged. These images featured their subjects in trim clothing, with proper posture, within genteel interior settings. "With their trappings of middle-class domesticity, these photographs served as public interventions in racial dialogues by indicating the respectable private lives of African Americans."[22] They circulated in public arenas in pamphlets, as cartes de visite, and as frontispieces in books.

It was also during the nineteenth century that photographs began to be used as facial recognition devices in legal cases, as dramatized in Dion Boucicault's popular 1859 play, *The Octoroon*, which was the first such dramatic work to feature a camera in the plot of the production. The widespread circulation of such photographs increased only after the repeal of the Fugitive Slave Act, which had made it dangerous for photographs of Black people to circulate with frequency in public domains.[23] The photographic images of colored people in the nineteenth century were thus various, often violent, and always participating in an economy where visuality (sight as a social fact) was accruing value through the medium of photography. How, then, to see the image of a figure like Edmonia Lewis?

To date, we know of eleven photographic portraits of Lewis that exist in archives.[24] As mentioned above, Lewis used photography in distinct ways: to develop her sculptural works (like many other sculptors of her day, she intermittently relied on photographs to make her sculptural portrait busts), to promote these objects (for example, she sold pictures of her sculpture of Col. Robert Gould Shaw in addition to plaster versions of the piece to finance her initial trip to Italy and may have seen a photo of him as a source), and to advertise herself as a professional artist. At times, she chose to gift photographs of herself as intimate mementos sent to other women. In using the international mail to transport her image across the Atlantic and beyond, Lewis showed, as Leigh Raiford notes, why "Black photographic self-representation must be understood . . . as a constant dialectic between private and public, personal and political, fiction and biography."[25] As an astute artist who lived from the sale of her work, Lewis no doubt thought about her own photographic portraits as complex representations. She keenly understood the role her own image played in other viewers' evaluations of her work and would have worked to shape and deploy her own image. She commissioned several of these self-portraits to advertise herself as a professional artist. These photos of Lewis have been kept in private archives, displayed in public places (such as museums) and on book covers, sent through the mail, and posted online, and may be held close to the bosom of many admirers.

Photographic images taken of Lewis were made into cartes de visite. The carte de visite was patented by André-Adolphe-Eugène Disdéri in 1854. Made of an albumen silver print from a glass negative, the photographs could be printed in multiples. Cartes de visite were relatively inexpensive to make and were printed on paperboard measuring approximately 7.5 × 9.5 inches, or sometimes smaller. Cartes de visite were printed in sets of four or eight, resembling a contact sheet. Images could then be cut and mounted on cardstock to create the carte de visite, which people left behind as evidence of having visited another's home or business. Sojourner Truth famously said she "sold the shadow to support the substance"—in other words, she sold her photograph to support her body and life.

Mathew Brady, who photographed Lewis's acquaintance Harriet Hosmer (see figure 3.3) and also gave us some of the now famous images of the Civil War, made cartes de visite in his New York studio.[26] The *London Times* reported in 1862 that "America swarms with the members of a mighty tribe of 'cameristas,' and the Civil War has developed their business in the same way that it has given an impetus to the manufacturers of metallic air-tight coffins and embalmers of the dead."[27] The afterlives of photographs are not always detrimental: The nineteenth-century practice of postmortem and memento mori (literally, "remember you must die") photography served as a form of commemoration and keepsake.[28] Given the long takes required for early photography, some eerie images of the living and the dead in the same frame resulted in the bodies of the living members being out-of-focus in comparison to those of the dead, who remained still longer and therefore could be rendered more vividly for the viewer. There are multiple ways to render the connections between the ubiquitous creative technologies of sculpture and photography: They were models and mirrors for each other: Photographic poses mimicked sculptural ones; "still" sculptures were literal models for photographs; photographs served as models for sculptural portraits; and so on.

In her own portraits, Lewis's various poses speak volumes. She appears as a middle-class subject (well dressed, formal, assertive), as a working professional (in her talma or velvet sculptor's cape), and as a woman of stature as she poses confidently with her arms folded over her chest, standing in a white dress and worn work boots. We are fortunate that the fame that grew from Lewis's art and entrepreneurial savvy enabled her to garner these professional photographs of herself. Her portraits complicate and enrich the archives of nineteenth-century women to the extent that her image is discordant with contemporary stereotypical images of sculptors, African American women, Indigenous women, Catholic subjects, and others. As an aggregate, these photographs of Lewis expand the bounded notions of the era: She is, by turns and at once, seen as an educated Indian, a woman sculptor, a Black Ojibwe, a mannish woman, an American expat, a pagan Catholic, a photographed free "colored" person. In truth, as with any of us, it would be difficult to portray Lewis's complicated and changing subjectivities in a single photograph or even in a series of them.

The first known photographs of Lewis were taken in Boston, then Chicago, and finally (as a curator at the Walters Art Museum in Baltimore discovered recently) in Rome. Lewis poses her petite frame differently in each print. These precious images provide proof of the artist's perspicacity, her prominence, her professionalism, and her profound will to persist. I am sure that there are more photographs awaiting retrieval, hidden in plain sight in basements and casements, at the bottom of glove boxes or steamer trunks, behind bookshelves and under floorboards, wrapped in hankies embroidered with roses, in attics and any manner of places where the remnants of the past accumulate.

Eventually, after she had become a celebrated artist, Lewis was able to command self-portraits by major photographers of her day, such as Rome's Fratelli d'Alessandri, who also photographed Pope Pius IX. Some of the earliest known photographic portraits (perhaps as early as 1864) were taken by Augustus Marshall, whose studio was located on Tremont Street in Boston, near hers. Then, photographer Henry Rocher took a series of photos, used in her cartes de visite, at his studio on State Street in Chicago. Virtually all of these photographic portraits of the artist date from the late 1860s to the mid-1870s—the zenith of Lewis's celebrity and the most productive decade of her career. I discuss several of them in detail below, isolating them to think about each shot.

Lewis worked in two Tremont Street locations in Boston—at number 89 and then number 120. The famous Studio Building that housed various artists was located at 110 Tremont Street, making the entire area into a Bohemian district. Augustus Marshall, a white photographer, advertised his studio as being among the best in the city for its beautiful light. In one image Marshall made, Lewis sits at a circular table covered with a dark damask cloth (figure 6.1). She gazes out at the viewer. Her doe eyes with their deep round pupils compel the viewer to contemplate her inner thoughts. No reference to her profession is visible within the frame; rather, this is simply a composed picture of a sagacious young woman sitting in an upright wooden chair wearing a puffed-sleeved crisp white dress. According to the Smithsonian National Museum of African American History and Culture, where the photograph resides, on the reverse of the carte de visite are graphite inscriptions including "Edmonia / Lewis / Sculptor" and the photographer's studio information in black ink: "MARSHALL / PHOTOGRAPHER, / Studio Building, / Cor. Tremont and Bromfield Sts., / BOSTON."

In another photograph from Marshall's studio (not included here) she occupies a circular heavy wooden chair bradded with golden fringe. It was this photographic image that the US Postal Service used to create Lewis's 2022 Black Heritage commemorative stamp (see figure 7.5). In this photograph, Lewis gazes beyond the frame, looking slightly over her left shoulder while seated in a curved chair made of dark wood; a fringe is affixed with brass brads to what we presume is a mahogany chair rail. This photograph is faded from exposure, making it seem as if Lewis's form is floating in front of the washed-away background. Her face is placid, and yet I detect a slight sparkle in her dark eyes. Light from above (key light) illuminates the just-off-center part of her lustrous waves of hair. The definitive vertical line of the part in her hair contrasts with the gentle tumble of undulating curls. Her silk cravat, crisply knotted and flaring down in two flat blades, creates a sharp contrast with the puffed bishop sleeves of her white muslin dress.

In the series of photographs taken by Henry Rocher in Chicago in the early 1870s, Lewis can be seen dressed in her dandified masculine work attire and

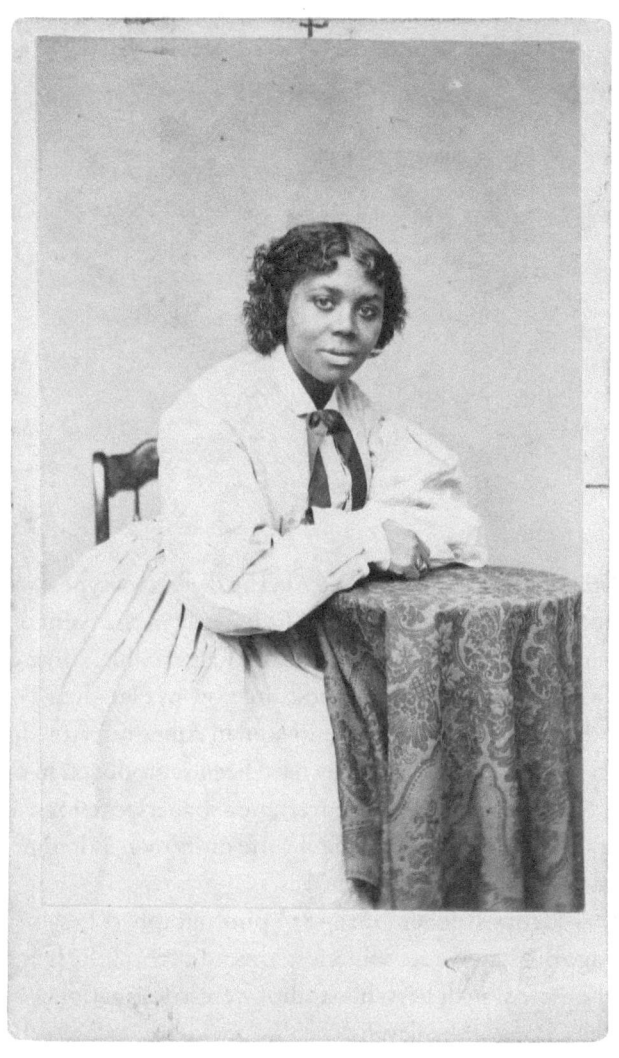

6.1 Augustus Marshall, carte de visite of Edmonia Lewis, made in Boston, ca. 1864–72. Albumen silver print on wove paper and cardboard, (image) 3⅝ × 2¼ in. Smithsonian National Museum of African American History and Culture, Washington, DC (2020.20.5).

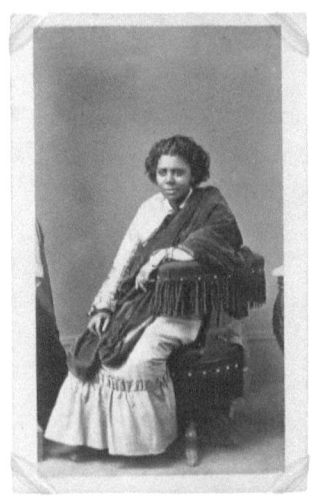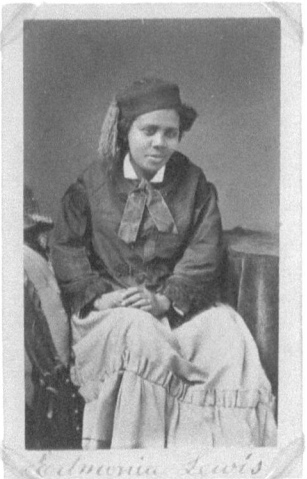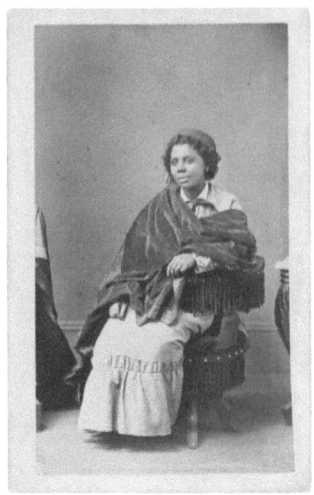

other outfits (figures 6.2–6.6). The daguerreotypes were printed as eight 3 × 2.5 inch images. Each can fit handily in the palm of one's hand. These cartes de visite feel more delicate than durable. Most of these tiny prints from Rocher's Chicago studio are now in Harvard's Fogg Museum; a few others are owned by the Smithsonian American Art Museum, and two are in private collections. They have been reproduced in our imaginations as well as printed on book covers, newspapers, catalogs, and elsewhere. Her image proliferates, taking on a life of its own as it appears across so many disparate platforms and places.

Henry Rocher (1826–87) photographed Lewis in downtown Chicago on State Street sometime around 1870, at the height of his career and the ascension of hers; his studios were a destination for famous actors and celebrities of the day. Rocher "was widely viewed," scholar David Shields reports, "as the most artistic portrait photographer of the 1870s . . . whose strength was posing. His abilities earned him exhibition gold medals in Vienna, Amsterdam, London, New York, and Philadelphia in the 1870s. His eminence was such that his work became a kind of benchmark against which subsequent photographers measured the development of the art of portraiture."[29] Because he photographed theatrical actors as well as celebrities such as Lewis, Rocher, like most of the studio photographers of the era, deployed props and accessories to enhance and stylize the participants in these portrait scenarios. Props seen in his portraits of Lewis include an ornate armless chair, cloth-covered tables, a velvet divan, and a tufted, fringed double-barreled chair with brass or copper brads. Such

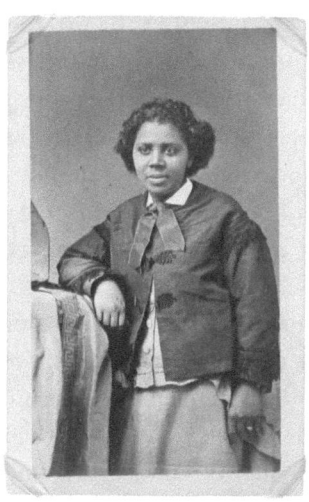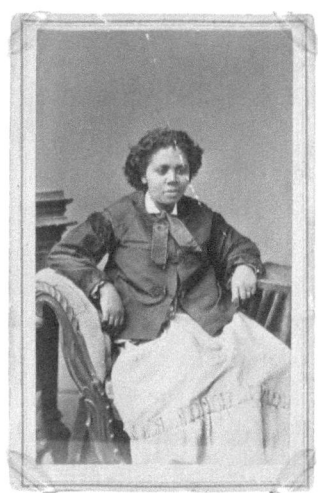

6.2 Henry Rocher, Edmonia Lewis, ca. 1870. Albumen silver print on card, 4 × 2½ in. Wisconsin Historical Society Archives, Madison.

6.3 Henry Rocher, Edmonia Lewis, ca. 1870. Albumen silver print on card, 3½ × 2¹⁄₁₆ in. Acquired by Harvard Art Museums / Fogg Museum, transfer from Special Collections, Fine Arts Library, Harvard College Library, Cambridge, Massachusetts; bequest of Evert Jansen Wendell, 2010.

6.4 Henry Rocher, Edmonia Lewis, ca. 1870. Albumen silver print on card, 3⁹⁄₁₆ × 2¹⁄₁₆ in. Acquired by Harvard Art Museums / Fogg Museum, transfer from Special Collections, Fine Arts Library, Harvard College Library, Cambridge, Massachusetts; bequest of Evert Jansen Wendell, 2010.

6.5 Henry Rocher, Edmonia Lewis, ca. 1870. Albumen silver print on card. Courtesy of a private collector.

6.6 Henry Rocher, Edmonia Lewis, ca. 1870. Albumen silver print on card, 3⅝ × 2 in. Acquired by Harvard Art Museums / Fogg Museum, transfer from Special Collections, Fine Arts Library, Harvard College Library, Cambridge, Massachusetts; bequest of Evert Jansen Wendell, 2010.

expensive "domestic" furnishings and decor helped to place the sitter in a refined context. This tradition also played out in painting, and these Rocher furnishings remind one of images wherein bejeweled enslaved persons play a part in propping up their propertied owners, serving as signifying objects of wealth, such as in the portrait of Elihu Yale (ca. 1719) that hung for years in the Corporation Room of Yale University in honor of the generous eighteenth-century benefactor for whom the university is named.[30]

The performative power of the pose is also part of the mise-en-scène, or costumed theatrical still. In these photographs, we can read the innovative specialties of both Rocher and Lewis. The photographs teem with texture and torque, as do some of her sculptures. Lewis turns her head, and we in turn project movement—imagining her body in motion and stasis. We are in the space of intermedial arts that complicated early art historical genres and techniques. As a resolutely neoclassical sculptor familiar with the rhetoric of the pose, anatomy, and bodily characteristics, Lewis had to be aware of her own and others' "differences" of race, gender, sexuality, and the like. One might try imitating these poses to see how they feel and imagine how Lewis might have felt being so posed. The body leans forward, the head is turned slightly toward the viewer, the arm is propped on a high table.

Lewis advertised not only her work but herself as a popular figure. The purpose of commissioning and printing the photographs may have been to spur sales, but I do not think they were made with only monetary profit in mind; rather, they were crafted with a Black gay's gaze as well. Edmonia Lewis looks out at us, changing our views. Each time I glance at these images, I think of them as interactive, moving moments at once personal, political, and performative. The ongoing circulation of images of Lewis, whether through digital distribution or other means, continues to foment desire for her. What sticks out for me in these photographs are Edmonia's elbows. Her nonchalant and slightly jaunty posture, elbows protruding from the picture plane . . . her crossed arms, a gesture of protection, guardedness, a gesture that hides her chest. This image reads as a strong, "unladylike" pose, a powerful and self-conscious stance.

The slight cock of her head in several of these photos makes it appear as if she is giving her viewers what we call in Black vernacular the "side eye"—along with a wry smile, the corner of her luscious lips curved upward. She appears defiant, certainly self-assured. These are modern poses befitting their wondrous modern subject. In 1877, Rocher explained to a British journal the effort necessary to get the public to accept his new style of portraiture: "In regard to the taste of the public: I will say that one or two years ago, I often countered difficulties upon showing the public what we call our 'composition' pictures. Many at that time were too accustomed to the old stereotyped photographic pose, but now it can be plainly observed that not one out of a hundred want this old-fashioned pose, but gladly accept what I think proper to make for them."[31] This description points to the collaborative, performative innovations possible in the studio setting, as well as the role the increasingly professional photographer took in creating the image.

Her costume in figure 6.4 consists of a cravat, lusciously draped heavy masculine sculptor's velvet cape—a talma to protect against the dirty white dust of the sculptor's labor—and a voluminous skirt with a nipped waist. In this Rocher carte de visite, she wears sculptor's clothes designed to protect the artist from the messy work that inevitably involved an excess of marble dust from chiseling. If one looks closely at the photographs of Lewis sitting in a chair in Rocher's studio, one can see that her feet hover just above the floor, suggesting her petite stature. The velvet cloak she dons almost overtakes her slight frame with its substantial drapery.

The 2008 exhibition at the National Portrait Gallery in Washington, DC, *Let Your Motto Be Resistance: African American Portraits*, included several of the cartes de visite of Edmonia Lewis produced by the Rocher Studio—a testament to her importance in the Black imagination. It is in this light that I wish to think about how photographs of Lewis have allowed her to *resist* both death and stereotypes, if not (temporary) erasure. Unfortunately, we do not know the sequence of the photographs taken in Rocher's studio (did she sit first, then stand? When did she don the hat? At what moment did she discard the velvet cape?) What we do know, however, is that Lewis posed in different "guises" and sentiments. I suspect she donned the hat toward the end of the session so as not to muss her coiffed natural hairstyle. The various poses lead the viewer to conjecture and imagine the staging of the images.

Gwendolyn DuBois Shaw first wrote about Rocher's photographs of Lewis in her book *Portraits of a People* (2006), noting, "The photograph embodies what philosopher Walter Benjamin has called a 'spell of personality' with its presentation of Lewis as a worldly woman, independent and liberated, artistic and original."[32] Writing of about six of the Rocher studio images of Lewis, Shaw observes: "One of the oft-repeated images that has become iconic of Lewis is the one in which she is posed standing with one arm resting on a table covered by cloth with a Greek key border [figure 6.5]...."

Her head is encircled by loosely curling dark locks of shortly cropped hair falling to just about her collar. Her heart-shaped face is distinguished by a broad forehead and firm brow. The unsmiling lips are purposely together, casting a faint shadow over a small, pointed chin."[33]

How does Lewis's image fit in a critical genealogy of photographs of other professional art sculptors of her day? While many of the predominately white sculptors were photographed standing next to their work, no such photograph of Edmonia Lewis has been found. She does, however, replicate the neoclassical stance in which a figure rests an arm on a plinth. Lewis adopts just such a stance in the Rocher image seen in figure 6.5. Her chosen pose echoes the contrapposto of posed sculptures that relied on a plinth or post to prop up the figure's body. The inclusion of tables, chairs, and other theatrical furniture served to put the subject in scale and to place the body in space. The representation of such features added to the air of finery and elegance accorded the subject.

To give more nuanced context to these photographs of Lewis, we can contrast her cartes de visite, or "advertisements of self," with the notorious written and sketched advertisements seeking runaway enslaved persons published in newspapers by slave traders in the previous decade—following the passage of the Fugitive Slave Act in 1850.[34] Again, we might think about how Lewis's circulation of her own image and work upends our understanding of Black Atlantic traffic in her day and ours: the difference between chattels purchased as insured cargo on slave ships crossing the Atlantic and Edmonia Lewis and her white marble statues, carried on those same currents from Africa's northern neighbor Italy back to the nouveau riche markets of the United States—a crossing that occurred at least eight times in Lewis's life.

The only known image of Lewis in Italy is a full-body standing portrait of her taken at the famed Fratelli d'Alessandri studio in Rome.[35] Here she wears seemingly more feminine attire: The outfit is lavish and her hair is out, crowning her steadfast gaze and a cross-armed power pose. In the photograph in figure 6.7, Edmonia stands centered in the frame next to an ornate side chair. She wears an elaborately embellished white or light-colored day dress with Pagoda sleeves, a bustle or polonaise, a Basque peplum, ruffles, and a high waistline, all of which create fancy layers for her fashionable, a la pointe de la mode look. She does not appear to wear jewelry (her hands are hidden), nor has she arranged any accessories in her hair, which she wears in a shorn, "natural" style that somewhat resembles the "Marcel" wave (a famous hairstyle achieved with the invention of the

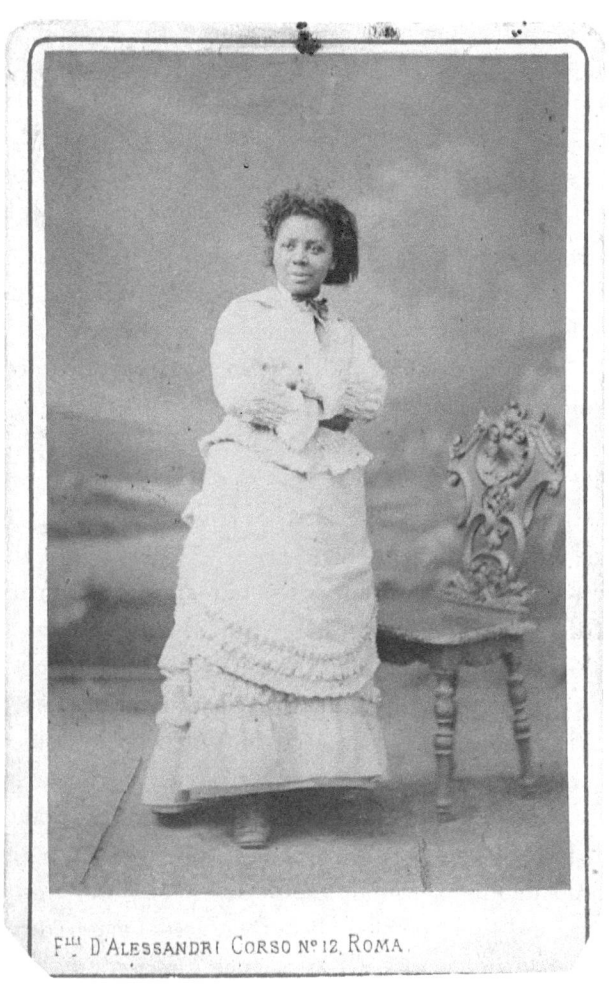

F.ˡˡⁱ D'ALESSANDRI CORSO Nº 12, ROMA.

6.7 Fratelli d'Alessandri, portrait of Edmonia Lewis, ca. 1874–76. Albumen print on card, 4 × 2½ in. The Walters Art Museum, Baltimore, Maryland; gift of an anonymous donor, 2011.

Marcel curling iron in France in 1872). Lewis had already been wearing her hair in this face-framing look for some time, perhaps even presaging the new style. Her stance is decidedly masculine with her arms crossed over her chest and her feet placed apart. A workmanlike leather boot can be seen on her right foot, which protrudes near the bottom of the frame. There seems to be a small bow or bustle just below her derriere. Does she wear a smirk as she stares out boldly from the photograph or is it a bemused smile that accompanies her rather regal, knowing look? And how to account for this photograph, which impossibly exudes the warmth of her personality? This "Roman portrait is wildfire," as Shaw quips.[36]

In her superb study of the postmodern artist Kara Walker, *Seeing the Unspeakable* (2004), Shaw compares a photograph of Walker with a description of Edmonia Lewis in a newspaper article. Shaw writes about the "fascination with the black female body at work, the notation of hairstyle, stature, . . . [and the] uncanny manner, that . . . [a] description of Walker echoes Henry T. Tuckerman's late-nineteenth-century description of . . . Lewis, whom he characterized as working in 'coarse but appropriate attire, with her black hair loose, and grasping in her tiny hand the chisel with which she does not disdain—perhaps with which she is obliged—to work, and with her large, black, sympathetic eyes brimful of simple unaffected enthusiasm.'"[37] There is a wealth of information about Lewis's appearance: The numerous descriptions range from the ridiculous to the sublime. We examine photographs of her that differ of course from the imaginative linguistic renderings of her printed in the press, in poems, and in other written texts. Photographs became a form of property that secured one's identity. In this sense, the sculptor's image serves as a supplement, visual cue, and authenticating document for a nineteenth-century cult of personality. These valuable stills, whether daguerreotypes or cartes de visite, were made of light, glass, silver, egg, copper, iodine, bromide vapors, mercury, salt, water, gold chloride, gelatin, and glue paper. As such, their actual materiality was unstable. We are lucky indeed to be able to touch these pictures of Lewis in her many "faces and phases."

As I have discussed, in life and in live performance, there is evidence that Lewis often stood next to her sculptures when they were shown at major exhibitions (such as her appearance next to her *Death of Cleopatra* when it was at the Philadelphia Centennial Exhibition in 1876) and could be seen working in her studio in Rome whenever visitors came to watch her sculpt. In lieu of not yet having a photograph of this particular juxtaposition, her image gets placed and sutured to her work in almost every instance (including throughout this book). This performative placing of her body in proximity to her sculptures (*about* her work) produces—in every sense of the term—entangled, entrenched relations among bodies, photographs, and sculptures. Such side-by-side-by-side associations expand our understanding of sculpture as embodied social phenomena and as part of the discursive formation of Lewis's oeuvre.[38] Lewis supplements her work and has a spectacular relationship to it as her very image substantiates the work.

Like Rebecca Schneider in *Performing Remains* (2011), I am interested in the attempt to virtually touch time through the residue of the gesture or the cross-temporality of the pose. Schneider writes about how the troubling, habitual line of binary opposition between "the live" and the "archival remain" might provoke us, even if momentarily, to look differently at the photos we pass by every day—whether hung in museums, plastered on billboards, scrunched into frames on our phones, glossed on the covers of magazines, packed away in drawers, embedded in archives, or awaiting surfers online. This is an invitation, in other words, to go in search of "photographs" in the live space of temporal lag—in the processionals of the Middle Ages, for example. Instead of looking for shrouds (the photography-equals-death school of thought), might we listen for photography's kin in rituals of reenactment?[39] I think about these photographs of Edmonia Lewis with a fierce attachment to what others might see as detritus from a purportedly bygone era; I hope we can see that, in certain hands, they function as well as beguilingly erotic material.

These totems allow us to imagine new object relations among these moving material realms. We might ask: Where, when, how, and why were they connected? For whose benefit and for what purposes? How can we characterize the politics and poetics of (re)producing photographic portraits of Lewis beside or within the purview of her sculptures? These appearances demonstrate how "a black artist always becomes an actor in her own show."[40] We know that she performed in relation to her work, and we may imagine these performances from the many extant descriptions of these events.[41] We have already noted the practical purpose, as in linking the artist and her work to viewing and buying publics, but there are other ways and venues in which these photographs of Lewis circulated.

We may compare and contrast Lewis's image with that of one of her contemporaries: Erastus Dow Palmer (1817–1904) (figure 6.8). If one were to close one's eyes and imagine a Victorian neoclassical sculptor, one might picture a figure resembling Palmer rather than Lewis. Even though both Lewis and Palmer were born in upstate New York and made sculptures of similar themes in the same neoclassical style, they have been remembered differently in the annals of art history.

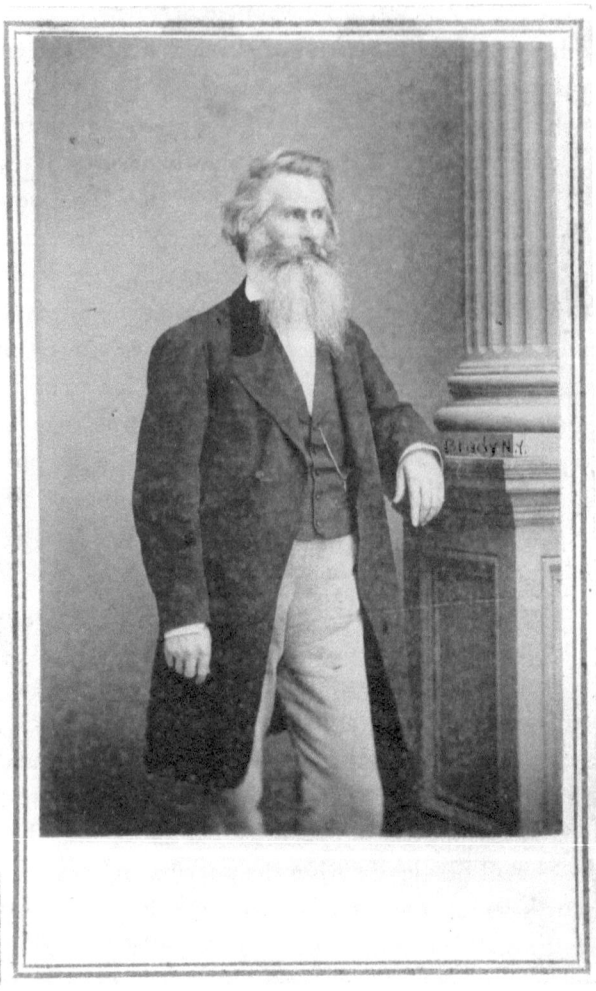

6.8 Mathew Brady Studio, Erastus Dow Palmer, ca. 1870s. Glass plate collodion photographic negative. Courtesy of Jeffrey Kraus Collection.

Palmer was said to have worked his way up from carpentry and wood machining to carving intricate portrait cameos. Soon he began making idealized marble works in the neoclassical style. Palmer made a popular work entitled *Indian Girl, or the Dawn of Christianity* (1855–56). This nubile statue's nudity was made chaste by its titular invocation of Christianity. Originally titled *The Dawn of Christianity upon the Aborigines*, the sculpture portrays a young woman disrobed to her waist with downcast eyes, looking curiously at a simple cross she holds in her right hand. Palmer published his ideas about the moral nature of sculpture in a popular journal of the period, and any whiff of impropriety in his work was largely excused with rapturous prose about the purity of his wholly American subjects. For example, one critic proclaimed that this work "has shown that the truly beautiful and refined of all races resemble each other; and we are not shocked by any offensive exhibition of the physical peculiarities of her race." The cross in the girl's right hand requires her to drop the clasped feathers in her left hand that denote her purportedly pagan religion.[42] A few years later, Palmer sculpted another well-known nude *The White Captive* (1858–59), which was donated to the then-new Metropolitan Museum of Art, becoming the inaugural sculpture in that august collection. Both of these works of nude women were sold in photographic form.[43] The Met has removed the work from view but describes it, in problematic terms, as depicting "a young woman who has been abducted in her sleep (her nightgown hangs from the tree trunk) and held captive by Native Americans. Bound at the wrists, she clenches her left fist behind her back in defiance. Palmer was commended for his choice of a 'thoroughly American' subject, which consciously alluded to ongoing frontier skirmishes between Indigenous peoples and white settlers."[44] He also showed work and won a prize at the 1876 Centennial International Exhibition, where Lewis triumphed with her *Death of Cleopatra*. Palmer was photographed by Mathew Brady.

Brady's image of him resembles the one of Lewis in which she stands with her arm resting on a tall table (see figure 6.5). Palmer stands next to a Doric column; Lewis next to the table covered by a cloth with a Greek key stripe. Contrasting her with Palmer is instructive in that he, too, was known for carving "thoroughly American" subjects, albeit from an utterly opposite point of view.[45] This work differs from all the many "colored" and Indigenous women Lewis carved as Palmer's contemporary, and specifically with Lewis's distinct and historic Nudes, which, though rendered in white marble, nevertheless defied the stereotype of the "white" woman in distress at the hands of "colored" men.

A "still" can solicit our affect. Every "description" is a translation, never seamless, always an interpretation that involves image manipulation and imagination. The image is never fixed. There is so much that exceeds the frame literally and figuratively. From the conditions of its making to the intended purpose, its (un)intended audiences, the meanings of this or any photograph emerge only belatedly. We have difficulty grasping it once and for all. To cite Leigh Raiford again:

> It is not that photographs "lie," but we unduly invest them with the burden of an all-knowing truth. We also need to consider what it means that a photograph is itself a mode of arrest and incarceration. Not just considering the margins and the center, a third method of reading compels us to interrogate photographic passage through time. The fecund irony of the "movement photograph"—the frozen document of a world-changing popular mobilization—reveals the complex work of photography in the long African American freedom struggle.[46]

As such, a photograph moves across space and time, changing formats, size, and medium, which is to say ontological and ideological meaning.

While Lewis appears as a single, singular subject in these portraits, they nevertheless were understood to be part of a collective community identity. Each individual image was always already connected intimately to ideas about race, class, and gender. Props used in studio portraits reappeared in other portraits with different sitters, showing the photograph to be resolutely theatrical, giving us haunted, spectral images then and now. The question of visualizing sexuality proved more problematic even as scientific images in and as profiles came to signify "criminality." For example, Francis Galton (1822–1911), Darwin's cousin who was knighted for his contributions to science in 1909, created a composite of images to prove individual, genetic propensities for criminality. These illustrations provided visual evidence for the biological basis for a criminal "type." The photograph was used to substantiate new "scientific" research areas such as physiognomy, phrenology, anthropology, and psychometrics—almost all of which also supported white supremacist hierarchies.[47]

When we scour the photographic archive, we are hard-pressed to locate many images that *tout court* resemble those of Lewis. If we were to follow the identitarian (racial) logic of comparison frequently used in art history, we might seek to compare these photographs to formal portraits of the most photographed Black man of the era, her friend the formerly enslaved Frederick Douglass. Or we might compare photos of Lewis to other sculptors, most of whom were white and male. We must ask: What is the iconography of working Black women? What of the etching of Afro-Indigenous Elleanor Eldridge, or depictions of other Native women, other artists, such as Elizabeth Keckley, the seamstress and modiste to Mary Todd Lincoln?

How *do* we image, imagine, and recognize an Afro-Indigenous "colored" female artist? Who might desire her image and for what purposes? It is a considerable gift to gaze on her face, to touch these scraps of printed paper. We look into and beyond the frame, analyzing her imprint, the ways her image moves us. To view Lewis's visage is to value a vestige of our past, to look at evidence of her shifting persona, her many "faces and phases."[48]

I wish there was many more like Miss Edmonie Lewis.

Addie Brown to Rebecca Primus, November 17, 1867

This chapter concludes with a wish: that there could be more like Miss Edmonia Lewis. The wish appears in a letter from Addie Brown (1841–70), an employee at Miss Porter's School for Girls in Farmington, Connecticut, to her "loving friend" Rebecca Primus (1837–1932), another free Black woman living in Hartford. These "extraordinary, ordinary" Black women exchanged more than 150 letters over a decades-long friendship that began in the late 1860s (figure 6.9).[49] Their letters, redacted and transcribed by eminent researcher Farah Jasmine Griffin, provide a remarkable record of a still-unsung Black "female world of love and ritual" (to quote the title of Carol Smith-Rosenberg's article about homoerotic moves between nineteenth-century women).[50] The cross-class written correspondence between Brown and Primus testifies to knowledge of Lewis in progressive New England circles. When the letter was composed and sent, Lewis had been gone from Boston for two years, and yet she remained a topic between these women. Indeed, reports of her exploits in Rome appeared regularly in the abolitionist press and Hartford had a sizable free Black population.

On the very same day that Brown mentions her wish for more women like Edmonia Lewis, she sent yet another letter to Primus, this one mentioning an explicit same-sex sexual encounter with one of the white female pupils at the exclusive Miss Porter's school. In this letter Brown talks candidly of sleeping with the young lady. She writes, in African American English: "If you think that is my bosom that captivated the girl that made her want to sleep with me she got sorely disappointed enjoying it for I had my back towards her all night and my night dress was button up so she could not get to my bosom." She continues: "I thought I told you about the girl sleeping with me. Whether I enjoyed it or not I can't say that I enjoyed it very much. I don't care about her sleeping with me again. I don't

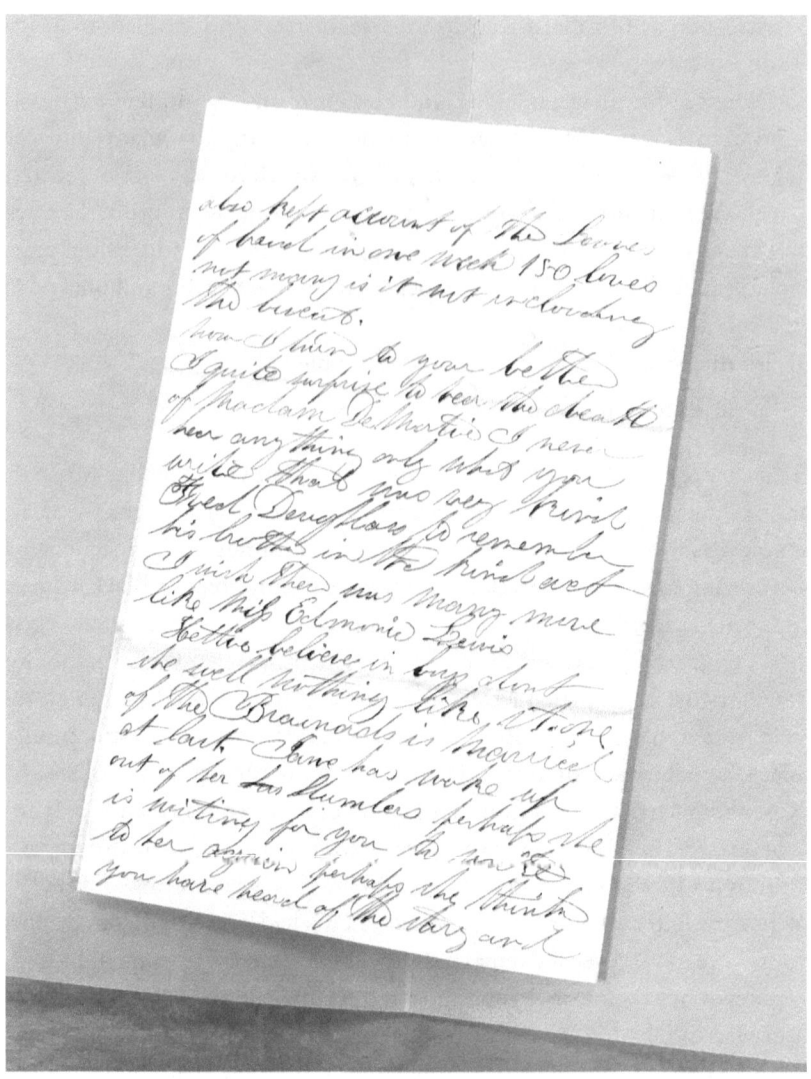

6.9 Letter from Addie Brown in Farmington, Connecticut, to Rebecca Primus in Hartford, Connecticut, dated November 17, 1867, on the occasion of receiving two cartes de visite sent by the artist Edmonia Lewis from Italy. Primus Family Papers, Connecticut Historical Society. Photograph by the author.

know what kind of excitement I refer to but I presume I know at the time." Such frank erotic discussions written by this Black female correspondent suggests the range of sexual desire possible among these women in the nineteenth century. Addie Brown's letter to Rebecca Primus documents the fact that Lewis had an audience of worldly Black women, that she had Black female admirers in the United States that connected her to an international network of literate devotees of her work. Primus's brother, Nelson, knew of Lewis and both Addie and Rebecca could easily have met her in Boston on a visit from Hartford.[51]

Another of these Black female admirers was writer and suffragette Frances Anne Rollin (1845–1901).[52] Rollin authored what is considered to be the first biography written by a Black person. The subject was a notable life of the Black abolitionist Martin Delaney that Rollin published under the pseudonym Frank A. Rollin in 1868. In that same year, she mentioned Lewis in her diary:

> 1868 Saturday, May 9. At home sewing until 12 o'clock then to the State House and wrote until four oclock, then to Mr Phillips could not see him as he was attending Mrs Rockwell in her sick chamber where she has been for three weeks. Went to Addie Howard's spent the afternoon with her did not get home until 8 o'clock Addie received today two Photographs of Edmonia Lewis from Rome taken in her Studio dress. Home and sewed like a trojan until 12 oclock."[53]

This entry is remarkable for its sense of comings and goings, indicating the busy daily life of a free nineteenth-century Black woman engaged in community building, making garments, writing, and being industrious; a woman aware of Lewis, noting down the arrival of cartes de visite for posterity. Addie Howard, we recall, accompanied Lewis to Richmond, Virginia, in 1865 to teach in the segregated schools. They had been friends since they met in Boston. This mention also shows that Lewis understood the importance of maintaining her relationships with other Black women in the country of her birth and situates her authoritatively in a world of global exchange fostered by communication technologies.

These exchanges between Primus and Brown and between Rollin and Howard give us proof of a group of Black women admirers among whom Edmonia Lewis circulated her "selfies," to use an anachronism to characterize her calling cards. The references in the letters testify to Lewis's use of photography to bolster her international celebrity and cultivate intimate relations.

Zanele Muholi

I share photography because I believe that every person should have a decent photo, and also that every person should be seen the way he or she wants to be seen. To be remembered, to be recognized. . . . I think the archive would be richer if we had many faces, many portraits, many life-stories narrated visually.

Zanele Muholi

In chapter 6, I read the photographic portraits of Edmonia Lewis as material objects that narrate her life story visually, to paraphrase Zanele Muholi (b. 1972). These images serve as part of Lewis's "biomythography" (Audre Lorde's neologism).[54] One could also compare the photographic images of Lewis with photographs made by Muholi, a South African queer artist, in their ongoing community project *Faces and Phases*. This project mobilizes large-format black-and-white photographic portraits of other Black and queer individuals as a form of activism. Muholi has championed the idea that photographic portraits of marginalized people do more than showcase or document a community: They also create community. It is this sentiment that I see as part of the function of the photographic images of Lewis.

Muholi uses their art (a) to document people who were thought not to exist (i.e., queer Black South Africans) and (b) to counter the pervasive ideas of such people's debasement. Circulating these photographic images is an aid to imagining the individual participants with whom Muholi collaborates as people possessing valor, and whose various phases suggest their mutability and power to counter negative images. Muholi's desire for "more images" unwittingly echoes the similar desire expressed by Lewis's correspondent Addie Brown for "many more like Miss Edmonie Lewis" (see figure 6.9). Both Muholi and Brown explicitly state a desire to foment a beloved community—they long for more like(nesses of) Black queer individuals, a hail that the photographic images of Lewis could be seen to answer. As we have discussed, the photographic images of Lewis differ from those of other colored and Indigenous folks of her era; in this, they are similar to the images of the distinct participants in Muholi's work.

As one of the first and very few photographers of queer culture in contemporary South Africa, Muholi carries on a project that we might imagine as having begun with Lewis's reproduction and circulation of her own image for creative purposes. As Dadwami Woubshet observes: "Perhaps the most constant feature among [Muholi's *Faces and Phases*] portraits is how the participants meet the camera's gaze directly and enact a look that is self-willed. On display is a wide range of eye-speak—communicating daring, defiance, pride, joy, gratitude, sensuality, serenity, wonder, anger, anguish, vulnerability, yearning—an aliveness palpable in each photograph and, in so many, simply moving to witness."[55] One can claim some of this variety of performative expression in the portraits made in collaboration with Muholi's camera for the photographs of Lewis discussed above that reveal her face over temporal phases and active attitudes.[56]

The use of the "solo" portrait allows us to focus on a single figure in detail: The singular images in Muholi's series harken back to Lewis's photographic portraits, which similarly deploy a single sitter in the service of continuing Black, feminist (and queer) communities. Muholi's photographs evoke a collective of individuals who cannot be dismissed as stereotypes. They provide proof of concept and of life even as they point to possibilities beyond the bordered image. Many have been published with an accompanying narrative that gives greater context to the images.

Muholi's *Faces and Phases* portraits always pose the participants being photographed in such a way that their gaze meets our own. This is especially true of the photograph of Lerato Dumse, who, like Lewis, survived a violent attack in their teens (figure 6i.1). In this striking image, Dumse looks out at us: The slight bend in the head allows the pupils of the eyes to arc up, giving more space for the eyebrows to express strength. The vertical black and white stripes on the shirt contrast with the plaid of the jacket with its wide and sharply cut lapels. Her hair is buzzed, allowing the beautifully rounded shape of her almost bald head to shine against the indistinct background of the photograph. This is a fine-and-dandy image that nevertheless carries a trace (perhaps at the edges of the eyes?) of what has been overcome, while clearly giving us an outlook portending what is yet to come. Like the work of Isaac Julien and Mark Nash discussed by Monica Miller, this "dandyish" portrait presents "not merely a vision of the empire looking back, but a vision looking *through* a shared history of

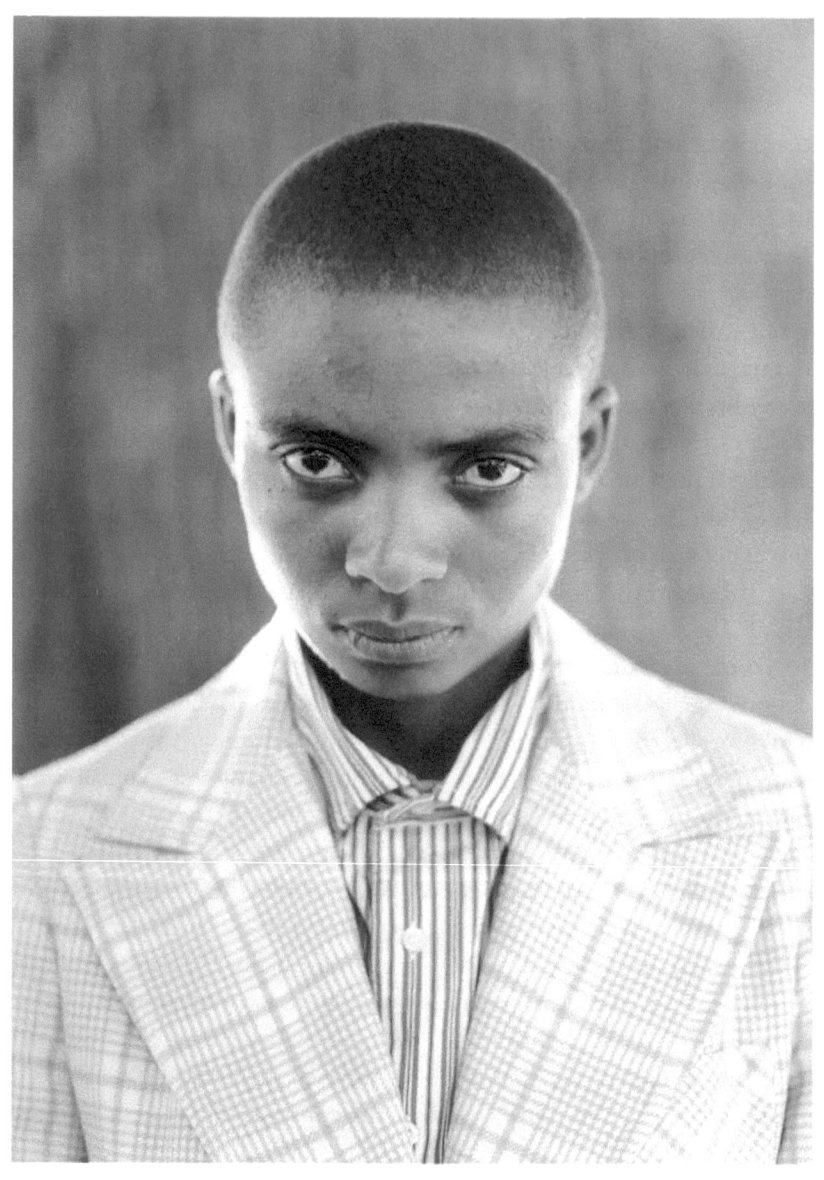

61.1 Zanele Muholi, *Lerato Dumse, Syracuse, New York* (*Faces and Phases* series), 2015. Silver gelatin print. Courtesy of the artist.

black representation toward an image of black cosmopolitanism that is simultaneously rooted and detached, celebratory and censorious."[57] The compelling portrait of Dumse stands as one of several hundred made thus far of the diasporic Black LGBTQI community and as an emblem of one of the many participants who have been inspired to take more photographs in the spirit of Muholi's on-going work.

A few years ago, my colleague Francesca Royster mailed me a reproduction of one of the Rocher photographs of Lewis, writing, "Isn't she cute?" on the top of the paper. More recently, Matt Richardson, who shared all his master's thesis research on Lewis with me, also suggested that he always thought of Lewis as queer. And the artist who created the cover art for this book, yétúndé ọlágbajú, has claimed Lewis as queer ancestor (looking particularly at the folds in Lewis's sculpture as a sign). The interaction among this community of readers mimics exchanges between the earlier, nineteenth-century Black desiring subjects who exchanged Lewis's cartes de visite. All wish to see Lewis as a "complex and beautiful subject of desire," to quote Deborah Willis, who uses this powerful phrase in declaring that the artist Carrie Mae Weems's photographs "show the art world that, although frequently pictured, the black woman has not been seen as complex and a beautiful subject of desire."[58] Here we gesture to a critical genealogy of Black beauty that begins with Lewis's photographic portraits, continues through the work of Muholi, and reverberates in photographic exchanges yet to be codified. As such, Lewis lives on in her photographic images, these chimerical, material tokens of affection laden, always, with complex questions of longing and belonging.

Engraving Edmonia

This is how you see me the space in which to place me /
The space in me
To see this space / see how you place me in you / This is
how to place you in the space in which to see

> **Layli Long Soldier,** "Ħe Sápa Three," in *Whereas*

Exquisite, that use of grave for engrave, as if the action of
the stonecutter and the place itself are one.

> **Paul Monette,** "3275," in *Last Watch of the Night*

7

Perhaps there is no more telling place than the site of
one's grave, the space where one is placed. Frequently,
this sacred space is marked with stones, elaborately
carved or lovingly or even hastily arranged depending on the circumstances. While all statues produce
meanings about the space where they are placed, the
gravestone is saturated with sentiment.[1] The grave is
among the most significant site-specific places that al-
ters space, as discussed in the chapter 2 interlude, on
Beverly Buchanan's environmental installations that
serve as commemorative stones. This chapter further

reflects on gravesites, not only because sculptors often were members of the stone-cutting profession that made headstones, but also because many more sculptors worked as professional carvers during Edmonia's lifetime as demand for this skill increased in conjunction with the invention in the nineteenth century of the pastoral cemetery. As the fortunes of individual bourgeois subjects rose, they sought to mark their lives with ever more grandiose monuments, many carved on commission by sculptors of note. As a Victorian stonecutter, Lewis ventured into this realm, making work to mark the lives of the no longer living. On at least two occasions, she was commissioned to produce such sculpture—to make meaningful headstones. These works differed from her posthumous portrait busts of Col. Robert Gould Shaw, John Brown, or Abraham Lincoln in that they were designed to be placed in designated cemeteries. In 1873 Lewis was asked to produce a memorial for Pelagie Rutgers, whose daughter Antoinette Thomas was a prominent Black socialite in St. Louis, Missouri. For this marker, Lewis designed a full-figure work entitled *The Virgin Mary at the Cross* (whereabouts unknown). That same year, "she finished two important statues erected over the gravesites of Lynch Blair at Graceland Cemetery in Chicago and Dr. Harriot K. Hunt in Mount Auburn Cemetery in Cambridge, Massachusetts."[2] In fact, Edmonia Lewis was the first woman and colored artist to carve a gravestone in the famed Mount Auburn Cemetery. She conceived of this commission as a site-specific commemoration of Dr. Harriot Hunt, whose family plot occupied several spaces in the pastoral cemetery.

Opened in 1831, Mount Auburn was the first such pastoral cemetery in the United States. This new type of burial place was modeled on the Cimetière du Père-Lachaise in Paris, which broke ground in 1804. At the time, this city graveyard represented an innovation in urban landscape design. "The site of this new necropolis covered acres," wrote John Gary Brown, "setting the standard that would be copied in London, Genoa and in Vienna. . . . The metamorphosis of the old graveyard into a culturally beneficial park led to the reintroduction of the word *cemetery*, a place of repose. . . . Many elements of culture—art, architecture, city planning, gardening, history—were considered . . . when designing the new burial grounds."[3] Accordingly, demand rose for funerary sculptures that could carve out distinctive plots in what were sometimes known as cities of the dead (to use the term associated with the aboveground plots of New Orleans, where the geography necessitated visible crypts—the famed "cities of the dead"). These monuments, markers, and tombs could be simple burial stones, elaborately carved headstones, or even architecturally distinct mausolea.

Many of these new, open-air burial grounds were necessitated by the overcrowding of church cemeteries and crypts. The pastoral urban cemetery was thus a Victorian innovation to transform congested places. These bucolic, pastoral, "parklike" expanses were still segregated by race, religion, station, and class, if not by age or gender. They became places for the performance of rituals activated by the living in memory of the dead. Having one's life commemorated to stone and placed deliberately among man-made ponds and the oaks, weeping willows, and sugar maples (to name only three of what are now more than 5,500 trees in Mount Auburn) literally naturalized death in modern ways.

Lewis's contribution to such new arrangements was to create a monument for Dr. Harriot Kezia Hunt (1805–75), one of the first female physicians in the country.[4] Like Lewis, who was forbidden to study at an art school, Hunt also had been refused training in her preferred profession when she was denied admission to the medical school at Harvard University. "Both single and self-supporting, Hunt and Lewis understood the difficulties of working in male-dominated professions," as the Mount Auburn website puts it.[5] Hunt learned medicine from a private tutor and opened her own clinic in Boston, where she treated patients during a decades-long career. Her commitment to women's rights was forged in her activism as an abolitionist in Massachusetts—two factors that no doubt influenced her decision to hire Edmonia Lewis to sculpt this significant final marker.[6]

Lewis's sculpture for the doctor's grave depicts, appropriately, Hygeia, the Greek goddess of health and hygiene. The statue features elaborately coiffed hair that shows parted ringlets in the front, while the back of the figure's head reveals a tightly coiled bun made from what appear to be long strands of hair. The right arm of the goddess (now missing its hand) extends outward, while her left hand gently grasps the folds of her flowing robes. This statue's stance is unconventional: Her left leg crosses over and in front of her right, standing leg in a kind of reverse contrapposto. She has long articulate toes that, on the left foot, protrude beyond the base of this feminized form. A serpent encircles Hygeia's ankles. The stance suggests a subtle insouciance and "unfeminine" boldness for a classical female figure. The goddess stands atop a large cylindrical base and is meant to be viewed from all sides. Her regal head bends slightly forward. Lewis's work is an exceptional depiction of a life-size female funereal figure who was

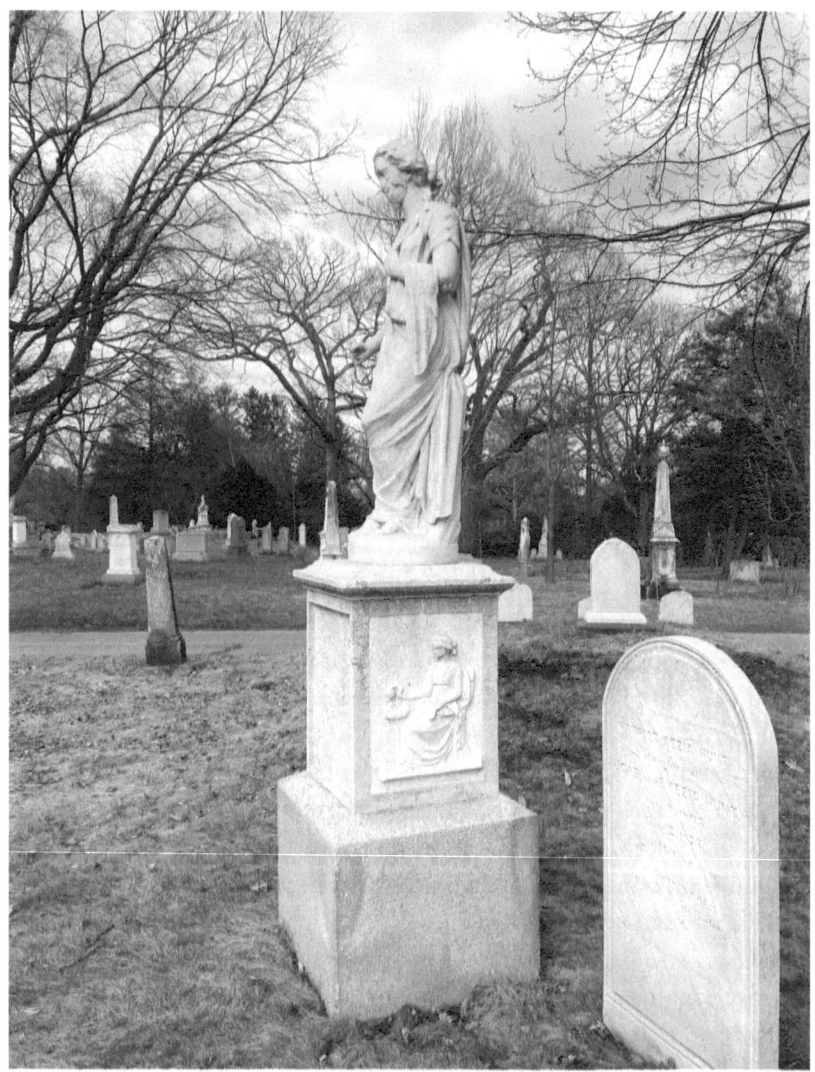

7.1 Edmonia Lewis, *Hygeia*, ca. 1872. Marble. Mount Auburn Cemetery, Cambridge, Massachusetts. Photograph by Tiya Miles.

not an angel (figure 7.1). The demeaner suggests a figure at ease, placid, composed, and beneficent—as if, heretically, she were beatified.

In our time, this once pristine and beautiful statue, *Hygeia* (ca. 1872), stands weather-beaten and broken. The face of the goddess has lost many of its distinctive features, even as she stands with poise. Lewis's *Hygiea* confronts us with questions about the preservation, performance, and placement of commemorative sculpture in the United States. Not only can stone statues be broken by acts of plunder, disfigured by displacement, refigured via restoration, repaired, and revived; they can be eroded by the outdoor environment as well. Lewis's lovely *Hygeia* is being destroyed as you read this by its ongoing exposure to the climate.

Foregoing chapters establish that statues are designed to move audiences to action, emotion, and commemoration. Their installations are almost always accompanied by dramatic live performances involving dedication speeches and unveilings, interactions in which the monument functions as "archive and the repertoire" at one and the same time. Such public sculptures mark accretions, multiple moments in time. These works' apparent stasis is in fact always part of a continuum of action that carries the traces of the living (even when they are meant as mnemonic devices for remembering the dead). As such, public sculptures both encapsulate and generate time as they revivify. They *do things* in the public sphere for those who interact with them. They may be alive with loss or other effectual emotions. Throughout this book, I seek to foster new readings of Lewis's neoclassical statues in part by thinking about sculpture in what Rosalind Krauss called the "expanded field of vision." Krauss's foundational essay claims that "the logic of sculpture, it would seem, is inseparable from the logic of the monument."[7] By virtue of this logic, Lewis did not have a destination in mind, nor did she produce most of her works to be part of particular architectural spaces. Lewis's sculptural monuments *moved* and were monumental as much because of their subject matter as because of their emplacement in public parks or at large fairs and international expositions.

Against Friedrich Nietzsche and others who conceive of stone monuments "as . . . efforts to stop time" that take up a "monumental" view of the past, as if such stone markers could "protest against the change of generations and against transitoriness," this book argues that transition and change are historical properties of moving stones.[8] Indeed, the very meaning of "sculpture" changes historically: Its ideological, aesthetic, and other boundaries are not fixed. What is clear is that Lewis's figurative sculptures—especially her statues—were part of a cultural moment of sculpture's import in both senses of the term.

In figure 7.2, we see a long stone slab rising slightly out of a patch of earth. It is a blank slate whose once distinct engraved words have been weathered and worn to the point of illegibility. This is Lewis's own gravesite, which occupies what I consider to be sacred ground near a

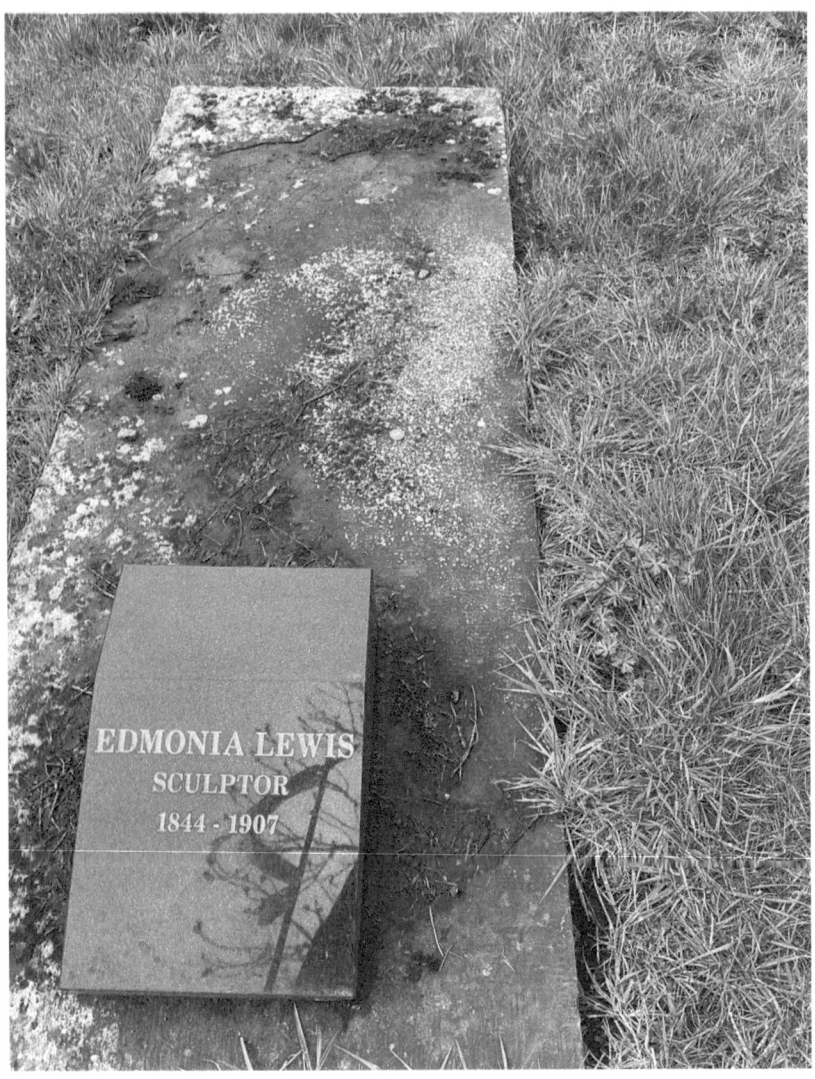

7.2 Edmonia Lewis's gravesite at St. Mary's Catholic Cemetery, London. Photograph by the author.

picturesque willow tree in a sprawling cemetery in London. At the time of her death, Lewis's resting place cost seven pounds sterling to secure; it is now one of more than 165,000 graves at St. Mary's Catholic Cemetery in Kensal Green. (Another famous Black Victorian, the Jamaican nurse and author Mary Seacole [1805–81], is also buried there.)[9] Much of Edmonia's story can be read in the aesthetic and temporal differences between the two headstones that now palimpsestically mark her burial spot. Here, we are viewing these grave sites simultaneously: They are sutured together, one newer burial stone partially supplanting what has become the older burial marker. They sit together on plot C350 on the far right side of the graveyard, within the shadow of a former industrial plant. This burial site marks a contested moment in Edmonia's story and its emplotment. Like so much of her art and life, it narrates the lost and the found, a covering and a re-covering—ceaseless change, movement in space over time.

The second headstone, placed in 2017 on Lewis's 1907 burial plot, is made of shimmering black onyx. Its letters have been etched in gold. This headstone slants upward toward the viewer: It *tops* the plain, horizontal gray stone slab now forming its base. The new headstone was placed at the behest of Bobbie Reno, another Edmonia Lewis devotee, who lives near Lewis's hometown in upstate New York.[10] Paid for in part with a GoFundMe campaign, the headstone writes over terms present on the first burial stone.

The story of this new engraving replicates Edmonia Lewis's history, which, as we know, was for many years somewhat overlooked and on the verge of being erased but is now being "singled out," burnished, and renewed for future generations. The comparatively upright monument produced by the London firm E. M. Lander is made of an expensive material, onyx, and is decidedly more aesthetically distinct and dimensional than the original stone. The black and gilt marker tilts *upward*, suggesting that it is metaphorically as well as literally *upstanding*. This retouched gravesite contrasts with Lewis's last will and testament, in which "Lewis identified herself as a 'Spinster and Sculptor,'" Talia Lavin has written. "She asked for a dark walnut coffin, and that a notice of her death be printed in the *Tablet*, a British Roman Catholic publication. The resulting announcement—a curt sentence fragment—made no mention of her myriad accomplishments and, as far as we know, did not reach those who sought her across the sea and throughout Europe."[11]

Lewis's work only appeared to have disappeared from the historical record. There are many reasons that she and her sculptures suffered "percepticide," to invoke Diana Taylor's term that glosses the politically potent and violently disappeared.[12] Lewis was subject to a profound lack of scholarly regard for colored women artists and, for some, the waning interest in the neoclassical style of sculpture she produced. Even the once ubiquitous marmorean souvenirs that flooded Western markets in the beginning of the twentieth century became unfashionable. Lewis never received the large-scale commissions for public sculpture awarded to some of her peers. Thus, during the nineteenth century's international era of "statuemania," which idolized neoclassical sculptures, Lewis maintained her reputation: But sometime in the 1880s she moved to Paris (a city she first visited in 1867) and then, in the last decade of the nineteenth century, to London, when and where her star supposedly waned.[13] And yet there are sitings and citings of her throughout the annals of art history, Black feminist organizing, activism, and other areas of inquiry.

Lewis's purported disappearance from the historical record would be a conundrum were it not for the racism, segregation, and sexism of the academic disciplines through which her story may have emerged. Our knowledge of Lewis has been preserved largely within the marginalized annals of African American, feminist, and queer art histories that are still emerging areas of inquiry.[14] Although the archival traces of her life, like many of her sculptures, remain damaged, cut, broken, scattered, lost, and obscured, seemingly undiscoverable, we can still be enthralled by imagining their existence. Few Lewis scholars can resist recounting the story of *The Death of Cleopatra*, which was carved in 1876 explicitly as an entry into the Centennial International Exhibition in Philadelphia. After its triumphant display there, it was shown again a few decades later in the 1893 World's Columbian Exposition in Chicago. The sculpture weighed several tons, and it proved too expensive for Lewis to ship back to Rome. Thereafter, the sculpture had an uncertain future: marking a racehorse's grave and ultimately being stored in a postal warehouse on the outskirts of Chicago before it was uncovered and finally installed in the Smithsonian American Art Museum, where it resides today. No doubt, there are other "forgotten, if not gone" Lewis sculptures that exist for now only in written or drawn documents.

We witness the changeable nature of statuary in movements to revise historic public tributes to a scarred past by dethroning statues representing prior leaders, oppressive histories, or racist ideologies. Recently, viewers around the globe have become accustomed to seeing sculpted stone monuments that weigh tons dangling precipitously from steel cranes, hanging in the air during their removal, or crumbling onto their plinths at the hands (or bulldozers) of justice. As these statues are cut down to size, so to speak, the act creates yet another moment when the material and its matter of production are sutured—they must be rejected together. Such stone monuments, once used to mobilize memories, now are being removed and obscured by contrapuntal projections and transformed from their places of prominence in public squares—many of them lay broken at the base like lies that have come tumbling down.

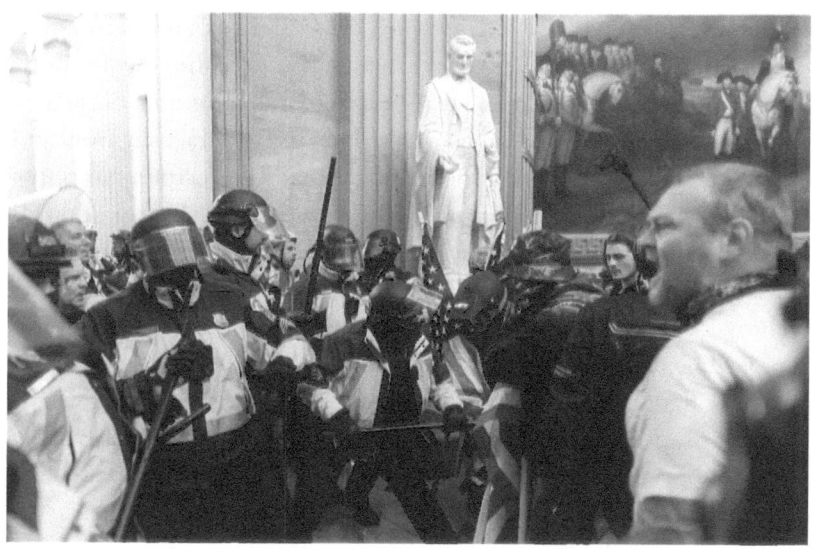

7.3 Vinnie Ream's marble statue of Abraham Lincoln (1871), captured in the background of an anonymous photograph taken at the Capitol Rotunda, Washington, DC, January 6, 2021. Courtesy of Getty Images.

The world has witnessed the university student activism in South Africa that called for the removal of the statue of Cecil Rhodes, thereby inaugurating the "Rhodes Must Fall, Fees Must Fall" movement among Cape Town university students in 2015; the deadly 2017 Unite the Right rally in Charlottesville, Virginia, in part galvanized by protest against a prominent statue of Robert E. Lee; and the insurrectionist violence that took place on January 6, 2021, at the US Capitol. At least one neoclassical sculpture known to Lewis in her lifetime played a role in the seditious events of January 6. Captured via haphazard cell phone and video images that recorded the fateful siege in the Capitol Rotunda was a statue of Abraham Lincoln (figure 7.3). The statue was made by a teenage Vinnie Ream (1847–1914), who knew Lewis and the group of nineteenth-century expat American women artists in Rome, since she spent a year there in the late 1870s.[15] The massive statue of Lincoln was installed in the Rotunda in January 1871.

Commissioned by the Senate several years after Lincoln's assassination for the sum of $10,000, the sculpture memorialized Lincoln as a liberator—in his outstretched hand he holds a copy of the Emancipation Proclamation. Standing seven feet tall, this Lincoln wears nineteenth-century garb elevated by a long flowing, classical robe. Lavinia "Vinnie" Ream was just eighteen years old when, living in DC, she convinced the then-living Lincoln to sit for a bust she carved in the summer of 1864. It was this bust that she used to bid on the lucrative contract she won, and that she then used as a model for the larger-than-life posthumous statue that stands in the Capitol Rotunda. The statue depicts Lincoln draped in a classical robe. His beard and hair are less full and straighter than in Lewis's acclaimed bust of the slain president. In Ream's work Lincoln's eyebrows are giant and unkempt. His beard covers his famous prominent jawline. Lincoln's neck is visible above the drapery that surrounds the entire figure, obscuring and simultaneously acting as the stand. The larger, notorious statue (notorious in that it was made by a young woman artist not born to wealth and of petite stature, for whom this was a first major commission) remained unscathed in the deadly melee on January 6, though it was in danger of being damaged, desecrated, or destroyed in the raid. Ream's neoclassical statue demonstrates the endurance of such moving stones as evidence for the ways nineteenth-century material culture still moves us and still matters.

Lewis's contemporary Nelson A. Primus (whose sister was Rebecca Primus, introduced in chapter 6) was an artist and a free Black person who knew Lewis in her lifetime. Nelson Primus was from Hartford, Connecticut, and after working in Boston became a painter in his final years in San Francisco. Although Nelson regretted he could not afford to study in Europe (as Lewis was able to do), he praised Lewis for her industry and talent. He also described a plan for a full-scale Lincoln memorial that Lewis was conceiving.[16] While this major work was never made, Lewis did make an excellent posthumous bust of Lincoln that resides in the San Jose Public Library.

Lewis's bust of Lincoln (1871) shows the president, slain in 1865, in contemporary dress with a vest, jacket, collared shirt, and jauntily tied neck scarf; deeply furrowed eyebrows cover eyes with carved pupils fixed in a stern gaze; a mole is prominent on his right cheek (figure 7.4). His chiseled chin juts out above the waving mass of his beard, which rings his face and blends into sideburns and hair set back from the figure's wide forehead. There are wrinkles around his eyes, and deep lines at his cheekbones echo the near grimace of the down-pulled lines by his strongly set lips. Lincoln's gaze is directed outward and his head rests directly above the shoulderless rendering of his costume. The visible modern clothing on the bust is rendered in a flat, two-dimensional style of carving that contrasts

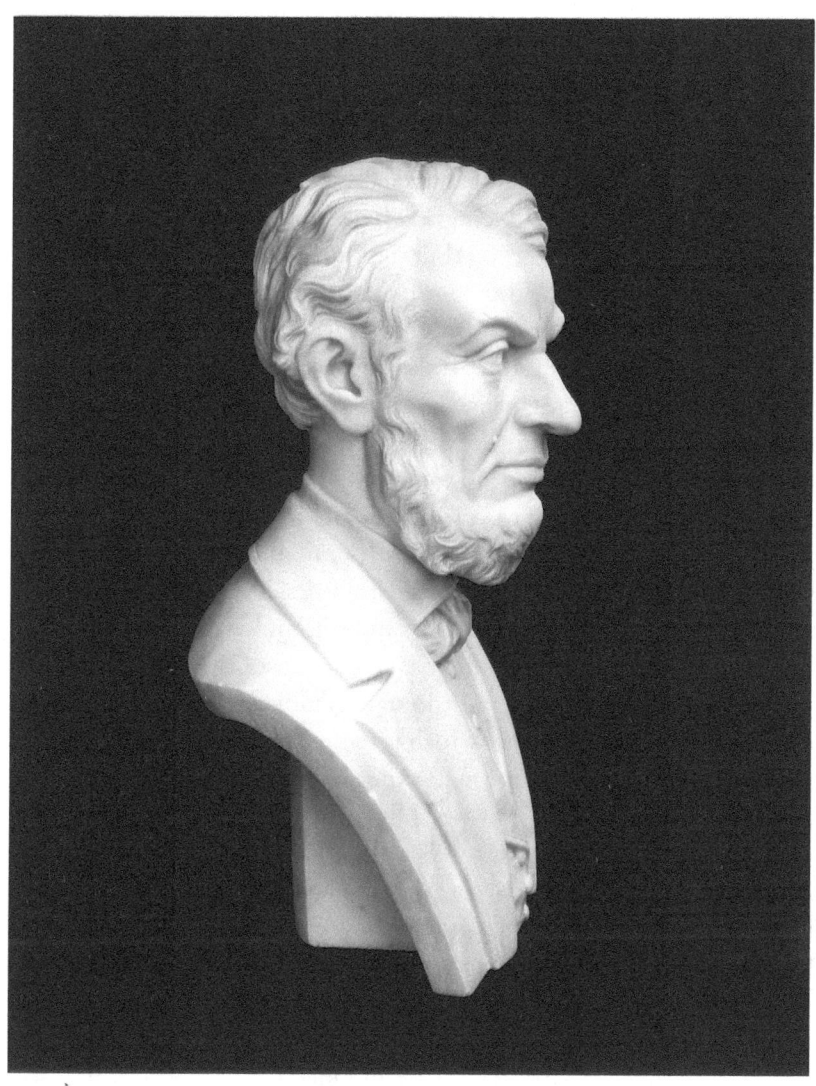

7.4 Edmonia Lewis, *Bust of Lincoln*, 1871. Marble, 21⁷⁄₁₆ × 13⅜ × 11⅝ in. San Jose Public Library, San Jose, California; purchase, with funds raised by the library in December 1873. Photograph by John Janca.

with his naturalist face. The clothing here is reminiscent (after the fact!) of the work of Harlem Renaissance artist Winhold Reiss (1886–1953), who sketched, in black on white, the below-the-neckline apparel worn by the vibrantly colored faces of his portrait subjects. This technique not only enlivened the realistically painted faces of his Harlem sitters (school-teachers, Charles Johnson, Georgia Douglas Johnson, W. E. B. Du Bois, Roland Hayes, and many others) but simultaneously showed them as real and surreal, naturalistic and artificial, or pictured and drawn.

Perhaps, rather ironically, sculptures can move and be moved. It can be useful to unmoor sculptures from what we often imagine to be their imperial, imperious permanence. In fact, sculpture participates in "monumental mobility" to quote the title of a book about the movements of the statue of Massasoit, made to commemorate the Wampanoag warrior and diplomat. The State of Massachusetts conscripted Massasoit's likeness in bronze to perform as a symbol of settler colonialism. The authors Lisa Blee and Jean O'Brien suggest that such statues, like the many historical narratives and public memories they embody and evoke, are not stable. The instability of such sculptures bears on many of the sculptures made by Edmonia Lewis. For not only do statues move from one place to another over and through time (which is to say, spatiotemporally, to recall the expansive dimension that marks time in language and thought), but popular statues have also been repeatedly copied, enlarged, or reduced—for example, to sit on interior mantels rather than in exterior city squares. Each shift in scale, material, or location changes the meaning of the object. Blee and O'Brien suggest that these ongoing iterations of statues demonstrate how "engaging with monuments allows us the opportunity to examine national stories, to grapple with the pain of suppressed and silenced truths, to determine which narratives fully reflect our shared past."[17] They may be formed of stone and metal and appear set in place, but monuments are not fixed.

While the United States is a nation formed by settler colonialism, the "mobility of *Massasoit* shows that such sites of memory contain monumental potential."[18] These figurative stones thus may be seen as engendering many moving affects. They are mnemonic devices, testaments to political divides, ways of doing history and public memory work. It was, after all, the Daughters of the American Revolution and the Ku Klux Klan (the latter founded on Christmas Eve 1865) that, during Reconstruction, began to honor the Southern "heroes" of the Confederacy with public statuary (and these new constructions were carried forward by the subsequent naming of many a US military base after the seditious men of the Confederacy, not to mention the National Garden of American Heroes proposed in 2020).[19]

It seems we find ourselves in the midst of a new era of moving stones as the once-overlooked genre of figurative sculpture undergoes a global revival. How many recent interventions involving commemorative statues have occurred across the world as activists have sought to alter the political geography instantiated via historic statues? In the United States, we continue to see how many people remain enthralled by centralized statues that memorialize white supremacist violence while attempts to monumentalize progressive figures, Black women, and Indigenous leaders garner criticism on the national stage. Efforts to represent these latter figures in a heroic style and to "change the names" that appear throughout the land, in order to rewrite history from the perspective not of the victors but of the vanquished, continue to meet with resistance.

The effort to document and categorize the nation's public statues is the mission of the Mellon Foundation's Monuments Project. Launched in October 2020, the Monuments Project seeks to transform "our commemorative landscape." As the foundation explains, "Statues are not just bodies in bronze, and monuments are not just stone pillars. They instruct. They lift up the stories of those who are unseen, and too often, propagate menacingly incomplete accounts of our country's past."[20] I note again the repeated fungibility between figurative statues and bodies that form and inform our understanding of their relatedness.

There is a profound parallelism here that Caroline Randall Williams references in her *New York Times* op-ed "You Want a Confederate Monument? My Body Is a Confederate Monument." Williams explains that our very bodies are also archival repositories of history.[21] Bodies, like statues, bear testimony to our inherent connection to American laws and customs. Both the blood and bloodshed of bodies bear witness to our historical connections, no less than do moving stones erected to re-member these events. In many ways, Lewis's sculptures—which poet Tyehimba Jess redacts as being about "apostles of eternal prayer and protestation"—can be seen as transforming what was written in stone, to use an ancient phrase.[22]

These references create a rationale that can be linked to renewed interest in Lewis's life and work: They testify to her impact on thinking about these issues of whom to sculpt and for what reason. And there has been interest in changing market forces around commissions such that new works redound to Black and Native professional artists, even as we have seen significant backlash against changing the national landscapes and cityscapes.[23]

The controversies surrounding activists such as Bree Newsome, who in 2015 removed the Confederate flag that flew outside the State House in South Carolina, and San Francisco 49ers' Colin Kaepernick, who began in 2016 to protest the singing of the National Anthem before football games by kneeling on the field, have underscored the importance of the politics of monuments. These acts proved to be potent embodied gestures that reactivated desires that may have motivated Lewis to show figures of freedom as well. The quest to do so continues, given that "historical closure on the issue of Black Freedom (distinguishable from American Freedom) remains in the subjunctive mode."[24] This might be another way of showing how Lewis's sculptures are still participating in the quest for Black and Native freedoms—the unfinished project for which art has a part to perform.

We see another example of the changeable nature of monumental stones in the larger-than-life carving known as the Confederate Memorial Carving in Stone Mountain Park. The depiction of Confederate leaders Stonewall Jackson, Robert E. Lee, and Jefferson Davis on horseback that constitutes this bright-white sculptural relief is fixed in the face of the mountain and is visible from the city of Atlanta, the site adjacent to the incorporated city of Stone Mountain. The Stone Mountain carving is the largest of more than seven hundred monuments that exist all across the United States built after Reconstruction to commemorate the Confederacy and, by extension, white supremacist violence. Stone Mountain was owned by the Venable family clan that in 1915 granted the Ku Klux Klan an easement on the top of the mountain for their rallies. The monument was carved over decades beginning in 1915 and not finished until 1972, testifying to the fact that the valorization of whiteness is long standing. The Stone Mountain carving is enshrined in the Georgia State Constitution, protecting it indefinitely from being defaced, tampered with, or destroyed.[25]

Natasha Trethewey, in her searing memoir of her mother's murder, *Memorial Drive*, remembers having to

> make [her] way down Memorial Drive [in Atlanta], a major east-west artery once named Fair Street. It originates in the middle of the city, Memorial, and winds east from downtown ending at Stone Mountain, the nation's largest monument to the Confederacy. A lasting

metaphor for the white mind of the South, Stone Mountain rises out of the ground like the head of a submerged giant—the nostalgic dream of Southern heroism and gallantry emblazoned on its brow: in bas-relief, enormous figures of Stonewall Jackson, Robert E. Lee, and Jefferson Davis.[26]

Tretheway's moving story tries to undo the power of such monuments to white supremacist racial patriarchy by countering them with the presence and power of her own memories and dreams. Although Stone Mountain still stands, its story has been altered irrevocably, tempered by such re-tellings and revisions. These glorifications of the Confederacy stand in contradistinction to Lewis's sculptures of sympathizers with the Union, abolitionists, and freed peoples. Her sculptures eschewed elevating the enslavers of her time.

I now perform an about-face as I move to focus on the significance of having a close-up of Lewis's face engraved on the US Postal Service's 2022 Black Heritage "forever" stamp (figure 7.5). Stamps were a Victorian invention: The first stamp was the Penny Black, made in 1840, which featured Queen Victoria's visage printed from an engraving by William Wyon. More than one hundred years later, in 1984, Maud Sulter created twelve heads for a series titled *Studies for a National Postage Stamp* meant to call attention to the many Black women suffering from AIDS and other afflictions, including domestic violence. Lewis's image on the US postage stamp helped valorize her and served as a form of redress. The stamp helped her image stick in the minds of those who purchased, used, and received it. Her image and life story may have been forgotten (by some), but she was never gone; rather, as Joseph Roach contends, she was imperfectly deferred. This miniature work of art is a commissioned commercial memorial based on the Marshall photograph of Lewis taken in Boston and discussed in chapter 6. It puts her visage in circulation around the globe anew—this time as an emblem of national and racial pride. The stamp affords us the opportunity to look at subsequent, residual performances of Lewis that recur in art and text by contemporary artists. Lewis appears in twentieth- and twenty-first century works of art *as* a work of art that pays tribute to her in bodily form. This repeated gesture then becomes part of her allure as an "artistic personality" whose aura continues to attract audiences' desires for her presence.

Many recent artistic renderings of Lewis feature her face rather than the sculptural works she produced. Whereas earlier, as I argue, she was

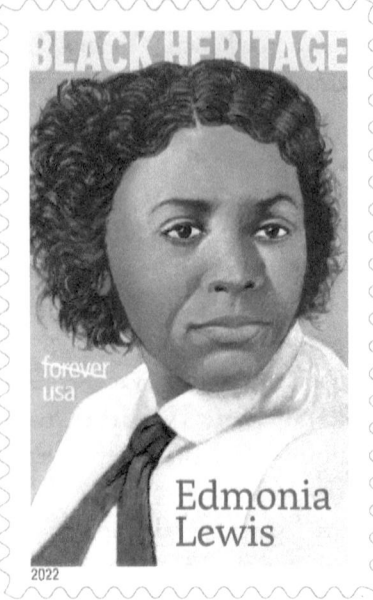

7.5 Antonio Alcalá, Edmonia Lewis Forever stamp (Black Heritage series). Casein-paint portrait based on a photograph by Augustus Marshall made in Boston between 1864 and 1871. Design based on art by Alex Bostic. The US Post Office, 2022.

pictured in proximity to her sculptures, now she is shown emerging as the embodied central subject to the exclusion of the art she made. However, the cover art of this book comes from an artist who has featured Lewis's sculpture as much as her portrait. In *For Edmonia Lewis: Together, Sculpting,* an ongoing community project and interactive website (launched on July 4, 2024), yétúndé ọlágbajú allows audiences to play with cutouts of both Lewis and her art. Ọlágbajú's online collaborative project features moving parts and permits viewers to make their own endlessly engaging collages out of bits of Lewis's oeuvre and image. Moving two-dimensional renderings of her sculptures, which have been copied and disarticulated from their "origin" and made manipulable, convert Lewis and her work into moving stones.

Although the collaborative commissioned cover for this book, titled *Edmonia Lewis: Shooting Star* (2024), features aspects of two different photographic images of Lewis alongside an outtake from one of her works—a close-up cutout of the rose from the base of her sculpture *Poor Cupid*—the artist, ọlágbajú, has fractured and fragmented as well as replicated, tinted, and rearranged these digitized fragments. As Tyehimba Jess does with poetic language, ọlágbajú translates Lewis's sculpture into new visual media. In other tributes to Lewis reviewed here, contemporary artists focus on Lewis more than her sculpture in their various citations. Both Jess and ọlágbajú transform Lewis herself into a work of art, thereby solidifying the work and life explored in this book and signified by its subtitle: "About the Art of Edmonia Lewis."

When he was teaching at Princeton University in the 1990s, poet Yusef Komunyakaa, his colleague Aleta Hayes, and composer Bill Banfield worked on a dramatic musical performance about Edmonia starring Hayes in the title role. This version of the sculptor's life was called "Ishkadooh." The show was workshopped in Toni Morrison's Princeton Atelier and eventually transformed into the opera *Edmonia: A Multidisciplinary Musical Dramatization*.[27] In this rendition, Edmonia is played by three different leads: a soprano as the young Edmonia, a modern dancer as the adult Edmonia, and a mezzo as the older Edmonia. In the show's finale in act 2, all three interpreters of Edmonia appear on stage together in a powerful instantiation of the artist's complex persona.

The footnotes to this book overflow with such an abundance of tributes to, and engagements with, Lewis's own visage and the statues she sculpted. We can say with certainty that in whatever form the archives take—print, material, ephemera, memories, drawings, collages, electronic and digital remarks, websites, and impossible haptic-optic and even sonic encounters—it appears that some material trace about the art of Edmonia Lewis will exist . . . forever.[28]

Interlude
Maud Sulter

She disappeared. It can happen to any of us.

Maud Sulter, on her character Hysteria, based on Edmonia Lewis

Queer Afro-Scottish poet and visual artist Maud Sulter (1960–2008) revived Lewis in her 1991 multimedia installation *Hysteria*. Sulter created the complex work as homage to Lewis during a Momart Fellowship at the Tate Liverpool. The exhibition toured across Britain from 1991 to 1992 with stops in Kendal, Birmingham, and Rochdale before concluding at the Royal Festival Hall in London. This mixed-media work comprised a haunting jazz soundscape, marble sculptural elements, large-scale

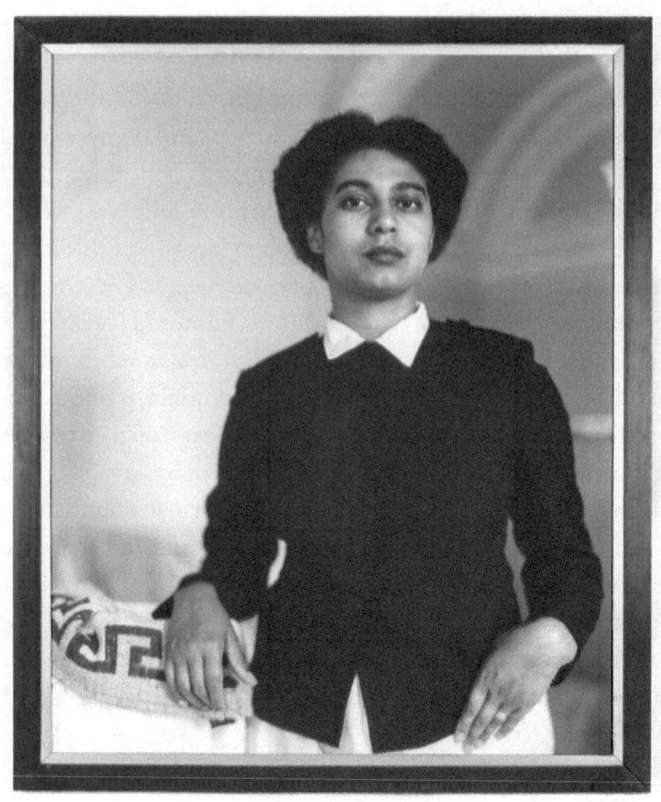

· Hysteria ·

7i.1 Maud Sulter, *Hysteria* (*Hysteria* series), 1991. Black-and-white photographic print, 58.3 × 45.7 in. © The Estate of Maud Sulter. Courtesy of ADAGP, Paris.

black-and-white photographs, and gilt labels—all collated carefully to honor a fictionalized composite Black female artist named Hysteria, who was based on and inspired by Edmonia Lewis (figure 7i.1). The eponymous piece also included a script for a film, substantiating the idea that Lewis's story lends itself to moving narratives that incorporate different media.

In line with most of Sulter's brilliant, multifaceted work, *Hysteria* sought to center Black women's narratives. In this regard, Lewis, about whom even less was known in the 1990s when Sulter was researching and making this piece, became an ideal subject. Like the other artists featured in the interludes of this book, Sulter owes something to Lewis's audacious existence. She, too, must be credited with linking her art and life to Lewis's and claiming the latter as a clear, queer precedent.,

A 1991 advertisement for the show in *Spare Rib* noted that *Hysteria* "consist[s] of large scale photoworks, marble plaques, scripted narrative and audio recording on compact disc." All these distinct components were installed in galleries as part of Sulter's fictive, interdisciplinary reenactment of these bits of Lewis's life. Through these multimedia components, "*Hysteria* tells the story of a 'blackwoman' artist who traveled from America to seek fame and fortune as a sculptor in Rome in the nineteenth century."[29] The narrative drew on fragments of Lewis's biography to create a new, amalgamated, and somewhat anonymized or mythic figure (Hysteria) who was also a successful nineteenth-century artist. Epitomizing her ethos and style, Sulter was invested in making "cross-temporal" portraiture in which she used her own body to portray "others." Tellingly, Sulter chose to embody the figure of Hysteria herself, as a kind of layered (self-)portrait in the guise of Lewis. Where, earlier, in chapter 1's interlude about Faith Ringgold, we saw how that artist elected to pose herself *next* to Lewis, Sulter decided to virtually *become* Edmonia in her embodied photographic performance.

Sulter also enlisted several of her friends to sit as the other subjects depicted in the dramatic, oversize still photographs that composed the installation *Hysteria*. These several semifictional figures drawn from Lewis's actual story included the Lawyer, his wife, Crone, and Hagar, whom Hysteria marries at the end of the filmscript. Sulter took Polaroids of her colleagues, such as the playwright and thespian Bernadine Evaristo (b. 1959), then had the photographs enlarged and printed as oversize black-and-white images (21 × 14.5 cm). As described in *Maud Sulter: Passion*, the catalogue for a posthumous exhibition of Sulter's photography, *Hysteria* was "a multi-media installation in which 16 photographs, [still-life tableaux] each with a marble title panel, . . . [are] displayed with a block of marble inscribed 'Temporis Filia Veritas' or 'Truth is the daughter of Time.' Fragments of a screenplay and music composed by Miles Ofuso Danso are included on the accompanying CD. *Hysteria* is loosely based on the social and artistic lives of Edmonia Lewis

(1844–1907), the celebrated nineteenth-century sculptor of African-American and Native American (Chippewa) heritage."[30] In 1992, a year after the work was installed, Sulter wrote, "*Hysteria* tells the tale of a nineteenth-century Black woman artist who sails from the Americas to Europe to seek fame and fortune as a sculptor. Having achieved a successful career she disappears."[31] The show received many positive reviews for its deft use of still-life tableaux and the way it engaged audiences complexly with its mixture of sight and sound.

It is no accident that Sulter envisioned this tribute to Edmonia as an exhibition for the gallery and also as a film with music. Simply stated, "Maud Sulter was one of many black women artists whose work put race, sexuality and identity at the heart of debates about art, aesthetics and the visual image and whose work critically intervened in the narratives of western art and its histories."[32] I suggest that subsequent artists have been drawn to Lewis's work because of open gaps that might mark the queer and radical aspects of her life. This is to say that Lewis, on first glance, does not necessarily appear to be a renegade (and indeed there is evidence to suggest she was something of a conformist); however, the very lack of definitive information leaves open the possibility of multiple, contradictory readings of the meaning of her work and life. Below is an abbreviation of Sulter's script that accompanied the exhibition. It is interesting that Sulter also thought about the medium of film as a means to render extraordinary, cinematic aspects of Lewis's life and work. It proceeds in almost stop-action freeze frames, as if it were composed of a series of stills, like photographs or sculptures frozen in time and yet meant to move, again.

Scene One

Time 1860's. Place Oberlin Ohio. We see the heavy wooden doors of the courtroom fly open. A group of toga clad figures carry Hysteria shoulder high. They are jubilant. As they move down the corridor they confront two young women of Hysteria's age. They are dressed in restrictive Victorian garb. Their long blond hair tied back tightly in plaits. Hysteria's lawyer—also dressed in strict Victorian dress—lifts the plaits high above the young women's heads. Hysteria is now standing in front of them. She raises a scythe and we hear it cut the air:

The frame freezes on the sight of a black fist clutching a handful of golden corn.

Scene Two

Roll opening credits . . . over . . .

Hysteria is now aboard ship. We see her silhouetted against the rigging. The ship docks. On the dockside we see her luggage. A variety of trunks and bags all labelled with the word Roma.

Deborah Cherry notes that "the screenplay is more a rebus than an explanation, and it runs discontinuously with the visual images. Sulter is not re-creating history or making documentary. She is once again experimenting with allegory, always duplicitous and treacherous in its entangled mazes of texts and images and its spiralling eddies of time." These "spiralling eddies of time" are akin to our readings of queer time and show these "blackwomen artists" connecting across impossible, moving spaces. Reassembling the "scattered remains strewn across history" involves the gathering and reusing of fragments, scraps, objects, images, sounds, voices that have survived, some almost by chance, some against the odds. The installations under discussion here neither visualize nor secure historical or contemporary personages, since "presence" cannot simply be inserted or asserted to fill what has hitherto been construed as "absence." It is the problem of erasure and the play of absence and presence that motivated much of Sulter's work. All of which engages in some fashion with questions of how, as she explains, "black women's contribution to culture is so often erased or marginalised. So it's important for me as an individual, and obviously as a black woman artist, to put black women back in the centre of the frame—both literally within the photographic image, but also within the cultural institutions where our work operates."[33] Sulter's installation, performance piece, and film script commemorate Lewis as a residual imprint.

Sulter's long-standing commitment to historicizing feminist art led her to curate a show honoring her predecessors in the form of a critical genealogy. Although this show honored women artists of many origins and genres, Sulter was ultimately concerned with "how black women's creativity is present then disappears." Sulter's interest in disappearance and revival led her to study different forms of commemoration. Sulter remembers "being in Pere Lachaise cemetery and reading the tombstones; seeing the tombstone of Rosa Bonheur (1822–99), which is also the tombstone of her partner, painter Anna Klumpke (1856–1942); seeing the tombstone of Gertrude Stein, where it's actually very difficult to see the other side of the tombstone designed by Francis Rose, which carries the name of Alice B. Toklas. And so that invisibility, even where there is presence, was something that I wanted to express through the portrayal of the artist recreating herself in the role of Calliope."[34]

In these curatorial interventions, Sulter exposed the way museums archive art.[35] Like innovative artist and curator Fred Wilson, who has, since the late 1980s, rearranged traditional museum collections as a means of reordering historical objects and subjects, Sulter has commented on the very spaces where her work was contextualized and framed.[36] Another tactic that both Sulter and Wilson deployed was to alter wall labels and create new works to reveal the otherwise masked and hidden ideological reasoning that governed many museum spaces. As Sulter notes, "As a black person and a woman I don't read history for facts, I read it for clues."[37] Such reconfigurations continue in the ongoing debates about the curatorial display of work by and about enslaved people, of stolen art and also Indigenous people—debates that necessarily influence how we think about Edmonia Lewis and exhibit her art.

Sulter astutely juxtaposes material not usually displayed together in museums. In redrawing and reinstalling items, she commented on curatorial elisions often having to do with racial slavery, imperialism, and patriarchy. In a 2023 essay I coauthored with Deborah Cherry, we concluded: "Sulter's approach seeks to re-distribute and literally reframe Victorian standards. *Museum* provides a concrete example of how a contemporary artist worked with one specific Victorian artwork and collection to offer new perspectives on that object. In doing so, the works become intertextually imbricated. Sharing the same museum space gives each work a new contextual relation such that Collier's work can no longer be imagined without Sulter's response."[38]

Maud Sulter revives the human capacity for creating scenarios and stories in our minds into which we project ourselves disidentified as heroes and heroines, victims, and champions. In much Eurocentric culture, long dominated by the values and representations of white patriarchy (which only provides roles for other people on and in its terms), she asks, "Where are representations of strong, creative black women?"[39] The antipatriarchal sentiment and foregrounding of "blackwomen" are in line with this artist's long-standing commitment to transforming visual narratives from the past. As an artist, curator, poet, photographer, historian, and activist, Sulter created work that put her at the forefront of Black feminist praxis in Britain.[40] Although I had long admired Sulter's art, I did not learn until a few years ago that she too had been drawn into the powerful orbit produced by Edmonia Lewis. Our mutual interest made me wonder: With what force, what felicity, and what counterfactual possibilities could Edmonia Lewis have reached beyond her grave to enlist us and so many others in her eternal revival?

Afterword

Now, I take leave of her image. It returns intermittently, translucent—as a fevered hallucination. I know that this book, with its endless archival returns, can never result in giving Lewis to me as a woman in full. Her body of work remains to be seen—given that so much of it is still missing, dispersed, fragmented, "a body in pieces," distributed across our restless Atlantic world. Lewis modeled others and, in so doing, herself became a model for becoming "free within ourselves." Edmonia Lewis is our lodestone. I yearn to touch her . . . work. In retrospect, I imagine her as a part of my past that I had forgotten but nevertheless had always been . . . waiting on, for and with. . . . It is in fleeting moments that I experience the impossibility of her touch re-covering mine. I so wish to embrace her; however, like sculpture in the round, at each turn, she recedes, thereby fomenting yet exceeding my queer desire. Left bereft, I seek out her warm brown hands that I might hold them in mine. I envision her as the woman in Lord Byron's famous 1814 idyll "She Walks in Beauty," the opening lines of which read: "She walks in beauty, like the night / Of cloudless climes and starry skies; / And all that's best of dark and bright / Meet in her aspect and her eyes." I can see her standing at sunset on the Scalinata della Trinità dei Monti in Rome, a shimmering, ancestral presence or precedent. Unwittingly I followed in her footsteps when I was there as a small child in 1969, on those very same steep stone steps that first opened to the public in 1725. When I traveled to Rome again, decades later, in 2023, I followed her trailblazed path as I bounded up the 135 stone steps from the Piazza di Spagna in search of her. I feel that I shall forever be indebted to her genius. Edmonia's gaze, like the blank, unseeing stares of some neoclassical statues or those produced in the rosette faces sculpted by Simone Leigh, can never return a longing look. I know that we are engaged in an impossible love affair. Closing, close, I situate Lewis, momentarily, momentously, in an ever expanding pantheon of colored artists: She stands as our complex and beautiful subject of desire. We are bound together through print, marble, and ink. I imagine that it was she who found me—improbably, across space, time, and distance. This fact does not prevent me or any of her many other admirers from putting her on a pedestal and re-creating her as our Galatea—willing her to animation—or making her into a monument as if she were the apotheosis of a moving stone.

Acknowledgments

This project has been long in the making. According to my *curriculum vitae* (for memory hardly serves me) the first public talk I gave about the art of Edmonia Lewis took place in 2005 when I gave the keynote address at the Interdisciplinary Nineteenth Century Studies Conference at Louisiana State University, Baton Rouge. The actual date of my first encounter with Lewis occurred a decade prior to that event, in 1995 in London, England. In 2010 Duke University Press published the first scholarly monograph on Lewis: Kirsten Buick's brilliant *Child of the Fire*. I was honored to have been asked to review her study for the *Women's Review of Books*. Buick's work continues to be the standard for future scholarship on Lewis as her readings remain essential. Indeed, I owe her a great debt.

From the nineteenth century to the present, a growing cadre of poets, performers, novelists, playwrights, scholars, and visual artists has worked to keep Lewis alive. Many are named in the endnotes of this book. Thank you to Romare Bearden, David Driskell, the Hendersons, Lorraine O'Grady, Dorothy Sterling, Judith Wilson, and Marilyn Richardson. My gratitude also goes to yétúndé ọlágbajú, whom I commissioned to make the cover art for this book, and to each of the artists highlighted: Beverly Buchanan, Simone Leigh, Kent Monkman, Zanele Muholi, Faith Ringgold, Maud Sulter, and Mickalene Thomas. There is no question that I have reaped numerous rewards from the generosity of many artists and scholars over these many years.

I have gleaned insights as well from audience members, students, librarians, and colleagues, and I am grateful for all their sage advice and probing questions. This book would not exist without the community they provided. In particular, I thank members of my various writing groups—Ayanna Flewellen, the late Elizabeth Freeman, Kali Handelman, Allyson Hobbs, Jane Jones, Beth Piatote, Leigh Raiford, Wendy Seppenson, and especially Abriel Louise Young. I benefited from using the Internet Archive and giving talks at the Henry Moore Foundation, Harvard, Yale, Princeton, and for many Victorian studies groups.

The photographs in this book benefited from work by Yutsha Dayal, Bryn Evans, Julien Fischer, and, preeminently, the photographer John Janca, who went above and beyond to refine the images included here. I owe a special shout-out to Dr. Gigi Otálvaro-Hormillosa, who helped to prepare the final manuscript for publication and whose grace under pressure is admirable. This project was improved by the brilliant scholarship and generous support of Caitlin Beach, Gloria Jean Bell, Deborah Cherry, Farah Jasmine Griffin, Kellie Jones, Tiya Miles, Steven Nelson, C. Riley Snorton, and Deborah Willis. I thank my expansive network of extraordinary colleagues and students at Stanford and elsewhere who have had a hand in making this book: Samer Al-Saber, Sukanya Banerjee, Dr. Bill Banfield, Stefanie Batiste, Isabel Bendek, Hershini Bhana Young, Janaka Bowman, Daphne Brooks, Kirsten Buick (again), Anne Cheng, Adrienne Childs, Indie Choudury, Soyica Colbert, Huey Copeland, Ann Cvetkovich, Cathy Davidson, Phillip DeLoria, Sarah Derbrew, Gwendolyn DuBois Shaw, Erica Edwards, Jacqueline Francis, Duana Fulwilley, Gretchen Gerzina, Michael Gillespie, Shaheen Haq, Shawyna Harris, Aleta Hayes, Janet Jarriel, Tyehimba Jess, E. Patrick Johnson, Alexis Jones, Meta Jones, Sir Isaac Julien, John Keene, Shawon Kinew, Marci Kwon, Kathleen McHugh, Kobena Mercer, Charmaine Nelson, Rachel Grace Newman, Ellen Oh, Tavia N'yongo, Carol Ockman, Venetria Patton, Pratibha Parmar, Richard J. Powell, Melissa Ragaine, Heika Raphael-Hernandez, Jeffrey Richmond-Moll, Joseph Roach, Aileen Robinson, the late Myrton Running-Wolf, Rose Salseda, Rebecca Schneider, Charlotte Sheedy, Amani Starnes, Mecca Sullivan, amara tabor-smith, Lava Thomas, Scott Trafton, Zoe Tweedie, Jennifer Tyburczy, Carole-Anne Tyler, Luke Williams, and Tristram Wolf. Matt Richardson deserves special mention for generously sending me a box of his former research on Lewis, which arrived one summer day to my great delight. I thank the anonymous readers for Duke University Press for their crucial interventions. Thank you to Matthew MacLellen for completing the index. All remaining mistakes are my own.

The ongoing help I have received from my colleagues in the Department of Theater and Performance Studies at Stanford is appreciated greatly: thank you to Eugene Buck, Katie Dooling, Harry Elam, Diana Looser, Jisha Menon, and Janet Pineda. I appreciate the invaluable help from workers at St. Mary's Cemetery, London, and from Kyle Burkett, Philip Curtin, and Michael Lara at the San Jose Public Library.

The Guggenheim Memorial Foundation awarded me a Fellowship in Fine Arts Research and the Bogliasco Foundation selected me for a Virginia Hamilton Fellowship—both of which afforded me research time in Italy. I acknowledge the generous support from the Stanford University Dean's Office of Humanities and Social Sciences, which provided me with a Cultivating Humanities Grant; the Office of the Vice President of the Arts for a Burt McMurtry Arts Initiative Award; and funding from the Center for Comparative Studies in Race and Ethnicity, Native American Studies, and the Institute for Diversity in the Arts. I thank the Programs in Feminist, Gender, and Sexuality Studies and American Studies, both of which provided me with summer research support. This book is all the better for the extraordinary opportunity to have worked with Stanford's Cantor Arts Center, where Marion Gill, Christina Linden, Kwang Mi Ro, Veronica Roberts, Vivian Sming, Lily Wong Soogrim, and my curatorial collaborator, Patrick Crowley, allowed me to curate the exhibition *Edmonia Lewis: Indelible Impressions*, which ran from September 17, 2025, to January 4, 2026.

At Duke University Press, I want to thank Ryan Kendall, Alejandra Mejía, Livia Tenzer, and Steven Baker for their excellent stewardship of this project. Ken Wissoker remains an incomparable editor to whom the fields he helped to develop owe so much. This book would not have been written without the continuing support of Elizabeth Alexander, Nick Boggs, Prudence Carter, Janet Neary, Allyson Hobbs, Yvonne Welbon, and Robyn Wiegman. I am grateful for my family: Alan and Melinda Brody, Michael Watkins, Joey Rivera, and Evangeline Franklin. I thank Judith Haughton and Sonia Lamothe, who tended to my late mother in her final hours. My father, Nathan Brody, remains an inspiration and North Star. I appreciate his views on art and life and thank him for his enduring love and support. I acknowledge the calming presence of the little doggies Suki and Juju, who, transmogrified, appear as the hummingbirds I see each morning in the garden. And last, and forever, I thank my spouse, Sio Alvarez, the love of my life, who, I am glad to say, resisted the temptation to change their name to "Edmonia Lewis" so that I would pay attention to them. Thank you to everyone who had a hand in this book.

Notes

Introduction

1   "Edmonia Lewis: An American Sculptor of Undoubted Genius, An Honor to the Colored Race; Sketch of Her Early Life and Art Studies—Some of her Greatest Works—Life in Italy," *San Francisco Chronicle*, September 7, 1879. In addition to her personal names, Lewis was referred to by a litany of terms and descriptions that sought to render her Other, such as "The Miscegan Sculptor," used in the *Daily Graphic: An Illustrated Evening Paper* (New York), 1873, 58.

2   Miles, "A Singular Maker's Many Migrations," 11.

3   *The Elevator*, August 30, 1873. Lewis and many of her contemporaries subscribed to the racial designation "colored." Throughout this book she will be referred to by multiple terms in accordance with the tangled and shifting historical record that continues to complicate all racial designations produced in various discourses.

4   "How Edmonia Lewis Became an Artist," unsigned tract, 1870 (emphasis in original), Harvard University Library, Gift of Hon. Charles Sumner, Boston. I thank Tiya Miles for sharing this document with me. Melissa Benbow analyzes this important document in her dissertation, "Before Black Bohemia."

5   On neoclassical sculpture, see Rheims, *19th Century Sculpture*, 15–48; also, GIlroy-Ware, *The Classical Body in Romantic Britain*.

6   Quoted in the *Lyon County Times* (Silver City, NV), December 25, 1878.

7   Quoted in "Seeking Equality Abroad," *New York Times,* December 29, 1878, 5.

8   S. Hall, *Writings on Visual Arts and Culture.* See also Henderson and Bearden, *A History of African-American Artists,* 55. Harry Henderson and Romare Bearden discuss Lewis's "accented" English, which they attribute to her having spoken the Ojibwe language as a child.

9   *Oxford English Dictionary,* "diaspora," updated 2014, https://www.oed.com/dictionary/diaspora_n?tl=true.

10   Erdrich, *Books and Islands in Ojibwe Country.*

11   See Gilroy, *The Black Atlantic*; Roach, *Cities of the Dead*; Mercer, *Travel and See*; and, especially, Copeland and Nelson, *Black Modernisms in the Transatlantic World.*

12   See Snead, "On Repetition in Black Culture"; Diawara, "Englishness and Blackness"; Powell, *Cutting a Figure*; Moten, *In the Break.* We could even think about the early cutter of profiles, the enslaved Moses Williams (1777–1825), who made silhouettes in Philadelphia, and the work of Kara Walker.

13   See Levi, *Cinema by Other Means.*

14   Campt and Jafa, "Love Is the Message, the Message Is Death."

15   See Gordon, *Indecent Exposures,* 20. In one early ad featuring another of Stanford's horse, Abe Edington, there is a reference to Abe being "driven by C. Martin." The horse in question was Sallie Gardner, pictured in the series of photographs "Sallie Gardner; or, The Horse in Motion" from 1878. The original horse, Occident, photographed in 1872, appears only in a woodcut as the original photograph was lost. See Solnit, *River of Shadows.*

16   See Handlin, *Statue of Liberty.* Bartholdi first devised a version of the statue when he was twenty-two years old, while working in Suez in the 1850s. It went through many iterations, becoming more classical and less "Egyptian" as it evolved. The statue was a feat of engineering. See also Amy Sherald's monumental oil painting *Trans Forming Liberty* (2024).

17   In my mind, McQueen's approach to the famous monumental sculpture renders the statue as an animated, moving stone. The eight-minute film plays with the size-distance problem of locating oneself in space and explores the idea of the statue's liberation from its prior historical suturing to contoured form and "stable" architecture. The word *statue* etymologically comes from the Latin verb *statuere* (to stand). Movement and stasis are perceptual and profoundly imbricated, even dependent modes that sculpture is situated uniquely to address. See Harasawa et al., "Effects of Content and Viewing Distance." See also

Garland-Thomson, *Staring*; Young, *Embodying Black Experience*; and Lingo, *Mochi's Edge and Bernini's Baroque*.

18 He also does this in *Baltimore* (2003), shot in the Baltimore Museum of Art, which owns a copy of Edmonia Lewis's sculpture *Night*, a version of her award-winning *Asleep*, discussed in chapter 4.

19 Julien and Gilroy-Ware, *Lessons of the Hour*, 28. See also Maidment and Seput, *Isaac Julien*.

20 Eisenstein, "A Dialectical Approach to Film Form," 1. In an interview between Mark Nash and Adam Finch, Nash notes how the multiscreen editing in Abel Gance's 1927 film *Napoléon* affected him and Julien when they both saw it in London in 1980. Gance used an experimental format he named Polyvision, which shifted from a single panoramic image shown across three screens to a variegated display of three distinct images on each screen. See Maidment and Seput, *Isaac Julien*, 84.

21 On the exhibition, titled *Vintage* and shown April 22–June 18, 2016, see "Isaac Julien at Jessica Silverman San Francisco," Contemporary Art Library, https://www.contemporaryartlibrary.org/project/isaac-julien-at-jessica-silverman-san-francisco-18494.

22 Reynolds quoted in Potts, *Sculptural Imagination*, 25.

23 Pollock, "The Grace of Time," 190; Pollock, *Differencing the Canon*.

24 Meisel, *Realizations*.

25 Kennedy, *People Who Led to My Plays*, 118.

26 Grosz, *Nick of Time*, 5.

27 Getsy, *Body Doubles*.

28 It reminds me of a passage I read in Harriot Hunt's autobiography, *Glances and Glimpses*. Hunt commissioned a headstone from Lewis. Hunt found a palazzo in Florence with a mirrored room that afforded viewers the chance to see multiple aspects of a single statue of exquisite beauty placed in the center of the space. "Each of these mirrors," she wrote, "reflects the statue at different angles, and consequently, exhibits some particular point more prominently or accurately than the others. Artists study the statue through the mirrors, and they can estimate the beauty of each separated part, and form a better judgment of the perfection of the whole." Hunt, *Glances and Glimpses*, 425.

29 The most recent research includes the exhibition catalogues Brody, *Edmonia Lewis*; and Harris and Richmond-Moll, *Edmonia Lewis*.

30 Mercer, *Travel and See*, 9.

31 Lyotard, *The Inhuman*.

32 See Levi, *Cinema by Other Means*; and Marks, *Touch*.

33 Moten, *In the Break*.

34 Meisel, *Realizations*; Brooks, *Bodies in Dissent*; Nead, *Haunted Gallery*.

35 In this context, we might also think about a renewed desire for depth, as in Rickerby Hinds's hip-hop tableaux vivants, work by Isaac Julien, and the commercial success of Avatar shown in 3-D—which seems to signal a move away from our immersion in flat digital screens toward the use of touch screens and 3-D technology that allows us to "visit" galleries, including the Smithsonian, where Lewis's famous sculpture *The Death of Cleopatra* is now installed. See Linscott, "Virtually and Actually Black"; and Linscott, "Extended Reality (XR)." Thanks to Michael Gillespie for these sources.

36 Beard, "Judgments in Stone." For Lewis's bust, see "Young Octavian," Smithsonian Museum of American Art, https://americanart.si.edu /artwork/young-octavian-14633.

37 Keeling, "Looking for M—."

38 Gaines, *Black Performance on the Outskirts of the Left*.

39 For the generic objectifying catalogue titles of actual museum collections, see for Lewis, *Voyage of the Sable Venus*. There are at least two explicit references to Edmonia's work in this devastating compendium of profound "found" titular artworks: a mention of *Forever Free* listed on page 92 and *The Old Arrow Maker and His Daughter* (93). Like *Moving Stones*, Robin Coste Lewis's narrative poem seeks to "explore and record not only the history of human thought, but also how normative and complicit artists, curators, and art institutions have been participating in—if not creating—this history . . . and as an homage includes titles of art *by* black women curators and artists, whether or not their art included a black female figure" (emphasis added). Lewis, "Preface," in *Voyage of the Sable Venus*, 35.

40 DeLoria, *Indians in Unexpected Places*, 1–14.

41 Miles, *Night Flyer*.

42 Snorton, *Black on Both Sides*, 7, 11.

43 One of the first articles to assert this "oddness" was the "black lesbian bibliography" section of "'Ain't I a Womon [sic]," *Off Our Backs: A Women's News Journal* 9, no. 6 (1979), 25. This section was written by J. R. Roberts. The work was expanded into *Black Lesbians: An Annotated Bibliography*, to which Roberts added a foreword by Barbara Smith. Artist yétúndé ọlágbajú sees the folds in Lewis's work as "holding erotic queer longings." Author's conversation with the artist, March 2024. Lewis is included in Summers, *Queer Encyolopedia of the Visual Arts*.

44 Gissing, *The Odd Women*.

45 An example comes from Naurice Frank Woods Jr., who, in an extensive footnote in his excellent biographical chapter on Lewis, critiques scholar Scott Trafton for seemingly "forcing a lesbian identity upon Lewis, using her associate with 'the flock' as a leading cause for assumption [and] . . . implying possible relationships with Adeline T. Howard and Adelia Gates, a painter who accompanied Lewis to Naples with Frederick Douglass and his wife during their visit to Italy. As with other attempts to define Lewis as a lesbian, Trafton offers no evidence to substantiate the claim." Woods, *Race and Racism in Nineteenth-Century Art*, 238.

46 Summers, *Queer Encyclopedia of the Visual Arts*. See also the Guerrilla Girls' *When Racism and Sexism Are No Longer Fashionable, How Much Will Your Art Collection Be Worth?* (1989), one of the group's public service messages that mentions Edmonia Lewis in a list of women artists. Guerrilla Girls, *Confessions of the Guerrilla Girls*, 58. The name "Edmonia Lewis" is also one of the group's adopted pseudonyms.

47 Lewis, quoted in Brown, *Rising Son*, 466.

48 Katz, *About Face*.

49 Dover, *American Negro Art*, 27, 28.

50 Without the scholarship of Black art historians, artists, and curators (many of whom were also feminists), Edmonia Lewis may well have remained "lost." This project would not exist without the work of Cedric Dover, Romare Bearden, Albert and Harry Henderson, Marilyn Richardson, Judith Wilson, Kirsten Buick, Kinshasa Cornwill, Samella Lewis, Richard Powell, Lisa Fearrington, Kimberly Pinder, Gwendolyn DuBois Shaw, David Driskell, Farah Jasmine Griffin, Regina Perry, Freida High Tesfagiorgis, Shawyna Harris, Tiya Miles, Leonard Simon, Charmaine Nelson, Naurice Frank Woods, Jr., Maud Sulter, Elizabeth Alexander and many, many more. I follow Kirsten Buick's call to focus on developing more complex models for understanding Lewis in relationship to her art. As such, I focus on Lewis's active doing of her art and identity. As Buick explains, "If we work from the premise that process is a space through which the artist moves freely, a context, which changes as much for the artist as it does for the audiences of objects created by the artists, then perhaps we can begin to conceptualize artistic intent as the infinitive 'to do.'" *Child of the Fire*, xvi.

51 Hartman, *Wayward Lives, Beautiful Experiments*, 226, 228 (emphasis in original).

52 Fittingly, Edmonia Lewis appears as a composite character in Iagiaba Scego's lyrical novel *La linea del colore* (2020), published in English as *The Color Line* (2022). Scego's fictionalized account continues Lew-

is's connection to African diasporas that resulted in a Black presence in Italy going back thousands of years. Scego's beautiful narrative alternates between the life of a character based on Edmonia and Sarah Parker-Remond and the story of a researcher, an Ethiopian woman. The novel cuts across time in order to imagine the composite nineteenth-century Black emigrant to Italy and the African woman from the area colonized by Italy.

53 Kirsten Buick provocatively suggests that "one can characterize Edmonia Lewis's slavery works by their 'distances': the time when they were created relative to the end of slavery; the place where they were created relative to where slavery occurred; even Lewis's own removed experience in that she was never a slave." Buick, *Child of the Fire*, 72. *Moving Stones* builds on Buick's foundational study as well as the dedicated work of Marilyn Richardson, who is completing a comprehensive biography of Lewis. My book has also benefited from insights in Charmaine Nelson's *The Color of Stone*, as well as the excellent biographical chapter in Naurice Frank Woods Jr.'s *Race and Racism in Nineteenth-Century Art*.

54 Eugene Warburg (1825–67) was a contemporary sculptor from New Orleans. He too worked in the neoclassical style. His brother Daniel was an engraver and a stonemason. Like Lewis, the brothers Warburg were "mixed race," though, as Paul Kaplan documents, Eugene, who owned slaves, sold some of them to finance his move to Europe in the 1850s. A small Parian marble sculpture of a character from Harriet Beecher Stowe's novel *Dred* exists, as well as stones laid to create the floor of a church in New Orleans, and there is a neoclassical portrait bust of John Young Mason, who served as the US minister to France. See Lewis, *African American Art and Artists*, 29. Also, this Warburg's seventh cousin, Aby, was the famous German art historian (discussed above; see note 23).

55 Laura U. Marks uses the term *haptic visuality* to describe how touch and sight work together. This relay between touch and sight of sculpture and, in Marks's work, even film invites us to understand perception as a moving form. See Marks, *Skin of the Film*.

56 Aria Dean, quoted in "Aria Dean Is Having Fun Being Herself," interview with M. H. Miller, *New York Times Style Magazine*, August 21, 2022, M273.

57 Here I am riffing on Meghan Trainor's pop song "It's All About That Bass," from her album *Title* (Epic Records, 2014).

58 Sharpe, *In the Wake*. See also the photographic work by Afro-Cuban artist Gisela Torres, *Looking for Edmonia (Self-Portrait)*, 2020, https://www.giselatorres.com/new-page-1; and the video about one of Lewis's sculptures by Madeleine Hunt-Ehrlich, *Cleopatra at the*

Mall (2024), https://www.metmuseum.org/art/collection/search
/909996.

59   This is also true of the Choctaw-Cherokee artist Jeffrey Gibson (b.
     1972), the first Native American artist to represent the United States
     at the Venice Biennale, in 2024, with his multimedia work entitled
     The Space in Which to Place Me. Cherokee artist America Meredith
     painted a portrait of her, and she was included in the Smithsonian
     Museum's exhibition *Hearts of Our People: Native Women Artists* in
     2020. The show was organized by a panel of Native curators. Sadly,
     it was open for only a month before the Renwick Gallery was closed
     due to the start of the COVID-19 pandemic.

60   Katz, *About Face*. One could also imagine Benjamin's backward facing
     "Angel of History" in this scenario; see *Illuminations*, 257–58.

61   Conwill, "Introduction," 14. This is the catalogue that accompanied
     Lynda Roscoe Hartigan's exhibition of the same name.

Chapter 1. A Head of Her Time

Interlude epigraph: Faith Ringgold, *Picasso's Studio, The French Collection Part I, #7.*

1   Founded in 1841, the London Library moved to St. James's Square in
     1845. London's history is significant for Lewis. Once known as Lon-
     dinium when it was part of the Roman Empire, London was ruled by
     Boudicca (a woman) when it was fighting against Roman incursions.
     The imperial cities of London and Rome, once linked, play a part in
     our story of ancient sculptures and the diasporic movements of our
     central figure, who lived in both cities during her lifetime. Roman
     rule of Britain ended in the fifth century. London then dates as the
     seat of government from 1066, becoming the home of Parliament and
     subsequently the capital of the United Kingdom in 1707. I thank my
     colleague Sarah Derbrew for help with this information. See Derbrew,
     Untangling Blackness in Greek Antiquity.

2   Muñoz, "Ephemera as Evidence."

3   The first use of the camera to capture evidence of a crime appeared
     on stage in Dion Boucicault's play about ocular evidence, entitled *The
     Octoroon* (1859). See Erdman, "Caught in the Eye of the Eternal."

4   The famous abolitionist Gerrit Smith (discussed in chapter 3) wrote
     a column, "Heads of the Colored People," in Frederick Douglass's
     newspaper, the *North Star*. The vignettes in his column, printed be-
     tween 1852 and 1854, described everyday black New Yorkers working
     in industries. In his biography of Douglass, David Blight writes, "In
     the term 'Heads,' Smith brilliantly parodied reigning racial theories

of the time, such as phrenology, which argued that the alleged racial superiority of whites stemmed from larger craniums." Blight, *Frederick Douglass*, 256. Douglass took issue with some of the entries as they could be read as stereotypical. For more on this problem of racial representation, see Blight, *Frederick Douglass*, 256–58.

5   Edmonia Lewis was indeed ahead of her time. The term *shadow archive* has been mobilized by Tavia Nyong'o, in *Afro-Fabulation*, 11–12.

6   Helfand, *Scrapbooks*, xvii.

7   Sutcliffe, "Charles Reade's Notebooks," 64–109.

8   This brings to mind the current battle waged by conservative gatekeepers who censor library materials by banning books.

9   Among the first of some 382 members to subscribe were notable Victorian writers John Stuart Mill, Harriet Martineau, and William Thackeray.

10   I wrote about these works by Reade in in my first book, *Impossible Purities: Blackness, Femininity, and Victorian Culture*, ch. 3, "Masking Faces."

11   Reading this page from my desk in Oakland, California, homeland of the Muwekma Ohlone peoples, I cannot help but think of the opening of Tommy Orange's novel *There, There* (2018), with its prominent list of violently decapitated Indian heads used as grotesque trophies of Western attempts at dominance.

12   Garvey, *Writing with Scissors*, 207.

13   Buick, *Child of the Fire*, 135.

14   Buick, *Child of the Fire*, 136.

15   James, *William Wetmore Story and His Friends*, 257.

16   Buick identifies an art historical problem when it comes to the so-called anomalous Black or "colored" artist, with that phrase understood as oxymoronic. How can we narrate the life and work of an artist for whom her racial identity was paramount (she signed her work as by a "colored artist") and whose achievement was notable often for its contribution to racial achievement in a post-Emancipation era when Black life did not matter? Buick astutely argues that, "had Lewis remained in the United States, she would have had to continue to rely on abolitionist patronage almost exclusively and the sale of her work would have been largely dependent upon her as a product of race. By going to Italy, however, she made herself part of an international art world, gained a measure of distance from her abolitionist patrons, and thus set the terms upon which she would practice her art—as part of highly visible community of *American* artists—that depended on a national rather than a racial identification." Buick, *Child of the Fire*, 3.

17 Buick, *Child of the Fire*, 80. Buick's "Longfellow, Lewis, and the Cultural Work of Hiawatha" (ibid., ch. 3) offers a brilliant analysis of the pitfalls of racial representation in critical examinations of Lewis's Native subjects. See also Berkhofer, *The White Man's Indian*; Dippie, *Vanishing American*; Nickerson, "Artistic Interpretations of Henry Wadsworth Longfellow's *The Song of Hiawatha*, 1855–1900"; Holland, "Mary Edmonia Lewis's 'Minnehaha'"; DeLoria, *Playing Indian*; and Hutchinson, "Strength and Resistance in Native American Women's Sculpture."

18 Hutchinson, *Shape of Power*, 180.

19 Again, Kirsten Buick's fine scholarship questions such analogies made by one contemporary of Lewis's. Since we know little of Lewis's story from her own words rather than from reportage, she may always be enigmatic, open to others' interpretations of her motivations and ideas (including this one). More recently, scholars such as Gloria Jane Bell (Métis) and other scholars have read Lewis vis-a-vis Indigenous contexts. See Bell, *Eternal Sovereigns*—especially her reading of Lewis's petite portrait bust of Minnehaha, owned now by the Metropolitan Museum of Art in New York City.

20 The original work purportedly was purchased by Lady Ashburton, sculptor Harriet Hosmer's lover. These small, intricate sculptures are too large for a mantel but suitable for a side table in a Victorian home.

21 Derrida, *Archive Fever*, 12. I showed the photo when I first spoke about Lewis in 2005 in a keynote for the Interdisciplinary Nineteenth-Century Studies Conference on my first trip to New Orleans.

22 Many adherents to "Afro-futurism," as well as many Black queer studies scholars, have talked about the significance of the as-if as a form of speculation.

23 See Noble, *Algorithms of Oppression*; and Benjamin, *Race After Technology*.

24 Lewis, *Voyage of the Sable Venus*, 35, 93.

25 Broun, "Foreword," 8. I understand this begs the question of what can be defined as "art" or sculpture outside a museum.

26 See Achille Mbembe, "The Power of the Archive and Its Limits," in *Refiguring the Archive*, ed. Carolyn Hamilton (Cape Town: David Philip; Kluwer Academic, 2002), 19, quoted in Matt Richardson, *The Queer Limit of Black Memory*, 5. The title of this section pays homage to Richardson's work.

27 Roach, *Cities of the Dead*.

28 See "The British Museum Story," British Museum, accessed August 4, 2025, britishmuseum.org/about-us/british-museum-story.

29 Schneider, *Performing Remains*, 99.

30 Benjamin, "On the Concept of History."

31 Sharpe, *In the Wake*, 20. See also Kessel, "Notes on the African Burial Ground Monument, New York City."

32 Here I reference a few key works in African American studies that have looked to the ocean as a crucible of modern forms of Blackness. These range from Hortense Spillers's use of the phrase "Africans becoming Americans" (in *Black, White, and in Color*), to Paul Gilroy's seminal work *The Black Atlantic*, to Joseph Roach's deployment of the term "circum-Atlantic" in *Cities of the Dead*, to work by Marxist historians Marcus Rediker and Peter Linebaugh (Rediker, *The Slave Ship*; Linebaugh and Rediker, *The Many-Headed Hydra*), as well as Omise'eke Natasha Tinsley's *Thiefing Sugar*; Saidiya Hartman's *Lose Your Mother*, and Christina Sharpe's *In the Wake*.

33 See work by Ayana Omilade Flewellen in "Research," Ayana Flewellen, accessed August 4, 2025, https://www.ayanaflewellen.com/research.

34 Taylor, *The Archive and the Repertoire*, 21. See also Schneider, *Performing Remains*.

35 For example, Stephen Best argues that "what in fact makes black culture in the archive historical is less its power to 'reference' the past than the simultaneity of excess and emptiness that it affords." Best, *None Like Us*, 87.

36 The archive's formation may even be "preposterous" in the sense developed by art historian Mieke Bal, who reads art productively through the dyads of the "past/present or present/past." See Bal, *Quoting Caravaggio*.

37 *Lorain County News*, April 4, 1866.

38 Woods, *Race and Racism in Nineteenth-Century Art*, 126–27.

39 Miles, "A Singular Maker's Many Migrations," 12. See also Kramer, "Indigenous Frameworks and New Directions, a Convening"; and Groat, "On Black-Indigenous Ancestry."

40 Lewis quoted in Woods, *Race and Racism in Nineteenth-Century Art*, 128.

41 See Buick, *Child of the Fire*, 122–23; and Sienkewicz, "Encountering Edmonia in the Correspondence of Florence Freeman."

42 "Samuel Lewis: Showman, Musician, Businessman," *Bozeman Magazine*. February 1, 2024, https://bozemanmagazine.com/articles/2024/02/01/119753-samuel-lewis-showman-musician-businessman.

43 Buick, *Child of the Fire*, 213.

44 Nelson Primus to his sister Rebecca, n.d., c. 1867, Connecticut Historical Society, Hartford, CT. Primus later moved to San Francisco, where he was able to sell some of his paintings while also working as a journeyman painter. See also Beeching, "The Primus Papers."

45 Lydia Maria Child to Harriet Winslow Sewall, July 10, 1868, Robie-Sewall Papers, Massachusetts Historical Society, Boston.

46 Lydia Maria Child to Harriet Winslow Sewall, June 24, 1868, Robie-Sewall Papers, Massachusetts Historical Society.

47 Lydia Maria Child to Sarah Black Sturgis Shaw, August 1870(?), Houghton Library, Harvard University, MS AM 1417 (305), quoted in Buick, *Child of the Fire*, 16.

48 Quoted in Lydia Maria Child, "Letter from L. Maria Child," *The Liberator*, February 19, 1864. For an excellent discussion of Lewis's work in Boston and her innovative contributions to abolitionist sculptures, see Beach, *Sculpture at the Ends of Slavery*.

49 "Edmonia Lewis: An American Sculptor of Undoubted Genius," *San Francisco Chronicle*, September 7, 1879.

50 Woods, *Race and Racism in Nineteenth-Century Art*.

51 Bontemps, *100 Years of Negro Freedom*, 121–22.

52 Frederick Douglass travel diary, February 1887, 58–59, Library of Congress.

53 See Woods, *Race and Racism in Nineteenth-Century Art*.

54 For more on ethnohistory and racial classification, see Hallowell, "Ojibwa Ontology, Behavior, and World View"; Bohaker, *Doodem and Council Fire*.

55 Painter, *Creating Black Americans*.

56 Fanon, *Black Skin, White Masks* (originally published in French as *Peau noire, masques blancs* in 1952).

57 Forbes, *History of Red-Black Peoples*.

58 Forbes, *African and Native Americans*, 3. Forbes mentions Lewis in his essay "Intellectual Self-Determination and Sovereignty."

59 Mays, *Afro-Indigenous History of the History of the United States*.

60 English, *To Describe a Life*, 81.

61 See Fong, "The Stories Outside the African Farm."

62 Bell, *Eternal Sovereigns*.

63 Douglass, *The Liberator*, April 20, 1849, 2.

64 Nelson, *Color of Stone*, ch. 7, "The Black Queen in the White Body: Edmonia Lewis and the Dead Queen."

65 Buick, *Child of the Fire*, 50–67.

66 Jefferson, *Notes on the State of Virginia*, 234.

67 Manning, *Relationscapes*.

68   Bernstein, *Racial Innocence*, 69; see also chapter 5, "The Scripts of Black Dolls."

69   Buick, *Child of the Fire*, 213.

70   Porter, *American Negro Art*, 57, 58. There are several versions of the hand-sculpting story.

71   Edmonia Lewis to Sarah Whitney, October 28, 1867, quoted in Henderson and Henderson, *Indomitable Spirit of Edmonia Lewis*, n.p. (epilogue, ch. 3, "Spite").

72   The manifesto appears in Faith Ringgold, *Le Café des Artistes*; see figure ii.1.

73   For information on Ringgold's earlier work, see Ringgold, *Politics Power*; and Wallace, "For the Women's House," 14–15. See also Farrington, *Faith Ringgold*. In *We Flew Over the Bridge*, Ringgold discusses having taught Edmonia Lewis's work to her students in New York.

74   Farrington, *Creating Their Own Image*, 154.

75   Farrington, *Creating Their Own Image*, 155.

76   Farrington, *Faith Ringgold*, 41.

77   Ringgold, *Le Café des Artistes*.

78   See Cameron et al., *Dancing at the Louvre*. Apparently, when Ringgold's autobiography was rejected by publishers in the 1980s, she decided to embed her story in her own art. For Tavia Nyong'o's term *afro-fabulation*, see Nyong'o, *Afro-Fabulation*.

79   Ringgold quoted in Graulich and Witzling, "Freedom to Say What She Pleases," 14.

80   In my decades-long quest in search of Edmonia Lewis, I have found her most often in the texts of other Black women artists and historians. Some of these texts include the compendium Dannett, *Profiles of Negro Womanhood*, which includes an illustration of Edmonia Lewis by Horace Varela.

81   "World's Fair Tribute, Life Size Bust of Phyllis Wheatley, Afro American; Letter from Edmonia Lewis," *Pittsburgh Mirror*, reprinted in *Plain Dealer* (Detroit), March 17, 1893.

82   Shaw, *Portraits of a People*, 29 (quoting Ringgold), 30.

Chapter 2. Animating Stones

1   See Bjornerud, *Turning to Stone*.

2   Here I am thinking not only of Lewis but also of Lorna Simpson's large-scale work *did time elapse* (2024), made of acrylic and screenprint on gessoed fiberglass.

3   Associated Press, "Rare Stone Discovered Outlining Ancient Rome's City Limits," *AP News*, July 16, 2021, https://apnews .com/article/europe-science-arts-and-entertainment-rome -9db54446337b9312b3f666a87cdc4efc.

4   See the National Death Valley Park website, "The Sailing Stones of Death Valley," National Park Foundation, accessed August 5, 2025, https:// www.nationalparks.org/connect/blog/sailing-stones-death-valley.

5   Bennett, *Vibrant Matter.*

6   Erdrich, *Books and Islands in Ojibwe Country*, 72. See also the web-site run by the University of Minnesota on Ojibwe language, "Ojibwe Language Program," University of Minnesota, https://cla.umn.edu /ais/undergraduate/language-programs/ojibwe-language-program.

7   See Bell, *Eternal Sovereigns.*

8   *Boston Post*, February 23, 1867.

9   Gloria Bell argues, in an unpublished essay, "Edmonia Lewis 'in the City of the Caesars': Sculpting Indigeneity in Rome" (2024; provided by Bell to the author) that Lewis's visits to the Vatican's collection of "Indian" artifacts, as well as her own work, "united her in Indigenous Turtle Island traditions of diplomacy and sovereignty reminding her of her ancestors and her responsibilities" (np).

10   Works on Michelangelo include Wilde, *Michelangelo*; Steinberg, *Michelangelo's Last Paintings*: Zöllner et al., *Michelangelo*; and Wallace, *Michelangelo.*

11   In another context, cultural critic Mel Chen also argues in favor of the animacy of stones. As Chen discusses, "Aristotle's exclusion of stones itself rubs up against other long-standing beliefs according to which stones are animate or potentially animate: his ontological dismissal anticipates the affective economies of current Western ontologies that are dominant in which stones might as well be nothing . . . that stones and other inanimates definitively occupy a *scalar* position (near zero) on the animacy hierarchy and when they are not excluded from it altogether and are not only treated as animacy's binary opposite." See Chen, *Animacies*, 4–5. We return to Chen's work at the end of chapter 4.

12   Here I paraphrase Sam Anderson's work quoted in Thompson, *Blanket*, 38–39.

13   Thompson, *Blanket*, 39.

14   Penny, *Materials of Sculpture*, 56.

15   Penny, *Materials of Sculpture*, 56.

16   Thompson, *Blanket*, 39.

17   *New York Times*, May 17, 1873, quoted in Henderson and Henderson, *Indomitable Spirit of Edmonia Lewis*, n.p. (book 2, ch. 29, "Media").

18   Cole, *Ambitious Form*, 102.

19   Buettner, "Precious Stones, Mineral Beings," 212.

20   Beard published an excerpt about Lewis in the *London Review of Books*, September 17, 2021, on the 114th anniversary of the day of Lewis's death in London's Hammersmith Infirmary.

21   "Sculpture in Rome: Works of American Ladies," *American Art Journal*, July 12, 1866, 182.

22   See "Young Octavian," Smithsonian American Art Museum, https://americanart.si.edu/artwork/young-octavian-14633.

23   Appadurai, "Grassroots Globalization and the Research Imagination."

24   Raiford, introduction to Raiford and Raphael-Hernandez, *Migrating the Black Body*.

25   As Kellie Jones suggests, "Placing the marker for 'globalism' in exhibitions . . . [can] also erase earlier transatlantic practices, at least on the part of African American artists, from Edmonia Lewis's Italian exhibitions and residency in the nineteenth-century to the coterie of artists of the African diaspora connected to the Harlem Renaissance and Negritude movements." Jones, *Eyeminded*, 287.

26   In her forthcoming project "Global Indigenous Arts in Unexpected Places," Gloria Bell makes a case for arguing that "the kind of self-conscious visibility performed by Lewis . . . is essential to understanding Indigenous art in the modern era." Unpublished proposal shared with the author, December 2024. Although she does not credit him, Bell riffs on Philip J. Deloria's work, in *Indians in Unexpected Places* and his *Becoming Mary Sully* (an exhibition at the Metropolitan Museum of Art). Phil Deloria wrote *Becoming Mary Sully* and then curated the Met exhibition *Mary Sully: Native Modern*, https://www.metmuseum.org/exhibitions/mary-sully-native-modern.

27   Orville W. Carroll, "Slave Auction Block at 'Green Hill' Plantation" (Virginia), quoted in McKittrick, *Demonic Grounds*, 65.

28   Might this be reminiscent of the pile of rocks compiled in the place of a Black girl's head in Simone Leigh and Chitra Ganesh's experimental short video *my dreams, my works, must wait till after hell* (2011), https://www.chitraganesh.com/video-2/project-two-2ggch? The film suggests the stacked relation between the girl's head and the rock pile. Her upper back faces us, while she and the rocks are laid out on a white slab: Is the girl living or dead? So, too, we might think about the photographic work of Laura Aguilar (1959–2018) with its explicit correspondences between rock and flesh, such as in her compelling

ink-jet print *Grounded #III* (2006) or her *American Ground Untitled* from 2007. Or, perhaps, the marker resonates with James Baldwin's short story "The Rock Pile" (1965).

29   Erdrich, *Books and Islands in Ojibwe Country*, 70.

30   Erdrich, *Books and Islands in Ojibwe Country*, 70. Erdrich explains that Ojibwemowin (Anishinaabemowin), "the primary language of philosophy and emotions, . . . is especially good at describing intellectual and dream states" (70). "Most Chippewas lived/live in the upper midwest, esp. Minnesota, Wisconsin, Michigan and also Canada . . . they spoke/ speak Ojibwe. This gets tricky though, as Ojibwe can refer to a broader category than just Chippewa. When you see Chippewa you can translate it as Ojibwe. When you see Ojibwe, you can usually assume the people being referred to are Chippewa but not always" (70).

31   Tiya Miles, private correspondence via email with M. Richardson, June 16, 2002. I shall be forever grateful to Professor Richardson for sharing a cache of research materials with me from his earlier doctoral work on Lewis.

32   Hallowell, "Ojibwa Ontology, Behavior, and World View," 22.

33   Bjornerud, *Turning to Stone*, 9.

34   Here, I am wary of reading the artist's "intention lodged like a stone whose only authority is a reaffirmation of noncontingent authority." Buick, *Child of the Fire*, xviii.

35   Buick, *Child of the Fire*, xxi.

36   Miles, *All That She Carried*, 268–69.

37   Lewis quoted in "Miss Edmonia Lewis," *The Elevator*, August 30, 1873; Erdrich, *Books and Islands in Ojibwe Country*, 72. While Naurice Frank Woods Jr. cites this same quotation as "evidence that she was instructed by nuns and possibly saw herself as Catholic at a young age" (*Race and Racism in Nineteenth-Century Art*, 234), I see it as evidence of her knowledge of the Ojibwe language. See Woods, *Race and Racism in Nineteenth-Century Art*.

38   Blaeser, *Traces in Blood, Bone, and Stone*.

39   Miles, *All That She Carried*, 19.

40   Douglass, *Narrative of the Life of Frederick Douglass*, 96.

41   Copeland, *Bound to Appear*, 41.

42   "Cast Cement," reproduced in Morris and Hockley, *We Wanted a Revolution*, 216.

43   "Beverly Buchanan—Ruins and Rituals, October 21, 2016–March 5, 2017," Brooklyn Museum, accessed August 5, 2025, https://www .brooklynmuseum.org/exhibitions/beverly_buchanan_ruins_rituals.

This show, mounted in 2016, is the most comprehensive exhibition of Buchanan's multimedia work to date.

44 Buchanan quoted in Wilson, "Coming of Age," 122. This statement reminds me of the piece *Still/Here* by the dancer-choreographer Bill T. Jones. This multimedia artistic performance piece celebrates living using videos and movement that feature people who were deemed terminally ill (including Jones, who has lived with HIV since the early 1990s). Bill T. Jones, *Still/Here*, premiered at the Brooklyn Academy of Music, New York, 1994.

45 "Beverly Buchanan: Marsh Ruins and Other Works," Nevada Museum of Art accessed August 5, 2025, https://www.nevadaart.org/art /collections/the-archive/CAE2205/finding-aids/.

46 McArthur and Staton, *Beverly Buchanan, 1978–1981*. Here I am thinking of Gilmore, *Golden Gulag*; and Trouillot, *Silencing the Past*.

47 De Certeau, *Practice of Everyday Life*, 1.

48 This is a riff on the line translated from Frantz Fanon's "The Fact of Blackness," in which he realizes that as a colonized Black man, he is but "an object in the midst of other objects." Fanon, *Black Skin, White Masks*, 109. Kim Hall, in *Things of Darkness*, uses the quotation to open her chapter about the ways in which images of "black faces on furniture, flasks, signs, lights, and other artifacts indicate that dark-skinned Africans were objects of symbolic importance and cultural exchange long before they became numerically a significant group in the English population . . . the appearance of actual black attendants in English portraiture is associated with an increase in consumer goods in the seventeenth century" (212). Throughout Hall's chapter 5, "An Object in the Midst of Other Objects: Race, Gender and Material Culture," she takes pains to explain that Blacks were imprisoned in a state of perpetual objectification that served only to reflect a white owner's cultural capital. By considering the role of jewels and crests that included Black images, she shows that they were objects of white supremacy.

Chapter 3. With Holding Hands

Chapter epigraph: Vasari, *The Lives of the Artists*, 343–44. The quote is from Vasari's entry on sculptor Properzia de' Rossi. I thank Wendy Sepponen for pointing me to this reference.

1 Dannett, *Profiles of Negro Womanhood*, 123. See also Willis, "Ruth and Faith."

2 Wolfe, *Edmonia Lewis*, 44.

3   In a prescient placing, Edmonia Lewis appears on the same page as a mention of Gerrit Smith purchasing land, in the important volume Harris et al., *The Black Book*, 127. The book was green-lighted by Random House editor Toni Morrison.

4   Samuel Coleridge-Taylor, a brilliant Black composer in London, wrote a trilogy of cantatas inspired by Hiawatha in 1899–1901. Like Lewis's homage to the more romantic and salutary aspects of Longfellow's epic poem, Coleridge-Taylor also dedicated one aspect of the score to "Hiawatha's Wedding Feast."

5   For more about the provenance of this work, see Driskell, *The Other Side of Color*, 23.

6   Buick, *Child of the Fire*, 202.

7   *San Francisco Chronicle*, 1873, quoted in Montesano, "Mystery of the San Jose Statues," 26.

8   "Miss Lewis," *The Elevator*, August 30, 1873, 2.

9   Quoted in Woods, *Race and Racism in Nineteenth-Century Art*, 183.

10   Lewis wrote to Maria Weston Chapman (1806–85) about her most famous abolitionist work, *Forever Free* (1867): "Until this group is given to Mr. Garrison—who has done so much for the race, if every black man in the United States would give a penny each, I could very soon be able to do *my* part. I will not take any *thing* for my labor. Mr. garrison [*sic*] has given his whole life for my father's people—and I think that I might give him a few months work. The cost of the group and the pedestal will be just one thousand dollars—I will give you the hundred." She also wrote to Chapman imploring her to help in collecting the sum of $800 for the group into which, Lewis proclaimed, she "had put all my *heart*." She explained that she had "done very little this winter and unless I receive this money from home–I will not be able to get on this year." Lewis to Chapman, February 5, 1867, Correspondence Manuscripts, Anti-Slavery Collection, Boston Public Library.

11   See Nochlin, *The Body*, 76

12   Gerrit Smith was said to be the wealthiest man in New York state at mid-century. Widowed at twenty-five, he married the sixteen-year-old Ann in 1822.

13   Capuano and Zemka, *Victorian Hands*.

14   They are sutured as a pair that cannot come apart (unlike a famous pair of hands sculpted by Rodin that can be reconfigured as individual entities and displayed separately).

15   Robert Browning to Harriet Hosmer, Florence, November, 16, 1854, reprinted in Carr, *Harriet Hosmer*, 46.

16   Hawthorne, *The Marble Faun*, 77; "Immortal Hands: Tiny but Iconic," Schlesinger Library, accessed February 21, 2024, radcliffe.harvard.edu /schlesinger-library/about-the-library.

17   "Immortal Hands," *Harvard Magazine*, July–August 2004, https:// www.harvardmagazine.com/2004/07/immortal-hands-html.

18   Robert Browning, "Andrea del Sarto," in *Men and Women* (London: Chapman and Hall, 1855). For more on literary descriptions, see Capuano and Zemka, *Victorian Hands*.

19   Dickerson et al., *Canova*, 47.

20   Christina Ferando, "The Deceptive Surface: Perception and Sculpture's 'Skin,'" *Images Re-Vues* 13 (2016), https://doi.org/10.4000 /imagesrevues.3931.

21   Bindman, "Lost Surfaces"; Beach, *Sculpture at the Ends of Slavery*. The latter book features Edmonia Lewis's *Forever Free* on its cover.

22   Jenkyns, *Dignity and Decadence*, 104.

23   Fein, "The Sense of Nearness," 2.

24   Nelson, *Color of Stone*.

25   Mills, *Racial Contract*, 16–17.

26   Jordan, *White over Black*.

27   See William Blake, "The Little Black Boy," in *Songs of Innocence and Experience* (London, 1794), The William Blake Archive, https:// blakearchive.org/copy/songsie.f?descId=songsie.f.illbk.06.

28   On the bust, see "Collection Archive: Edmonia Lewis," Mount Stuart, accessed October 23, 2025, https://www.mountstuart.com /collections-archive/edmonia-lewis. For scholarship about color and racial theory in art, see Liverani, *Myth and Politics in Ancient Near Eastern Historiography*; Verri et al., "The 'Treu Head'"; and Brinkmann et al., *Circumlitio*. Major advances in this field have been made by the Tracking Colour project, led by Jan Stubbe Østergaard at the Ny Carlsberg Glyptotek in Copenhagen, whose bibliographic materials and preliminary reports can be found at www.trackingcolour.com. See Derbew, *Untangling Blackness in Greek Antiquity*.

29   Quoted in Dukore, *Dramatic Theory and Criticism*, 560.

30   Beach, *Sculpture at the Ends of Slavery*, 9.

31   Buick, "Question of Realism," 24–28.

32   "The Exposition," *Inter Ocean* (Chicago), September 26, 1878, quoted in Woods, *Race and Racism in Nineteenth-Century Art*, 195.

33   *Newport Rhode Island Daily News*, September 19, 1878, 4.

34   Atkins, "The Invitation," in *Stone Mirrors*, 120.

35   Fulwiley, *Tabula Raza*.

36   See Blight, *Frederick Douglass*.

37   For a discussion of recent figurations of John Brown in Rome (and a mention of Lewis), see Finley, "Dreaming Diasporas." One version of Lewis's bust of Brown is held by the Smithsonian American Art Museum. See "John Brown (sculpture)," Smithsonian, https://www.si.edu/object/john-brown-sculpture:siris_ari_419440.

38   Originally published in an article by Katherine Mayo in the *New York Evening Post*, November 13, 1909, reprinted in "John Brown's Raid Fifty Years Ago," *Magazine of History* 10, no. 6 (1909): 309–41. Brackett's bust of Brown is held at Tufts University. See "The Magnet and the Iron: John Brown and George L. Stearns, the Stories Behind the Busts," Tufts, https://exhibits.tufts.edu/spotlight/john-brown-tufts/feature/the-bust-of-john-brown.

39   H. E. S., letter in the *St. Louis Dispatch*, November 20, 1878. p. 2.

40   See Best and Marcus, "Surface Reading."

41   Copeland, *Bound to Appear*, 201; Campt, *Listening to Images*.

42   For more on the art of making moccasins, see the series of videos at Justine Woods (Métis), "Making of Moccasins," Bata Shoe Museum, accessed August 7, 2025, https://batashoemuseum.ca/the-making-of-moccasins/.

43   Buick, *Child of the Fire*, 204.

44   Quoted in Lydia Maria Child, letter to Harriet Sewall, Massachusetts Historical Society, Robie-Sewall Papers. The patronizing (in both senses of the term) white abolitionist Lydia Maria Child, who knew Lewis throughout her life, supported her within limits.

45   See Ruskin, *Stones of Venice*.

46   Murray, postscript to *Emancipation and the Freed in American Sculpture*, 22.

47   Murray, postscript, 22.

48   Murray, postscript, 23.

49   John P. Samson, "Doing the Centennial," *Christian Recorder*, October 19, 1876, 8.

50   Fuss, *Inside Out*.

51   Schechner, *Performance Studies*, 280.

52   In *The Body in Pain: The Making and Unmaking of the World*, Elaine Scarry theorizes that the distinction between hands as weapons or tools depends on the surfaces that they impact: "The fist that kneads bread is a tool and the fist that hits a face is a weapon." Scarry, *Body in Pain*, 173.

53 Henderson and Henderson, *Indomitable Spirit of Edmonia Lewis*, under heading "Beyond Prayers."

54 Jess, "Edmonia Lewis: Provenance."

55 Langston, *From the Virginia Plantation to the National Capital*, 177.

56 Jess, "Edmonia Lewis: Provenance."

57 Spivak, "Acting Bits / Identity Talk," 18.

58 *The Elevator*, December 3, 1869.

59 Droth et al., *Sculpture Victorious*, 42.

60 "How Edmonia Lewis Became an Artist," n.p.

61 Morris and Morris, "Camping Out with Miss Chief," 265–84.

62 See "Biography," Kent Monkman, accessed August 7, 2025, https://www.kentmonkman.com/biography. See also Rymhs, "Kent Monkman's *The Big Four* as Automobiography"; and Scott, "Pornoarcheology of Kent Monkman's *Group of Seven Inches*."

63 See Monkman and Gordon, *Memoirs of Miss Chief Eagle Testickle*.

64 "Kent Monkman with Amber Jamilla Musser," *Brooklyn Rail*, November 2020, https://brooklynrail.org/2020/11/art/KENT-MONKMAN-with-Amber-Jamilla-Musser/.

65 Mark Rifkin, Daniel Heath Justice, and Bethany Schnieder are the coeditors of a special double issue, entitled "Sexuality, Nationality, and Indigeneity" of *GLQ* 16, nos. 1–2 (2010). The journal was held at Canadian customs and had to have its cover, by Monkman, amended to eliminate its purported pornographic properties.

66 Myburgh, "Here and Now," 395.

67 My transcription from the film, with bracketed definition added.

Chapter 4. About the Nude

1 *The Image of the Black in Western Art*, a multivolume work edited by David Bindman and Henry Louis Gates Jr., for the most part eschews engagement with this topic: only one nude image of a Black female subject appears in volume 4, *From the American Revolution to World War I*, and it is painting done by a Swiss artist. The Guerrilla Girls, a feminist collective founded in the 1980s and still active today, knew of Lewis and her work. One of their many "public service messages" mentions her in the list of "women and artists of color" whose work might have been purchased for less than only one of white, male Jasper Johns paintings at auction. They also include her in their book, *Guerrilla Girls Bedside Companion to the History of Western Art*, in the chapter on nineteenth-century art, titled, appropriately for Lewis, "Girls Going Places." The

page on Lewis shows images of her *Death of Cleopatra* (1876) and *Forever Free* (1867). The Guerrilla Girls' public service ad asks, "Do women have to be naked to get into the Met. Museum [*sic*]?" They note that "less than **5%** of the **artists** in the Modern Art sections are women, but **85% of** the **nudes** are female." Guerrilla Girls, *Do Women Have to Be Naked to Get into the Met. Museum?*, poster, 1989.

2　　Jones, "Nancy Elizabeth Prophet and Augusta Savage."

3　　Clark, *The Nude*. See also Winckelmann, *History of the Art of Antiquity*.

4　　See Clark, *The Nude*; Nead, *Female Nude*; Tyburczy, *Sex Museums*; and Ware, *Classical Body in Romantic Britain*.

5　　On these generic types, see Nichols, *Greece and Rome at the Crystal Palace*; and Prettejohn, *Modernity of Ancient Sculpture*.

6　　Beauvoir, *The Second Sex*.

7　　Cheng, *Second Skin*, 12.

8　　Savage, *Standing Soldiers, Kneeling Slaves*, 58.

9　　Richardson, "Edmonia Lewis at McGrawville."

10　*St. Louis Dispatch*, November 20, 1878, 2.

11　Alexander, *Black Interior*, 118. This story is one all too familiar. The same denials persisted in the early twentieth century, as a letter (reprinted in Alexander, *Black Interior*) from the head of the Fontainebleau School of Art written in 1923 to W. E. B. Du Bois about the Black sculptor Augusta Savage reveals.

12　Wayne Craven recounts this history in his study *Sculpture in America*: "[Sculpture] . . . it seemed much too unladylike an occupation. Aside from the physical labor involved, there was also the business of learning human anatomy, which meant dissecting corpses and drawing and modeling from the nude. But Harriet Hosmer was immune to all talk of her scandalous behavior and followed her own gay course. In the late 1840s she went into Boston regularly to take lessons with the sculptor Paul Stevenson, but she was unsuccessful in her attempts to enter medical school. Not until 1850, when she renewed her school friendship with Cornelia Crow in St. Louis, was she finally able to study anatomy. Dr. J. N. McDowell . . . was soon convinced of the extraordinary young woman's sincerity; although he could not allow her to enter the all-male classes at the medical school in Columbia, Missouri, he met with her each day in his office for private study." Craven, *Sculpture in America*, 326.

13　Carr, *Harriet Hosmer*; Sherwood, *Harriet Hosmer*; and Culkin, *Harriet Hosmer*.

14　"Miss Edmonia Lewis," *The Elevator* (San Francisco), 1873.

15 Brooks, *Bodies in Dissent*.

16 Canova quoted in Dickerson et al., *Canova*.

17 Wilson, "Getting Down to Get Over," cited in O'Grady, "Olympia's Maid," 176.

18 O'Grady, "Olympia's Maid." Faith Ringgold noted in the story quilt *The Picnic at Giverny, The French Collection Part I, #3* (1991) "that there are enough paintings of beautiful nude women. . . . I now want to see nude men painted by women, or nude men in paintings with clothed women."

19 Collins, *Art of History*, 40.

20 "Fact and Fancies," *Milwaukee Daily Sentinel*, August 3, 1876, 2.

21 Hine, "Rape and the Inner Lives of Black Women in the Middle West."

22 See Brody, *Impossible Purities*; and Forman, "Who's Your Mama?"

23 Collins, *Art of History*, 50.

24 Here I am thinking of Daphne Brooks's brilliant chapter "The Deeds Done in My Body," about the nineteenth-century actress Adah Isaacs Menken. Brooks discusses Menken's "passing" performances, some of which incorporated poses by Canova, and argues that Menken performed "costumed as nude." Brooks, *Bodies in Dissent*, 167.

25 Story, *Roba di Roma*.

26 Unlike many of her contemporaries on the continent, such as Jean-Baptiste Carpeaux, Francesco Pezzicar, and especially Charles-Henri-Joseph Cordier, and despite her talent for "life-like sculpturing," Lewis rarely used darker materials to render her "colored" subjects.

27 Browning, "The Greek Slave."

28 This lithograph is among the illustrations in Brett Todd and Kate Mason, "St. Louis Hotel & Exchange: Auctioning Off Lives," ed. Kathryn O'Dwyer, New Orleans Historical, accessed October 23, 2025, https://neworleanshistorical.org/items/show/926.

29 Roach, "Slave Spectacles and Tragic Octoroons," 167–87.

30 Blake, *History of Slavery*, 50.

31 Murell, *Posing Modernity*.

32 The American sculptor John Quincy Adams Ward (1830–1910) produced one of the most notable Black male figures of the period in his bronze cast sculpture *The Freedman* (1863), which, along with Lewis's *Forever Free* was among the very earliest representations of a formerly enslaved Black male figure. Ward advised, "No matter how the figure is to be draped, always model it in the nude first, so as to feel the masses and movement of the figure." This was part of the realism that clothed nudes in classicism.

33   I borrow this term from the exhibition catalogue *Kerry James Marshall: Mastry*, edited by Helen Molesworth.

34   Quoted in Henderson and Henderson, *Indomitable Spirit of Edmonia Lewis*, n.p. (book 2, chapter 26).

35   Three copies of this statue were made, variously named *Asleep*, *Sleep*, and *Night*. *Night* is in the collection of the Baltimore Museum of Art.

36   Bernstein, *Racial Innocence*.

37   The pose resembles the figures in Jules-Robert Auguste's watercolor *Les Amies* (1835) or Courbet's painting *The Happy Lovers* (1844).

38   Mirzoeff, *Bodyscape*.

39   Canova, in whose studio Lewis worked in Rome, was said to be Queen Victoria's favorite sculptor. (The studio is now a restaurant named "Canova" that remembers Canova without, as yet, any mention of its other famous occupant, Edmonia Lewis). The studio is not far from a hospital opened during Lewis's time in Rome.

40   Robin Bernstein's analysis of "racialized innocence" is relevant here. See Bernstein, *Racial Innocence*.

41   Craven, *Sculpture in America*, 328.

42   Cole, *Ambitious Form*, 107.

43   Quoted in Beeching, "The Primus Papers." See also Primus Family Papers, 1853–1924, Ms 44012, Connecticut Historical Society, Hartford, CT.

44   Buick, *Child of the Fire*, 70.

45   Kent Monkman's time-traveling narrator imagines a scene between the nineteenth-century French painter Eugene Delacroix and Miss Chief Testickle in which the latter "brought in my helpers, the little people from our forests, whom Delacroix adoringly called 'sweet putti.'" Monkman and Gordan, *Memoirs of Miss Chief Eagle Testickle*, 136.

46   The putto's tracing carries forward all the way to the postmodern figures recurring in the work of auteur Sir Isaac Julien, who uses male cupids as a leitmotif in many of his films. See also Ware, *Classical Body in Romantic Britain*.

47   Lin Vertefeuille, "The Putto—Angels in Art," Virtual Library on the Ringling Museum, 2005, https://ringlingdocents.org/putto.htm. See also Dempsey, *Inventing the Renaissance Putto*.

48   See "Poor Cupid," Smithsonian American Art Museum, https://americanart.si.edu/artwork/poor-cupid-14631.

49 Perhaps it is this association that pervades the melancholic use of putti as a leitmotif in the auteur Sir Isaac Julien's films, such as *Looking for Langston* (1989) and the experimental short *The Attendant* (1992).

50 Ovid, *Metamorphoses*, trans. Charles Martin, book 1, line 428.

51 Powers's *The Greek Slave* is held by the National Gallery of Art, Washington, DC; see https://www.nga.gov/artworks/166484-greek-slave.

52 Murray, *Emancipation and the Freed in American Sculpture*, 3. Murray's is an invaluable text for anyone interested in the representation of Blacks in American Art. Freeman Henry Morris Murray was also the first Black art historian. He discussed Edmonia Lewis's work. For more on *The Greek Slave*, see Droth and Hatt, "The Greek Slave by Hiram Powers."

53 At the time, this statue was seen as the most captivating expression of an idealized female nude. It was shown at the 1851 Great Exhibition in London and was once "rescued" from a fire while on display at P. T. Barnum's American Museum in New York. The sculpture was viewed by thousands in cities from New Orleans to Boston during its famous two-year tour of America between 1847 and 1849.

54 Buick, *Child of the Fire*, 67.

55 Brown, *Rising Son*.

56 Genesis 16:1–16, 21: 8–21.

57 Ovid, *Metamorphoses*, book 10, lines 243–97.

58 See Getsy, *Body Doubles*.

59 An interesting comparison could be made here with the series by Laura Aguilar, including works such as "Clothed/Unclothed #34" (1994), two gelatin silver prints that form a diptych showing a queer family, clothed and unclothed.

60 Murrell, *Posing Modernity*, 40.

61 Murrell, *Posing Modernity*, 58.

62 A major controversy about this statement has raged since it became well known in academic and popular texts in the 1970s. See Painter, *Sojourner Truth*.

63 See Halberstam, *Female Masculinity*.

64 Miles, *All That She Carried*, 274.

65 Henderson and Henderson, *Indomitable Spirit of Edmonia Lewis*, n.p. (book 2, chapter 30).

66 *San Jose Daily Mercury*, October 7, 1873.

67 *The Elevator* (San Francisco), August 1873.

68 *Pacific Appeal* (San Francisco), September 6, 1873.

69   See Driskell, *Two Centuries of Black American Art*; Leonard Simon
        (1937–2014), who was the registrar at the Cantor Museum and a dear
        colleague at University of California, Riverside, and who taught
        Lewis's work, completed the catalog notes for the exhibition. See also
        Novo, "The Indian Maiden Visits San Jose."

70   Undated item, "Edmonia Lewis File Clippings," California Room, San
        Jose Public Library, San Jose, CA. I am grateful to Emma Larson for
        assisting me with documentation from the Frances Lehman Loeb Art
        Gallery at my alma mater, Vassar College. See the exhibition catalogue
        with introduction by William H. Gerdts and with entries by Nicolai
        Cikovsky Jr., Marie H. Morrison, and Carol Ockman; Gerdts et al.,
        The White Marmorean Flock.

71   Robin Pogrebin, "Mickalene Thomas Takes L.A.," *New York Times
        Magazine*, April 16, 2024.

72   Angela Flournoy, "Mickalene Thomas Is Reinventing Nudes," *New
        York Times Magazine*, October 13, 2021.

73   See Bogus, "Dyke Hands."

74   Chen, *Animacies*, 216.

75   Murrell, *Posing Modernity*, 171.

76   Thomas et al., *Mickalene Thomas.*

77   Gay, "Wild and Somewhat Disruptive," 7.

Chapter 5. A Rose Somebody Knows

Second chapter epigraph: This is my memorized memory of a nursery rhyme that served as an elocution lesson I learned when I was
three years old living in South Kensington, London. I attended a
weekly "Dance and Deportment" class where "mummies and nannies"
watched as a gaggle of young girls recited the lines from the ancient
rhyme and learned to curtsy before the Queen. While I have long
thought that ballet made me gay, perhaps this performance ushered
in my introduction to fem training.

Interlude epigraph: Simone Leigh, quoted in Jasmine Liu, "In Historic
First, Simone Leigh and Sonia Boyce Win Venice Biennale's Golden
Lions," *Hyperallergic*, April 25, 2022, https://hyperallergic.com/727225
/simone-leigh-and-sonia-boyce-win-venice-biennale-golden-lions/.

1   I conceived of this chapter title before knowing that one of Emily
        Dickinson's first poems is titled "Nobody Knows This Little Rose,"
        also a philosophical meditation on the nature of life and death, and
        before having seen Maud Sulter's collection of images of roses in her

archive at the Tate Britain. I hope this reading also recalls the roses referenced in two of Tiya Miles's works, her novel *The Cherokee Rose* (2015) about the Trail of Tears and relations between three female characters on a Georgia Plantation, and a central historical figure, Rose, in *All That She Carried* (2021).

2   "Sonnet 130," Shakespeare's Sonnets, Folger Shakespeare Library, https://www.folger.edu/explore/shakespeares-works/shakespeares -sonnets/read/130/.

3   Cixous, *The Laugh of the Medusa*.

4   Buick, *Child of the Fire*, 1999.

5   Pollock, *Vision and Difference*, 135.

6   Richardson quoted in Nelson, *Color of Stone*, 176.

7   DeMaria Smith, "HRH Cleopatra."

8   K. Hall, *Things of Darkness*, 77.

9   James, "A Gust of Grace," 76. I chose to color Lewis's sculpted roses that appear on the cover of this book lavender for precisely this reason.

10   The research on the hieroglyphs may have been aided by Lewis's possible friendship with the British writer and Egyptologist Amelia Blanford Edwards (1831–92). For a connection with Cleopatra and roses in Lewis's art, see Terry Blackhawk, "After 'The Death of Cleopatra' by Edmonia Lewis," in *Body and Field*, 81.

11   Pollock, *Vision and Difference*, 135.

12   For more on the punctum, see Barthes, *Camera Lucida*. Barthes explains that "occasionally . . . a detail attracts me. I feel that its mere presence changes my reading, that I am looking at a new photograph, marked in my eyes with a higher value. This 'detail' is the *punctum*." Moreover, "in order to perceive the *punctum*, no analysis would be of use to me (but perhaps memory sometimes would)" (42).

13   The major scholarly works that have debated the racial significance of Cleopatra's nose include Thurman, *Cleopatra's Nose*; Boorstin, *Cleopatra's Nose;* Royster, *Becoming Cleopatra*; and Nelson, *Color of Stone*.

14   Trafton, *Egypt Land*, 165, 168 (in the chapter "Undressing Cleopatra: Race, Sex and Bodily Interiority in Nineteenth-Century American Egyptomania").

15   Cooper, *A Voice from the South by a Black Woman of the South*, 275 (emphasis in original).

16   Cooper, *A Voice from the South by a Black Woman of the South*, 101.

17   Mossell, *The Work of the Afro-American Woman*, 22.

18   Cooper, *A Voice from the South by a Black Woman of the South*, 276 (emphasis added).

19   Griffin, *Beloved Sisters and Loving Friends*, 8.

20   See Cobb, "Optics of Respectability," chapter 2 in *Picture Freedom*, 71; Farrington, *Creating Their Own Image*, 51.

21   Douglass quoted in Cobb, "Optics of Respectability," 79.

22   Ruskin quoted in Pollock, *Vision and Difference*, 135, 137.

23   Conwill, introduction, 11.

24   Brooks, "On Creating a Usable Past." See also Walker, *In Search of Our Mothers' Gardens*.

25   "Portrait of a Woman," St. Louis Art Museum, accessed August 10, 2025, https://www.slam.org/collection/objects/29143/.

26   *Cincinnati Daily Star*, Friday evening, September 27, 1878, p. 2.

27   *Cincinnati Enquirer*, September 18, 1879, p. 8. Likewise, we might conceive of the veil itself as code for the veiled sexuality of the figure and its maker, as Marni Kessler argues in *Sheer Presence*.

28   Lee, *Perceptual Drift*, 76 (quoting James, "A Gust of Grace"), 77.

29   See Hammonds, "Black (W)holes and the Geometry of Black Female Sexuality."

30   Leigh, *Simone Leigh*.

31   Leigh, *Simone Leigh*.

32   James, "A Gust of Grace," 76.

33   See Brody, "Effaced into Flesh."

34   Tinsley, *Thiefing Sugar*, 22 (emphasis in original), 18. It is little wonder that Tinsley titled her next book *The Color Pynk: Black Femme Art for Survival*, which pays homage to the pansexual artist Janelle Monae.

35   Tinsley, *Color Pynk*, 2. On Marsha P. Johnson, see Johnson and Servera, *Blacktino Queer Performance*; and Tourmaline, *Marsha*.

36   Should it surprise us that the prescient Maud Sulter (1962–2008) dissected Victorian artist John Collier's massive oil painting *The Death of Cleopatra* (1890) in her photographic series *Museum* (1990)?

37   Transgender Day of Remembrance was founded in 1999 by a small group, including Gwendolyn Ann Smith, Nancy Nangeroni, and Jahaira DeAlto, to memorialize the murders of Black transgender women Rita Hester in Allston, Massachusetts, and Chanelle Pickett in Watertown, Massachusetts. Wikipedia, "Transgender Day of Remembrance," last modified October 19, 2025, 15:27 (CST), https://en.wikipedia.org/wiki/Transgender_Day_of_Remembrance. See also Micah Bazant, "To My Siblings, on Trans Day of Visibility," Forward Together, March 29, 2018, https://forwardtogether.org/siblings-trans-day-visibility/.

38   Stein, "Sacred Emily" (1913), 178–88. See Stein's repeated variations on this statement, including "she would carve on the tree Rose is a Rose is a Rose is a Rose until it went all the way around" (Stein, *World Is Round*); "Civilization begins with a rose. A rose is a rose is a rose is a rose. It continues blooming and it fastens clearly on excellent examples" (Stein, "As Fine as Melanctha," on the central stories in *Three Lives* (1922), about a Black woman).

39   Stein, *Three Lives* (1909). Maud Sulter cites Stein's operatic prose poem *Four Saints in Three Acts* as part of her series *Museum* (1990), which was made in response to an 1890 painting, *The Death of Cleopatra*. See note 36 in this chapter.

40   Griffin, "Textual Healing," 519–36.

41   Allen, "A Single Rose," 77.

Chapter 6. About Photography

Interlude epigraph: Zanele Muholi, quoted in "Zanele Muholi: To Tell the Truth," *Musée*, March 15, 2017, https://museemagazine.com /features/2017/3/15/whm-zanele-muholi.

1   On visual technologies, see Mirzoeff, *Bodyscape*; Crary, *Techniques of the Observer*; Gitelman, *Scripts, Grooves, and Writing Machines*; Willis, *Reflections in Black*; and Willis, *Black Venus 2010*.

2   Angus, *Camera Geologica*, 20.

3   Frederick Douglass, "Negro Portraits," *The Liberator*, April 20, 1849. See also Stauffer et al., *Picturing Frederick Douglass*; and Julien and Gilroy-War, *Lessons of the Hour*.

4   Edmonia Lewis, Rome, to Maria Weston Chapman, February 5, 1867, Letter/Correspondence Manuscripts, Anti-Slavery Collection, Boston Public Library.

5   Novo, "The Indian Maiden Visits San Jose," 24.

6   *The Commonwealth* (Boston), February 4, 1865.

7   For an excellent discussion of Lewis's early abolitionist work in Boston, see Beach, *Sculpture at the Ends of Slavery*.

8   Originally the title of a 2016 issue of *Aperture* magazine edited by Sarah Elizabeth Lewis, the phrase has grown to encompass "a civic initiative that generates original research, curricula, and programs that reveal the foundational role that visual culture plays in generating equity and justice in America." See "About the Initiative," Vision and Justice, accessed August 10, 2025, https://visionandjustice.org/about. Photography's origins shift. Scholars tend to agree that the technology was

invented by Louis-Jacques-Mandé Daguerre (whose name is preserved in the word *daguerreotype*) in 1835. Within just a few years, by 1839, more photographers in Europe and America began using it, including for making portraits of human subjects. The first photographic portrait studio opened in Boston, Massachusetts, in 1842.

9   As Sarah Elizabeth Lewis explains in *Unseen Truth*, 63–64: "Racial dominance in the United States had turned visual perception into a weapon with a legacy we still live with today. Aesthetics were marshaled to create, solidify, and naturalize the structure of racial hierarchies. In 1854, Douglass had decried the use of pictures by the American School of Ethnology to legitimate caricatures and stereotypes, to 'read the Negro out of the human family.' In that year, the widely known, circulated, distributed, and consumed antebellum racial treatise entitled *Types of Mankind* (1854), by Josiah Clark Nott and George Gliddon, sought to prove polygenesis—the idea that races have different origins, that there is no common, equal family of humankind. The treatise included a diagram of this idea, placing, . . . the famous Apollo Belvedere sculpture—which President Woodrow Wilson wanted to purchase for his home—next to a chimpanzee and a black man to show a hierarchy of human races."

10   Susan Tallman, "The Uses of Portraiture," *New York Review of Books*, October 7, 2021.

11   A major exhibition at the Museum of Modern Art in New York in 2011 compared sculpture and photography. As the catalogue for the show explained, "Sculpture was among the first such subjects to be treated in the history of photography . . . [such that] the photography of sculpture became its own art." This exhibition glossed over the role of Renty and his associates who effectively became sculpture for insidious ideology, or the previously explored homology between rocks and/as people. Again, photographic technology is not neutral: it encodes power relations not only within the image, but also about, around, and via the context and the processing of the produced image. Marcoci, *Original Copy*.

12   Willis, *Reflections in Black*, xvi.

13   See Weems, *To Make Their Own Way in the World*.

14   Collins, *Art of History*, 77.

15   Schneider, "Louis Aggasiz and the American School of Ethnoeroticism."

16   Collins, "Reclaiming Venus," 73, 77.

17   The photos have been moved to a South Carolina Museum. See Starlette Thomas, "Harvard Forced to Get the Picture After Losing Lawsuit over 19th Century Image of Renty Taylor," *goodfaithmedia*, June 16, 2025,

https://goodfaithmedia.org/harvard-forced-to-get-the-picture-after -losing-lawsuit-over-19th-century-image-of-renty-taylor/.

18   Young, *Embodying Black Experience*, 94.

19   Delmez, *Carrie Mae Weems*, 132.

20   Invaluable scholarly sources on this growing area of research that have informed my thinking include: Shaw, *Portraits of a People*; Shaw, *Seeing the Unspeakable*; Powell, *Cutting a Figure*; Wallace and Smith, *Pictures and Progress*; Kim and Andrews, *Black American Portraits*; and Smith, *At the Edge of Sight*. I completed this work before the benefit of reading Best, "An Emancipatory Form."

21   Raiford, *Imprisoned in a Luminous Glare*, 10.

22   Raiford, *Imprisoned in a Luminous Glare*, 10.

23   Lewis, *Unseen Truth*.

24   The eleven photographs can be viewed in the blog post by antje, "Looking at Edmonia Lewis," Discovering Edmonia Lewis, February 22, 2021, https://edmonialewis.org/elBlog/index.php/2021/02 /22/looking-at-edmonia-lewis/.

25   Raiford, *Imprisoned in a Luminous Glare*.

26   For more on Brady's studio and its significance in this period, see Lewis, *Unseen Truth*, 25; and Wilson, *Mathew Brady*. A memorial to the photographer, which represents his influence on America in the nineteenth century, was installed on September 17, 2022, in the Congressional Cemetery.

27   *The Times* (London), August 30, 1862.

28   Photography plays a ubiquitous and ethically ambiguous role as a captive technology (to say nothing of its connection to destructive industries such as mining). Here I am thinking of the role of photography in fixing criminality, as an instrument of war, and in facial recognition and its ubiquity in postmodern life.

29   See David S. Shields, "Henry Rocher," Broadway Photographs, accessed August 10, 2025, broadway.library.sc.edu/content/henry -rocher.html.

30   See Alexander, *Trayvon Generation*. See also Hall, Roach, and Childs, *Ornamental Blackness*. The portrait is *Elihu Yale with Members of His Family and an Enslaved Child*, attributed to John Verelst, in the collection of the Yale Center for British Art; see https://collections .britishart.yale.edu/catalog/tms:107.

31   Rocher quoted in Shields, "Background."

32   Shaw, *Portraits of a People*, 172. Joseph Roach claims something similar in *It*, his book about celebrity.

33   Shaw, *Portraits of a People*, 170.

34   Wood, *Blind Memory*.

35   See Shaw, "That Roman Portrait Is Wildfire."

36   Shaw, "That Roman Portrait Is Wildfire."

37   Shaw, *Seeing the Unspeakable*, 131–32.

38   See Shaw, *Portraits of a People*, 170–73. We can compare these images online at antje, "Looking at Edmonia Lewis."

39   Schneider, *Performing Remains*.

40   Gaines, *Black Performance on the Outskirts of the Left*.

41   *Black Hands on White Marble* is the title of a play about Lewis but also a phrase frequently noted in articles past and present about her work and life.

42   Shawon Kinew (Ojibways of Onigaming First Nation, pizhiw doodem) wrote about this work in a 2019 project that asked Indigenous artists and curators to comment on representations of Indigenous and "Western" themes in the Metropolitan collection. Kinew, a professor of art history at Harvard, notes: "It is difficult to untether this sculpture from the ongoing legacy of colonization, including thousands of Missing and Murdered Indigenous Women and Girls (MMIWG). I am struck by the honesty of the artwork, the careful pairing of sexuality and religion, wherein the body and soul of this nubile neophyte are the desired sites of transformation." Shawon Kinew, "Shawon Kinew on *Indian Girl, or The Dawn of Christianity*," in "Native Perspective," The Met, September 11, 2019, https://www.metmuseum.org/perspectives/native-perspectives.

43   Tolles, *American Sculpture in the Metropolitan Museum of Art*. This text does not include Lewis, who was added to the collection belatedly, in the twentieth century. Two curators—Shawnya Harris at the University of Georgia Museum and Jeffrey Richmond-Moll at the Peabody Essex Museum—are organizing the first solo show of Lewis's work in more than a century with the assistance of the Crystal Bridges Museum of American Art in Bentonville, Arkansas. The show, *Edmonia Lewis: Said in Stone*, is set to open in February 2026.

44   "The White Captive," The Met, accessed October 24, 2025, https://www.metmuseum.org/art/collection/search/11680.

45   See *Catalogue of the Palmer Marbles*, 11–12.

46   Raiford, *Imprisoned in a Luminous Glare*, 10.

47   See Stocking, *Victorian Anthropology*; Willis, "Skeletons in the Anthropological Closet"; and Baker, *From Savage to Negro*.

48   *Faces and Phases* is the title of Zanele Muholi's ongoing artistic series
       of black-and-white photographic prints. Started in 2006 as a form of
       activism, the series documents Muholi's queer community in South
       Africa. See the interlude in this chapter; and Muholi, *Zanele Muholi:*
       Faces and Phases.

49   Griffin, *Beloved Sisters and Loving Friends*.

50   Smith-Rosenberg, "The Female World of Love and Ritual." When I
       was a student volunteer in the archives of the Connecticut Histori-
       cal Society, located on 1 Elizabeth Street in Hartford, less than a mile
       from my parents' home, I came across the correspondence between
       these Black female contemporaries who, I eventually learned, knew
       of Edmonia Lewis.

51   The African American daguerreotypist Augustus Washington had
       several studios in Hartford in the early part of his career. An ar-
       dent abolitionist, he took one of the most striking portraits of John
       Brown.

52   Rollin's diary from 1868 is preserved in the National Museum of Afri-
       can American History, https://nmaahc.si.edu/object/nmaahc_2018
       .101.1.

53   Quoted in Sterling, *We Are Your Sisters*, 459.

54   Lorde, *Zami*.

55   Woubshet, "Right to Look," 149. For more on Muholi, see Young, *Il-*
       legible Will; and Muholi, *Zanele Muholi: Somnyama Ngonyama*.

56   We may think of Lewis posing there subsequently as a prelude to Car-
       rie Mae Weems's future photographs taken in Rome for her *Roaming*
       series from 2006. Even though Weems's haunting series does not in-
       clude explicit images of the Spanish Steps, it is easy to imagine her
       statuesque persona mattering in that location. For a comparison of
       Weems and Lewis, see Morse, "Roman Studios."

57   Miller, *Slaves to Fashion*, 243.

58   Willis, "Photographing Between the Lines," 33.

Chapter 7. Engraving Edmonia

1   Krauss, *Originality of the Avant-Garde*, 33. I allude as well to Layli
       Long Soldier (Oglala Lakota), whose poem "Ȟe Sápa Three," like
       Stein's "Rose," is a calligram. The lines are written to frame an open
       space—"the space in which to place me." Long Soldier, "Ȟe Sápa
       Three," in *Whereas*. This line from the poem provides the title for the
       historic installation by Jeffrey Gibson (Choctaw/Cherokee) at the
       2024 Venice Biennale, making Gibson the first Indigenous artist to

represent the country in the US Pavillion. See the catalogue Winograd and Crouch, *Jeffrey Gibson*.

2   Woods, *Race and Racism in Nineteenth-Century Art*, 188.

3   Brown, *Soul in Stone*, 4–5.

4   Lewis was commissioned to make a headstone for a wealthy Black woman in St. Louis that ended up in a lawsuit brought by the family, which was dissatisfied with her work.

5   "Hygeia Monument and Edmonia Lewis," Mount Auburn Cemetery, accessed August 11, 2025, https://www.mountauburn.org/notable -residents/explore-the-african-american-heritage-trail/hygeia -monument/.

6   See Hunt's autobiography, *Glances and Glimpses*.

7   Krauss, *Originality of the Avant-Garde*, 276–90. More recently, she has claimed that "sculpture is a verb;" Krauss, "Sculpture Is a Verb."

8   Levinson, *Written in Stone*, 7.

9   See Seacole, *Wonderful Adventures of Mary Seacole in Many Lands*. Like Lewis, Seacole traveled extensively. After leaving her birthland of Jamaica, she owned a tavern in the goldfields of Cruces, Panama, worked as a professional nurse with Florence Nightingale in the Crimea, and ultimately made her home in London.

10   Reno is the author of the illustrated children's book, *Edmonia Lewis: A Sculptor of Determination and Courage* (New York: Troy Bookmakers, 2017).

11   Talia Lavin, "The Decades-Long Quest to Find and Honor Edmonia Lewis's Grave," *Hyperallergic*, March 28, 2018, https://hyperallergic .com/434881/edmonia-lewis-grave/.

12   Taylor, *Disappearing Acts*.

13   Droth et al., *Sculpture Victorious*.

14   In a letter to Sylvia Dannett, dated November 12, 1963, Louis Ambler of Harvard's Fogg Art Museum remarked that, at that time, Lewis's *Bust of Longfellow*, which had been on display before the Widener Library was built, was missing. "No one seems to know where it is," she wrote. "The sculpture has probably been moved to another location in that immense building." Quoted in Dannett, *Profiles of Negro Womanhood*, 336–37.

15   See Nelson, *Color of Stone*; Dabakis, *Sisterhood of Sculptors*.

16   Nelson Primus to his family in Hartford, CT, 1866, quoted in Beeching, "The Primus Papers."

17   Blee and O'Brien, *Monumental Mobility*.

18   Blee and O'Brien, *Monumental Mobility*, 213.

19   Foner, *Reconstruction*. See Michael Schaffer, "'Completely Unwork-
      able': Sculpture Experts Say Trump's $34 Million Statue Garden Has
      Major Problems," *Politico*, May 31, 2025, https://www.politico.com
      /news/magazine/2025/05/31/trump-sculpture-garden-american
      -heroes-china-00372297.

20   Mellon Foundation, quoted in "Mellon Foundation Pledges $250
      Million to Rethink Nation's Monuments," NPR, October 5, 2020,
      https://www.npr.org/sections/live-updates-protests-for-racial
      -justice/2020/10/05/920339144/mellon-foundation-pledges-250
      -million-to-rethink-nations-monuments. These ideas are explored
      further in the LACMA × Snapchat: Monumental Perspectives ini-
      tiative (2021–24), which used augmented-reality memorials to re-
      think monuments (see https://www.lacma.org/art/exhibition/lacma
      -snapchat-monumental-perspectives), and the exhibition *Monuments*
      (October 23, 2025–May 3, 2026) at MOCA, Los Angeles, curated with
      The Brick, that exhibits actual decommissioned monuments taken
      down during the uprisings fomented by the calls for racial justice in
      2020 (see https://www.moca.org/exhibition/monuments). See also
      Farber and Lum, *Monument Lab*.

21   Caroline Randall Williams, "You Want a Confederate Monument? My
      Body Is a Confederate Monument," *New York Times*, June 26, 2020.

22   Jess, "Edmonia Lewis," in *Olio*, 201.

23   For example, the National Garden of American Heroes proposed in
      2020 by President Trump and funded in the July 2025 One Big Beau-
      tiful Bill Act, is a response to the removal of Confederate and other
      monuments.

24   Buick, *Child of the Fire*, 45.

25   Elizabeth Alexander writes about Stone Mountain in her book *The
      Trayvon Generation*, where, in the chapter "Here Lies," she notes that
      Kara Walker, who was born near Stone Mountain, claims the monu-
      ment as a major influence for her art.

26   Trethewey, *Memorial Drive*, 9.

27   Personal correspondence and playbill for the World Premiere at In-
      terlochen Arts Academy, May 3 and 4, 2023 (author's collection).

28   Many other artworks pay homage to Lewis, including Synthia
      St. James's colored lithograph made in the 1990s, *Wildfire*, and her
      self-published book in the form of a monologue, *I Am Edmonia Lewis
      and My Name Is Wildfire* (2018). There are many iterations of Lewis
      in contemporary culture, including graphic novels, musical projects,
      T-shirts, and a video game; and her photograph appears in the final

season of the HBO series *And Just Like That*. See also work by Lubaina Himid, Marlene Smith, Madeleine Hunt-Ehrlich, and America Meredith; Gisela Torres's photography series *Conjure* (2020); Alberta White's sculpture *Remembering Wildfire* (2024); as well as a song tribute by Susan Anders and the Zia Singers.

29   "Hysteria by Maud Sulter," *Spare Rib*, April 19, 1991; from Maud Sulter's archive, shared with the author (see note 40 below).

30   Cherry, *Maud Sulter*, 146.

31   Cherry, *Maud Sulter*, 146.

32   Cherry, *Maud Sulter*, 10.

33   Cherry, *Maud Sulter*, 14, 27, 13.

34   Haworth-Booth, "Maud Sulter: An Interview," 264.

35   See Brody and Cherry, "Resonance and Reverberation in Maud Sulter's *MUSEUM*."

36   See Berger, *Fred Wilson*.

37   Cherry, *Maud Sulter*, 42.

38   Brody and Cherry, "Resonance and Reverberation in Maud Sulter's *MUSEUM*."

39   Cherry, *Maud Sulter*.

40   Marlene Smith curated some of these early works. I benefited from a cache of xeroxed materials sent to me by Maud Sulter in 1997 in conjunction with the publication of my first book, *Impossible Purities: Blackness, Femininity, and Victorian Culture*, which featured her photograph *Calliope* (1989) from the *Zabat* series on the cover; and from a visit to the new Sulter archive housed at the Tate Britain.

Bibliography

Alexander, Elizabeth. *The Black Interior: Essays*. St. Paul, MN: Graywolf Press, 2004.

Alexander, Elizabeth. *The Trayvon Generation*. New York: Grand Central, 2022.

Allen, Sarah, and Yasufumi Nakamori, eds. *Zanele Muholi*. London: Tate Enterprises, 2020.

Allen, S. D. "A Single Rose." In *Erotique Noire: Black Erotica*, edited by Miriam DeCosta-Willis, Reginald Martin, and Roseann P. Bell. New York: Doubleday Press, 1992.

Angus, Siobhan. *Camera Geologica: An Elemental History of Photography*. Durham, NC: Duke University Press, 2024.

Appadurai, Arjun. "Grassroots Globalization and the Research Imagination." *Public Culture* 12, no. 1 (2000): 1–19.

Atkins, Jeanne. *Stone Mirrors: The Sculpture and Silence of Edmonia Lewis*. New York: Atheneum Books for Young Readers, 2017.

Bad-Object Choices, ed. *How Do I Look? Queer Film and Video*. Seattle: Bay Press, 1991.

Baker, Lee. *From Savage to Negro: Anthropology and the Construction of Race, 1896–1954*. Berkeley: University of California Press, 1998.

Bal, Mieke. *Quoting Caravaggio: Contemporary Art, Preposterous History*. Chicago: University of Chicago Press, 1999.

Barthes, Roland. *Camera Lucida: Reflections on Photography*. Translated by Richard Howard. New York: Hill and Wang, 1981.

Beach, Caitlin. *Sculpture at the Ends of Slavery*. Berkeley: University of California Press, 2022.

Beard, Mary. "Judgements in Stone: Two Contrasting Styles of Edmonia Lewis, the First African American Woman Sculptor." *Times Literary Supplement*, September 17, 2021.

Beauvoir, Simone de. *The Second Sex*. Translated by Constance Borde and Sheila Malovany-Chevallier. New York: Penguin, 2011.

Beeching, Barbara Jean. "The Primus Papers: An Introduction to Hartford's Nineteenth Century Black Community." MA thesis, Trinity College, 1995.

Bell, Gloria Jane. *Eternal Sovereigns: Indigenous Artists, Activists, and Travelers Reframing Rome*. Durham, NC: Duke University Press, 2024.

Benbow Flowers, Melissa. "Before Black Bohemia: Edmonia Lewis in the Post-Bellum, Pre-Harlem Period." PhD diss., University of Delaware, 2024.

Benjamin, Ruha. *Race After Technology: Abolitionist Tools for the New Jim Code*. Cambridge: Polity Press, 2019.

Benjamin, Walter. "On the Concept of History." In *Illuminations: Essays and Reflections*, edited by Hannah Arendt, translated by Harry Zohn. New York: Schocken Books, 1986. Thesis VII.

Bennett, Jane. *Vibrant Matter: A Political Ecology of Things*. Durham, NC: Duke University Press, 2010.

Berger, Maurice, ed. *Fred Wilson: Objects and Installations*. Baltimore: Center for Visual Art and Culture, University of Maryland, Baltimore County, 2002.

Berkhofer, Robert F. *The White Man's Indian: Images of the American Indian, from Columbus to the Present*. New York: Vintage Books, 1979.

Bernstein, Robin. *Racial Innocence: Performing American Childhood from Slavery to Civil Rights*. New York: New York University Press, 2011.

Best, Makeda. "An Emancipatory Form: The Carte de Visite." In *Edmonia Lewis: Said in Stone*, edited by Jeffrey Richmond-Moll and Shawnya Harris. Chicago: University of Chicago Press, 2026.

Best, Stephen. *None Like Us: Blackness, Belonging, Aesthetic Life*. Durham, NC: Duke University Press, 2018.

Best, Stephen, and Sharon Marcus. "Surface Reading: An Introduction." *Representations* 8, no. 1 (2009): 1–21.

Bindman, David. "Lost Surfaces: Canova and Colour." *Oxford Art Journal* 39, no. 2 (2016): 229–41.

Bindman, David, and Henry Louis Gates Jr., eds. *The Image of the Black in Western Art*, Vol. 4, *From the American Revolution to World War I*, Parts 1 and 2. Cambridge, MA: Harvard University Press, 2012.

Bjornerud, Marcia. *Turning to Stone: Discovering the Subtle Wisdom of Rocks*. New York: Flatiron Books, 2024.

Blackhawk, Terry. *Body and Field: Poems*. Ann Arbor: Michigan State University Press, 1999.

Blaeser, Kimberly. *Traces in Blood, Bone, and Stone: Contemporary Ojibwe Poetry*. Bemidji, MN: Loonfeather Press, 2006.

Blake, W. O. *The History of Slavery, and the Slave Trade, Ancient and Modern*. Columbus, OH: H. Miller, 1861.

Blee, Lisa, and Jean M. O'Brien. *Monumental Mobility: The Memory Work of Massasoit*. Chapel Hill: University of North Carolina Press, 2019.

Blight, David W. *Frederick Douglass: Prophet of Freedom*. New York: Simon and Schuster, 2018.

Bogus, S. Diane. "Dyke Hands." In *Black Noire / Black Erotica*, edited by Miriam Decosta-Willis, Reginald Martin, and Roseann P. Bell. New York: Doubleday, 1992.

Bohaker, Heidi. *Doodem and Council Fire: Anishinaabe Governance Through Alliance*. Toronto: University of Toronto Press, 2020.

Bontemps, Arna. *100 Years of Negro Freedom*. New York: Dodd, Mead, 1961.

Boorstin, Daniel. *Cleopatra's Nose: Essays on the Unexpected*. New York: Knopf, 1994.

Brinkmann, Vinzenz, Oliver Primavesi, and Max Hollein, eds. *Circumlitio: The Polychromy of Antique and Medieval Sculpture*. Munich: Hirmer Verlag GmbH, 2010.

Brody, Jennifer DeVere. "Black Cat Fever: Manifestations of Manet's *Olympia*." *Theater Journal* 53, no. 1 (2001): 95–118.

Brody, Jennifer DeVere, ed. *Edmonia Lewis: Indelible Impressions*. Stanford, CA: Cantor Arts Center, 2025.

Brody, Jennifer DeVere. "Effaced into Flesh: Black Women's Subjectivity." *Genders*, no. 24 (1996): 184–205.

Brody, Jennifer DeVere. *Impossible Purities: Blackness, Femininity, and Victorian Culture*. Durham, NC: Duke University Press, 1998.

Brody, Jennifer DeVere, and Deborah Cherry. "Resonance and Reverberation in Maud Sulter's *MUSEUM*." In *Approaching Race and Empire in Collections of Nineteenth-Century Art and Design: A Resource Pack for Museums and Galleries*, edited by Kate Nichols, Victoria Osborne, and Sabrina Rahman. London: British Art Network, 2023. https://britishartnetwork .org.uk/wp-content/uploads/2023/11/Digital-Museum-Resource-1.pdf.

Brooks, Daphne. *Bodies in Dissent: Spectacular Performances of Race and Freedom*. Durham, NC: Duke University Press, 2006.

Brooks, Van Wyck. "On Creating a Usable Past." *The Dial*, April 11, 1918, 337–41.

Broun, Elizabeth. "Foreword." In *African American Art: Harlem Renaissance, Civil Rights Era, and Beyond*, by Richard Powell and Virginia Mecklenburg. Washington, DC: Smithsonian American Art Museum, 2012.

Brown, Bill. *A Sense of Things: The Object Matter of American Literature*. Chicago: University of Chicago Press, 2004.

Brown, Bill. "Thing Theory." *Critical Inquiry* 28, no. 1 (2001): 1–22.

Brown, John Gary. *Soul in Stone: Cemetery Art from America's Heartland.* Lawrence: University Press of Kansas, 1994.

Brown, William Wells. *The Rising Son; or, The Antecedents and Advancement of the Colored Race.* Boston: A. G. Brown, 1874.

Browning, Elizabeth Barrett. "The Greek Slave." In *Poems*, Vol. 2. London: Edward Moxon, 1850.

Browning, Robert. "Andrea del Sarto." In *Men and Women.* London: Chapman and Hall, 1855.

Buettner, Brigette. "Precious Stones, Mineral Beings: Performative Materiality in Fifteenth-Century Northern Art." In *The Matter of Art: Materials, Practices, Cultural Logics, c. 1250–1750*, edited by Christy Anderson, Anne Dunlop, and Pamela H. Smith. Manchester: Manchester University Press, 2015.

Buick, Kirsten Pai. *Child of the Fire: Mary Edmonia Lewis and the Problem of Art History's Black and Indian Subject.* Durham, NC: Duke University Press, 2010.

Buick, Kirsten Pai. "The Question of Realism." In *Edmonia Lewis: Indelible Impressions*, edited by Jennifer DeVere Brody. Chicago: University of Chicago Press, 2026.

Cameron, Dan, Richard J. Powell, Michele Wallace, et al. *Dancing at the Louvre: Faith Ringgold's French Collection and Other Story Quilts.* New York: New Museum of Contemporary Art, 1998.

Campt, Tina M. *Listening to Images.* Durham, NC: Duke University Press, 2017.

Campt, Tina M., and Arthur Jafa. "Love Is the Message, the Message Is Death." *e-flux journal*, no. 81 (2017). https://www.e-flux.com/journal.

Capuano, Peter J., and Sue Zemka. *Victorian Hands: The Manual Turn in Nineteenth-Century Body Studies.* Columbus: Ohio State University Press, 2020.

Carr, Cornelia, ed. *Harriet Hosmer: Letters and Memories.* New York: Moffat, Yard, and Company, 1912.

Catalogue of the Palmer Marbles at the Hall Belonging to the Church of the Divine Unity, 548 Broadway, New York, November, 1856. Albany, NY: J. Munsell, 1856.

Chen, Mel Y. *Animacies: Biopolitics, Racial Mattering, and Queer Affect.* Durham, NC: Duke University Press, 2012.

Cheng, Anne. *Second Skin: Josephine Baker and the Modern Surface.* New York: Oxford University Press, 2011.

Cherry, Deborah. *Beyond the Frame: Feminism and the Visual.* London: Routledge, 2000.

Cherry, Deborah, ed. *Maud Sulter: Passion.* Exhibition catalogue. London: Altitude Editions, 2015.

Cherry, Deborah. "Troubling Presence: Body, Sound, and Space in Installation Art of the Mid-1990s." *RACAR* 25, nos. 1–2 (1998): 12–30.

Cixous, Hélène. *The Laugh of the Medusa*. Brooklyn, NY: Petroleuse House, 1976.

Clark, Kenneth. *The Nude: A Study in Ideal Form*. Princeton, NJ: Princeton University Press, 1956.

Cobb, Jasmine N. *Picture Freedom: Remaking Black Visuality in the Early Nineteenth Century*. New York: New York University Press, 2015.

Cole, Michael W. *Ambitious Form: Giambologna, Ammannati, and Danti in Florence*. Princeton, NJ: Princeton University Press, 2011.

Collins, Lisa Gail. *The Art of History: African American Women Artists Engage the Past*. New Brunswick, NJ: Rutgers University Press, 2002.

Collins, Lisa Gail. "Reclaiming Venus: The Presence of Sarah Bartmann in Contemporary Art." In *Black Venus, 2010: They Called Her "Hottentot,"* edited by Deborah Willis. Philadelphia: Temple University Press, 2010.

Conwill, Kinshasa Holman. Introduction to *Free Within Ourselves: African American Artists in the Collection of the National Museum of Art*, by Regina A. Perry. Washington, DC: Smithsonian Institution, 1992.

Cooper, Anna Julia. *A Voice from the South; by a Black Woman of the South*. Xenia, OH: Aldine Printing House, 1892.

Copeland, Huey. *Bound to Appear: Art, Slavery, and the Site of Blackness in Multicultural America*. Chicago: University of Chicago Press, 2013.

Copeland, Huey, and Steven Nelson, eds. *Black Modernisms in the Transatlantic World*. New Haven, CT: Yale University Press, 2023.

Crary, Jonathan. *Techniques of the Observer*. Cambridge, MA: MIT Press, 1992.

Craven, Wayne. *Sculpture in America*. Revised ed. Newark: University of Delaware Press; London: Cornwall Books, 1983.

Culkin, Kate. *Harriet Hosmer: A Cultural Biography*. Amherst: University of Massachusetts Press, 2010.

Cvetkovich, Ann. *An Archive of Feelings: Trauma, Sexuality, and Lesbian Public Archives*. Durham, NC: Duke University Press, 2003.

Dabakis, Melissa. *A Sisterhood of Sculptors: American Artists in Nineteenth-Century Rome*. University Park: Pennsylvania State University Press, 2014.

Danbolt, Mathias, Jane Rowley, and Louise Wolthers. *Lost and Found: Queerying the Archive*. Copenhagen: Museum Tusculanum Press, 2010.

Dannett, Sylvia G. L., ed. *Profiles of Negro Womanhood*, Vol. 1: *1619–1900*. Negro Heritage Library. Yonkers, NY: Educational Heritage, 1964.

de Certeau, Michel. *The Practice of Everyday Life*. Translated by Steven Rendall. Berkeley: University of California Press, 1984.

Delmez, Kathryn E., ed. *Carrie Mae Weems: Three Decades of Photography and Video*. New Haven, CT: Yale University Press, 2012.

Delmez, Kathryn E. Introduction to *Carrie Mae Weems: Three Decades of Photography and Video*, edited by Kathryn E. Delmez. New Haven, CT: Yale University Press, 2012.

Deloria, Philip J. *Becoming Mary Sully: Toward an American Indian Abstract.* Seattle: University of Washington Press, 2019.

Deloria, Philip J. *Indians in Unexpected Places.* Lawrence: University Press of Kansas, 2004.

Deloria, Philip J. *Playing Indian.* New Haven, CT: Yale University Press, 1998.

DeMaria Smith, Margaret Mary. "HRH Cleopatra: The Last of the Ptolemies and the Egyptian Paintings of Sir Lawrence Alma-Tadema." In *Cleopatra: A Sphinx Revisited*, edited by Margaret M. Miles. Berkeley: University of California Press, 2011. http://www.jstor.org/stable/10 .1525/j.ctt1pnvmm.12.

Dempsey, Charles. *Inventing the Renaissance Putto.* Chapel Hill: University of North Carolina Press, 2015.

Derbrew, Sarah. *Untangling Blackness in Greek Antiquity.* Cambridge: Cambridge University Press, 2022.

Derrida, Jacques. *Archive Fever: A Freudian Impression.* Chicago: University of Chicago Press, 1998.

Diawara, Mantia. "Englishness and Blackness: Cricket as Discourse on Colonialism." *Callaloo* 13, no. 4 (1990): 830–44.

Dickerson, C. D., III, Emerson Bowyer, Anthony Sigel, and Elyse Nelson. *Canova: Sketching in Clay.* New Haven, CT: Yale University Press, 2024.

Dippie, Brian W. *The Vanishing American: White Attitudes and U.S. Indian Policy.* Lawrence: University Press of Kansas, 1982.

Donkor, Emmanuel Eyram, Kwame Opoku-Bounsu, and Felix Annor Anim. "Space as a Unique Context for Sculpture Theory and Praxis in Ghana." *Journal of Fine and Studio Art* 6, no. 2 (2016): 9–18.

Douglass, Frederick. *Narrative of the Life of Frederick Douglass, An American Slave, Written by Himself.* Boston: Anti-Slavery Office, 1845.

Dover, Cedric. *American Negro Art.* Greenwich, CT: New York Graphic Society, 1960.

Driskell, David C. *The Other Side of Color.* San Francisco: Pomegranate Press, 2001.

Driskell, David C. *Two Centuries of Black American Art.* Los Angeles: Los Angeles County Museum of Art, 1976.

Droth, Martina, Jason Edwards, and Michael Hatt, eds. *Sculpture Victorious: Art in an Age of Invention, 1937–1901.* New Haven, CT: Yale Center for British Art, 2014.

Droth, Martina, and Michael Hatt. "The Greek Slave by Hiram Powers: A Transatlantic Object." *Nineteenth-Century Art Worldwide* 15, no. 2 (2016). https://www.19thc-artworldwide.org/summer16/droth-hatt -intro-to-the-greek-slave-by-hiram-powers-a-transatlantic-object.

Dukore, Bernard F., ed. *Dramatic Theory and Criticism: Greeks to Grotowski.* New York: Holt, Reinhart and Winston, 1974.

Eisenstein, Sergei. "A Dialectical Approach to Film Form." In *Film Form: Essays in Film Theory*. New York: Harcourt, Brace, 1949.

English, Darby. *To Describe a Life: Notes on the Intersection of Art and Race Terror*. New Haven, CT: Yale University Press, 2019.

Erdman, Harley. "Caught in the Eye of the Eternal: Justice, Race, and the Camera from *The Octoroon* to Rodney King." *Theater Journal* 45, no. 3 (1993): 333–48.

Erdrich, Louise. *Books and Islands in Ojibwe Country: Traveling Through the Land of My Ancestors*. New York: HarperCollins, 2014.

Fanon, Frantz. *Black Skin, White Masks*. Translated by Richard Philcox. New York: Grove Press, 2008.

Farber, Paul M., and Ken Lum. *Monument Lab: Creative Speculations for Philadelphia*. Philadelphia: Temple University Press, 2026.

Farrington, Lisa E. *Creating Their Own Image: The History of African-American Women Artists*. New York: Oxford University Press, 2005.

Farrington, Lisa E. *Faith Ringgold*. San Francisco: Pomegranate Press, 1992.

Fein, Kathryn. "'The Sense of Nearness': Harriet Hosmer's Clasped Hands and the Materials and Bodies of Nineteenth-Century Life Casting." *British Art Studies*, no. 14 (November 2019).

Finley, Cheryl. "Dreaming Diasporas." In *Migrating the Black Body: The African Diaspora and Visual Culture*, edited by Leigh Raiford and Heike Raphael Hernandez. Seattle: University of Washington Press, 2017.

Foner, Eric. *Reconstruction: America's Unfinished Revolution, 1863–1877*. New York: Harper and Row, 1988.

Fong, Ryan D. "The Stories Outside the African Farm: Indigeneity, Orality, and Unsettling the Victorian." *Victorian Studies* 62, no. 3 (2020): 421–32.

Forbes, Jack D. *Africans and Native Americans: The Language of Race and the Evolution of Red-Black Peoples*. Champaign: University of Illinois Press, 1993.

Forbes, Jack D. *A History of Red-Black People*s. New York: Oxford University Press, 1993.

Forbes, Jack D. "Intellectual Self-Determination and Sovereignty: Implications for Native Studies and for Native Intellectuals." *Wicazo Sa Review* 13, no. 1 (1998): 11–23. https://doi.org/10.2307/1409026.

Forman, P. Gabrielle. "Who's Your Mama? 'White' Mulatta Genealogies, Early Photography, and Anti-Passing Narratives of Slavery and Freedom." *American Literary History* 14, no. 3 (2002): 505–39.

Freeman, Elizabeth. *Time Binds: Queer Temporalities, Queer Histories*. Durham, NC: Duke University Press, 2010.

Fulwiley, Duana. *Tabula Raza: Mapping Race and Human Diversity in American Genome Science*. Berkeley: University of California Press, 2024.

Fuss, Diana, ed. *Inside Out: Lesbian and Gay Theories*. London: Routledge, 1991.

Gaines, Malik. *Black Performance on the Outskirts of the Left: A History of the Impossible*. New York: New York University Press, 2017.

Garland-Thomson, Rosemarie. *Staring: How We Look*. Oxford: Oxford University Press, 2009.

Garvey, Ellen G. *Writing with Scissors: American Scrapbooks from the Civil War to the Harlem Renaissance*. New York: Oxford University Press, 2013.

Gay, Roxane. "Wild and Somewhat Disruptive." In *Mickalene Thomas*, edited by Roxane Gay and Kellie Jones. London: Phaidon Press, 2021.

Gerdts, William H., Nicolai Cikovsky Jr., Marie H. Morrison, and Carol Ockman. *The White Marmorean Flock: Nineteenth-Century American Women Neoclassical Sculptors*. Poughkeepsie, NY: Merchants Press, 1972.

Getsy, David. *Body Doubles: Sculpture in Britain, 1877–1905*. New Haven, CT: Yale University Press, 2004.

Gilmore, Ruth Wilson. *Golden Gulag: Prisons, Surplus, Crisis, and Opposition in Globalizing California*. Berkeley: University of California Press, 2007.

Gilroy, Paul. *The Black Atlantic: Modernity and Double-Consciousness*. Cambridge, MA: Harvard University Press, 1993.

Gilroy-Ware, Cora. *The Classical Body in Romantic Britain*. New Haven, CT: Yale University Press, 2020.

Gissing, George. *The Odd Women*. London: Macmillan Press, 1893.

Gitelman, Lisa. *Scripts, Grooves, and Writing Machines: Representing Technology in the Edison Era*. Stanford, CA: Stanford University Press, 2000.

Glissant, Édouard. *A Poetics of Relation*. Translated by Betsy Wing. Ann Arbor: University of Michigan Press, 1999.

Gordon, Sarah. *Indecent Exposures*. New Haven, CT: Yale University Press, 2015.

Graulich, Melody, and Mara Witzling. "The Freedom to Say What She Pleases: A Conversation with Faith Ringgold." *NWSA Journal* 6, no. 1 (1994): 1–27.

Griffin, Farah Jasmine, ed. *Beloved Sisters and Loving Friends: Letters from Rebecca Primus of Royal Oak, Maryland, to Addie Brown of Hartford, Connecticut, 1854–1868*. New York: Knopf, 1999.

Griffin, Farah Jasmine. "Textual Healing: Claiming Black Women's Bodies, the Erotic, and Resistance in Contemporary Novels of Slavery." *Callaloo* 19, no. 2 (1996): 519–36.

Groat, Cody. "On Black-Indigenous Ancestry: Tracing Descent, Legislating Identity." In *Edmonia Lewis: Said in Stone*, edited by Jeffrey Richmond-Moll and Shawnya Harris. Chicago: University of Chicago Press, 2026.

Grosz, Liz. *The Nick of Time: Politics, Evolution, and the Untimely*. Durham, NC: Duke University Press, 2004.

Guerrilla Girls. *Confessions of the Guerrilla Girls*. London: Pandora Books, 1995.

Guerrilla Girls. *The Guerrilla Girls Bedside Companion to the History of Western Art*. New York: Penguin Press, 1998.

Halberstam, Jack. *Female Masculinity*. Durham, NC: Duke University Press, 1998.

Hall, Kim. *Things of Darkness: Economies of Race and Gender in Early Modern England*. Ithaca, NY: Cornell University Press, 1995.

Hall, Kim, Joseph Roach, and Adrienne L. Childs. *Ornamental Blackness: The Black Figure in European Decorative Arts*. New Haven, CT: Yale University Press, 2025.

Hall, Stuart. *Writings on Visual Arts and Culture: Detour to the Imaginary*. Durham, NC: Duke University Press, 2024.

Hallowell, A. Irving. "Ojibwa Ontology, Behavior, and World View." In *Readings in Indigenous Religions*, edited by Graham Harvey. New York: Bloomsbury Academic Press, 2002.

Hammonds, Evelynn. "Black (W)holes and the Geometry of Black Female Sexuality." *differences* 6, nos. 2–3 (1994): 126–45.

Handlin, Oscar. *Statue of Liberty*. New York: Newsweek, 1971.

Harasawa, Masamitsu, Yasuhito Sawahata, Kazuteru Komine, and Satoshi Shioiri. "Effects of Content and Viewing Distance on the Preferred Size of Moving Images." *Journal of Vision* 20, no. 3 (2020). https://doi.org/10.1167/jov.20.3.6&APS/APS.

Harris, Middleton, Morris Levitt, Roger Furman, and Ernest Smith, eds. *The Black Book*. New York: Random House, 1973.

Harris, Shawnya, and Jeffrey Richmond-Moll, eds. *Edmonia Lewis: Said in Stone*. Chicago: University of Chicago Press, 2026.

Hartman, Saidiya. *Lose Your Mother: A Journey Along the Atlantic Slave Route*. New York: Farrar, Strauss and Giroux, 2007.

Hartman, Saidiya. *Wayward Lives, Beautiful Experiments: Intimate Histories of Social Upheaval*. New York: W. W. Norton, 2019.

Hawthorne, Nathaniel. *The Marble Faun; or, The Romance of Monte Beni*. Boston, 1860.

Haworth-Booth, Mark. "Maud Sulter: An Interview." *History of Photography* 16, no. 3 (1992): 263–66.

Helfand, Jessica. *Scrapbooks: An American History*. New Haven, CT: Yale University Press, 2008.

Henderson, Harry B., and Romare Bearden. *A History of African-American Artists from 1792 to the Present*. New York: Pantheon, 1993.

Henderson, Harry B., and Albert Henderson. *The Indomitable Spirit of Edmonia Lewis: A Narrative Biography*. Milford, CT: Published by the authors, 2012.

Hine, Darlene Clark. "Rape and the Inner Lives of Black Women in the Middle West: Preliminary Thoughts on the Culture of Dissemblance." *Signs: Journal of Women in Culture and Society* 14, no. 4 (1989): 912–20.

Hobbs, Allyson. *A Chosen Exile: A History of Racial Passing in American Life.* Cambridge, MA: Harvard University Press, 2014.

Holland, Juanita Marie. "Mary Edmonia Lewis's 'Minnehaha': Gender, Race and the 'Indian Maid.'" *Bulletin of the Detroit Institute of Arts* 69, nos. 1–2 (1995): 1–2, 26–35.

Hutchinson, Elizabeth. "Strength and Resistance in Native American Women's Sculpture." In *The Shape of Power: Stories of Race and American Sculpture*, edited by Karen Lemmey, Tobias Wofford, and Grace Yasumura. Washington, DC: Smithsonian American Art Museum, 2024.

Hunt, Harriot Kesia. *Glances and Glimpses, or Fifty Years Social, Including Twenty Years Professional Life.* Boston: John P. Jewett and Company, 1856.

Jacobs, Harriet A. *Incidents in the Life of a Slave Girl: Written by Herself.* Edited by L. Maria Child. London: Hodson and Son, 1862.

Jafa, Arthur, and Tina M. Campt. "Love Is the Message, the Message Is Death: A Conversation." In *Black Futures*, edited by Kimberly Drew and Jenna Wortham. New York: Random House, 2020.

James, Erica Moiah. "A Gust of Grace: Simone Leigh's *Las Meninas*." In *Perceptual Drift: Black Art and an Ethics of Looking*, edited by Key Jo Lee. New Haven, CT: Yale University Press, 2022.

James, Henry. *William Wetmore Story and His Friends.* Boston: Houghton, Mifflin, 1903.

Jefferson, Thomas. *Notes on the State of Virginia.* London: Printed for John Stockdale, 1786.

Jenkyns, Richard. *Dignity and Decadence: Victorian Art and the Classical Inheritance.* Cambridge, MA: Harvard University Press, 1992.

Jess, Tyehimba. "Edmonia Lewis: Provenance," *Callaloo* 38, no. 3 (2015): 431–32.

Jess, Tyehimba. *Olio.* Seattle: Wave Books, 2020.

Johnson, E. Patrick, and Ramon Rivera Servera, eds. *Blacktino Queer Performance.* Durham, NC: Duke University Press, 2016.

Jones, Kellie. *Eyeminded: Living and Writing Contemporary Art.* Durham, NC: Duke University Press, 2011.

Jones, Kellie. "Nancy Elizabeth Prophet and Augusta Savage: Sculptural Habits of Black Modernism." In *Black Modernisms in the Transatlantic Black World*, edited by Huey Copeland and Steven Nelson. New Haven, CT: Yale University Press, 2023.

Jones, Lynette A. *Haptics.* Cambridge, MA: MIT Press, 2018.

Jordan, Winthrop D. *White over Black: Attitudes Toward the Negro, 1550–1812.* Chapel Hill: University of North Carolina Press, 1968.

Julien, Isaac, and Cora Gilroy-Ware, eds. *Lessons of the Hour: Frederick Douglass.* London: Isaac Julien Studio, 2021.

Katz, Jonathan, ed. *About Face: Stonewall, Revolt, and New Queer Art*. Chicago: Alphawood Foundation, 2024.

Keeling, Kara. "Looking for M—: Queer Temporality, Black Political Possibility, and Poetry from the Future." *GLQ: A Journal of Lesbian and Gay Studies* 15, no. 4 (2009): 571–72.

Kennedy, Adrienne. *People Who Led to My Plays*. New York: Theatre Communications Group, 1987.

Kessel, Erich. "Notes on the African Burial Ground Monument, New York City." *Theater Journal* 74, no. 3 (2022): 47–57.

Kessler, Marni. *Sheer Presence: The Veil in the Age of Manet*. Minneapolis: University of Minnesota Press, 2006.

Kim, Christine Y., and Myrtle Elizabeth Andrews, eds. *Black American Portraits*. Los Angeles: Los Angeles County Museum of Art, 2023.

Kramer, Karen. "Indigenous Frameworks and New Directions, A Convening." In *Edmonia Lewis: Said in Stone*, edited by Jeffry Richmond-Moll and Shawnya L. Harris. Chicago: University of Chicago Press, 2026.

Krauss, Rosalind. *The Originality of the Avant-Garde and Other Modernist Myths*. Cambridge, MA: MIT Press, 1985.

Krauss, Rosalind. "Sculpture Is a Verb: Remembering Richard." *October*, no. 189 (Summer 2024): 199–202.

Kwon, Miwon. *One Place After Another: Site-Specific Art and Locational Identity*. Cambridge, MA: MIT Press, 2002.

Langston, John Mercer. *From the Virginia Plantation to the National Capitol, or The First and Only Negro Representative in Congress from the Old Dominion*. Hartford, CT: American Publishing Company, 1894.

Lee, Key Jo. *Perceptual Drift: Black Art and an Ethics of Looking*. New Haven, CT: Yale University Press, 2022.

Leigh, Simone. *Simone Leigh*. Edited by Eva Respini. New York: DelMonico Books, 2023.

Lemmey, Karen, Tobias Wofford, and Grace Yasumura, eds. *The Shape of Power: Stories of Race and American Sculpture*. Washington, DC: Smithsonian American Art Museum, 2024.

Levi, Pavle. *Cinema by Other Means*. New York: Oxford University Press, 2012.

Levinson, Sanford. *Written in Stone: Public Monuments in Changing Societies*. Durham, NC: Duke University Press, 1998.

Lewis, Robin Coste. "The Voyage of the Sable Venus." In *The Voyage of the Sable Venus and Other Poems*. New York: Knopf, 2015.

Lewis, Samella. *African American Art and Artists*. Berkeley: University of California Press, 2003.

Lewis, Sarah Elizabeth. *The Unseen Truth: When Race Changed Sight in America*. Cambridge, MA: Harvard University Press, 2024.

Linebaugh, Peter, and Marcus Rediker. *The Many-Headed Hydra: Sailors, Slaves, Commoners, and the Hidden History of the Revolutionary Atlantic.* Boston: Beacon Press, 2000.

Lingo, Estelle. *Mochi's Edge and Bernini's Baroque.* Seattle: University of Washington Press, 2017.

Linscott, Charles P. "Extended Reality (XR): Inside of Media, Inside the Mind." In *Now Media: The Evolution of Electronic Communication*, edited by Babara K. Kaye and Norman J. Medoff. London: Taylor and Francis, 2022.

Linscott, Charles P. "Virtually and Actually Black: On VR and Racial Empathy." *ASAP Journal* 4, no.2 (2019): 303–6.

Liverani, Mario. *Myth and Politics in Ancient Near Eastern Historiography.* Ithaca, NY: Cornell University Press, 2004.

Long Soldier, Layli. *Whereas: Poems.* Minneapolis: Graywolf Press, 2017.

Lorde, Audre. "Poetry Is Not a Luxury." In *Sister Outsider: Collected Essays.* New York: Crossing Press, 2007.

Lorde, Audre. *Zami: A New Spelling of My Name.* New York: Kitchen Table Press, 1983.

Lyotard, Jean-François. *The Inhuman: Reflections on Time.* Translated by Geoffrey Bennington and Rachel Bowlby. Stanford, CA: Stanford University Press, 1992.

Maidment, Isabella, and Vladimir Seput, eds. *Isaac Julien: What Freedom Is to Me.* London: Tate Publishing, 2023.

Manning, Erin. *Relationscapes: Movement, Art, Philosophy.* Cambridge, MA: MIT Press, 2009.

Marcoci, Roxana. *The Original Copy: Photography of Sculpture, 1839 to Today.* New York: Museum of Modern Art, 2011.

Marks, Laura U. *The Skin of the Film: Intercultural Cinema, Embodiment, and the Senses.* Durham, NC: Duke University Press, 2000.

Marks, Laura U. *Touch: Sensuous Theory.* Minneapolis: University of Minnesota Press, 2002.

Mays, Kyle T. *An Afro-Indigenous History of the United States.* Boston: Beacon, 2021.

McArthur, Park, and Jennifer Burris Staton, eds. *Beverly Buchanan, 1978–1981.* Mexico City: Athénée Press, 2015.

McKittrick, Katherine. *Demonic Grounds: Black Women and the Cartographies of Struggle.* Minneapolis: University of Minnesota Press, 2006.

Meisel, Martin. *Realizations: Narrative, Pictorial, and Theatrical Arts in Nineteenth-Century England.* Princeton, NJ: Princeton University Press, 1984.

Mercer, Kobena. *Alain Locke and the Visual Arts.* New Haven, CT: Yale University Press, 2023.

Mercer, Kobena. "Black Hair Style / Politics." *new formations*, no. 3 (1987): 33–54.

Mercer, Kobena. *Travel and See: Black Diaspora Art Practices Since the 1980s.* Durham, NC: Duke University Press, 2016.

Miles, Tiya. *All That She Carried: The Journey of Ashley's Sack, a Black Family Keepsake.* New York: Random House, 2021.

Miles, Tiya. *The Cherokee Rose: A Novel of Gardens and Ghosts.* Winston-Salem, NC: John F. Blair, 2015.

Miles, Tiya. *Night Flyer: Harriet Tubman and the Faith Dreams of a Free People.* New York: Penguin, 2024.

Miles, Tiya. "A Singular Maker's Many Migrations." In *Edmonia Lewis: Indelible Impressions,* edited by Jennifer DeVere Brody. Stanford, CA: Cantor Arts Center, 2025.

Miles, Tiya. *Wild Girls: How the Outdoors Shaped the Women Who Challenged a Nation.* New York: W. W. Norton, 2024.

Miller, Monica L. *Slaves to Fashion: Black Dandyism and the Styling of Black Diasporic Identity.* Durham, NC: Duke University Press, 2009.

Mills, Charles W. *The Racial Contract.* Ithaca, NY: Cornell University Press, 1997.

Mirzoeff, Nicholas. *Bodyscape: Art, Modernity, and the Ideal Figure.* New York: Routledge, 1995.

"The Miscegen Sculptor." *Daily Graphic: An Illustrated Evening Newspaper* (New York), July 10, 1873.

Molesworth, Helen. "Eros and the Readymade." In *The Lure of the Object,* edited by Stephen Melville. Williamstown, MA: Clark Art Institute, 2005.

Molesworth Helen, ed. *Kerry James Marshall: Mastry.* New York: Skira Rizzoli, 2016.

Monette, Paul. *Last Watch of the Night: Essays Too Personal and Otherwise.* New York: Harcourt Brace, 1994.

Monkman, Kent, and Gisèle Gordon. *The Memoirs of Miss Chief Eagle Testickle: A True and Exact Accounting of the History of Turtle Island.* Toronto: McClelland and Stewart, 2023.

Montesano, Philip M. "The Mystery of the San Jose Statues." *Urban West,* March–April, 1968, 26.

Morris, Catherine, and Rujeko Hockley, eds. *We Wanted a Revolution: Black Radical Women, 1967–85: A Sourcebook.* Brooklyn: Brooklyn Museum; distributed by Duke University Press, 2017.

Morris, Kate, and Lina Morris. "Camping Out with Miss Chief: Kent Monkman's Ironic Journey." *Studies in American Humor* 6, no. 2 (2020): 265–84.

Morrison, Toni. *Beloved.* New York: Knopf, 1987.

Morse, Heidi. "Roman Studios: The Black Woman Artist in the Eternal City, from Edmonia Lewis to Carrie Mae Weems." In *Classicisms in the Black Atlantic,* edited by Ian Moyer, Adam Lecznar, and Heidi Morse. Oxford: Oxford University Press, 2020.

Mossell, Gertrude Bustill. *The Work of the Afro-American Woman*. 2nd ed. Philadelphia: George S. Ferguson Company, 1908.

Moten, Fred. *In the Break: The Aesthetics of Black Radical Tradition*. Minneapolis: University of Minnesota Press, 2003.

Muholi, Zanele. *Zanele Muholi: Faces and Phases, 2006–2014*. Göttingen: Steidl, 2015.

Muholi, Zanele. *Zanele Muholi: Somnyama Ngonyama, Hail the Dark Lioness*. New York: Aperture, 2018.

Mulvey, Laura. "Visual Pleasure and Narrative Cinema." *Screen* 16, no. 3 (1975): 6–18.

Muñoz, José Esteban. "Ephemera as Evidence: Introductory Notes on Queer Acts." *Women and Performance* 8, no. 1 (1996): 5–16.

Murell, Denise. *Posing Modernity: The Black Model from Manet and Matisse to Today*. New Haven, CT: Yale University Press, 2018.

Murray, Freeman Henry Morris. *Emancipation and the Freed in American Sculpture : A Study in Interpretation*. Published by the author, 1916. Reprint, Books for Libraries Press, 1972.

Myburgh, Brittany. "Here and Now: Indigenous Canadian Perspectives and New Media Works by Ruben Komangapik, Kent Monkman, and Adrian Duke." *Leonardo* 51, no. 4 (2018): 394–98.

Ndiaye, Taylor. "Sites of Survival." *MoMA Magazine*, October 8, 2025.

Nead, Lynda. *The Female Nude: Art, Obscenity, and Sexuality*. London: Routledge, 1992.

Nead, Lynda. *The Haunted Gallery: Painting, Photography, Film c. 1900*. New Haven, CT: Yale University Press, 2007.

Nelson, Charmaine. *The Color of Stone: Sculpting the Black Female Subject in Nineteenth-Century America*. Minneapolis: University of Minnesota Press, 2007.

Nichols, Kate. *Greece and Rome at the Crystal Palace*. Cambridge: Cambridge University Press, 2015.

Nickerson, Cynthia D. "Artistic Interpretations of Henry Wadsworth Longfellow's *The Song of Hiawatha*, 1855–1900." *American Art Journal* 16, no. 3 (1984): 49–77.

Noble, Umoja. *Algorithms of Oppression: How Search Engines Reinforce Racism*. New York: New York University Press, 2018.

Nochlin, Linda. *The Body*. London: Thames and Hudson, 2024.

Nott, Josiah Clark, and George Gliddon. *Types of Mankind; or, Ethnological Researches Based Upon the Ancient Monuments, Paintings, Sculptures, and Crania of Races, and Upon Their Natural, Geographical, Philological and Biblical History*. Philadelphia: Lippincott, Grambo & Co., 1854.

Novo, Marla. "The Indian Maiden Visits San Jose: Rediscovering Edmonia Lewis." Master's thesis, San Jose State University, 1995.

Nyong'o, Tavia. *Afro-Fabulation: The Queer Drama of Black Life*. New York: New York University Press, 2019.

O'Grady, Lorraine. "Olympia's Maid: Reclaiming the Black Female Body." *AfterImage* 20, no. 1 (1992): 268–86.

Orange, Tommy. *There, There*. New York: Vintage Books, 2018.

Ovid. *Metamorphoses*. Translated and edited by Charles Martin. New York: W. W. Norton, 2010.

Painter, Nell Irvin. *Creating Black Americans: Afro-American History and Its Meanings, 1619 to the Present*. New York: Oxford University Press, 2006.

Painter, Nell Irvin. *Sojourner Truth: A Life, A Symbol*. 2nd ed. New York: W. W. Norton, 2024.

Penny, Nicholas. *The Materials of Sculpture*. New Haven, CT: Yale University Press, 1996.

Perry, Imani. *Looking for Lorraine: The Radiant and Radical Life of Lorraine Hansberry*. Boston: Beacon Press, 2018.

Perry, Regina. *Free Within Ourselves: African-American Artists in the Collection of the National Museum of American Art*. Washington, DC: Smithsonian Institution, 1992.

Philip, M. NourbSe. *Zong!* Middletown, CT: Wesleyan University Press, 2008.

Pointon, Marcia. *Naked Authority: The Body in Western Painting, 1830–1908*. Cambridge: Cambridge University Press, 1990.

Pollock, Griselda. *Differencing the Canon: Feminist Desire and the Writing of Art's Histories*. London: Routledge, 1999.

Pollock, Griselda. "The Grace of Time: Narrativity, Sexuality, and a Visual Encounter in the Virtual Feminist Museum." *Art History* 26, no. 2 (2003): 174–213.

Pollock, Griselda. *Vision and Difference: Femininity, Feminisms, and Histories of Art*. London: Routledge, 1988.

Porter, James. *American Negro Art*. New York: Arno Press, 1969.

Potts, Alex. *The Sculptural Imagination: Figurative, Modernist, Minimalist*. New Haven, CT: Yale University Press, 2000.

Powell, Richard J. *Cutting a Figure: Fashioning Black Portraiture*. Chicago: University of Chicago Press, 2008.

Powell, Richard J., and Jock Reynolds. *To Conserve a Legacy: Art from Historically Black Colleges*. Andover, MA: Addison Gallery of American Art, 1999.

Prettejohn, Elizabeth. *The Modernity of Ancient Sculpture: Greek Sculpture and Modern Art from Winckelmann to Picasso*. London: I. B. Tauris, 2012.

Raiford, Leigh, and Heike Raphael-Hernandez, eds. *Migrating the Black Body: The African Diaspora and Visual Culture*. Seattle: University of Washington Press, 2017.

Raiford, Leigh. *Imprisoned in a Luminous Glare: Photography and the African American Freedom Struggle*. Chapel Hill: University of North Carolina Press, 2011.

Rediker, Marcus. *The Slave Ship: A Human History*. New York: Viking, 2007.

Rheims, Maurice. *19th Century Sculpture*. Translated by Robert E. Wolf. New York: Harry N. Abrams, 1977.

Richardson, Marilyn. "Edmonia Lewis at McGrawville: The Early Education of a Nineteenth-Century Black Woman Artist." *Nineteenth-Century Contexts* 22, no. 2 (2000): 239–56.

Richardson, Matt. *The Queer Limit of Black Memory: Black Lesbian Literature and Irresolution*. Columbus: Ohio State University Press, 2013.

Ringgold, Faith. *Politics Power*. New York: Weiss, 2022.

Ringgold, Faith. *We Flew over the Bridge: The Memoirs of Faith Ringgold*. Durham, NC: Duke University Press, 2005.

Roach, Joseph. *Cities of the Dead: Circum-Atlantic Performance*. New York: Columbia University Press, 1996.

Roach, Joseph. *It*. Ann Arbor: University of Michigan Press, 2007.

Roach, Joseph. "Slave Spectacles and Tragic Octoroons: A Cultural Genealogy of Antebellum Performance." *Theatre Survey* 33, no. 2 (1992): 167–87.

Roberts, J. R. *Black Lesbians: An Annotated Bibliography*. Foreword by Barbara Smith. Tallahassee, FL: Naiad Press, 1981.

Royster, Francesca. *Becoming Cleopatra: The Shifting of an Icon*. New York: Palgrave Macmillan, 2003.

Ruskin, John. *The Stones of Venice*. 3 vols. London: Smith and Elder, 1867.

Rymhs, Deena. "Kent Monkman's *The Big Four* as Automobiography." *a/b: Auto/Biography Studies* 31, no. 3 (2016): 465–85.

Savage, Kirk. *Standing Soldiers, Kneeling Slaves: Race, War, and Monument in Nineteenth-Century America*. Princeton, NJ: Princeton University Press, 1997.

Scarry, Elaine. *The Body in Pain: The Making and Unmaking of the World*. Oxford: Oxford University Press, 1985.

Scego, Igiaba. *The Color Line*. Translated by John Cullen and Gregory Conti. New York: Other Press, 2022.

Scego, Igiaba. *La linea del colore: Il grand tour di Lafanu Brown*. Milan: Bompiani, 2020.

Schechner, Richard. *Performance Studies: An Introduction*. 3rd ed. New York: Routledge, 2013.

Schneider, Rebecca. *The Explicit Body in Performance*. New York: Routledge, 1997.

Schneider, Rebecca. *Performing Remains: Art and War in Times of Theatrical Reenactment*. New York: Routledge, 2011.

Schneider, Suzanne. "Louis Aggasiz and the American School of Ethno-eroticism: Polygenesis, Pornography, and Other Perfidious Influences." In *Pictures and Progress: Early Photography and the Making of African American Identity*, edited by Maurice Wallace and Shawn Michelle Smith. Durham, NC: Duke University Press, 2012.

Schuller, Kyla. *The Biopolitics of Feeling: Race, Sex, and Science in the Nineteenth Century*. Durham, NC: Duke University Press, 2018.

Scott, B. L. "Pornoarcheology of Kent Monkman's *Group of Seven Inches*." *Porn Studies* 8, no. 3 (2021): 296–313.

Seacole, Mary. *The Wonderful Adventures of Mrs. Seacole in Many Lands*. London: James Blackwood Paternoster Row, 1857.

Sharpe, Christina. *In the Wake: On Blackness and Being*. Durham, NC: Duke University Press, 2016.

Shaw, Gwendolyn DuBois. *Portraits of a People: Picturing African Americans in the Nineteenth Century*. Andover, MA: Addison Gallery of American Art, Phillips Academy, 2006.

Shaw, Gwedolyn DuBois. *Seeing the Unspeakable: The Art of Kara Walker*. Durham, NC: Duke University Press, 2004.

Shaw, Gwendolyn DuBois. "That Roman Portrait Is Wildfire." In *Edmonia Lewis: Indelible Impressions*, edited by Jennifer DeVere Brody. Stanford, CA: Cantor Arts Center, 2025.

Sherwood, Dolly. *Harriet Hosmer: American Sculptor, 1830–1908*. Columbia: University of Missouri Press 1991.

Shields, David S. "Background: The Picture in the Picture." Broadway Photographs, accessed February 13, 2026. https://broadway.library.sc.edu/content/background-picture-picture.html.

Sienkewicz, Julia. "Beyond the Mohawk Warrior: Reinterpreting Benjamin West's Evocations of American Indians." *Interdisciplinary Studies in the Long Nineteenth Century* 19, no. 9 (2009). https://doi.org/10.16995/ntn.515.

Sienkewicz, Julia. "Encountering Edmonia Lewis in the Correspondence of Florence Freeman." *Panorama: Journal of the Association of Historians of American Art* 11, no. 1 (2025): 1–13.

Smith, Shawn Michelle. *At the Edge of Sight: Photography and the Unseen*. Durham, NC: Duke University Press, 2013.

Smith-Rosenberg, Carol. "The Female World of Love and Ritual." *Signs: A Journal of Women and Gender* 1, no. 1 (1975): 1–29.

Snead, James A. "On Repetition in Black Culture." *Black American Literature Forum* 15, no. 4 (Winter 1981): 146–54.

Snorton, C. Riley. *Black on Both Sides: A Racial History of Trans Identity*. Minneapolis: University of Minnesota Press, 2017.

Solnit, Rebecca. *River of Shadows: Eadwaerd Muybridge and the Technological Wild West*. New York: Penguin Press, 2003.

Soyinka, Wole. "Do Statues Die?" In *Isaac Julien: What Freedom Means to Me*, edited by Isabella Maidment. London: Tate Britain, 2023.

Spillers, Hortense J. *Black, White, and in Color: Essays on American Literature and Culture*. Chicago: University of Chicago Press, 2003.

Spivak, Gayatri Chakravorty. "Acting Bits / Identity Talk." *Critical Inquiry* 18, no. 4 (1992): 770–803.

Stauffer, John, Zoe Trodd, and Celeste-Marie Bernier, eds. *Picturing Frederick Douglass: An Illustrated Biography of the Nineteenth Century's Most Photographed American*. New York: Liveright, 2015.

Stein, Gertrude. "Sacred Emily." In *Geography and Plays*. Boston: Four Seas Co., 1922.

Stein, Gertrude. *Three Lives*. New York: Grafton Press, 1909. Reprint, New York: Vintage Press, 1958.

Stein, Gertrude. *The World Is Round*. New York: William R. Scott, 1939.

Steinberg, Leo. *Michelangelo's Last Paintings*. New York: Oxford University Press, 1975.

Sterling, Dorothy, ed. *We Are Your Sisters: Black Women in the Nineteenth Century*. New York: W. W. Norton, 1984.

St. James, Synthia. *I Am Edmonia Lewis and My Name Is Wildfire*. San Bernadino, CA: Published by the author, 2018.

Stocking, George W., Jr. *Victorian Anthropology*. New York: Free Press, 1991.

Story, William Wetmore. *Roba di Roma*. London: Chapman and Hall, 1862.

Stowe, Harriet Beecher. *Dred: A Tale of the Great Dismal Swamp*. Boston: Phillips, Sampson and Company, 1856.

Sulter, Maud. "Interview with Mark Haworth-Booth." In *Maud Sulter: Passion*, edited by Deborah Cherry. London: Altitude Editions Press, 2015.

Summers, Claude J., ed. *The Queer Encyclopedia of the Visual Arts*. San Francisco: Cleis Press, 2004.

Sutcliffe, Emerson Grant. "Charles Reade's Notebooks." *Studies in Philology* 27, no. 1 (1930): 64–109.

Taylor, Diana. *The Archive and the Repertoire: Performing Cultural Memory in the Americas*. Durham, NC: Duke University Press, 2003.

Taylor, Diana. *Disappearing Acts: Spectacles of Gender and Nationalism in Argentina's "Dirty War."* Durham, NC: Duke University Press, 1997.

Thomas, Mickalene, Beverly Guy-Sheftall, Kristian Conteras, et al. *Mickalene Thomas: All About Love*. London: Hayward Gallery, 2024.

Thomas, Keith. Introduction to *A Cultural History of Gesture*, edited by Jan Bremmer and Herman Roodenburg. Ithaca, NY: Cornell University Press 1991.

Thompson, Kara. *Blanket*. New York: Bloomsbury Academic, 2019.

Thurman, Judith. *Cleopatra's Nose: 39 Varieties of Desire*. New York: Farrar, Straus and Giroux, 2007.

Tinsley, Omise'eke Natasha. *The Color Pynk: Black Femme Art for Survival*. Austin: University of Texas Press, 2022.

Tinsley, Omise'eke Natasha. *Thiefing Sugar: Eroticism Between Women in Caribbean Literature*. Durham, NC: Duke University Press: 2010.

Tolles, Thayer, ed. *American Sculpture in the Metropolitan Museum of Art*. Vol. 1: *A Catalogue of Works by Artists Before 1865*. New York: Metropolitan Museum of Art, 1999.

Tourmaline. *Marsha: The Joy and Defiance of Marsha P. Johnson*. New York: Tiny Reparations Books, 2025.

Trafton, Scott. *Egypt Land: Race and Nineteenth-Century American Egyptomania*. Durham, NC: Duke University Press, 2004.

Trethewey, Natasha. *Memorial Drive: A Daughter's Memoir*. New York: Ecco, 2020.

Trouillot, Michel-Rolph. *Silencing the Past: Power and the Production of History*. Boston: Beacon Press, 1995.

Tyburczy, Jennifer. *Sex Museums: The Politics and Performance of Display*. Chicago: University of Chicago Press, 2016.

Vasari, Giorgio. *The Lives of the Artists*. Translated by Julia Conway Bondanella and Peter Bondanella. London: Oxford World Classics, 1991.

Verri, Giovanni, Thorsten Opper, and Thibaut Deviese. "The 'Treu Head': A Case Study in Roman Sculptural Polychromy." *British Museum Technical Research Bulletin* 4 (2010): 39–52.

Wagner, Ann Middleton. *Mother Stone: The Vitality of Modern British Sculpture*. New Haven, CT: Yale University Press, 2005.

Walker, Alice. *In Search of Our Mothers' Gardens: Womanist Prose*. San Diego, CA: Harcourt Brace Jovanovich, 1983.

Wallace, Maurice, and Shawn Michelle Smith, eds. *Pictures and Progress: Early Photography and the Making of African-American Identity*. Durham, NC: Duke University Press, 2012.

Wallace, Michele. "For the Women's House: An Interview with Faith Ringgold." *Feminist Art Journal* (April 1972): 14–15.

Wallace, William E. *Michelangelo: The Artist, the Man, and His Times*. Cambridge: Cambridge University Press, 2010.

Walsh, Linda. "The 'Hard Form' of Sculpture: Marble, Matter, and Spirit in European Sculpture from Enlightenment through Romanticism." *Modern Intellectual History* 5, no. 3 (2008): 455–48.

Walters, Wendy, and Elyse Nelson, eds. *Fictions of Emancipation: Carpeaux's "Why Born Enslaved!" Reconsidered*. New York: Metropolitan Museum of Art, 2023.

Weems, Carrie Mae. *To Make Their Own Way in the World: The Enduring Legacy of the Zealy Daguerreotypes*. Cambridge, MA: Peabody Museum Press, 2020.

Wilde, Johannes. *Michelangelo: Six Lectures.* Oxford: Clarendon Press, 1978.

Willis, Deborah, ed. *Black Venus 2010: They Called Her "Hottentot."* Philadelphia: Temple University Press, 2010.

Willis, Deborah. "Photographing Between the Lines: Beauty, Politics, and the Poetic Vision of Carrie Mae Weems." In *Carrie Mae Weems: Three Decades of Photography and Video*, edited by Kathryn E. Delmez. New Haven, CT: Yale University Press, 2012.

Willis, Deborah. *Reflections in Black: A History of Black Photographers, 1840 to the Present.* New York: W. W. Norton, 2000.

Willis, Deborah. "Ruth and Faith: Power in Their Hands." *Scholar and Feminist On-Line* 19, no. 1 (2023). https://sfonline.barnard.edu/ruth-and-faith-power-in-their-hands/.

Willis, Deborah, and Barbara Krauthamer, eds. *Envisioning Emancipation: Black Americans and the End of Slavery.* Philadelphia: Temple University Press, 2012.

Willis, William Shedrick. "Skeletons in the Anthropological Closet." In *Reinventing Anthropology*, edited by Dell Hymes. New York: Pantheon Books, 1972.

Wilson, Judith. "Coming of Age: Look at Three Contemporary Artists." *Essence*, May 1986.

Wilson, Judith. "Getting Down to Get Over: Romare Bearden's Use of Pornography and the Problem of the Black Female Body in U.S. Afro-Art." In *Black Popular Culture*, edited by Gina Dent. Seattle: Bay Press, 1992.

Wilson, Robert. *Mathew Brady: Portraits of a Nation.* New York: Bloomsbury, 2013.

Winckelmann, Johann Joachim. *History of the Art of Antiquity* (1764). Translated by Harry Francis Mallgrave. Los Angeles: Getty Research Institute, 2006.

Winograd, Abigail, and Christian Ayne Crouch, eds. *Jeffrey Gibson: The Space in Which to Place Me.* New York: Delmonico Books, 2025.

Wolfe, Rinna. *Edmonia Lewis: Wildfire in Marble.* Parsippany, NJ: Dillon Press, 1998.

Wolff, Tristram. "Romantic Stone Speech and the Appeal of the Inorganic." *ELH* 84, no. 3 (2017): 617–47.

Wood, Marcus. *Blind Memory: Visual Representations of Slavery in England and America, 1780–1965.* London: Routledge, 2000.

Woods, Naurice Frank, Jr. "An African Queen at the Philadelphia Centennial Exposition 1876: Edmonia Lewis's *The Death of Cleopatra*." *Meridians* 9, no. 1 (2009): 62–82.

Woods, Naurice Frank, Jr. *Race and Racism in Nineteenth-Century Art: The Ascendency of Robert Duncanson, Edward Bannister, and Edmonia Lewis.* Jackson: University Press of Mississippi, 2021.

Woubshet, Dagwami. "The Right to Look." In *About Face: Stonewall, Revolt, and New Queer Art,* edited by Jonathan Katz. New York: Monacelli Press, 2024.

Wynter, Andrew. "Cartes de Visite." *Photographic News* 6, no. 178 (1862): 135.

Wynter, Sylvia. *On Being Human as Praxis.* Edited by Katherine McKittrick. Durham, NC: Duke University Press, 2015.

Wynter, Sylvia. *We Must Learn to Sit Down Together and Talk About a Little Culture: Decolonising Essays, 1967–1984.* Leeds: Peepal Tree Press, 2022.

Yellin, Jean Fagan. *Harriet Jacobs: A Life.* New York: Basic Civitas Books, 2004.

Young, Harvey. *Embodying Black Experience: Stillness, Critical Memory, and the Black Body.* Ann Arbor: University of Michigan Press, 2010.

Young, Hershini Bhana. *Illegible Will: Coercive Spectacles of Labor in South Africa and the Diaspora.* Durham, NC: Duke University Press, 2017.

Yusoff, Kathryn. *A Billion Black Anthropocenes or None.* Minneapolis: University of Minnesota Press, 2018.

Zöllner, Frank, Christof Thoenes, and Thomas Pöpper. *Michelangelo: Complete Works.* Cologne: Taschen, 2007.

Index

Page references in *italics* refer to figures. EL is Edmonia Lewis.

skin color, 85

Slave Trade, The (Slaves on the West Coast of Africa) (Biard), 8

slavery: African people, 68; allegories, 126; emancipation and manumissions, 93–94, 113; epistemology, 67; Fugitive Slave Act, 167, 176; humanity and, 68; markets, 115; museums, 7; prohibitions, 94; racialization, 68–69; readymade (Copeland), 69; representations, 126; *The Slave Trade (Slaves on the West Coast of Africa)* (Biard), 8. *See also* abolitionism

Sloane, Hans, 34

Smith, Ann Carroll Fitzhugh, 78, *79*, 80–81

Smith, Elizabeth, 146

Smith, Gerrit, 78, *79*, 80–81, 89, 227n4, 237n3, 237n12

Smith, Marlene, 255n40

Smith-Rosenberg, Carol, 183

Smithsonian American Art Museum, 32–33, 143, 152, 172, 198

Smithsonian National Museum of African American History and Culture, 170

"social problem" novels, 25

Song of Hiawatha, The (Longfellow), xvi, 29, 31, 75, 77

Sonnet 130 (Shakespeare), 140

Sotheby's, 115

South Africa, 186, 187, 199, 203, 252n48

sovereignty, 68

Space in Which to Place Me, The (Gibson), 227n59

spinsterhood, 16

spirituality, 110–11, 149

Spivak, Gayatri, 99

stamps, 205

Stanford, Leland, Sr., 5

Stanford University, 133

STAR (Street Transvestite Action Revolutionaries), 156

stasis, 5, 222n17

stasis and movement, 10

Statue of Liberty (Bartholdi), 6

statues: lighting, 11

Stein, Gertrude, 154, 157–58, 248nn38–39

still, 4, 181

still life (*nature morte*), 140, 155

Still/Here (Jones), 236n44

St. Louis Art Museum, 148

St. Louis Dispatch, 91–92

St. Mary's Catholic Cemetery (Kensal Green), 1, 196, *196*

Stoker, Bram, 22

Stone Mountain Park (Georgia), 204–5, 254n25

stones: aboutness, 57, 58; as ancestors, 66; being (Chen), 137; body and, 58; EL's work, 58–59, 66, 67; habitus, 57; headstones, 19, 192, 212; language, 65; living history, 64; materiality, 58, 59, 61; movement, 58, 66, 68, 70; Ojibwe people and culture, 66, 68; performativity, 57; in philosophy, 233n11; place, 57–58; *Green Hill, Slave Auction Block, 378 Pannills Road (State Route 728), Long Island, Campbell County, VA* (Boucher), 64–65, *65*. *See also* sculpture

story, 72

Story, William Wetmore, 40

Stowe, Harriet Beecher, 122, 226n54

street transvestite activist revolutionary (STAR), 156

student activism, 199

Studies for a National Postage Stamp (Sulter), 205

subjectivity: EL and, 2, 3, 4, 15, 17, 27, 28, 33, 43, 46, 55, 66, 89, 99, 110, 169; Indigenous and African conceptions, 68

Sulter, Maud, 20, 207–13, 245n1, 247n36, 248n39, 255n40; *Hysteria*, 207–11, *208*; *Maud Sulter: Passion*, 209–10; *Studies for a National Postage Stamp*, 205

surface, 92

survival, 68

tableaux vivants, 8, 10, 11, 224n35

Tablet (Catholic publication), 197

Tate Britain, 246n1

Tate Liverpool, 208

Taylor, Diana, 197

Taylor, Renty, 165

temporality: archives, 35–36, 46; asynchronicity, 159; dislocation, 11; gesture, 12; graves, 196–97; Julien's work, 8; queerness, 9, 159; race, 71; sculpture, 12, 70–71

Testickle, Miss Chief Eagle. *See* Monkman, Kent/Miss Chief Eagle Testickle (Cree)

texture, 92, 174

Thackeray, William, 228n9

There, There (Orange), 228n11

thingliness, 69

Thomas, Antoinette, 192

Thomas, Mickalene: overview, 20, 101, 129; hands, 137; interlude on, 135–38; *Mickalene Thomas: All About Love* (exhibition), 137; photographs of, 135–36, *136*

Thompson, Kara, 59

Three Lives (Stein), 158

Tibetan painting, 49

Tinsley, Omise'eke Natasha, 155–56, 247n34

Tinted Venus, The (Gibson), 84

Toklas, Alice B., 212

touch: artists, 74; EL's work and, 95; erotics of, 19; sculpture, 74, 92; *ultima mano* (last hand), 83. *See also* hands; haptics

Tourmaline, 156, 247n35

Tracking Colour project, 238n28

Trafton, Scott, 144, 225n45

trans people: National Transgender Day of Remembrance, 157, 247n37; Roses Program (Transgender Law Center), 157; "Give Us Our Roses While We're Still Here" (Parker), 157

transatlanticism, 2, 176; *The Harlem Renaissance and Transatlantic Modernism* (exhibition), 9

Transgender Law Center, 157

Trethewey, Natasha, 204

Trump, Donald, and administration, 33, 254n23

truth, 152, 182

Truth, Sojourner, 130, 167

Tubman, Harriet, 16

Tuckerman, Henry T., 178

Two Centuries of Black American Art (exhibition), 134

Uncle Tom's Cabin (Stowe), 122

Unite the Right (march), 199

United States: 54th Regiment Massachusetts, xv, 38, 44, 47, 61; enslavement's end in, 37–38; race, 38; sculpture, 203; USPS, 205

"Untitled (Double Portrait of Artist with Frustula Sculpture)" (Buchanan), 70

Vasari, Giorgio, 73

Vassar College, 134

Vatican, 110, 233n9

Venice Biennale, 153, 155

Venus verticordia (Rossetti), 147–48

Verelst, John, 250n30

Vertefeuille, Lin, 124

Vesey, Denmark, 89

Victoria, Queen, 205, 243n39

Victorian era: art projection, 5; cemeteries, 192–93; children, 121–22; difference (discourse on), 86–87; homes, 229n20; hysteria, 11; nudity, 112, 135; representation, 11; sculpture's whiteness, 84; stamps, 205; tableaux vivants, 8, 10, 11

Vielmetter, Susanne, 135

violence, 99, 157

vision: expanded field, 14; objects, 57; perception, 13

visual technologies, 13

Vizenor, Gerald, 68

"Voyage of the Sable Venus" (Coste Lewis), 32

Walker, Alice, 148

Walker, Kara, 178, 254n25

Wall Column (Buchanan), 69–70

Wall Fragments (Buchanan), 70, 71

Walters Art Museum, 169

Warburg, Aby, 10

Warburg, Eugene, 226n54

Ward, John Quincy Adams: *The Freedman*, 242n32

war(s): Civil War, 126; Greek War of Independence, 126

Washington, Augustus, 164, 252n51

Waterson, Anna, 108

"way out of no way" (proverb), 46

wayward, as term, 18

Weems, Carrie Mae, 166, 189, 252n56

Westernism, 50

Wheatley, Phyllis, 38, 45, 54, 86, 144–45

White Captive, The (Palmer), 181

white (hue) in sculpture, 11, 84, 86, 176

whiteness (racial): Blackness vs., 130; children, 121–22; EL's work and, 45, 93; heteropatriarchy, 27; vs. Indigenous people, 31; marble, 121; Monkman's revisions, 101–2; nude sculptures, 107; nudes, 130; otherness, 93; patriarchy, 212; photography, 164; privilege, 93; property, 43; sculpture, 31, 80, 83–84, 86, 88, 107, 114, 121, 203; skin toning in art, 93; *The White Captive* (Palmer), 181; white supremacy, 84, 164, 203, 205

Whitney, Anne, 40
Wilberforce House Museum (England), 7
Williams, Caroline Randall, 203
Williams, Moses, 222n12
Willis, Deborah, 165, 189
Wilson, Fred, 212
Wilson, Judith, 111
Wilson, Woodrow, 249n9
Woffington, Peg, 26
"Woman Playing at Man" (Reade), 26
women: archives and, 32; artists, 73, 106, 109, 130; Black, 17, 32; butch pleasure, 137; colonialism, 155; Cult of True Womanhood, 46; education (access to), 193; in EL's work, 128; gender ambiguity, 26; masculinity, 131; poetry, 83, 140; pregnancy, 128; representations, 126; rights, 193; roses, 141–42; struggles and suffering, 46, 127
Woods, Frank Naurice Woods, Jr., 42–43, 87, 225n45, 235n37
Woolf, Virginia, 22
World's Columbian Exposition (Chicago, 1893), 198
Woubshet, Dadwami, 187
Wynter, Andrew, 161
Wyon, William, 205

Yale, Elihu, 174, 250n30
Yale University, 174
Young, Harvey, 166
youthfulness, 79

Zealy, J. T., 165, 166